Edward Livingston Youmans, John E. Tyndall, Arthur Henfrey

The Culture demanded by Modern Life

Edward Livingston Youmans, John E. Tyndall, Arthur Henfrey

The Culture demanded by Modern Life

ISBN/EAN: 9783337816117

Printed in Europe, USA, Canada, Australia, Japan

Cover: Foto ©Andreas Hilbeck / pixelio.de

More available books at **www.hansebooks.com**

THE
CULTURE DEMANDED
BY
MODERN LIFE;

A SERIES OF ADDRESSES AND ARGUMENTS

ON

THE CLAIMS OF SCIENTIFIC EDUCATION.

BY PROFESSORS TYNDALL, HENFREY, HUXLEY, PAGET, WHEWELL, FARADAY, LIEBIG, DRAPER, DE MORGAN; DRS. BARNARD, HODGSON, CARPENTER, HOOKER, ACLAND, FORBES, HERBERT SPENCER, SIR JOHN HERSCHEL, SIR CHARLES LYELL, DR. SEGUIN, MR. MILL, ETC.

WITH AN INTRODUCTION ON MENTAL DISCIPLINE IN EDUCATION BY

E. L. YOUMANS.

"Scientific Education, apart from professional objects, is but a preparation for judging rightly of man, and of his requirements and interests."

John Stuart Mill.

NEW YORK:
D. APPLETON AND COMPANY,
90, 92 & 94 GRAND STREET.
1870.

PREFACE.

THE system of Popular Education in this country has become an established fact, and the extensive provisions for it in all the States show how generally and thoroughly it is appreciated. But the movement which led to it proceeded from the feeling of a *want to be supplied*, rather than from any clear perception of the character of the thing wanted. While the struggle was to get it accepted, any thing passing under the name of Education—any thing learned from books at stated times and in set places—was sufficient.

But the first step being taken and the System secured, the question inevitably arises as to its character, defects, and the means of its improvement; and this is now the supreme consideration. Deeper than all questions of Reconstruction, Suffrage, and Finance, is the question, *What kind of culture shall the growing mind of the nation have?* The recent and extensive organization of Normal Schools for the more thorough and systematic preparation of Teachers, is proof of a general desire to improve the methods and raise the standard of popular instruction; and there are many other indications of a growing disposition to carry educational inquiries down to first principles, and to bring the system into better harmony with the needs of the times.

Among other imperfections of the prevailing education, in all its grades, one of the most serious is a lack of the study of Nature. The importance of giving a larger space to scientific subjects, in our educational courses, is being every year more and more felt and acknowledged. In place of the excess of verbal acquisition and mechanical recitation, we need more thinking about things; in place of the passive acceptance of mere book and tutorial authority, more cultivation of independent judgment; in place of the arbitrary presentation of unrelated subjects, the branches of knowledge require to be dealt with in a more rational and connected order; and in place of much that is irrelevant, antiquated, and unpractical in our systems of study, there is needed a larger infusion of the living and available truth which belongs to the present time. A conviction of the extent of its defects and needs has led many of the most eminent thinkers to criticise the existing Educational Systems, and to urge the claims of the various sciences to increasing consideration. These opinions have generally been expressed in the form of lectures and incidental arguments, which are not convenient of access; and a belief that it would be a useful service at the present time to collect some of the most important of them, has led to the present compilation.

Most of the lectures in this volume have not been before published in this country, and the authors of several have kindly revised their productions for the present work. It may be added that several of the discussions are important not only as presenting the claims and educational value of their subjects, but also as suggesting the best methods of their study. Professor Liebig's late lecture on the "Development of Ideas in Physical Science" has so direct a bearing upon the position and claims of science, especially in this country, as to deserve a place in the present collection; and an excellent translation of it has been expressly made for this volume.

Nearly all the discussions it contains have been made within the last dozen years, and several of them quite recently; so that they may be regarded as outgrowths and exponents of the present state of thought. Those of Tyndall, Paget, Faraday, Whewell, and Hodgson, were parts of a course delivered before the Royal Institution of Great Britain, on the claims of the various sciences as means of the education of all classes. Although the reader may miss in this volume the connection and coherency of a systematic treatise on the subject by a single writer, and even note some minor points of disagreement, yet he will find that each statement is a section of a comprehensive and essentially harmonious argument which presents an attractive variety of treatment; while the stamp of various and powerful minds, each speaking upon the subject with which he is best acquainted, must give the general discussion far greater authority than the work of any one man, no matter how able, could possibly possess.

The lecture on "The Scientific Study of Human Nature," and the introductory essay on "Mental Discipline in Education" have been contributed by the editor, not because he thought himself at all competent to do justice to these interesting topics, but because, holding them to be of the first importance, he was unable to find any discussion of them in a form appropriate to the volume. In the Introduction he has attempted to show that a course of study, mainly scientific, not only meets the full requirements of mental training, but also affords the kind of culture or mental discipline which is especially needed in this country at the present time. He has there presented the phases of discipline as *successive*, and the course of subjects should undoubtedly conform to the order stated; yet, as President Hill, of Harvard, has pointed out in his admirable pamphlet on "The True Order of Studies," the pupil's mind requires to be variously exercised from the outset;—several different lines of acquisition being carried along together. The organization of a scheme of study adapted to American wants is the educational problem immediately before us, and the present volume, it is hoped, will contribute valuable suggestions toward its solution.

NEW YORK, *May* 1, 1867.

CONTENTS.

PREFACE, ...

INTRODUCTION—ON MENTAL DISCIPLINE IN EDUCATION, ... 1

PROFESSOR TYNDALL ON THE STUDY OF PHYSICS, 57

PROFESSOR HENFREY ON THE STUDY OF BOTANY, 87

PROFESSOR HUXLEY ON THE STUDY OF ZOOLOGY, 117

DR. JAMES PAGET ON THE STUDY OF PHYSIOLOGY, 147

DR. FARADAY ON THE EDUCATION OF THE JUDGMENT, ... 185

DR. WHEWELL ON THE EDUCATIONAL HISTORY OF SCIENCE, ... 225

DR. HODGSON ON THE STUDY OF ECONOMIC SCIENCE, 253

MR. HERBERT SPENCER ON POLITICAL EDUCATION, 295

DR. BARNARD ON EARLY MENTAL TRAINING, . . 309

PROFESSOR LIEBIG ON THE DEVELOPMENT OF SCIENTIFIC IDEAS, ... 345

E. L. YOUMANS ON THE SCIENTIFIC STUDY OF HUMAN NATURE, ... 371

APPENDIX.

PAGE

Sir John Herschel on University Studies, ... 415
Dr. George E. Paget on the General Influence of Scientific Culture, . 418
Herbert Spencer on the Order of Discovery in the Progress of Knowledge, 425
Dr. Draper on the Deficiencies of Clerical Education, ... 427
Dr. Seguin on the Physiological Basis of Primary Education, . . 431
Dr. Wayland on Modern Collegiate Studies, ... 434
Professor De Morgan on Thoroughness of Intellectual Attainment, . 438
Professor Edward Forbes on the Educational Uses of Museums, . . 443
Prince Albert on the Educational Claims of Science, ... 444
Dr. Hill on the Cultivation of the Senses, ... 445
Professor Goldwin Smith on Classical and Modern Culture, ... 449
Dr. Acland on Early Physiological Study, ... 450
Lord Macaulay on the Study of Classical Languages, ... 451

EXTRACTS FROM EVIDENCE BEFORE THE ENGLISH PUBLIC SCHOOLS' COMMISSION.

Evidence of Dr. Carpenter, ... 452
Evidence of Sir Charles Lyell, ... 459
Evidence of Dr. Faraday, ... 462
Evidence of Professor Owen 466
Evidence of Dr. Hooker, ... 470

MENTAL DISCIPLINE IN EDUCATION.

"If we consult reason, experience, and the common testimony of ancient and modern times, none of our intellectual studies tend to cultivate *a smaller number of the faculties, in a more partial or feeble manner, than Mathematics.* This is acknowledged by every writer on Education of the least pretension to judgment and experience."

SIR WILLIAM HAMILTON.

From the "vast preponderance of encouragement to Classical reading which the condition of English culture offers," it will be seen "how important it is for those who know that *mere Classical reading is a narrow and enfeebling Education* to resist any attempts to add to this preponderance, by diminishing the encouragement which the University gives to studies of a larger or more vigorous kind."

DR. WHEWELL.

"To suppose that deciding whether a Mathematical or a Classical Education is the best, is deciding what is the proper curriculum, is much the same thing as to suppose that the whole of dietetics lies in ascertaining whether or not bread is more nutritive than potatoes."

HERBERT SPENCER.

INTRODUCTION.

All educational inquiries assume that man is individually improvable, and therefore collectively progressive. Through varied experiences he is slowly civilized, and there is a growth of knowledge with the course of ages. But while thought is ever advancing, it is the nature of institutions to fix the mental states of particular times; and there hence arises a tendency to conflict between growing ideas and the external arrangements which are designed to express and embody them. Thought refuses to be stationary; institutions refuse to change, and war is the consequence.

This fact is familiarly illustrated in the case of government. Ideas and character, having outgrown the arbitrary institutions of the remoter past, there has arisen between them an antagonism, of the results of which modern history is full. So, too, religious conceptions having developed beyond the ecclesiastical organizations to which they at first gave rise, a struggle arose in the sixteenth century, which, resulting in the Protestant Reformation, has persisted under various aspects to the present time. And so it is also with the traditional systems of mental culture. Educational institutions which have been bequeathed to us by the past, and which may have been suited to their times, have fallen out of harmony with the intellectual necessities of modern life, and a conflict has arisen which is deepening in intensity with the rapid growth of knowledge and the general progress of society.

The friends of educational improvement maintain that the system of culture which prevails in our higher institutions of learning, and which is limited chiefly to the acquisition of the mathematics, and of the ancient languages and literature, was shaped ages ago in a state of things so widely different from the present, that it has become inadequate to existing requirements. They urge that since its establishment the human mind has made immense advances; has changed its attitude to nature and entered upon a new career; that realm after realm of new truth has been discovered; that ideas of government, religion, and society have been profoundly modified, and that new revelations of man's powers and possibilities, and nobler expectations of his future, have arisen. As man is a being of action, it is demanded that his education shall be a preparation for action. As the highest use of knowledge is for guidance, it is insisted that our Collegiate establishments shall give a leading place to those subjects of study which will afford a better preparation for the duties and work of the age in which we live.

The adherents of the traditional system reply that all this is but the unreasoning clamor of a restless and innovating age, which wholly misconceives the true aim of a higher culture, and would reduce every thing to the standard of a low and sordid utility. They maintain that knowledge is to be acquired not on account of its capability of useful application, but for its own intrinsic interest; that the purpose of a liberal education is not to prepare for a vocation or profession, but to train the intellectual faculties. They, therefore, hold that *Mental Discipline* is the true object of a higher culture, and that for its attainment the study of the ancient classics and mathematics is superior to all other means. From the tone assumed by its defenders, when speaking of its incomparable fitness to develop all the mental faculties, it might be inferred that this scheme of study was formed by the help of a perfected science of the human mind. Nothing, however, could be more erroneous. Not only was that system devised ages anterior to any thing like true mental science, but it antedates by centuries the whole body of modern knowledge. There was abundance of vague metaphysics, but hardly a germ of that positive knowledge of the laws of mind, which could serve as a valid basis of education. The predominant culture of modern times had its origin, more than eight hundred years ago, in a superstition of the middle ages. A mystical reverence was attached to the sacred number *seven*, which was supposed to be a key to the order of the universe. That there were seven cardinal virtues, seven deadly sins, seven sacraments, seven days in the week, seven metals, seven planets, and seven apertures in a man's head, was believed to afford sufficient reason for making the course of liberal study consist of seven arts, and occupy seven years. Following another fancy about the relation of three to four, in a certain geometrical figure, these seven arts were divided into two groups. The first three, Grammar, Logic, and Rhetoric, comprised what was called the Trivium; and the remaining four, Arithmetic, Geometry, Astronomy, and Music (the latter as a branch of Arithmetic), formed the Quadrivium. This scheme has been handed down from age to age, and with but slight changes, still predominates in the higher institutions of learning, and still powerfully reacts upon the inferior schools.

Passing by various embarrassing questions suggested by the hypothesis that the one perfect method of bringing the human mind to its highest condition has not only been found, but has been actually organized into educational institutions for hundreds of years—a hypothesis which discredits the whole movement of modern intellect in its educational bearings—let us take up this question of mental discipline. The subject is not only intrinsically important, but its importance is greatly heightened when an old and widely-established system, challenged by the spirit of the age, yields the point of the usefulness of the knowledge it imparts, and offers as its sole defence its superior merits as a system of mental training; and still more important does it become when the idea is so constantly and vehemently iterated as to acquire all the force and tenacity of a superstition, and breed a regular cant of education, which serves as the stereotyped apology for numberless indefensible projects and crudities of instruction. The writer recently opened a huge volume on Heraldry, and the very first passage which struck his eye in the preface, urged the claims of that subject to more general study on the ground of its excellence as a mental discipline.

I propose, in the present Introduction, *first*, to point out the defects of the traditional system as a means of disciplining the mind; and, *second*, to show the superior claims of scientific education for this purpose.

The claims put forth in behalf of the prevailing scheme are as multitudinous and diverse as the tastes and capacities of those who offer them—a natural result, perhaps, in the absence of any considerations so decisive as to command general agreement; but those most commonly urged are, that the grammatical acquisition of the dead languages best disciplines the memory and judgment, and the study of mathematics the reason. Let us briefly notice these points first:

That the acquisition of words exercises the memory is of course true—those of living languages as well as dead ones, but their assumed merit for discipline raises the question *how* they exercise it. Memory is the capability of recalling past mental impressions, and depends chiefly upon the relations subsisting among these impressions in the mind. If they are arbitrary, the power of recall depends upon multiplicity of repetition, and involves a maximum outlay of mental force in acquisition. If, however, ideas are arranged in the mind in a natural order of connection and dependence, this principle becomes the most important element in commanding past acquisitions. The conditions are then reversed; the outlay of effort in acquisition is reduced, and the power of recall increased. Now the memory cultivated in the common acquirement of language, is of this lowest kind. The relation between words and the ideas, or objects, of which they are the signs, is accidental and arbitrary. Although philological science is beginning dimly to trace out certain natural relations between words and the things they signify, it will not be claimed that this is made at all available in the ordinary study of Latin and Greek; indeed, the most thorough-going advocates of these studies claim that their disciplinal value is in the ratio of the naked retentive power which they call into exercise. But the memory cannot be best disciplined by a mental procedure which neglects its highest law. If the power of recovering past states of consciousness depends upon the natural and necessary connections among ideas, then those studies are best suited for a rational discipline of this power which involve these natural relations among objects. On both grounds the sciences are preferable to dead languages, as instruments of culture. For if it be held desirable merely to task the memory by a dead pull at arbitrary facts (and there are not wanting those who hold to this notion of discipline), then it is only necessary to use the innumerable facts of science, without regard to order; but when we take into account the immense importance of methodizing mental acquisition, and utilizing the principle of natural association among the elements of knowledge, the immeasurable superiority of the sciences for this purpose becomes at once apparent. This is happily illustrated by some observations of Dr. Arnold, respecting the memory of geography. He says:

"And this deeper knowledge becomes far easier to remember. For my own part I find it extremely difficult to remember the positions of towns, when I have no other association with them than their situations relatively to each other. But let me once understand the real geography of a country—its organic structure, if I may so call it; the form of its skeleton, that is, of its hills; the magnitude and course of its veins and arteries, that is, of its streams and rivers; let me conceive of it as a whole made up of connected parts; and then the positions of towns viewed in reference to these parts becomes at once easily remembered, and lively and intelligible besides."

If now it be said that it is not mere memory of words that is contended for, but the discipline and judgment afforded by the grammatical study of the structure of language, the crushing answer is that a dead language is unnecessary for this discipline, which is far better secured by the systematic study and thorough logical analysis of the vernacular tongue.* Perhaps there is no point in education in which there is so universal and intense an agreement among independent thinkers, as in condemning the folly of beginning the acquisition of foreign languages, living or dead, by the study of their grammar—the method in general use among those who defend it as a mental discipline. The usual school-practice of thrusting the young into the grammar, even of their native tongue, is well known to be one of the most efficient means of the artificial production of stupidity; but the habit of introducing them to a foreign language through this gateway, is a still more flagrant outrage. The natural method of acquiring speech is the way we all acquire it; the knowledge of words first, then their combination into sentences, to be followed by the practical use of the language; rules and precepts may then be intelligently applied. But to begin with these is to put the complex before the simple, the abstract before the concrete, generals before particulars, and, in short, to invert the natural order of mental processes, and to work the mind backward, under the plea of disciplining it. An eminent living authority in philology, Professor Latham, in a lecture before the Royal Institution of Great Britain, observed:

"In the ordinary teaching of what is called the grammar of the English language, there are two elements. There is something professed to be taught which is not; and there is something which, from being already learned better than any man can teach it, requires no lessons. The latter is the use and practice of the English tongue. The former is the principles of grammar. The facts, that language is more or less regular; that there is such a thing as grammar; that certain expressions should be avoided, are all matters worth knowing. And they are all taught even by the worst method of teaching. But are these the proper

* See Prof. Jewell's able paper on the "Logical Analysis of the English Language," in Proceedings of N. Y. University Convocation.

objects of systematic teaching? Is the importance of their acquisition equivalent to the time, the trouble, and the displacement of more valuable subjects, which are involved in their explanation? I think not. Gross vulgarity of language is a fault to be prevented; but the proper prevention is to be got from habit—not rules. The proprieties of the English language are to be learned, like the proprieties of English manners, by conversation and intercourse; and a proper school for both is the best society in which the learner is placed. If this be good, systematic teaching is superfluous; if bad, insufficient. There *are* unquestionably points where a young person may doubt as to the grammatical propriety of a certain expression. In this case let him ask some one older, and more instructed. Grammar, as an *art*, is undoubtedly the art of speaking and writing correctly—but then, as an art, it is only required for foreign languages. For our own we have the necessary practice and familiarity.

"The true claim of English grammar, to form part and parcel of an English education, stands or falls with the value of the philological knowledge to which grammatical studies may serve as an introduction, and with the value of scientific grammar, as a disciplinal study. I have no fear of being supposed to undervalue its importance in this respect. Indeed, in assuming that it is very great, I also assume that wherever grammar is studied as grammar, the language which the grammar so studied should represent, must be the mother tongue of the student, whatever that mother tongue may be. This study is the study of a theory; and for this reason it should be complicated as little as possible by points of practice. *For this reason a man's mother tongue is the best medium for the elements of scientific philology*, simply because it is the one which he knows best in practice."

It thus appears that to secure the disciplinary uses of grammatical study, not even a foreign language is necessary, much less a dead one.

When it is remembered that the Hebrew language had no grammar till a thousand years after Christ; that the. masterpieces of Greek literature were produced before Aristotle first laid the grammatical foundations of that language; that the Romans acquired the Greek without grammatical aid, by reading and conversation; that the most eminent scholars of the middle ages and later, Alfred, Abelard, Beauclerc, Roger Bacon, Chaucer, Dante, Petrarch, Lipsius, Buddeus, and the Scaligers—Latin scholars, who have never since been surpassed, learned this language without the assistance of grammar; that Lilly's grammar, in doggerel Latin verse, was thrust upon the English schools by royal edict of Henry VIII., against the vehement protest of men like Ascham, and that the decline of eminent Latinists in that country was coincident with the general establishment of this method of teaching; that Dante, Petrarch, and Boccaccio gave to the world their immortal works two hundred years before the appearance of the first Italian grammar; that Shakespeare, Milton, Dryden, Addison, Pope, Young, Thomson, Johnson, Burns, and others, whose names will live as long as the English language, had not in their childhood learned any English grammar; that Corneille, Moliere, La Fontaine, Pascal, Bossuet, Boileau, and Racine, wrote their masterpieces long before the publication of any French grammar; that men like Collet, Wolsey, Erasmus, Milton, Locke, Gibbon, Condillac, Lemare, Abbe Sicard, Basil Hall, Horne Tooke, Adam Smith, and a host of others, have emphatically condemned the method of acquiring language through the study of grammar; that the most eminent masters of language, Demosthenes, Seneca, Malherbe, Clarendon, Montesquieu, Fenelon, Voltaire, Rousseau, Montaigne,

Boileau, Dante, Galileo, Franklin, Gibbon, Robertson, Pope, Burns, Byron, and Moore, acknowledge that they attained their excellences of style by the study and imitation of the best models of writing; and finally, that mere grammarians are generally bad writers: when we recall facts like these, we can begin to rate at something like their true value the claims of the grammatical study of defunct forms of speech for mental training. That there is a useful discipline in the critical study of language, as in the critical study of most other things, is not denied; but that it has either the transcendent importance usually assumed, or that it cannot be substantially acquired by the mastery of modern tongues, is what the advocates of the dead languages have failed to prove.*

Let us now notice the discipline of mathematics, the claims of which to an important place in a liberal scheme of education are of course unquestionable. Dealing with conceptions of quantity under various forms of expression, and with a varying application to universal phenomena, they are an indispensable key to universal science, and their basis is, therefore, a broad and solid utility. But the devotees of tradition are not satisfied with this; they make extravagant claims for mathematics, on the ground of the discipline they afford, and then usurp for them an educational predominance to which they are not entitled. In their subordinate place they are invaluable; as a too engrossing subject of study, injurious. Mathematics are suited to form habits of continuous attention by dealing with trains of proof, to help the imagination steadily to grasp abstract relations, and to familiarize the mind

* For confirmation of the statements in this paragraph see "Marcel on Language," in two volumes. London: Chapman & Hall, 1853. It is not creditable to American education that this able work has not been republished here.

with a system of necessary truth. But they do not afford a complete exercise of the reasoning powers. They begin with axioms, self-evident truths, established principles, and proceed to their conclusions along a track each step of which is an intuitive certainty. But it so happens that in our mental dealings with the experiences of life, the first, the most important, and most difficult thing is to get the data or premises from which to reason. The primary question is, What are the facts, the pertinent facts, and all the facts, which bear upon the inquiry? This is the supreme step; for, until this is done, reasoning is futile, and it may be added that, when this is done, the formation of conclusions is a comparatively simple process. Now mathematical training cannot help to this important preliminary work; it leaves its cultivator to the blind acceptance or blind rejection of his premises. Those, therefore, who have exclusively pursued these studies, so as to form mathematical habits of thinking, have no preparation for the practical emergencies of thought, where contingencies are to be taken into account, where probable evidence is to be weighed, and conclusions from imperfect knowledge are to be formed and acted upon. The pure mathematician is therefore liable to a one-sided and erratic judgment of affairs. An exclusive mathematical discipline must, therefore, be held as an actual disqualification for the work of life.*

* Dugald Stewart remarks: "How accurate soever the logical process may be, if our first principles be rashly assumed, or if our terms be indefinite and ambiguous, there is no absurdity so great that we may not be brought to adopt it; and it unfortunately happens that, while mathematical studies exercise the faculty of reasoning or deduction, they give no employment to the other powers of the understanding concerned in the investigation of truth. On the contrary, they are apt to produce a facility in the admission of data, and a circumscription of the field of speculation by partial and arbitrary definitions. . . . I think I have observed a peculiar proneness in mathematicians to avail themselves of

It is important to notice that, so far as the mode of exercising the mind is concerned, mathematical discipline does not correct the defects of lingual discipline, but rather confirms them. We hence see how it was that mathematics so perfectly harmonized with philology as to have been early and naturally incorporated with it in the same scheme of culture. Both begin with the unquestioning acceptance of data—axioms, definitions, rules; both reason deductively from foregone assumptions, and therefore both habituate to the passive acceptance of authority—the highest mental desideratum in the theological ages and establishments which gave origin to the traditional curriculum.

To those familiar with the literature of this discussion, the objections here presented will not be new; but there are certain considerations growing out of the recent progress of thought, which have a powerful bearing upon the question, and which it is desirable now to present. And first, What is the real significance of the phrase 'discipline of the mind'?

By mental discipline in education is meant, that systematic and protracted exercise of the mental powers which is suited to raise them to their highest degree of healthful capability, and impart a permanent direction to

principles sanctioned by some imposing names, and to avoid all discussion which might tend to an examination of ultimate truths, or involve a rigorous analysis of their ideas. . . . In the course of my own experience I have not met with a mere mathematician, who was not credulous to a fault; credulous not only with respect to human testimony, but credulous also in matters of opinion; and prone, on all subjects which he had not carefully studied, to repose too much faith in illustrations and consecrated names." Pascal also observes: "It is rare that mathematicians are observant, or that observant minds are mathematical, because mathematicians would treat matters of observation by rule of mathematic, and make themselves ridiculous by attempting to commence by definitions, and by principles."

their activity. The mind takes a set or stamp from the character of the knowledge it acquires, and the mode of activity which these acquisitions involve, and, in this way, mental habits are formed. But, what is the basis of this great fact of mental habits, by which so spiritual an agency as mind becomes fettered? It is a property of the *organic constitution*, and its consideration brings us down to the firm physiological basis of the whole subject.

There are two methods of studying mind. The old metaphysical method simply takes note of the mental effects which are manifested in consciousness, but modern psychology goes deeper, and takes into account the conditions under which these manifestations arise. It no longer admits of denial or cavil, that the Author of our being has seen fit to connect mind and intelligence with a nervous mechanism: in studying mental phenomena, therefore, in connection with this mechanism, we are studying them in the relation which God has established, and, therefore, in the only true relation. There is still a powerful prejudice against this proceeding. Literature and Theology continue to pour their contempt upon that 'matter' which infinite wisdom has consecrated to the high purpose of manifesting mental effects, while the scientific study of the organ of thought has been, until very recently, outlawed by the state.* Yet nothing is more certain than that in future, mind is to be studied in connection with the organism by which it is conditioned: when we begin to deal with the problem of mental discipline, metaphysics no longer avail; it is the organism with which we have finally to deal.

When it is said that the brain is the organ of the mind, it is meant that in thinking, remembering, reasoning, *the brain acts*. It is now admitted that all impressions made

* Human dissections having been, until lately, illegal.

upon the brain, and all actions occurring within it, are accompanied by physical changes. Thought usually goes on so quietly, and seems so far removed from bodily activity, that we are easily betrayed into the notion that it is carried on in a region of pure spirit; but this is far from being the truth. The changes of states of consciousness, the course of thought, and all processes of the understanding, are carried on by a constant succession of nerve-excitements and nerve-discharges. The brain is not a chaos of parts thrown together at random; it consists of hundreds of millions of cells and fibres, organized into symmetrical order, so as to produce innumerable connections, crossings, and junctions of exquisite delicacy. The simple elements of mind are built up into complex knowledge by the law of association of ideas; and the mental associations are formed by combinations of currents in the brain, and are made permanent by the growth and modification of cells at the points of union. When a child associates the sight, weight, and ring of a dollar, with the written word and verbal sound that represent it so firmly together in its mind that any one of these sensations will instantly bring up the others, it is said to 'learn' it. But the real fact of the case is, that the currents formed by visible impressions, vocal movements and sounds, are often repeated together, and are thus combined in the brain, and fixed by specific growths at their points of union, and in this way the mental associations are cemented by cerebral nutrition. And thus the child goes on multiplying its experiences of the properties of objects and of localities, persons, actions, conduct; he observes, compares, contrasts, infers, and judges, and all this growing and complex mass of acquisition is definitely combined in the growing and perfecting organ of the mind.

The basis of educability, and hence of mental discipline, is, therefore, to be sought in the properties of that nervous substance by which mind is manifested. That basis is the law that cerebral effects are strengthened and made lasting by repetition. When an impression is made upon the brain, a change is produced, and an effect remains in the nerve substance; if it be repeated, the change is deepened, and the effect becomes more lasting. If we have a perception of an object, or if we perform an action only once, the nervous change is so slight that the idea may perhaps never reappear, and the act never be repeated; if experienced twice, the tendency to recur is increased; if many times, this tendency is so deepened, and the links of association become so extended, that the idea will be often obtruded into thought, and the action may take place involuntarily. Intellectual 'capacity' is thus at bottom an affair of physical impressibility, or nervous adhesiveness. Regard being had to the law that all nutritive operations involve repose, cohesion or completeness of association depends upon repetition. Of course, constitutions differ widely in this property, some requiring many more repetitions than others, to secure acquirement.* This view leads to important practical conclusions.

* To illustrate the two modes of viewing mental phenomena, I will quote a couple of extracts from eminent authorities, reprobating the pernicious practice of 'cramming' for examinations. Dr. Whewell, content with the metaphysical method, observes: "I may add my decided opinion that no system of education which is governed entirely or even mainly by examinations, occupying short times with long intervening intervals, can ever be otherwise than bad mental discipline. Intellectual education requires that the mind should be habitually employed in the acquisition of knowledge, with a certain considerable degree of clear insight and independent activity."

Mr. Bain takes the psychological view, and reaches the vital dynamics of the case. He says: "The system of cramming is a scheme for making temporary acquisitions, regardless of the endurance of them. Excitable brains, that

When it is perceived that what we have to deal with in mental acquirement is organic processes, which have a definite time-rate of procedure, so that, however vigorously the currents are sustained by keeping at a thing, acquisition is not increased in the same degree; when we see that new attainments are easiest and most rapid during early life—the time of most vigorous growth of the body generally; that thinking exhausts the brain as really as working exhausts the muscles, and that rest and nutrition are as much needed in one case as the other; when we see that rapidity of attainment and tenacity of memory involve the question of cerebral adhesions, and note how widely constitutions differ in these capabilities, how they depend upon blood, stock, and health, and vary with numberless conditions, we become aware how inexorably the problem of mental attainment is hedged round with limitations, and the vague notion that there are no bounds to acquisition except imperfect application, disappears forever.*

The doctrine of mental limitations, which we thus find grounded in the organic constitution, puts the philosophy of education at once on the basis of the economy of mental power. The student is constantly told that his time is limited, and exhorted not to waste it; but his forces of acquisition are equally limited, and it becomes a question of still higher importance how to economize these, for it

can command a very great concentration of force upon a subject, will be proportionably improved for the time being. By drawing upon the strength of the future, we are able to fix temporarily a great variety of impressions during the exaltation of cerebral power that the excitement gives. The occasion past, the brain must lie idle for a corresponding length of time, while a large portion of the excited impressions will gradually perish away. This system is exceedingly unfavorable to permanent acquisitions; for these the brain should be carefully husbanded, and temporarily drawn upon. Every period of undue excitement and feverish susceptibility is a time of great waste for the plastic energy of the mind."

* See page 348.

is possible sedulously to save the moments while squandering half the energies of the mind in bad application. Obviously if intellectual power has its fixed bounds, the supreme question is, How can the highest results be attained within those bounds?

Nature's method of economizing power is by repetition of actions in constantly varying conditions. The celestial order is maintained by endless repetition of axial and orbital revolutions. The operations of the world are carried on by using over and over again the same stock of resources; matter and force circle round and round through the mineral, vegetable, and animal phases; in the growing plant leaves undergo constant transformation into other organs, while the animal skull is formed of modified vertebral spines. And so in the unfoldings of the mental world, Nature is constantly falling back upon old acquisitions, and using them to produce new effects. In the process of acquirement, ideas and aptitudes once mastered are constantly wrought into higher and more complex combinations. The organ of thought being a vast reduplication of the same simple elements, the growth of thought results from an endless repetition of the same simple operations.

The child, through numberless repetitions of effort, at length gets the aptitude of using its hands for ordinary purposes. But this faculty once secured, serves for life in all the ordinary emergencies of action. The necessity for new and varied movements involves no new acquisitions; within the range of ordinary activity the early aptitudes suffice. But if in any case manipulations of special delicacy and precision are required, as in learning to draw, a new acquisition must be made. Yet here the same thing occurs. The new acquirement may be utilized in other similar applications; if the child have first learned to draw, the aptitude will serve also in learning to write.

Again, the instrumental performer, by long drill, acquires a great number of movements, according to the range of his musical sensibility, so that learning new pieces is but little else than new combinations of old sequences—the new acquisition being, in fact, but a new grouping of old acquisitions. So also in the purely intellectual operations. In learning geometry, the mind having grasped the preliminary definitions, axioms, and postulates, uses them over and over in solving the successive problems; while mathematical genius consists mainly in the ready ability to identify the old elements under the disguises of the new cases. In fixing the conception of a new mineral, plant, or animal, the naturalist recalls the characteristics of known specimens which most nearly resemble them, and superadds to these the new features. The same thing holds in learning languages. The mastery of Latin reduces the labor of acquiring Italian, French, and Spanish, into which it largely enters; and we find new words to be easy in proportion as they consist of old familiar articulations. In historical studies, revolutions, campaigns, negotiations, and political measures, are repeated by the same nation at successive epochs, and by one government after another, so that a new history is but a varied reading of old ones; the really new features bearing but a small proportion to those already fixed in the student's mind. The vast mental economy which would arise throughout civilization by the general adoption of decimal coinage, weights, and measures, is but another illustration of the principle; a few simple arithmetical acquisitions would serve the requirements of all who deal with relations of quantity. In short, our reason has been aptly defined as 'the power of using old facts in new circumstances,' and this is the secret of the production of vast effects with limited resources.*

Now this principle, as it affords the true key to intellectual progress, must become the organizing law of education. We find that extent of mental attainment depends, not alone upon intellectual effort, but upon the order of relations among objects of thought. Of course, menta capacity is the first factor in acquisition, but that being given, the scale of possible attainment depends absolutely upon the order of the course of study. Education cannot make capacity, but it controls the conditions by which the least or the most can be made of it. If the methods of study be such that the mind encounters broad breaks in its course, and is abruptly shifted into new lines of effort, so that past conceptions are not carried on to a progressive unfolding, mental growth is checked and power lost. The extent to which one fact or principle is a repetition or outgrowth of another, in the serial relation of subjects, determines the rate of mental movement, which can only become steady and rapid in continuous ranges of effort. As in the outward world, the past creates the future along unbroken lines of dynamic sequence and causation, so in the mental world, there must be a corresponding continuity of movement by which the past creates the future in intellectual evolution.

We have here the touchstone of educational systems, and the fatal condemnation of the current theory of discipline. How grossly that theory violates the law of mental economy, and, indeed, actually *provides* for waste of power, will be apparent by glancing briefly at its origin. The notion of mental gymnastics was borrowed from

* For a full working out of this doctrine, see Bain's "Senses and Intellect."

that of bodily gymnastics. In early times, useful labor being regarded as menial and degrading, the superior classes sought the activity needed for health in various artificial exercises. The old Greek gymnastics was a system of athletic exercises cultivated for the attainment of physical development, and had no reference to the preparation of men for the occupations of industry. The ancient philosophers held that it was as degrading to seek useful knowledge as to practise useful arts; hence, subjects of study were chosen as intellectual gymnastics and to acquire mental discipline, and this, not as a preparation for valuable mental labor, but as an end in itself. Not the game, but the excitement of the chase; not the truth, but the exhilaration of its pursuit, were the mottoes of culture. Under these circumstances no vulgar question of economy could arise; mental power was ostentatiously wasted, and with the necessary consequences—truth unsought was not found; the ends of culture being ignored, there was neither conquest of nature nor progress of society.

Not only does the principle of vicarious discipline involve enormous mental waste, but the system of studies employed to secure it grossly violates the great law of acquisition, which should become the basis of education. That system is neither an outgrowth of the proper education of childhood, nor does it flow on into the intellectual life of manhood: it is a foreign body of thought, uncongenial and unaffiliated, thrust into the academic period, and destroying the unity and continuity of the mental career. The young student is detached from all his early mental connections, expatriated to Greece and Rome for a course of years, becomes charged with antiquated ideas, and then returns to resume his relation with the onflowing current of events in his own age. The radical defect of the traditional system is, that it fails to recognize and grasp the controlling ends of culture. Misled by the fallacy that, through a scheme of aimless exercises for discipline, mental power may be accumulated for universal application, it sees no necessity of organizing education with explicit reference to ultimate and definite purposes, and it thus forfeits its right of control over the educational interests of the time. For that there are great and well-defined aims, revealed with more clearness in this age than ever before, to which a higher mental culture should be subservient, does not admit of intelligent question. If the classical system grasps the conception of education, in its ends as well as its beginnings, as a preparation for the activities of life; and of discipline, as the formation of habits to guide a constantly unfolding mental career; and of knowledge, as consisting of a chain of relations, along which the mind is to move in accomplishing that career; if it unfolds the order of the world, and puts the student in command of the ripest and richest results of past thinking; if it qualifies best for the relations of parenthood, citizenship, and the multiform responsibilities of social relation; if it equips for the intelligent and courageous consideration of those vital questions which the progress of knowledge and aspiration are forcing upon society; if it fits most effectually for these supreme ends, then, indeed, it affords a proper discipline for the needs of the time; but if the student, after having faithfully mastered his collegiate tasks, finds upon entering the world of action, that his acquisitions are not available—that he has to leave them behind him and begin anew, then his preparation has been a bad one; time has been irretrievably lost, power irrecoverably wasted, and the chances are high that he will give the go-by to modern knowledge, and thin down his intellectual life to the languid nursing of his classical memories.

It is well known that, in numerous cases, the success of educated men may be directly traced to neglect of the regular college studies, or to their neutralization by the vigorous pursuit of other subjects; and equally notorious that in numberless other cases, where the student has surrendered himself to college influences and conquered his *curriculum*, exactly in proportion to his fidelity has been his defeat. He has mastered a disqualifying culture. In hundreds of instances it has been the lot of the writer to listen to expressions of bitter regret on the part of college graduates at the misdirected studies and the misapplied time which their 'liberal' education had involved. "O that I had some knowledge of those imminent questions that are urging themselves on public attention, in place of my *college lumber!*" is a stereotyped exclamation in these cases. And this turn of expression discloses the worst aspect of the matter, for the lumber cannot be got rid of. The mind is not a reservoir to be emptied and refilled at pleasure. The student has not been preparing a soil for future sowing; he has sown it, and to extirpate the roots will consume half a lifetime. In the most plastic period of receptivity he has been making acquisitions and forming habits which, by coercing his attention and engrossing his thoughts, will operate powerfully to obstruct subsequent mental operations; for if they do not help, they must inevitably hinder.

In the preceding pages, after pointing out some of the special disciplinary defects of the traditional scheme of study, I have endeavored to show that in its very conception of mental training there is involved enormous waste of power, and in its course of study a total non-recognition of the great law by which alone the highest mental attainment can be reached. I have also shown that this erroneous conception of discipline, by ignoring the great ends of culture, and the adaptation of studies to them, not only wastes power, but gives a false preparation for life. It remains now to indicate how these errors and defects may be remedied by scientific education.

Let it be remembered that this culture does not deny the importance of mental discipline, but only the wasteful policy of vicarious discipline. The question has three aspects. The ancients employed the useless fact A for disciplinary purposes, and ignored the useful fact B. The adherents of the current theory propose to learn first the useless fact A to get the discipline necessary to acquire the useful fact B; while a rational system ignores useless A and attacks B at once, making it serve both for knowledge and discipline. The ancient view was more reasonable than that which has grown out of it. It wanted one acquisition, and it made it; the prevailing method wants one, and makes two; and as it costs as much effort to learn a useless fact as a useful one, by this method half the power is wasted.

The moment that the conception of *value* attaches to power, the idea of its *economy* inevitably arises, and this is fatal to its vicarious application. Hence gymnastics are never thought of as a preparation for industrial occupation. The employer who should resort to them would quickly come to bankruptcy, for he knows that the laborer has but a limited amount of power, all of which it is necessary to utilize; and he understands that the needed aptness comes in the regular course of occupation, and in that way alone. In the world of business, where results become quickly apparent, and a wrong policy works speedy disaster, the notion of discipline *for* a special activity, and not *through* it, could not be entertained, and it only lingers in the world of mind and education because *there* effects are more remote, complex, and indefinite, and the consequences of a wrong principle are less readily detected. With the growing perception of the relation between human thought and human life, it will be seen that by far the most priceless of all things is mental power; while one of the highest offices of education must be strictly to economize and wisely to expend it. Science made the basis of culture, will accomplish this result.

We have affirmed the broad principle of mental limitations, but let none suppose that its necessary corollary is narrow and stinted mental results. It has been explained how this consequence is to be escaped. A limited outlay of energy with results so vast as to seem out of all proportion with it, is exactly the miraculous problem which Nature has solved. It was at first supposed that prodigious quantities of power were required to work the Atlantic cable—an error which probably led to its destruction; but electricians have been recently startled by the discovery that the force generated in a lady's thimble, or even in a percussion-cap, is sufficient to operate the ocean telegraph. The lesson of this experience is, that a knowledge of the laws of power is essential to prevent waste of power; and this is no more true in physical dynamics than in mental. Let none indulge apprehensions that this doctrine of limits to acquirement darkens the future of education, or derogates from man's mental dignity. What the human mind has already accomplished is our starting-point. Working waywardly, in isolation, by arbitrary methods, upon chaotic materials, and in ignorance of the mighty secret of its power, grand results have nevertheless been achieved, and they are the indices of attainment under the worst conditions. But in the new revelation of a cosmical order, and of the correlation and interdependence of all truth, Science utters a pregnant prophecy of the mind's future destiny, and vindicates her right to take control of its future unfolding.

The ideal of the higher education demanded by the present age, especially in this country, where it is becoming most general, is a scheme of study, which, while it represents the present state of knowledge, and affords a varied cultivation and a harmonious discipline, shall at the same time best prepare for the responsible work of life. For this, the study of languages and mathematics is necessary, but far from sufficient. Other sciences are to be supplied and a curriculum framed, which, conforming to the true logical order of subjects on the one hand, shall equally conform to the order of unfolding the mental faculties on the other, thus reaching an integral discipline through living and applicable knowledge.

There is great significance in the fact that the prevailing higher culture is without a foundation. Professing to devote itself exclusively to the moulding and evolution of mind—sinking knowledge itself into nothingness in comparison with this effect—its method does not reach back to those beginnings of culture which far outweigh in importance all subsequent action. And this is no trifling criticism of that method. Is it possible for a truly philosophical system of training the mental powers to have been organized for centuries in all the higher institutions, and not have reacted with controlling power upon the processes of primary instruction? Here a true method *must* begin, and here scientific education *does* begin. Commencing early, and commencing with Nature, it lays the foundation of culture in the systematic exercise of the observing powers. In childhood there is a vast capability of accumulating simple facts. The higher forms of mental activity not having come into exercise, the whole plastic power of the brain is devoted to the storing up of perceptions, while the vigor of cerebral growth insures the highest intensity of mental adhesiveness. The capability of grasping relations being low, it makes but little difference at first what objects are presented to attention; words or things, with meaning or without, and in the most arbitrary order, stick readily in the memory. Skilful guidance at this period is of the very highest importance. When curiosity is freshest, and the perceptions keenest, and memory most impressible, before the maturity of the reflective powers, the opening mind should be led to the art of noticing the aspects, properties, and simple relations of the surrounding objects of Nature. This should be guided into a growing habit, and the young pupil gradually trained to know how to observe, and what to observe among all the objects of its unfolding experience. It should be encouraged to collect many of the little curiosities which awaken its attention, and required carefully to preserve them; but to do all this judiciously is delicate work. The custodian of the child must know something of the objects of Nature, and much of the nature of the young pupil. Above all other things, teachers qualified to do this work are the desperate need of the age. To perfect the object-method, and train instructors to its discriminating use, is one of the great functions of Normal Schools, and must become the practical basis of a rational system of education. Let it be remembered that there is nothing forced or artificial here: the scenes of childish pleasure and exuberant activity furnish the objects of thought. In creating an interest in these things a bent is given in the true direction; the valuable habit of observing and seeking is formed, while the numberless disconnected shreds of knowledge are incipient acquisitions, which will grow with time into the ripened forms of science.

With such a preparation, the transition is natural to the regular study of the sciences, in which the observing and reasoning powers are to be systematically cultivated. For this purpose the first to be taken up are mathematics, physics, or natural philosophy, and chemistry, as they deal with the clearest and simplest conceptions, and depend upon the fewest and most definite conditions. The adaptation of mathematics to cultivate deductive reasoning has been noticed. Physics trains equally to accuracy and precision of thought; but, beginning with observation, it exercises the reason *inductively*. From particulars we pass to generals; from observed facts to principles, by the mental process of induction, which is a powerful instrumentality. When we contemplate the vast extent of the facts which form the body of the various sciences, and the marvellous rapidity with which they are still accumulating, the task of their acquisition seems appalling, and utterly beyond all grasp of the intellect. But there is an order of Nature by which individual facts are connected and bound together, and there is a corresponding capacity in the human mind of seizing upon those relations, of binding the facts into groups, and of dealing with them, as it were, at wholesale or in masses. This is the faculty of generalization, by which wide-reaching principles replace or *represent* the infinitude of details, which they include. Indeed, the advance of science essentially consists in the successive establishment of such general principles which rise one above another in higher and higher stages, until a few simple laws are found to explain and represent the wide range of phenomena to which they apply. But now mark, that while in this way knowledge is simplified, the mind is called into higher action. The abstraction of a common law from many facts, while it relieves the memory of the burden of a large portion of them, makes a greater demand upon the understanding. In proportion as knowledge is compressed in bulk, its quality becomes, as it were, more intense; and just to the degree to which this operation is carried, is greater intellectual effort required to master it. Thus, in gaining command of the facts of nature and rising to a comprehension of the order of the universe, we are at the same time securing the highest and most salutary form of mental discipline; and a form of it, it may be added, for which the traditional system of culture makes no provision.

The physical sciences, moreover, afford a discipline in deductive reasoning, the same as mathematics, but of a still more valuable character. For while mathematics deals with the smallest number of ideas, those of space and number, which may be abstracted entirely from all material existence, physics includes, in addition to these, the conceptions of matter and force, although it deals with them in their universal properties and forms; and it thus comes nearer to the realities of experience. Deduction is the most common and practical form of mental activity. We are constantly reasoning from our general notions or opinions to particular facts and circumstances. Induction lays the mental foundation by showing us how correctly to arrive at these general notions; deduction guides their constant application;—the physical sciences afford the best training-ground for both.

It is needless to dilate here upon the various benefits, moral as well as intellectual, to be gained by the systematic pursuit of physical studies, as they are abundantly illustrated in the various lectures of the present volume. I may refer, however, to their great value in an experimental point of view. They afford scope for the keenest and closest observation; they link thought to action, and bring the results of thinking to inexorable tests.

The mental advantages to be derived from a more thorough study of the physical sciences have been very clearly and impressively presented in a late discourse by Mr. John Stuart Mill,* and his view so strongly confirms the present argument as to justify extended quotation:

"The most obvious part of the value of scientific instruction, the mere information that it gives, speaks for itself. We are born into a world which we have not made; a world whose phenomena take place according to fixed laws, of which we do not bring any knowledge into the world with us. In such a world we are appointed to live, and in it all our work is to be done. Our whole working power depends on knowing the laws of the world—in other words, the properties of the things which we have to work with, and to work among, and to work upon. We may and do rely, for the greater part of this knowledge, on the few who in each department make its acquisition their main business in life. But unless an elementary knowledge of scientific truths is diffused among the public, they never know what is certain and what is not, or who are entitled to speak with authority and who are not: and they either have no faith at all in the testimony of science, or are the ready dupes of charlatans and impostors. They alternate between ignorant distrust, and blind, often misplaced, confidence. Besides, who is there who would not wish to understand the meaning of the common physical facts that take place under his eye?

* Inaugural Address delivered to the University of St. Andrew, February 1, 1867. By John Stuart Mill.

Who would not wish to know why a pump raises water, why a lever moves heavy weights, why it is hot at the tropics and cold at the poles, why the moon is sometimes dark and sometimes bright, what is the cause of the tides? Do we not feel that he who is totally ignorant of these things, let him be ever so skilled in a special profession, is not an educated man but an ignoramus? It is surely no small part of education to put us in intelligent possession of the most important and most universally interesting facts of the universe, so that the world which surrounds us may not be a sealed book to us, uninteresting because unintelligible. This, however, is but the simplest and most obvious part of the utility of science, and the part which, if neglected in youth, may be the most easily made up for afterward. It is more important to understand the value of scientific instruction as a training and disciplining process, to fit the intellect for the proper work of a human being. Facts are the materials of our knowledge, but the mind itself is the instrument: and it is easier to acquire facts, than to judge what they prove, and how, through the facts which we know, to get to those which we want to know.

"The most incessant occupation of the human intellect throughout life is the ascertainment of truth. We are always needing to know what is actually true about something or other. It is not given to us all to discover great general truths that are a light to all men and to future generations; though with a better general education the number of those who could do so would be far greater than it is. But we all require the ability to judge between the conflicting opinions which are offered to us as vital truths; to choose what doctrines we will receive in the matter of religion, for example; to judge whether we ought to be Tories, Whigs, or Radicals, or to what length it is our duty to go with each; to form a rational conviction on great questions of legislation and internal policy, and on the manner in which our country should behave to dependencies and to foreign nations. And the need we have of knowing how to discriminate truth, is not confined to the larger truths. All through life it is our most pressing interest to find out the truth about all the matters we are concerned with. If we are farmers we want to find what will truly improve our soil; if merchants, what will truly influence the markets of our commodities; if judges, or jurymen, or advocates, who it was that truly did an unlawful act, or to whom a disputed right truly belongs. Every time we have to make a new resolution or alter an old one, in any situation in life, we shall go wrong unless we know the truth about the facts on which our resolution depends. Now, however different these searches for truth may look, and however unlike they really are in their subject-matter, the methods of getting at truth, and the tests of truth, are in all cases much the same. There are but two roads by which truth can be discovered: observation, and reasoning; observation, of course, including experiment. We all observe, and we all reason, and therefore, more or less successfully, we all ascertain truths: but most of us do it very ill, and could not get on at all were we not able to fall back on others who do it better. If we could not do it in any degree, we should be mere instruments in the hands of those who could: they would be able to reduce us to slavery. Then how shall we best learn to do this? By being shown the way in which it has already been successfully done. The processes by which truth is attained, reasoning and observation, have been carried to their greatest known perfection in the physical sciences. As classical literature furnishes the most perfect types of the art of expression, so do the physical sciences those of the art of thinking. Mathematics, and its application to astronomy and natural philosophy, are the most complete example of the discovery of truths by reasoning; experimental science, of their discovery by direct observation. In all these cases we know that we can trust the operation, because the conclusions to which it has led have been found true by subsequent trial. It is by the study of these, then, that we may hope to qualify ourselves for distinguishing truth, in cases where there do not exist the same ready means of verification.

"In what consists the principal and most characteristic difference between one human intellect and another? In their ability to judge correctly of evidence. Our direct perceptions of truth are so limited; we know so few things by immediate intuition, or, as it used to be called, by simple apprehension—that we depend for almost all our valuable knowledge, on evidence external to itself; and most of us are very unsafe hands at estimating evidence, where an appeal cannot be made to actual eyesight. The intellectual part of our education has nothing more important to do than to correct or mitigate this almost universal infirmity—this summary and substance of nearly all purely intellectual weakness. To do this with effect needs all the resources which the most perfect system of intellectual training can command. Those resources, as every teacher knows, are but of three kinds: first, models; secondly, rules; thirdly, appropriate practice. The models of the art of estimating evidence are furnished by science; the rules are suggested by science; and the study of science is the most fundamental portion of the practice. . . . The logical value of experimental science is comparatively a new subject, yet there is no intellectual discipline more important than that which the experimental sciences afford. Their whole occupation consists in doing well, what all of us, during the whole of life, are engaged in doing, for the most part badly. All men do not affect to be reasoners, but all profess, and really attempt, to draw inferences from experience: yet hardly any one, who has not been a student of the physical sciences, sets out with any just idea of what the process of interpreting experience really is. If a fact has occurred once or oftener, and another fact has followed it, people think they have got an experiment, and are well on the road toward showing that the one fact is the cause of the other. If they did but know the immense amount of precaution necessary to a scientific experiment; with what sedulous care the accompanying circumstances are contrived and varied, so as to exclude every agency but that which is the subject of the experiment—or, when disturbing agencies cannot be excluded, the minute accuracy with which their influence is calculated and allowed for, in order that the residue may contain nothing but what is due to the one agency under examination; if these things were attended to, people would be much less easily satisfied that their opinions have the evidence of experience; many popular notions and generalizations which are in all mouths, would be thought a great deal less certain than they are supposed to be; but we should begin to lay the foundation of really experimental knowledge, on things which are now the subjects of mere vague discussion, where one side finds as much to say and says it as confidently as another, and each person's opinion is less determined by evidence than by his accidental interest or prepossession. In politics, for instance, it is evident to whoever comes to the study from that of the experimental sciences, that no political conclusions of any value for practice can be arrived at by direct experience. Such specific experience as we can have, serves only to verify, and even that insufficiently, the conclusions of reasoning. Take any active force you please in politics, take the liberties of England, or free trade; how should we know that either of these things conduced to prosperity, if we could discern no tendency in the things themselves to produce it? If we had only the evidence of what is called our experience, such prosperity as we enjoy might be owing to a hundred other causes, and might have been obstructed, not promoted, by these. All true political science is, in one sense of the phrase, *a priori*, being deduced from the tendencies of things, tendencies known either through our general experience of human nature, or as the result of an analysis of the course of history, considered as a progressive evolution. It requires, therefore, the union of induction and deduction, and the mind that is equal to it must have been well disciplined in both. But familiarity with scientific experiment at least does the useful service of inspiring a wholesome skepticism about the conclusions which the mere surface of experience suggests."

The discipline of observation and strict reasoning afforded by the exact sciences, mathematics, physics, and chemistry, pure and applied, being secured, we then pass to the study of the biological sciences, botany, zoology, physiology, geology. A new order of truths and new circumstances of knowledge are here encountered, to which the sciences just considered are an indispensable introduction, but for which, the mental habits they form are not an adequate preparation. We are still carefully to observe, still to reason from facts to general principles, but the facts, though equally positive, are now so different—so complex, inaccessible, and indefinite, as to embarrass inference, and call for a higher exercise of the judgment. Experiment or active observation, which plays so prominent a part in physics and chemistry, is here greatly limited; we cannot isolate the phenomena, and turn them round and round, and inside out, so as to compel a revelation of their secrets: hence, in proportion as the sources of error become more numerous and fallacies more insidious, a subtler exercise of the reason is demanded—more circumspection in weighing evidence and checking conclusions, and a severer necessity for suspension of judgment. As the biological sciences deal with the laws of life and the phenomena of living beings, man in his animal constitution and relations, is included in their subject-matter, while the problems presented exercise the mind in a manner similar to the formation of judgments upon human affairs. Complete or demonstrative induction being impossible, we are compelled to form conclusions from only a part of the facts involved, and to anticipate the agreement of the rest. This is reasoning *from analogy*, a powerful but perilous mode of proceeding; one which we are compelled constantly to adopt in our mental treatment of the concerns of life, and for which biological studies are eminently suited to give the requisite discipline.

Another advantage of the study of these subjects is afforded by the comprehensiveness and perfection of their *classifications.* No other subjects compare with zoology and botany in these respects. Not only do they furnish inexhaustible material for the exercise of memory, but by the presentation of facts in their natural relations, they exercise it in its highest and most perfect form. It is maintained by Agassiz that classifications in natural history are but reports of the order of Nature—expressions of her profoundest plan; and he even goes so far as to interpret them as a divine ideal programme of constructions, of which the living world is but the execution. However this may be, it is certain that they open to us the broadest view of the relations and harmonies of organic nature, and are best fitted to discipline the mind in dealing with large co-ordinations, and the comprehensive arrangement of objects of thought, whether in the arts, the professions, business, or science. But here, again, I may say, it is unnecessary to expatiate upon advantages which the reader will find more fully and lucidly treated by Professors Henfrey, Huxley, and Paget, in the body of the present work.

Dr. Whewell, in his defence of the absorbing attention given to mathematics and physics, in the University of Cambridge, has urged the necessity of admitting, as means of education, only those subjects, the truths of which are demonstrated and settled forever. But what is the extent of the field of the absolutely unquestionable? Mathematics do indeed present truths upon which rational beings can never disagree; but supposing that the student becomes a little inquisitive, and ventures to ask something about the grounds and origin of these truths, he is instantly launched into the arena of polemical strife, and his teacher, from being a frigid expositor of self-evident principles, is suddenly transformed into an ardent partisan. Dr. Whewell has been the life-long champion of certain views respecting the nature of mathematical conceptions, which are sharply contested, and have certainly no more than held their own in philosophical conflict. In the field of physics, also, has not the present generation witnessed one of the deepest and most comprehensive revolutions which the history of science records—the acceptance of a totally new view of the nature and relations of forces? What, indeed, is the object of education, the *leading out* of the mind, if not to arouse thought and provoke inquiry, as well as to direct them? Is the student's mind a tank to be filled, or an organism to be quickened? It may be well-pleasing to indolent and arrogant pedagogues never to have their assertions questioned, but it is wholesome neither for themselves nor their students.

Important as may be the mental preparation for dealing with certainties, it is still more important to prepare for dealing with uncertainties: to ignore this, arrests education at an inferior stage, and but ill prepares for the emergencies of practical life. It is matter of notoriety that the so-called liberal culture is no adequate protection against numerous fallacies and impostures which are current in society; and to so great an extent is this true that it is common to question whether, after all, for our real needs, education is better than ignorance. But there is an 'educated ignorance,' which, for the great end of guiding to action and ruling the conduct, is as worthless as blank ignorance. Take the charlatanries of medical treatment; take the question of so-called 'spiritual manifestations,' and we find persons of reputed culture and good sense venturing opinions, adopting practices, and professing to 'investigate,' in the completest ignorance of all the conditions of thinking —all the canons of inquiry which have conducted to truth in this high and complex range of subjects.

To meet these and kindred emergencies of our social experience, we require an education not merely in dead languages, mathematics, and physics, with perhaps a superadded smattering of physiology and geology, but such a training in the fundamental organic sciences as shall constitute a thorough *biological discipline.*

The direct and powerful bearing of biological studies upon an understanding of the nature and relations of man has been so well stated by Mr. Mill, in the address already referred to, in speaking of the educational claims of physiology, that I cannot forbear making another extract :

"The first is physiology; the science of the laws of organic and animal life, and especially of the structure and functions of the human body. It would be absurd to pretend that a profound knowledge of this difficult subject can be acquired in youth, or as a part of general education. Yet an acquaintance with its leading truths is one of those acquirements which ought not to be the exclusive property of a particular profession. The value of such knowledge for daily uses has been made familiar to us all by the sanitary discussions of late years. There is hardly one among us who may not, in some position of authority, be required to form an opinion and take part in public action on sanitary subjects. And the importance of understanding the true conditions of health and disease—of knowing how to acquire and preserve that healthy habit of body which the most tedious and costly medical treatment so often fails to restore when once lost, should secure a place in general education for the principal maxims of hygiene, and some of those even of practical medicine. For those who aim at high intellectual cultivation, the study of physiology has still greater recommendations, and is, in the present state of advancement of the higher studies, a real necessity. The practice which it gives in the study of nature is such as no other physical science affords in the same kind, and is the best introduction to the difficult questions of politics and social life. Scientific education, apart from professional objects, is but a preparation for judging rightly of Man, and of his requirements and interests. But to this final pursuit, which has been called *par excellence* the proper study of mankind, physiology is the most serviceable of the sciences, because it is the nearest. Its subject is already Man: the same complex and manifold being, whose properties are not independent of circumstance, and immovable from age to age, like those of the ellipse and hyperbola, or of sulphur and phosphorus, but are infinitely various, indefinitely modifiable by art or accident, graduating by the nicest shades into one another, and reacting upon one another in a thousand ways, so that they are seldom capable of being isolated and observed separately. With the difficulties of the study of a being so constituted, the physiologist, and he alone among scientific inquirers, is already familiar. Take what view we will of man as a spiritual being, one part of his nature is far more like another than either of them is like any thing else. In the organic world we study nature under disadvantages very similar to those which affect the study of moral and political phenomena: our means of making experiments are almost as limited, while the extreme complexity of the facts makes the conclusions of general reasoning unusually precarious, on account of the vast number of circumstances that conspire to determine every result. Yet in spite of these obstacles, it is found possible in physiology to arrive at a considerable number of well-ascertained and important truths. This, therefore, is an excellent school in which to study the means of overcoming similar difficulties elsewhere. It is in physiology, too, that we are first introduced to some of the conceptions which play the greatest part in the moral and social sciences, but which do not occur at all in those of inorganic nature. As, for instance, the idea of predisposition, and of predisposing causes, as distinguished from exciting causes. The operation of all moral forces is immensely influenced by predisposition: without that element, it is impossible to explain the commonest facts of history and social life. Physiology is also the first science in which we recognize the influence of habit—the tendency of something to happen again merely because it has happened before. From physiology, too, we get our clearest notion of what is meant by development or evolution. The growth of a plant or animal from the first germ is the typical specimen of a phenomenon which rules through the whole course of the history of man and society—increase of function, through expansion and differentiation of structure by internal forces. I cannot enter into the subject at greater length; it is enough if I throw out hints which may be germs of further thought in yourselves. Those who aim at high intellectual achievements may be assured that no part of their time will be less wasted, than that which they employ in becoming familiar with the methods and with the main conceptions of the science of organization and life.

"Physiology, at its upper extremity, touches on Psychology, or the Philosophy of Mind: and without raising any disputed questions about the limits between Matter and Spirit, the nerves and brain are admitted to have so intimate a connection with the mental operations, that the student of the last cannot dispense with a considerable knowledge of the first. The value of psychology itself need hardly be expatiated upon in a Scottish university; for it has always been there studied with brilliant success. Almost every thing which has been contributed from these islands toward its advancement since Locke and Berkeley, has until very lately, and much of it even in the present generation, proceeded from Scottish authors and Scottish professors. Psychology, in truth, is simply the knowledge of the laws of human nature. If there is any thing that deserves to be studied by man, it is his own nature and that of his fellow-men: and if it is worth studying at all, it is worth studying scientifically, so as to reach the fundamental laws which underlie and govern all the rest. With regard to the suitableness of this subject for general education, a distinction must be made. There are certain observed laws of our thoughts and of our feelings which rest upon experimental evidence, and, once seized, are a clue to the interpretation of much that we are conscious of in ourselves, and observe in one another. Such, for example, are the laws of association. Psychology, so far as it consists of such laws (I speak of the laws themselves, not of their disputed applications) is as positive and certain a science as chemistry, and fit to be taught as such."

The discipline and the knowledge conferred by study of the preceding group of sciences form the true preparation for that higher class of studies, mental, moral, political, and literary, which completes the course of a true liberal education. Although not themselves ranked as sciences, these extensive and important subjects are constantly becoming more and more scientific in their conceptions and methods, and hence form the natural sequel of a systematic scientific culture. Physiology passes insensibly into psychology, the central science, upon which hinge logic, sociology, political economy, history, ethics, æsthetics, and literature. Mental phenomena are manifestations of life, and their laws are derivatives of the laws of life; only through a knowledge of the former, therefore, is it possible to reach a true understanding of the latter. Logic treats of the laws of evidence and proof, by which things and their relations are truly represented in thought.* Sociology considers the relations among human beings and the forces which act upon them in society, and it hence only becomes possible through a prior knowledge

* See page 45

of the vital and mental organization of man;—political economy, a branch of this subject, treating of industrial and commercial questions, depends upon the same conditions. History is a record of the course of human experience in its multiform phases, and the key to its right interpretation is that knowledge of the character of the Actor and the circumstances of action which it is the prerogative of science alone to give. Ethics, or moral science, determines the principles which should guide the right ruling of conduct, and depends upon every science which can throw light on the progress of the intellect, the evolution of the emotions, and the limits of moral liberty and responsibility imposed by the conditions of physical organization or social circumstances. Æsthetics, which regards the beautiful in nature, and gives rise to the fine arts, depends upon the laws of feeling and sensibility. Its principles are founded in the constitution of human nature, and will probably be yet reduced to a scientific system. To work out its great ideas of 'unity,' 'harmony,' 'proportion,' and the laws of beauty, it awaits a better psychology, and a deeper penetration into the true spirit of nature. Literature is that great body of expression of thought upon a vast variety of subjects, the proper judgment of which depends upon the extent and accuracy of our knowledge of the truth of things in reality, conception, and expression.

Thus does scientific culture reach its ultimate and exalted ends. Its course is along a line of connections which are causal and dynamic; its ideas constantly flowing on and widening out until they embrace all the higher subjects of human interest and inquiry. The order of dependence of facts and principles must here imperatively determine the true order of study. To pass directly from languages and mathematics to the complex questions of man and society, is to violate the continuity of Nature's logic; to carry false methods of reasoning and judgment into the highest spheres of thought, and to provide for those errors of theory and vices of practice which are so lamentably conspicuous in the management of social and public affairs. Only by that scientific discipline which confers a steadfast faith in the universality of law, and only as the discipline of mathematical and physical studies is corrected and amplified by familiarity with biological conceptions, will it be possible to secure a class of thinkers who can grapple with the upper grade of questions, in which the best welfare of society is involved. The culture afforded by these higher subjects is also varied, copious, and quickening. They give breadth, adaptiveness, and enlarged effect to the discipline of the preparatory sciences, and cultivate mental pliancy, readiness of judgment, and practical sagacity.

If it be objected that this scheme is too vast, I reply, *first*, the student is not expected to grasp the details of the various sciences, but only to master their leading principles. At least one science, however, should be thoroughly acquired by every well-educated person—should be carried into detail, pursued experimentally, and pushed to its boundaries. The student should be brought face to face with the stern problems of Nature, and taught to wrestle with the difficulties she offers; only thus can he truly know how much is meant by the word 'truth,' and get the discipline that will give value to his other scientific studies. But while the thorough attainment of a single science may serve for training in method, it is highly desirable, and in a mental point of view completely possible, to master two, say inorganic chemistry and botany. They represent separate orders of scientific truths; both are attractive to fascination, and their opportunities of study are universal.

But, *secondly*, this scheme is not too extended, because its arrangement economizes mental power in the highest degree. Wasting no force for mere discipline, it gives the entire energies of the mind to the direct attainment of knowledge, while the natural sequence of subjects, and the constant reappearance and re-employment of old acquisitions in the track of progress, guarantees a rapidity of mental advancement and a comprehensiveness of attainment without parallel in past experience. With a reverent acquiescence in the finite limitations of mind, science nevertheless gives the clue to reaches of thought and splendors of achievement which old routinists regard with incredulity. When Nature becomes the subject of study, the love of Nature its stimulus, and the order of Nature its guide, then will results in education rival the achievements of Science in the fields of its noblest triumphs.

What now is the basis of relative valuations among subjects of thought? These subjects fall into three categories—1st, the objects of Nature; 2d, their mental representations; 3d, the devices for marking and distinguishing them; and the various terms employed to express these relations may be thus exhibited:

The External World,........	Mind,..................	Language.
Things,...................	Ideas,.................	Words.
Presentation,..............	Re-presentation,..........	Re-representation.
Physics,...................	Metaphysics,............	Philology.
Objective Realities,..........	Subjective Symbols,.......	Artificial Symbols
Objects and Relations to be known,...........	Nature's Instruments for the work,........	Man's Instruments for the work.

In this scheme we build upon the solid foundation of objective nature, and place first that which we find first in the order of the world—the fabric of being into which we are introduced at birth—which was here before we came and will remain when we are gone. Man's first and his life-long concern is with his environment, the objective universe of God, the theatre of his activity, ownership, ambition, enjoyment, and the multifarious instrumentality of his experience and education. It is a realm of law, and therefore he can understand and control it: a scene of irresistible forces which crush him if he is ignorant, and serve him if he is wise. But in what manner are created intelligences to deal with the organism of nature in which they have such varied and vital interests? By its ideal re-creation for the individual. The brain duplicates the universe in miniature; hence the passage from things to thoughts; from objective realities to their ideal symbols. We here, as it were, take one step away from outward nature and enter a world of representation, which is of great importance to us because of the still greater importance of that which it represents. The overlooking of this fact has been the error of ages. Men have been fascinated with the curious phenomenon of mental representation, and have dwelt upon it in utter neglect of *that which is represented.* Confessedly of high interest, they have forgotten that it is forever subordinate to the original order for which it stands. Losing themselves in the contemplation of this mystery, metaphysicians have often fallen into a kind of skeptical hallucination as to whether, after all, there *are* any realities back of the ideas; or, granting an external world, they have held it to be of very trifling account, as all its truths are to be excogitated from the realm of pure ideas. Modern psychology inverts this order, and teaches not only that a knowledge of nature depends upon the direct study of nature, but that our knowledge of mind itself, of the relations among ideas, depends upon our prior understanding of the relations of phenomena and of the laws of action in the environment. It was this danger of being beguiled with mere symbols that called forth the sagacious adjuration of Newton: "Oh, physics, beware of metaphysics!" Mr. Mill thus points out the mischievous consequences of the error in the case of logic:

"The notion that what is of primary importance to the logician in a proposition, is the relation between the two *ideas* corresponding to the subject and predicate (instead of the relation between the two *phenomena* which they respectively express), seems to me one of the most fatal errors ever introduced into the philosophy of logic; and the principal cause why the theory of the science has made such inconsiderable progress during the last two centuries. The treatises on logic, and on the branches of mental philosophy connected with logic, which have been produced since the intrusion of this cardinal error, though sometimes written by men of extraordinary abilities and attainments, almost always tacitly imply a theory that the investigation of truth consists in contemplating and handling our ideas, or conceptions of things themselves; a doctrine tantamount to the assertion that the only mode of acquiring knowledge of nature is to study it at second-hand, as represented in our own minds. Meanwhile, inquiries into every kind of natural phenomena were incessantly establishing great and fruitful truths on most important subjects by processes upon which these views of the nature of Judgment and Reasoning threw no light." * .

Another step brings us to language—the system of marks and labels for thought—the "signs of ideas."

* Mill's "System of Logic," vol. i., p. 98.

These are the implements furnished by art for dealing with *ideas* of *things*. Through the association of ideas with visible symbols, language becomes the embodiment of thought, and there arises a relation among words growing out of the relations among ideas, which again grow out of the relations among things. Both rest upon the order of nature which science reveals; but that order is twice refracted through distorting media, and although the semblance of science is to be found in both, yet so many imperfections are introduced at each change, that we are only safe by keeping the intellectual eye steadily fixed upon the primal source of truth. The overshadowing error of present education, is the propensity to accept *words* in place of the ideas and things for which they stand, and from which they borrow all their value. This false estimate has been well characterized by the observation that "words are the counters of wise men, but the money of fools." Of course, most of the realities of knowledge are inaccessible to us; we know them only through their verbal signs; but all the more necessary is it that we should never forget that we are dealing with third-hand representations. Words are the *tools* of the thinker, which he must know how to handle, or they are useless; but the sensible mechanic remembers that his tools are for nothing but use, and hence spends the least possible time in grinding and polishing them. Words are the *vehicles of thought*; but as the farmer, who, having ten-thousand dollars to invest in his business, should put nine-thousand of it in wagons to carry his produce to market, reserving only one-thousand to buy a farm, would be justly chargeable with stupidity, so the student who invests the principal share of his time and power in variously-constructed vehicles of thought, with a corresponding neglect of what they are to carry, is chargeable with an analogous folly. So much of the study of language, and in such forms as are necessary to its intelligent use, is demanded in education; but while this places the study upon explicit grounds of utility, by the principle of utility should it be limited. But the lingual student, captivated by the interest of word-studies, loses the end in the means. A plough was sent to a barbarian tribe: they hung it over with ornaments, and fell down and worshipped it. In much the same manner is language treated in education.*

The old scholasticism sported with symbols, ideal and verbal; science makes a serious inquest into the realities for which they stand. The greatest secular event in history was this inversion of values among subjects of thought, and the rise of science and conquest of nature which followed; and an event of no less moment will be the carrying out of this great intellectual movement in education.

As respects discipline, these considerations present the question thus: shall it consist in the mere futile flourishing of the instruments of inquiry, or shall it be obtained by their employment upon the ends for which they are designed?

In this discussion I use the term Science in its true and largest meaning, which is nothing less than a right interpretation of nature—a comprehension of the workings of law wherever law prevails. Knowledge grows. Its germs are found in the lowest grades of ignorance, and develop first into the improved form of common information,

* "There is no study that could prove more successful in producing often thorough idleness and vacancy of mind, parrot-like repetition and sing-song knowledge, to the abeyance and destruction of the intellectual powers, as well as to the loss and paralysis of the outward senses, than our traditional study and idolatry of language."—*Professor Halford Vaughan.*

which then unfolds into the definite and perfected condition of science. It matters nothing whether the subjects are stones or stars, human souls, or the complications of social relation;—that most perfect knowledge of each which reveals its uniformities constitutes its special science, and that comprehensive view of the relations which each sustains to all in the cosmical order, realizes the broadest import of the conception. Science, therefore, is the revelation to reason of the policy by which God administers the affairs of the world. But how inadequate is the conception of it generally entertained, even among men of eminent literary cultivation, who seem to think the highest object of understanding the things of nature is merely to slake a petty curiosity! *

A common form of misapprehension is that which limits science to the consideration of 'mere matter,' and then reproaches it with being a cold materializing pursuit. But science deals with forces as well as matter; and when those who make this reproach will indicate just how much remains when the actions of power upon matter are exhausted, they will, perhaps, widen their conceptions upon

* Mr. Carlyle writes: "For many years it has been one of my constant regrets, that no schoolmaster of mine had a knowledge of natural history, so far at least as to have taught me the grasses that grow by the wayside, and the little winged and wingless neighbors that are continually meeting me, with a salutation which I cannot answer, as things are! Why didn't somebody teach me the constellations, too, and make me at home in the starry heavens, which are always overhead, and which I don't half know to this day? I love to prophesy that there will come a time, when not in Edinburgh only, but in all Scottish and European towns and villages, the schoolmaster will be strictly required to possess these two capabilities (neither Greek nor Latin more strict!) and that no ingenuous little denizen of this universe be thenceforward debarred from his right of liberty in these two departments, and doomed to look on them as if across grated fences all his life!" No hint is here given of that transcendent order of truth to which surrounding objects are but the portals.

the subject. Not only do the great lines of scientific thought converge to the supreme end of elucidating the regnant subjects of man and society, but its influence is powerfully felt even in the highest regions of philosophical speculation.* Yet it is by denying this, and insisting that science consists in collecting stones, labelling plants, and dabbling in chemical messes, that the adherents of tradition strive to render it obnoxious to popular prejudice. In defending the policy of the Great English Schools which contemptuously ignore almost the whole body of modern knowledge, the able Head-master of Rugby puts the case

* Professor Masson, in his lively little work, "Recent British Philosophy," remarks: "In no age so conspicuously as in our own has there been a crowding in of new scientific conceptions of all kinds to exercise a perturbing influence on Speculative Philosophy. They have come in almost too fast for Philosophy's powers of reception. She has visibly reeled amid their shocks, and has not yet recovered her equilibrium. Within those years alone which we have been engaged in surveying there have been developments of native British science, not to speak of influxes of scientific ideas, hints, and probabilities from without, in the midst of which British Philosophy has looked about her, scared and bewildered, and has felt that some of her oldest statements about herself, and some of the most important terms in her vocabulary, require re-explication. I think that I can even mark the precise year 1848 as a point whence the appearance of an unusual amount of unsteadying thought may be dated—as if, in that year of simultaneous European irritability, not only were the nations agitated politically, as the newspapers saw, but conceptions of an intellectual kind that had long been forming themselves underneath in the depths were shaken up to the surface in scientific journals and books. There are several vital points on which no one can now think, even were he receiving four thousand a year for doing so, as he might very creditably have thought seventeen years ago. There have been during that period, in consequence of revelations by scientific research in this direction and in that, some most notable enlargements of our views of physical nature and of history—enlargements even to the breaking down of what had formerly been a wall in the minds of most, and the substitution on that side of a sheer vista of open space. But there is no need of dating from 1848, or from any other year in particular. In all that we have recently seen of the kind there has been but the prolongation of an action from Science upon Philosophy that had been going on for a considerable time before."

on the explicit ground that science deals only with the lower utilities, while classical studies carry us up to the sphere of life and man; that science only *instructs*, while they *humanize*. But we have seen that such a view is indefensible. Science being the most perfect form of thought, and man its proper subject, the sharply-defined question is, whether he is to be studied by the lower or the higher method. Is the most thorough acquaintance with humanity to be gained by cutting the student off from the life of his own age, and setting him to tunnel through dead languages, to get such imperfect and distorted glimpses as he may of man and society in their antiquated forms; or by equipping him with the best resources of modern thought, and putting him to the direct and systematic study of men and society as they present themselves to observation and experience. In all other departments it is held desirable, as far as possible, to place directly before the student his materials of inquiry: why abandon the principle in the case of its highest application?

Our question thus assumes another aspect: for the best discipline of the human mind, shall we make use of those higher forms and completer methods of knowledge which constitute the science of the present age, or shall we use the lower and looser knowledge and cruder methods of the past?

Science also has great advantage, as a means of mental discipline, in the *incentives* to which it appeals for arousing mental activity, its motives to effort being such as the pupil can be made most readily to appreciate and feel. The reasons for studying the dead languages are not such as to act with inspiring force upon beginners: hence motives to exertion have largely to be supplied by external authority, which necessitates in the school-discipline a decided coercive element, while those who administer it, having little sympathy with 'new-light' notions about making study pleasurable, lighten the student's tasks by the enlivening assurance that wearisome toil is evermore the price of great results.

This is the old ascetic misconception of the controlling aims of life—false everywhere, fatal in education. The free and healthy exercise of the faculties and functions is so pleasurable as to be universally spoken of as a 'play'; who then has the right to turn it into dreary and repulsive task-work? The love of enjoyment is the deepest and most powerful impulse of our nature, and the educational system which does not recognize and build upon it violates the highest claim of that nature. The first thing to be done by the teacher is to awaken the pupil's interest, to engage his sympathies and kindle his enthusiasm, for these are the motors of intellectual progress; it is then easy to enchain his attention, to store his mind with knowledge, and carry mental cultivation up to the point of discipline.

This is of the first importance. Flogging has been the accompaniment of education for centuries; and although the humanizing agencies are slowly bringing us out of this barbaric dispensation, yet the penal policy, or that which makes the fear of pain, in one shape or other, the chief incentive to effort, is still prevalent. This not only appeals to the lowest motives, but is self-defeating. Painful feelings are anti-vital, depressing, fatal to mental spontaneity, and therefore a hindrance to acquisition: agreeable emotions, on the other hand, are stimulating, and favor nervous impressibility and spontaneous impulsion. The instinctive love of pleasurable activity which is so marked in youth becomes therefore a most powerful means of mental improvement. Government appeals to the dread of punishment as a motive to right conduct; but who will compare the influence it thus exerts upon the beneficent activities of society with the general stimulation to this result which springs from the desire of happiness? A scientific system of culture, which deals with the immediate objects and the living agencies of the world, is suited to employ this higher class of motives. The interest of an unperverted mind in the things of twenty centuries ago can never equal its interest in the things of to-day. It cannot for a moment be admitted that an empty and useless shell of a fact has the same relation to the mind that a living and applicable one has. Nothing can arouse, quicken, and mould it like the realities with which it has to deal. It has been well said that "everywhere throughout nature we find faculties developed through the performance of those functions which it is their office to perform, not through artificial exercises devised to fit them for those functions." A system of culture, therefore, which ignores the thousand immediate pressures and solicitations upon feeling and thought, by which human beings are stirred, can neither shape the mind into harmony with its actual circumstances, nor reach the deepest springs of impulse and exertion. The intellect follows the lead of the heart; and with the slow emergence of right ideas respecting the uses of the world, we shall discover that the real scene of human action and enjoyment is also the true source of inspiration and of the noblest incentives to effort. The end of a rational culture being to adjust the student's relations to his own age, it will employ for the purpose all those subjects which come home to him most directly, and that these are best fitted for rousing and sustaining a pleasurable mental activity is both declared by reason and confirmed by experience.

And this leads me finally to observe that a mental culture, based upon science, and applied to the great questions of the time, will give a type of mental discipline marked by the elements of vigor and courage, and suited to brace the mind for the serious work which comes before it with the advance of society. In this respect the classical cultivation is so faulty as hardly to deserve the name of discipline. Its ideal is European, and is shaped into accordance with the requirements of the European system: it is that of the refined and elegant scholar, fitted for meditative retirement in some cloistered seclusion or 'sacred shade,' immersed in the past, and disinclined to meddle with the present. But what Sydney Smith calls "the safe and elegant imbecility of classical learning," is not the preparation needed by the cultivated mind of this country. Here all the cumbrous machinery for taking care of people and superseding thought—Monarchy, Nobility, and State-Church, are gone, and we are thrown back upon first principles, to work out the great problem of a self-governing society, for weal or for woe. The finished classical scholar blinks the issues, and shirks the responsibilities of his time. He is disgusted with the 'noise and confusion' of this degenerate utilitarian age, and longs to bury himself in the quietness of the past. "In proportion as the material interests of the present moment become more and more engrossing, more and more tyrannical in their exactions, in the same proportion it becomes more necessary that man should fall back on the common interests of humanity, and free himself from the trammels of the present by living in the past," says the advocate of the English universities, Dr. Donaldson. But this will not do *here*. Not to 'fall back,' but to press forward should be the motto of American education. Not to escape the present and live in the past, but resolutely to accept the present, thanking God for its opportunities, and to live rather in the future, is the high requirement of mental duty. And herein is the character of the two systems shown, that while the one looks forever backward, the other leads steadfastly forward. Science, therefore, piercing the future, and working toward it through the present, engages naturally with those great subjects of public interest which are no longer to be postponed or evaded.

The classicists are fond of presenting the issue as be tween liberal culture and money-making, and triumphantly contrast the refined and generous feelings which cluster around the former, with the vulgar and sordid motives which characterize the latter. But the real issue is far different from this. The mind of our age is confronted with a host of urgent questions, such as the Perils of Misgovernment, the Limits of Legislation, the Management of Criminals, of the Insane, the Congenitally Defective, and the Pauper Class; the operation of Charities, the Philosophy of Philanthropy, the relations of Sex and Race, International Ethics, the Freedom of Trade, the Rights of Industry, Property in Ideas, Public Hygiene, Primary Education, Religious Liberty, the Rights of Invention, Political Representation, and many others, which inosculate and interfuse into the great total of practical inquiry which challenges the intellect of our times; and it is this which the classical scholar evades, when he shrinks from the present and retires into the past. And well he may; for the mastery of the languages and literatures of Greece and Rome, and culture in unprogressive studies, furnish neither suitable ideas nor mental habits for this kind of work. Science, grounding itself in the order and truth of nature, armed with the appropriate knowledge, and inspired with the hope of a better future, to which it sees all things tending, enters the great field as properly its own, and will train its votaries to that breadth of view, that robust boldness of treatment, and that patient and dispassionate temper which the imminent questions of the times so decisively demand.

In his late instructive lecture on the "Development of Ideas in Physical Science," Professor Liebig shows that it has been a slow organic growth, depending upon deeper conditions than the mere favor or opposition of Church or State. He shows that in Greece the progress of science was arrested by its slave-system; points out the necessity of abounding wealth to give leisure for thought and culture, and the importance of those social conditions which bring into intimate intercourse all classes of thinkers and workers, upon the mutual co-operation of which the advance of science and of society depends. He says: "*Freedom*, that is the absence of all restrictions which can prevent men from using to their advantage the powers which God has given them, is the mightiest of all the conditions of progress in civilization and culture;" and he adds that, "it can hardly be doubted that among the peoples of the North American Free States, all the conditions exist for their development to the highest point of culture and civilization attainable by man."

These are weighty considerations for the educators of this country. Institutions are but expressions of ideas and habits; and the European policy, governmental and ecclesiastical, is grounded upon a culture suited to its necessities, and which has grown up with it in the course of ages. Both idolize the past; both worship precedent and authority, and both dread independent inquiry into first principles: one recoils from Freedom, as the other from Science. Freedom and Science, on the other hand, have had a coeval destiny; have suffered together, and grown together. Both break from prescription and throw themselves upon Nature, and the watchword of both is Progress, which consists not in rejecting the past, but in subordinating and outgrowing it, in assimilating and reorganizing its truth, and leaving behind its obsolete forms. In the last century we threw off the trammels of the repressive system, and entered upon the experiment of Free Institutions; but it avails little to shift the external forms if the old ideas are not replaced by new growths of thought and feeling. Our system of Popular Education is the first great constructive measure of National Progress, and this has yet to be moulded to its purposes through a system of higher institutions, organized into harmony with the genius of American circumstances and the great requirements of the period.

In the preceding pages I have quoted Mr. J. S. Mill's able presentation of the claims of Scientific Studies; but lest I be accused of partiality in the use of his authority, it is proper to add that in the same address he makes also a strong argument for the Classics. It is not pertinent here to criticise this branch of his argument, as the claims of the classics are put less on the usual ground of 'discipline' than on certain high utilities of scholarship. But while, as the reader has seen, Mr. Mill urges the importance of Scientific Studies *for all*, an examination of his argument for the Classics will show that it is applicable only to those who, like himself, are professional scholars, and devote their lives to Philological, Historical, or Critical Studies.

ON THE IMPORTANCE OF THE STUDY OF PHYSICS.

A LECTURE DELIVERED AT THE ROYAL INSTITUTION OF GREAT BRITAIN.

BY

JOHN TYNDALL, LL.D., F.R.S.

ON THE STUDY OF PHYSICS.

THERE is a word in the title of this Lecture which does not clearly convey the idea by which I shall be guided in its delivery. I hold in my hand a soiled proof of the syllabus of the present course, and the title of the present Lecture is there stated to be "On the Importance of the Study of Physics as a *Means* of Education." The corrected proof, however, contains the following title: —"On the Importance of the Study of Physics as a *Branch* of Education." Small as this editorial alteration may seem, the two words appear to me to suggest two radically distinct modes of viewing the subject before us. The term Education is sometimes applied to a single faculty or organ, and if we know wherein the education of a single organ or faculty consists, this knowledge will enable us to form a clearer notion regarding the education of the sum of all the faculties, or of the mind. When, for example, we speak of the education of the voice, what do we mean? There are certain membranes at the top of the windpipe which are capable of being thrown into vibration by the air forced between them from the lungs, and thus caused to produce sound. These membranes are, to some extent, under the control of the will: it is found that they can be so modified by exercise as to produce notes of a clearer and more melodious character, and this exercise we call the education of the voice. We may choose for our exercise a new song or an old song, a festive song or a solemn chant; and, the education of the voice being the object we have in view, the songs may be regarded as the *means* by which this education is accomplished. I think this expresses the state of the case more clearly than if we were to call the songs a *branch* of education. Regarding also the education of the human mind as the improvement and development of the mental faculties, I consider the study of Physics to be a means towards the attainment of these objects. Of course, from this point of view, I degrade Physics into an implement of culture, and I mean to do so, to a great extent. Viewing the development of the mental faculties as the end of mental education, it will be my endeavour to state to you some of the claims of Physical Science as a means towards the attainment of this end.

I do not think that it is the mission of this age, or of any other particular age, to lay down a system of education which shall hold good for all ages. The basis of human nature is, perhaps, permanent, but not so the forms under which the spirit of humanity manifests itself. It is sometimes peaceful, sometimes warlike, sometimes religious, sometimes sceptical, and history is simply the record of its mutations.

> "The eternal Pan
> Who layeth the world's incessant plan
> Halteth never in one shape,
> But for ever doth escape
> Into new forms."

This appears to be the law of things throughout the

universe, and it is therefore no proof of fickleness or destructiveness, properly so called, if the implements of human culture change with the times, and the requirements of the present age be found different from those of the preceding. Unless you are prepared to say that the past world, or some portion of it, has been the final expression of human competency; that the wisdom of man has already reached its climax; that the intellect of to-day possesses feebler powers, or a narrower scope than the intellect of earlier times; you cannot, with reason, demand an unconditional acceptance of the systems of the past, nor are you justified in divorcing me from the world and times in which I live, and confining my conversation to the times gone by. Who can blame me if I cherish the belief that the world is still young; that there are great possibilities in store for it; that the Englishman of to-day is made of as good stuff, and has as high and independent a vocation to fulfil, as had the ancient Greek or Roman? While thankfully accepting what antiquity has to offer, let us never forget that the present century has just as good a right to its forms of thought and methods of culture as any former centuries had to theirs, and that the same sources of power are open to us to-day as were ever open to humanity in any age of the world.

In the earliest religious writings, we find man described as a mixture of the earthy and the divine. The existence of the latter implies, in his case, that of the former: and hence the holiest and most self-denying saint must, to a certain extent, protect himself against hunger and cold. But every attempt to restrict man to the dominion of the senses has failed, and will continue to fail. He is the repository of forces which push him beyond the world of sense. He has an intellect as well as a palate, and the demands of the latter being satisfied, the former inevitably puts in its claim. We cannot quench these desires of the intellect. They are stimulated by the phenomena which surround us as the body is by oxygen; and in the presence of these phenomena we thirst for knowledge as an Arab longs for water when he smells the Nile. The Chaldean shepherds could not rest contented with their bread and milk, but found that they had other wants to satisfy. The stars shed their light upon the shepherd and his flock, but in both cases with very different results. The quadruped cropped the green herbage and slept contented; but that power which had already made man the lord of the quadruped was appealed to night after night, and thus the intellectual germ which lay in the nature of these Chaldeans was stimulated and developed.

Surely, it might be urged, if man be not made, and stars scattered, by guess-work, there is strong reason for assuming that it was intended that mental power should be developed in this way. But if this be granted, it must be admitted that we have the very highest sanction for the prosecution of physical research. Sanction, indeed, is a term too weak to express the inference suggested by a comparison of Man's powers with his position upon earth; it points to an imperative command to search and to examine, rather than to a mere toleration of physical inquiry.

The term Physics, as made use of in the present Lecture, refers to that portion of natural science which lies midway between astronomy and chemistry. The former, indeed, is Physics applied to masses of enormous weight, while the latter is Physics applied to atoms and molecules. The subjects of Physics proper are, therefore, those which lie nearest to human perception:—the light and heat of the sun, colour, sound, motion, the loadstone, electrical attractions and repulsions, thunder and lightning, rain, snow, dew, and so forth. The senses of Man stand between these phenomena, between the external world, and the world of thought. He takes his facts from Nature and transfers them to the domain of mind: he looks at them, compares them, observes their mutual relations and connexions, and thus brings them clearer and clearer before his mental eye, until, finally, by a kind of inspiration, he alights upon the cause which unites them. This is the last act of the mind, in this centripetal direction, in its progress from the multiplicity of facts to the central cause on which they depend. But, having guessed the cause, he is not yet contented: he now sets out from his centre and travels in the other direction: he sees that if his guess be true, certain consequences must follow from it, and he appeals to the law and testimony of experiment whether the thing is so. Thus he completes the circuit of thought,—from without inward, from multiplicity to unity, and from within outward, from unity to multiplicity. He traverses the line between cause and effect both ways, and, in so doing, calls all his reasoning powers into play. The mental effort involved in these processes may be justly compared to those exercises of the body which invoke the co-operation of every muscle, and thus confer upon the whole frame the benefits of healthy action.

The first experiment a man makes is a physical experiment: the suction-pump is but an imitation of the first act of every new-born infant. Nor do I think it calculated to lesson that infant's reverence, or to make him a worse citizen, when his riper experience shows him that the atmosphere was his helper in extracting the first draught from his mother's breast. The child grows, but is still an experimenter: he grasps at the moon, and his failure teaches him to respect distance. At length his little fingers acquire sufficient mechanical tact to lay hold of a spoon. He thrusts the instrument into his mouth; hurts his little gums, and thus learns the impenetrability of matter. He lets the spoon fall, and jumps with delight to hear it rattle against the table. The experiment made by accident is repeated with intention, and thus the young Newton receives his first lessons upon sound and gravitation. There are pains and penalties, however, in the path of the young inquirer: he is sure to go wrong, and Nature is just as sure to inform him of the fact. He falls down stairs, burns his fingers, cuts his hand, scalds his tongue, and in this way learns the conditions of his physical well being. This is Nature's way of proceeding, and it is wonderful what progress her pupil makes. His enjoyments for a time are physical, and the confectioner's shop occupies the foreground of human happiness; but the blossoms of a finer life are already beginning to unfold themselves, and the relation of cause and effect dawns upon the boy. He begins to see that the present condition of things is not final, but depends upon one that has gone before, and will be succeeded by another. He becomes a puzzle to himself; and to satisfy his newly-awakened curiosity, asks all manner of inconvenient questions. The needs and tendencies of human nature express themselves through these early yearnings of the child. He desires to know the character and causes of the phenomena presented to him; and unless this desire has been granted for the express purpose of having it repressed, unless the attractions of natural phenomena be like the blush of the forbidden fruit, conferred merely for the purpose of exercising our self-denial by letting them alone; then I claim for the study of Physics the recognition that it answers to an impulse implanted by Nature in the human constitution, and he who would oppose such study must be prepared to exhibit the credentials which authorize him to contravene Nature's manifest designs. Such credentials were never given; and the opposition, where it exists, is in most, if not in all cases, due to the fact, that at the time when the opponent of Science was beginning to inquire like the little boy, it was so arranged by human institutions that the train of thought suggested by natural objects should, in his case, be utterly supplanted by another. But is this unavoidable? Is the knowledge of grammatical concord and government so utterly antagonistic to the scientific discernment of the same two principles in Nature, as to render the complete extrusion of the one necessary to the existence of the other?

A few days ago, a Master of Arts, who is still a young man, and therefore the recipient of a modern education, stated to me that for the first twenty years of his life he had been taught nothing regarding Light, Heat, Magnetism, or Electricity: twelve of these years had been spent among the ancients, all connexion being thus severed between him and natural phenomena. Now, we cannot, without prejudice to humanity, separate the present from the past. The nineteenth century strikes its roots into the centuries gone by, and draws nutriment from them. The world cannot afford to lose the record of any great deed or utterance; for such deeds and such utterances are prolific throughout all time. We cannot yield the companionship of our loftier brothers of antiquity,—of our Socrates and Cato,—whose lives provoke us to sympathetic greatness across the interval of two thousand years. As long as the ancient languages are the means of access to the ancient mind, they must ever be of priceless value to humanity; but it is as the avenues of ancient thought, and not as the instruments of modern culture, that they are chiefly valuable to Man. Surely these avenues might be kept open without demanding such sacrifices as that above referred to. We have conquered and possessed ourselves of continents of land, concerning which antiquity knew nothing; and if new continents of thought reveal themselves to the exploring human spirit, shall we not possess them also? In these latter days, the study of Physics has given us glimpses of the methods of Nature which were quite hidden from the ancients, and it would be treason to the trust committed to us, if we were to sacrifice the hopes and aspirations of the Present out of deference to the Past.

At an agricultural college in Hampshire, with which I was connected for some time, and which is now converted into a school for the general education of youth, a Society was formed among the boys, which met weekly for the purpose of reading reports and papers upon various subjects. The Society had its president and treasurer; and abstracts of its proceedings were published in a little monthly periodical issuing from the school press. One of the most remarkable features of these weekly meetings was, that after the general business had been concluded, each member of the Society enjoyed the right of asking questions on any subject on which he desired information. The questions were either written out previously in a book devoted to the purpose, or, if a question happened to suggest itself during the meeting, it was written upon a slip of paper and handed in to the Secretary, who afterwards read all the questions aloud. A number of teachers were usually present, and they and the boys made a common stock of their wisdom in furnishing replies. As might be expected from an assemblage of eighty or ninety boys, varying from eighteen to eight years old, many extraordinary questions were proposed. To the eye which loves to detect in the tendencies of the young the instincts of humanity generally, such questions are not without a certain philosophic interest, and I have therefore thought it not derogatory to the present course of Lectures to copy a few of these questions, and to introduce them here. They run as follows :—

What are the duties of the Astronomer Royal?

What is frost?

Why are thunder and lightning more frequent in summer than in winter?

What occasions falling stars?

What is the cause of the sensation called "pins and needles"?

What is the cause of waterspouts?

What is the cause of hiccup?

If a towel be wetted with water, why does the wet portion become darker than before?

What is meant by Lancashire witches?

Does the dew rise or fall?

What is the principle of the hydraulic press?

Is there more oxygen in the air in summer than in winter?

What are those rings which we see round the gas and sun?

What is thunder?

How is it that a black hat can be moved by forming round it a magnetic circle, while a white hat remains stationary?

What is the cause of perspiration?

Is it true that men were once monkeys?

What is the difference between the *soul* and the *mind?*

Is it contrary to the rules of Vegetarianism to eat eggs?

In looking over these questions, which were wholly unprompted, and have been copied almost at random from the book already alluded to, we see that many of them are suggested directly by natural objects, and are not such merely as had an interest conferred on them by previous culture. Now the fact is beyond the boy's control, and so certainly is the desire to know its cause. The sole question then is, is this desire to be gratified or not? Take, for example, the case of the wetted towel, which at first sight appears to be one of the most unpromising questions in the list. Shall we tell the proposer to repress his curiosity, as the subject is improper for him to know, and thus interpose our wisdom to rescue the boy from the consequences of Nature's implanting a desire which acts to his prejudice? Or, recognising the propriety of the question, how are we to answer it? It is impossible to do so without reference to the laws of optics—impossible to answer it without making the boy to some extent a natural philosopher. You may say that the effect is due to the reflection of light at the common surface of two media of different refractive indices. But this answer presupposes on the part of the boy a knowledge of what reflection and refraction are, or reduces you to the necessity of explaining them. On looking more closely into the matter, we find that our wet towel belongs to a class of phenomena exhibited by tabasheer and hydrophane, which have long excited the interest of philosophers. These bodies are opaque when dry, but when dipped into water or beech-nut oil they become transparent. The towel is white for the same reason that snow is white, that foam is white, that pounded quartz or glass is white, and that the salt we use at table is white. On quitting one medium and entering another, a portion of light is always reflected, but with this restriction, the media must possess different refractive indices. Thus, when we immerse glass in water, light is reflected from the common surface of both, and it is this light which enables us to see the glass. But take a transparent solid and immerse it in a liquid of the same refractive index as itself, it will immediately disappear. I remember once dropping the eyeball of an ox into water; it vanished as if by magic, a bystander actually supposing that the mass had been instantly dissolved. This, however, was not the case, and a comparison of the refractive index of the vitreous humour with that of water cleared up the whole matter. The indices were identical, and hence the light pursued its way through both bodies as if they formed one continuous mass. In the case of snow, powdered quartz, or salt, we have a transparent solid body mixed with air; at every transition from solid to air, or from air to solid, a portion of light is reflected; this takes place so often that the light is wholly intercepted, and thus from the mixture of two transparent bodies we obtain an opaque one. The case of the towel is precisely similar. The tissue is composed of semi-transparent vegetable fibres, with the interstices between them filled with air; repeated reflection takes place at the limiting surfaces of air and fibre, and hence the towel becomes opaque like snow or salt. But if we fill the interstices of the towel with water, we diminish the reflection; a portion of the light enters the mass, and the darkness of the towel is due to its increased transparency. Thus the hydrophane, tabasheer, the tracing paper used by engineers, and many other considerations of the highest scientific interest, are involved in the simple enquiry of this unsuspecting little boy.

Again, take the question regarding the rising or falling of the dew—a question long agitated, and finally set at rest by the beautiful researches of Wells and Melloni. I do not think that any boy of average intelligence will be satisfied with the simple answer that the dew falls. He will wish to learn how you know that it falls, and, if acquainted with the notions of the middle ages, may refer to the opinion of Father Laurus, that, if you fill a goose egg with the morning dew and expose it to the sun, it will rise like a balloon—a swan's egg being better for the experiment than a goose egg. It is impossible to give the boy a clear notion of the beautiful phenomenon to which his question refers, without first making him acquainted with the radiation and conduction of heat. Take, for example, a blade of grass, from which one of these orient pearls is depending. During the day the grass, and the earth beneath it, possess a certain amount of warmth imparted by the sun; during a serene night, heat is radiated from the surface of the grass into space, and to supply the loss, there is a flow of heat from the interior portions of the blade towards its surface. Thus the surface loses heat by radiation, and gains heat by conduction. Now, in the case before us, the power of radiation is great, whereas the power of conduction is small; the consequence is that the blade loses more than it gains, and hence becomes more and more refrigerated. The light vapour floating around the surface so cooled is precipitated upon it, and there accumulates to form the little pearly globe which we call a dew-drop.

Thus the boy finds the simple and homely fact which addressed his senses to be the outcome and flower of the deepest laws. The fact becomes, in a measure, sanctified as an object of thought, and invested for him with a beauty for evermore. He thus learns that things which, at first sight, seem to stand isolated and without apparent brotherhood in Nature are united by their causes, and finds the detection of these analogies a source of perpetual delight.

To enlist pleasure on the side of intellectual performance is a point of the utmost importance; for the exercise of the mind, like that of the body, depends for its value upon the spirit in which it is accomplished. Every physician knows that something more than mere mechanical motion is comprehended under the idea of healthful exercise—that, indeed, being most healthful which makes us forget all ulterior ends in the mere enjoyment of it. What, for example, could be substituted for the jubilant shout of the playground, where the boy plays for the mere love of playing, and without reference to physiological laws; while kindly Nature accomplishes her ends unconsciously, and makes his very indifference beneficial to him? You may have more systematic motions, you may devise means for the more perfect traction of each particular muscle, but you cannot create the joy and gladness of the game, and where these are absent, the charm and the health of the exercise are gone. The case is similar with mental education. Why then should the mind of youth be so completely warped from its healthful and happy action, so utterly withdrawn from those studies to which its earliest tendencies point, and in the cultivation of which the concurrence of its ardour would powerfully tend to the augmentation of its strength, as to leave the man in after-life, unless enlightened by his visits to an Institution such as that in which we are now assembled, in absolute ignorance as to whether the material world is governed by law or chance, or indeed whether those phenomena which excited his youthful questionings be not really the jugglery of Jotuns, or of some other power similar in kind?

The study of Physics, as already intimated, consists of two processes, which are complementary to each other—the tracing of facts to their causes, and the logical advance from the cause to the fact. In the former process, called *induction*, certain moral qualities come into play. It requires patient industry, and an humble and conscientious acceptance of what Nature reveals. The first condition of success is an honest receptivity and a willingness to abandon all preconceived notions, however cherished, if they be found to contradict the truth. And if a man be not capable of this self-renunciation—this loyal surrender of himself to Nature, he lacks, in my opinion, the first mark of a true philosopher. Thus the earnest prosecutor of science, who does not work with the idea of producing a sensation in the world, who loves the truth better than the transitory blaze of to-day's fame, who comes to his task with a single eye, finds in that task an indirect means of the highest moral culture. And although the virtue of the act depends upon its privacy, this sacrifice of self, this upright determination to accept the truth, no matter how it may present itself—even at the hands of a scientific foe, if necessary—carries with it its own reward. When prejudice is put under foot, and the stains of personal bias have been washed away—when a man consents to lay aside his vanity and to become Nature's organ—his elevation is the instant consequence of his humility. You may, it is true, point to the quarrels of scientific men, to their struggles for priority, to that unpleasant egotism which screams around its little property of discovery like a scared plover about its young. I will not deny all this; but let it be set down to its proper account, to the weakness—or, if you will—to the wickedness of Man, but not to the charge of Physical Science.

The second process in physical investigation is *deduction,* or the advance of the mind from fixed principles to the conclusions which flow from them. The rules of logic are the formal statement of this process, which, however, was practised by every healthy mind before ever such rules were written. In the study of Physics, induction and deduction are perpetually married to each other. The man observes,—he strips facts of their peculiarities of form, and tries to unite them by their essences; having effected this, he at once deduces, and thus checks his induction. Here the grand difference between the methods at present followed, and those of the ancients, becomes manifest. They were one-sided in these matters: they omitted the process of induction, and substituted conjecture for observation. They do not seem to have possessed sufficient patience to watch the slow processes of Nature, and to make themselves acquainted with the conditions under which she operates. Ignorant of these conditions, they could never penetrate her secrets nor master her laws. This mastery not only enables us to turn her forces against each other, so as to protect ourselves from their hostile action, but makes them our slaves. By the study of Physics we have opened to us treasuries of power of which antiquity never dreamed: we lord it over Matter, but in so doing we have become better acquainted with the laws of Mind; for to the mental philosopher material Nature furnishes a screen against which the human spirit projects its own image, and thus becomes capable of self-inspection.

Thus, then, as a means of intellectual culture, the study of Physics exercises and sharpens observation: it brings the most exhaustive logic into play: it compares, abstracts, and generalizes, and provides a mental imagery admirably suited to these processes. The strictest precision of thought is everywhere enforced, and prudence, foresight, and sagacity are demanded. By its appeals to experiment, it continually checks itself, and builds upon a sure foundation.

Thus far we have regarded the study of Physics as an agent of intellectual culture; but like other things in Nature, it subserves more than a single end. The colours of the clouds delight the eye, and, no doubt, accomplish moral purposes also; but the self-same clouds hold within their fleeces the moisture by which our fields are rendered fruitful. The sunbeams excite our interest and invite our investigation; but they also extend their beneficent influences to our fruits and corn, and thus accomplish, not only intellectual ends, but minister, at the same time, to our material necessities. And so it is with scientific research. While the love of science is a sufficient incentive to the pursuit of science, and the investigator, in the prosecution of his inquiries, is raised above all material considerations, the results of his labours may exercise a potent influence upon the physical condition of Man. This is more often the arrangement of Nature, than of the scientific investigator himself; for he usually pursues his object without regard to its practical applications. And let him who is dazzled by such applications—who sees in the steam-engine and the electric telegraph the highest embodiment of human genius and the only legitimate object of scientific research, beware of prescribing conditions to the investigator. Let him beware of attempting to substitute for that simple love with which the votary of science pursues his task, the calculations of what he is pleased to call utility. The scientific man must approach Nature in his own way; for if you invade his freedom by your so-called practical considerations, it may be at the expense of those qualities on which his success as a discoverer depends. Let the self-styled practical man look to those from the fecundity of whose thought he, and thousands like him, have sprung into existence. Were they inspired in their first inquiries by the calculations of utility? Not one of them. They were often forced to live low and lie hard, and to seek a compensation for their penury in the delight which their favourite pursuits afforded them. In the words of one well qualified to speak upon this subject, "I say not merely look at the pittance of men like John Dalton, or the voluntary starvation of the late Graff; but compare what is considered as competency or affluence by your Faradays, Liebigs, and Herschels, with the expected results of a life of successful commercial enterprise: then compare the amount of mind put forth, the work done for society in either case, and you will be constrained to allow that the former belong to a class of workers who, properly speaking, are not paid, and cannot be paid for their work, as indeed it is of a sort to which no payment could stimulate."

But while the scientific investigator, who, standing upon the frontiers of human knowledge, and aiming at the conquest of fresh soil from the surrounding region of the unknown, makes the *discovery* of truth his exclusive object for the time, he cannot but feel the deepest interest in the practical application of the truth discovered. There is something ennobling in the triumph of Mind over Matter: apart even from its uses to society, there is something sublime in the idea of Man having tamed that wild force which rushes through the telegraphic wire, and made it the minister of his will. Our attainments in these directions appear to be commensurate with our needs. We had already subdued horse and mule, and obtained from them all the service which it was in their power to render: we must either stand still, or find more potent agents to execute our purposes. To stand still, however, was not in the plan of Him who made motion a condition of life, and, as if by His high arrangement, the steam-engine appeared. Remember that these are but new things; that it is not long since we struck into the scientific methods which produced these extraordinary results. We cannot for an instant regard them as the final achievements of science, but rather as an earnest of what she is yet to do. They mark our first great advances upon the dominion of Nature. Animal strength fails, but here are the forces which hold the world together, and the instincts and successes of Man assure him that these forces are his when he is wise enough to command them.

In the title of this Lecture, the study of Physics as a branch of education "for all classes" is spoken of. I am not quite sure that I understand the meaning intended to be conveyed by the words "all classes;" and I have regarded the question with reference to those mental qualities which have been distributed without reference to class. As an instrument of intellectual culture, the study of Physics is profitable to all: as bearing upon special functions, its value, though not so great, is still more tangible. Why, for example, should Members of Parliament be ignorant of the subjects concerning which they are called upon to legislate? In this land of practical physics, why should they be unable to form an independent opinion upon a physical question? Why should the senator be left at the mercy of interested disputants when a scientific question is discussed, until he deems the nap a blessing which rescues him from the bewilderments of the committee-room? The education which does not supply the want here referred to, fails in its duty to England. With regard to our working people, in the ordinary sense of the term working, the study of Physics would, I imagine, be profitable, not only as a means of mental culture, but also as a moral influence to woo these people from pursuits which now degrade them. A man's reformation oftener depends upon the indirect than upon the direct action of the will. The will must be exerted in the choice of employment which shall break the force of temptation by erecting a barrier against it. The drunkard, for example, is in a perilous condition if he content himself merely with saying, or swearing, that he will avoid strong drink. His thoughts, if not attracted by another force, will revert to the public-house, and to rescue him permanently from this you must give him an equivalent. By investing the objects of hourly intercourse with an interest which prompts reflection, new enjoyments would be opened to the working man, and every one of these would be a point of force to protect him against temptation. Besides this, our factories and our foundries present an extensive field of observation, and were those who work in them rendered capable, by previous culture, of appreciating what they see, the results to science would be incalculable. Who can say what intellectual Samsons are at the present moment toiling with closed eyes in the mills and forges of Manchester and Birmingham? Grant these Samsons sight, give them some knowledge of Physics, and you multiply the chances of discovery, and with them the prospects of national advancement. In our multitudinous technical operations, we are constantly playing with forces where our ignorance is often the cause of our destruction. There are agencies at work in a locomotive of which the maker of it probably never dreamed, but which nevertheless may be sufficient to convert it into an engine of death. Again, when we reflect on the intellectual condition of the people who work in our coal mines, those terrific explosions which occur from time to time need not astonish us. If these men possessed sufficient physical knowledge, I doubt not, from the operatives themselves would emanate a system by which these shocking accidents might be effectually avoided. If they possessed the knowledge, their personal interests would furnish the necessary stimulus to its practical application, and thus two ends would be served at the same time—the elevation of the men and the diminution of the calamity.

In what I have said regarding mental processes, I have described things as they reveal themselves to my own eyes, and have been enacted in my own limited practice. In doing this, I have been supported by the belief that there is one mind common to us all; and that if I be true to the expression of this mind, even in a small particular, the truth will attest itself by a response in the convictions of my hearers. There may be the same difference between the utterance of two individuals of different ranges of intellectual power and experience on a subject like the present, as between "The Descent from the Cross," by Rubens, and the portrait of a spaniel dog. Nevertheless, if the portrait of the spaniel be true to nature, it recommends itself as truth to the human mind, and excites, in some degree, the interest that truth ever inspires. Thus far I have endeavoured to keep all tints and features which really do not belong to the portrait of my spaniel, apart from it, and I ask your permission to proceed a little further in the same manner, and to refer to a fact or two in addition to those already cited, which presented themselves to my notice during my brief career as a teacher in the establishment already alluded to. The facts, though extremely humble, and deviating in some slight degree from the strict subject of the present discourse, may yet serve to illustrate an educational principle.

One of the duties which fell to my share, during the period to which I have referred, was the instruction of a class in mathematics, and I usually found that Euclid and the ancient geometry generally, when addressed to the understanding, formed a very attractive study for youth. But it was my habitual practice to withdraw the boys from the routine of the book, and to appeal to their self-power in the treatment of questions not comprehended in that routine. At first, the change from the beaten track usually excited a little aversion: the youth felt like a child amid strangers; but in no single instance have I found this aversion to continue. When utterly disheartened, I have encouraged the boy by that anecdote of Newton, where he attributes the difference between him and other men, mainly to his own patience; or of Mirabeau, when he ordered his servant, who had stated something to be impossible, never to use that stupid word again. Thus cheered, he has returned to his task with a smile, which perhaps had something of doubt in it, but which, nevertheless, evinced a resolution to try again. I have seen the boy's eye brighten, and, at length, with a pleasure of which the ecstacy of Archimedes was but a simple expansion, heard him exclaim, "I have it, sir." The consciousness of self-power, thus awakened, was of immense value; and, animated by it, the progress of the class was astonishing. It was often my custom to give the boys their choice of pursuing their propositions in the book, or of trying their strength on others not to be found there. Never in a single instance have I known the book to be chosen. I was ever ready to assist when I deemed help needful, but my offers of assistance were habitually declined. The boys had tasted the sweets of intellectual conquest, and demanded victories of their own. I have seen their diagrams scratched on the walls, cut into the beams upon the playground, and numberless other illustrations of the living interest they took in the subject. As regards experience in teaching, I was a mere fledgling at that time: I knew nothing of the rules of pedagogics, as the Germans name it; but I adhered to the spirit indicated at the commencement of this discourse, and endeavoured to make geometry a *means* and not a *branch* of education. The experiment was successful, and some of the most delightful hours of my existence have been spent in marking the vigorous and cheerful expansion of mental power, when appealed to in the manner I have described.

And then again, the pleasure we all experienced was enhanced when we applied our mathematical knowledge to the solution of physical problems. Many objects of hourly contact had thus a new interest and significance imparted to them. The swing, the see-saw, the tension of the giant-stride ropes, the fall and rebound of the football, the advantage of a small boy over a large one when turning short, particularly in slippery weather; all became subjects of investigation. Supposing a lady to stand before a looking-glass, of the same height as herself, it was required to know how much of the glass was really useful to the lady? and we learned, with great pleasure, the economic fact that she might dispense with the lower half and see her whole figure notwithstanding. We also felt deep interest in ascertaining from the hum of a bee the number of times the little insect flaps its wings in a second. Following up our researches upon the pendulum, we were interested to learn how Colonel Sabine had made it the means of determining the figure of the earth; and we were also startled by the inference which the pendulum enabled us to draw, that if the diurnal velocity of the earth were seventeen times its present amount, the centrifugal force at the equator would be precisely equal to the force of gravitation, and that hence an inhabitant of those regions would have the same tendency to fall upwards as downwards. All these things were sources of wonder and delight to us: we could not but admire the perseverance of Man which had accomplished so much; and then when we remembered that we were gifted with the same powers, and had the same great field to work in, our hopes arose that at some future day we might possibly push the subject a little further, and add our own victories to the conquests already won.

I know I ought to apologize to you for dwelling so long upon this subject. But the days I spent among these youthful philosophers made a deep impression on me. I learned among them something of myself and of human nature, and obtained some notion of a teacher's vocation. If there be one profession in England of paramount importance, I believe it to be that of the schoolmaster; and if there be a position where selfishness and incompetence do most serious mischief, by lowering the moral tone and exciting contempt and cunning where reverence and noble truthfulness ought to be the feelings evoked, it is that of the governor of a school. When a man of enlarged heart and mind comes among boys,—when he allows his being to stream through them, and observes the operation of his own character evidenced in the elevation of theirs,—it would be idle to talk of the position of such a man being honourable. It is a blessed position. The man is a blessing to himself and to all around him. Such men, I believe, are to be found in England, and it behoves those who busy themselves with the mechanics of education at the present day, to seek them out. For no matter what means of culture may be chosen, whether physical or philological, success must ever mainly depend upon the amount of life, love. and earnestness, which the teacher himself brings with him to his vocation.*

* The following extract from a journal is, I think, too good to be omitted here. The writer of it—a pupil of Dirichlet and Steiner—would doubtless have felt himself more at home in dealing with elliptic functions than with the definitions of Euclid. But the manner in which he contrived to render the latter mysteries evident to a light-headed little boy, does credit to another faculty than his mere mathematical one, and will, I trust, prove as pleasant to the reader as it has to me. "K—— stammers distressingly, and this has impeded his progress very much. I have often passed him in the class, knowing that I could not get any intelligible answer from him, and had it not been for his eloquent eyes, which said, 'I know it, Sir, if I could but speak,' I might have mistaken him for a dunce, and thus done him great injustice. Through his love of mischief, however, and his inability to cope with his schoolfellows, on account of his defective utterance, it was evident that he was losing interest in his work, or rather that he had never felt much interest in it, and it became necessary to awaken him. One day, after he had been more noisy and mischievous than usual, I told him rather sternly to put on his cap and follow me. He did so, and I walked forward, while he, in a state of anxious suspense, walked behind me. After some moments' silence, I asked, 'Do you know, K——, what I am going to do with you?' 'Ne—ne—ne—no, Sir,' he replied. 'Well,' I said, 'I will tell you. I have spoken to you often enough, to no purpose, and now I intend to make you do better for the future.' We walked forward for some distance, and at length, putting my arm quietly around his neck, I broke silence once more, 'Can you tell me what an angle is, my boy?' 'Ye—ye—ye—yes, Sir, an angle is a—a—a—a—,' he could get no further, and turned his eyes upon me beseechingly. 'Well,' I replied to this silent appeal, 'go and pull two stalks of grass and show me what an angle is.' This he did, and with the grass stalks continued to answer my questions on the geometrical definitions. We turned into a stubble field—by this time he had lost all fear, and could speak quite distinctly—'What is a right angled triangle?' I asked. 'It has all its angles right angles, Sir.' 'Indeed,' I replied, taking my arm from around his neck, 'it has three right angles, has it? will you just kneel down?' He saw his mistake, stammered 'two,' looked at me piteously and hesitated. 'On your knees,

Such are some of the thoughts which have floated before me, in a more or less distracted manner, in reference to the present hour; and nobody can be more conscious of their manifold imperfections than I am myself. I have throughout been less anxious to make out a case for Physics than to state the truth; and I confess that the Lecture of this day week causes me to doubt, whether you are not entitled to expect from me a more emphatic statement of the claims of the science which I now represent, than that which I have laid before you. When I saw your Lecturer reduced to the necessity of pleading for Science, and meekly claiming for it, from the Institution which we are accustomed to regard as the highest in this land, a recognition equal to that accorded to Philology, I confess that the effect was to excite a certain revolutionary tendency in a mind which is usually tranquil almost to apathy in these matters. As the pole of a magnet acting upon soft iron induces in the latter a condition opposed to its own, so the irrationality of those who cast this slight upon Science tends to excite an opposite error on the part of their antagonists, and to cause them, in retaliation, to underrate the real merits of Philology. But is there no mind in England large enough to see the value of both, and to secure for each of them fair play? Let us

Sir,' I cried, and he knelt down, while I, falling on my knees beside him, said, 'Now pull up some stubble, and make me a triangle having either two or three right angles.' At once he saw his error, and the absurdity of our position, as we knelt together, making geometrical diagrams with stubble. Springing to his feet, he shook with laughter—'It has only one right angle, Sir—only one, of course!' I responded, 'Of course.' With my arm round his neck, we turned homewards, and continued our lesson successfully. 'This is the punishment I had in store for you,' I said, when we reached home. 'Now go, and transgress no more,' to which his eyes responded, 'I will, Sir.'"

not make this a fight of partisans—let the gleaned wealth of antiquity be showered into the open breast; but while we "unsphere the spirit of Plato" and listen with delight to the lordly music of the past, let us honour by adequate recognition the genius of our own time. Let me again remind you that the claims of that science which finds in me to-day its unripened advocate, are based upon the natural relations subsisting between Man and the world in which he dwells. Here, on the one side, we have the apparently lawless shifting of phenomena; on the other side, mind, which requires law for its equilibrium, and in obedience to its own indestructible instincts, believes that these phenomena are reducible to law. To chasten this apparent chaos is a problem which man's Creator has set before him. The world was built in order: it is the visual record of its Maker's logic, and to us have been trusted the will and power to grapple with the mighty argument. Descending for a moment from this high ground to considerations which lie closer to us as a nation—as a land of gas and furnaces, of steam and electricity: as a land which science, practically applied, has made great in peace and mighty in war:—I ask you whether this "land of old and just renown," has not a right to expect from her institutions a culture which shall embrace something more than declension and conjugation? They can place physical science upon its proper basis; they can check the habit, now too common, of regarding science solely as an instrument of material prosperity; they can dwell with effect upon its nobler use, and raise the national mind to the contemplation of it as the last development of that "increasing purpose" which runs through the ages and widens the thoughts of men.

ON THE EDUCATIONAL CLAIMS OF BOTANICAL SCIENCE.

A LECTURE DELIVERED BEFORE THE LONDON SOCIETY OF ARTS.

BY

ARTHUR HENFREY, ESQ., F.R.S., F.L.S.

ON THE STUDY OF BOTANY.

THE classification of the sciences, and the investigation of their relations one to another, must necessarily be a subject of great interest to those who pursue the special branches of knowledge in a philosophical spirit, not as the means of acquiring a body of abstruse ideas, but for the purpose of contributing to the common stock of classified facts and natural laws upon which the education, and consequently the civilization, of the human race depends.

A votary of the Natural History sciences is especially led to the examination of the general relations of his pursuits, from the great degree in which they seem to the common observer to be removed from the practical business of life. It is a question to which his social and sympathetic feelings especially attract him; and, therefore, it is with great gratification that I avail myself of this opportunity of insisting publicly upon the claims of Botany to the attention of all engaged in education.

The most remarkable of the classifications of the sciences which have been given to the world, may be briefly characterized by arrangement under three heads, indicating the totally distinct points of view from which they set out, viz.:—

1. Those based upon the sources of knowledge.

2. Those based upon the purpose for which the knowledge is sought; and

3. Those based upon the nature of the objects studied.

1. The classifications of the first kind,—those which arrange the various branches of knowledge according to the character of the intellectual methods and processes by means of which they are cultivated, are termed subjective, as regarding alone the nature of the recipient mind, or subject.

If we disregard the technicalities of metaphysics, or rather psychology, we may conveniently restrict our analysis of this, to the distinction of two qualities, those of *perception* and *reflection.*

By perception, by the aid of the senses, we observe facts: these facts may be either independent of our influence, when we call the *observation* proper; or they may be the result of special contrivance on our parts, when the mode of observation is called *experimentation;* and, again, we may receive information of observed facts by *testimony* of others. All these processes involve the acquisition of *experience,* direct or indirect, of phenomena; the sciences pursued especially by their means are called *experimental,* and the truths of experience are *facts.*

Reflection is the action of the reasoning faculty, according to its own laws, upon the simple ideas furnished by perception, dealing with certain properties of these, which it abstracts from the facts of perception, and, by the comparison and classification of them, arriving at generalizations, principles, laws, and the like, known by the collective name of *theory.* Those sciences which depend almost entirely (for none do solely) upon the reason, are called *rational, abstract,* or *theoretical* sciences

Now, when we consider that there exists no science purely abstract from its origin, and that the measure of advancement of every science is the degree to which it has co-ordinated the ideas with which it deals under general propositions and laws, it becomes obvious that the division into *experimental* and abstract is totally inapplicable to the existing state of science.

2. The classifications according to purpose, the division into *speculative* and *applied* or *practical* sciences, fail almost in the same way, since the progression of every science is marked, step by step, by the removal of certain truths from the position of abstract theories, interesting only to the learned, into the rank of axioms from which practical results of the greatest value to mankind are derived.

3. The third point of view is that from which we regard only the objects of our study, without considering either the faculties or processes by which we obtain our knowledge, or the advantages we may derive from its acquisition.

When we reflect upon the ordinary operations of our reasoning faculties, upon the common rules of logic, it becomes evident that this last mode of classification is the only one that can be called *rational,* since it is the only one which proceeds, according to the indispensable rule, of advancing from the most simple to the more complex of the ideas, which we wish to co-ordinate in our minds. The other two modes, the division into experimental and rational, abstract and applied sciences, must not only, from their nature, continually shift their ground as knowledge progresses, but they both set out from considerations of a highly complex character, which it would be vain to attempt to analyze, until a very large portion of the whole field of human inquiry has been cleared.

The objective mode of classification, which seems to have been first promulgated in a full and adequate manner by Descartes, has been revived of late years from a long oblivion, and it asserts its claim so clearly and evidently, and proves to harmonize so completely with the general direction which scientific inquiry has taken in modern times, that those who have once become acquainted with its characters can scarcely hesitate to adopt it.

The principle is laid down by Descartes in his "Method," in the following terms:—"To conduct my thoughts in order, commencing with the objects which are simplest and easiest to know, so as to rise gradually to the knowledge of the more compound;" and in a subsequent chapter he traces the course of his inquiries through mathematics, general physics, botany, zoology, and the sciences relative to man, according to the progressive complexity of the objects of his study.

In the chain or series thus formed, there not only exists a logical sequence, a relation of progression of the number of *kinds* of ideas with which we have to deal, but there is a relation of dependence, insomuch that each science rests upon that preceding it for a certain proportion of its data, and in turn constitutes the necessary basis for that which follows,—added to which we find the history of the development of the individual sciences bringing a striking confirmation of the validity of the principle, by showing that, although the first steps were made almost simultaneously in all the great divisions of science here laid down, the most simple have, from their nature, outstripped, in exact proportion to their relative simplicity, those which involve more complicated classes of generalities; so that, as it has been well expressed, the *logical antecedents* have always been the *historical antecedents*.*

The objective classification of the sciences may be briefly explained here.

The primary divisions depend upon the groups or classes of truths, which must be arranged according to their simplicity, or, what amounts to the same, their generality: in other words, the small number of qualities attached to the notions with which they deal.

The mathematical sciences deal with ideas which may be abstracted entirely from all material existence, retaining only the conceptions of space and number.

The physical sciences require, in addition, the actual recognition of matter, or force, or both, in addition to relations in space and time, but they are still confined to *universal* properties of matter.

The biological sciences are distinguished, in a most marked manner, by their dependence; the laws of life relate to objects having relations in space and time, and having material existence; they display, moreover, in their existence, a dependence upon physical laws, which form their medium; but they are distinguished by the presence of organization and life, characterized by a peculiar mobility and power of resistance to the physical forces, and an individuality of a different kind from that found in inorganic matter.

* This is the view of Comte, but there are other conditions which have determined the order in which the various relations among phenomena were discovered. Mr. Herbert Spencer has stated these further conditions, and the point is so important, that I have placed an extract from his statement in the Appendix.—[ED.]

The sciences relating to man, to human society, are removed another step, by the interference, among all the preceding laws, of those relating to the human mind in its fullest sense.

We thus obtain four groups. The following table illustrates these remarks :—

Truths	Abstract or absolute		Mathematical Sciences.
	Relative	to Matter	Physical Sciences.
		to Life	Biological Sciences.
		to Man	Social Sciences.

These four groups include respectively a number of secondary sciences derived from, dependent on, or forming essential constituents of the groups. With these we shall only so far engage ourselves here as relates to the subdivisions of biological science. Certain common characters run through these, life and organization being attributes of all the objects with which they are conversant. Physiology and morphology traverse the whole field of organic nature, animal as well as vegetable. But as animals and vegetables exhibit, in mass, a manifest difference in the degree of complexity of the vital powers and the organization,—since the animal kingdom exhibits qualities which are superadded to, and conjoined with those which it shares with the vegetable kingdom,—it becomes necessary to distinguish the branches of biology relating to these, and to divide these sciences under two heads, Botany and Zoology.

The greater simplicity of the physiological processes of vegetables, is alone sufficient to indicate their inferiority, or antecedent position in the scale of natural objects; and this is further confirmed, in accordance with the principle of objective classification, by their greater generality, since they extend through the succeeding group, in the vegetative or organic life of animals, while the animal life proper is restricted to the latter. And this physiological distinction is in agreement with a morphological or anatomical difference; for not only is the apparatus of organic life more complicated in animals, but these possess a system of organs, the nervous system, which is not represented in any way in vegetables, and constitutes the especial instrument or seat of that kind of spontaneity which is the most striking characteristic of animal life.

These observations will suffice to give an indication of the place which Botany holds in the natural classification of the sciences generally, according to the objects of their investigation.

Let us turn now to the *methods* employed in the various sciences, in order to ascertain the relative position of that with which we are engaged, in this respect also. Those sciences devoted to the investigation of purely abstract truths, the mathematical sciences, are free from the necessity of applying the perceptive faculties, or senses, since the objects of their pursuit are ideas from which have been abstracted all qualities having material existence. Those sciences, geometry and algebra, proceed by reasoning, and calculation, which has been well designated an abridged mode of reasoning. When we advance to the examination of material phenomena, the faculties of observation come into play, and, in the first place, in application to facts over which we can exercise no control; thus, in astronomy, pure observation is added to the reasoning and calculation used in mathematics. In the investigation of the physical phenomena of our own globe, however, we have greater scope, and are able to prepare facts for observation—to *experiment*, as it is termed. In the biological sciences, reasoning, observation, and experiment, all have place; but observation of unprepared facts is far more employed than experiment. Observation, however, as used in biology, is very different in its character from observation in physics. Not to speak of the greater complexity of phenomena, increasing in great proportion the danger of errors of sense, or first perceptions, a new difficulty arises from the character of the objects observed. In physics, observation of any given object—a ray of light, a chemical salt, or the like—is sufficient to afford us conclusions as to all existing objects of the same kind: any one specimen will serve as a type of the rest; and a renewal of the observation, under precisely the same condition, will only repeat and verify it. But in the case of animals or plants, no single example will serve as a *type* of its *kind*. Thus, in astronomy, a single observed fact becomes a datum; in terrestrial physics, any given example of an object may be experimented on, and all the characters of the kind of object ascertained; while in biology, the individual example, transitory and always undergoing change, being incapable of affording, at any given time, all the characters of its kind, it becomes necessary to derive the specific type—the *permanent unity*, as it was called by Buffon—from comparison of a more or less considerable number of examples, of all ages and placed in all conditions. Here, then, we are compelled to generalize, from the very first step in our progress.

The words, light, heat, iron, gold, oxygen, or the like, do not necessarily connote any attributes, imply no classification or grouping of separate things; so that we could not say, "a light" (except colloquially in the sense of a source of light, which would imply a generalization), "a gold," "an oxygen," &c. But when we speak of a horse, an oak, or any animal or vegetable, we use a general name, connoting certain characters or attributes, belonging to a class of objects, that is, an indefinite number of objects, separated by those attributes from all other objects.

Now, as the classes or kinds of objects forming the basis of all reasoning toward laws in botany and zoology exist in enormous numbers, it is evident that *comparative observation*, by means of which the groups are established, must occupy a most prominent place in their processes, since the classification of things is one of the necessary preliminaries to the induction which seeks the ascertainment of law.

In dwelling upon these differences, however, it is important to point out that the methods of all the sciences are fundamentally one, modified only in secondary particulars; and the division of the sciences into deductive and inductive indicates merely a difference in the degree of advancement of the respective sciences towards perfection. Every science is at first inductive; but in proportion to the small number of qualities possessed by its objects, it rises more quickly to certain abstract generalizations, which suffice to represent all the necessary characteristics of its individual objects or unities, and then deduction enables us to derive all the possible conditions of their relations from these. Mathematics have long stood in this position. Physics lagged behind long, from the overhaste of the ancients to reach their generalizations without passing through the series of inductions from facts which were indispensably requisite for the secure foundation of deductive physics. In these days, however, induction having performed a vast amount of work since Bacon gave the great impulse to its application, deduction finds a large and increasing domain in physics, where observation is only applied for the purpose of verification. On the other hand, deduction as yet finds little scope in biology, and the attempts of the German "philosophers of nature" are not of a character to attract us to the pursuit of this method; nevertheless, it is evident that when the bases have been securely laid by induction, deduction finds as great a scope here as elsewhere.

A few words must still be added respecting the inductive method in natural history. Bacon defines induction as "constructing axioms from the senses and particulars, by ascending continually and gradually till it finally arrives at the most general axioms," and subsequently he warns us against what he calls "anticipations," meaning hypotheses. But, however valuable his cautions were in the state of science in those days, it is evident that this precept of avoiding "anticipations" is the advice to abdicate the most valuable attributes of the human mind. Indeed, he remarks in a later passage, that his "method of discovering the sciences is such as to leave little to the acuteness and strength of wit, and indeed, rather to level wit and intellect." And those who have possessed acuteness and strength of wit, and who have most advanced the natural sciences since his day, have, in return, departed from the rigorous method of induction, and by this alone rendered possible the rapid progress of their sciences.

For in natural history—to speak of this alone—it is rarely in our power to ascertain *all* the particulars requisite for any given induction—it is scarcely ever possible to use this *demonstrative induction.* We are constantly obliged to derive a general consequence from a portion of the particular cases which it ought to rest upon, and in such cases we *anticipate* the agreement of the rest, basing the hypothesis upon *analogy*—one of the most important instruments in biological reasonings. In this way we arrive, not at absolute certainties, but at great probabilities, which are then tested by the various modes of verification, before they are admitted into the rank of truths. Thus this reasoning from analogy or *tentative induction,* comes to occupy a front rank with us, and is in reality of far greater utility for the advancement of science than the pure demonstrative induction; at the same time, it is a process which requires to be employed with the greatest circumspection, and under the most rigid control both of observation and reasoning. And this gives the methods of natural history a high value as intellectual discipline; for the cases in which inductions have to be made, or judgments to be formed in common life, are most frequently of this kind. Of the particulars which will be comprised in our generalization, only a certain number are accessible to observation.

We will now direct our attention to some further considerations regarding the relations of botany, as one of the biological sciences, to those preceding it in the classification we have adopted. That branch of physics which immediately precedes it is chemistry, the most special of the physical sciences, and its relations with this it will be sufficient for us to examine among the antecedents.

Chemistry, like the biological sciences, penetrates into the intimate constitution of natural bodies, and moreover, the bodies subject to its domain exhibit a kind of individuality not dependent upon ideas of number, density, colour, &c. alone, but upon this said intimate constitution. We arrive here at the formation of certain abstract notions, for the purpose of classification, which include in the particulars from which they are derived, both statical and dynamical characters. These abstractions refer to the idea of a *species*, which, however, is far more general here than in botany or zoology. A species in chemistry is a definite compound of two or more elements, in obedience to certain general laws, possessing certain definite characters, by which it may be known from all other species; the relation between the objects represented in this conception is one of identity in all respects but that of simple material continuity; the individuality of separate natural objects belonging to the given species depends solely upon their being mechanically separated from each other. There do indeed exist *varieties* in chemical species analogous to the varieties of species in living nature, but these partake of the same unstable individuality, and depend upon physical causes of great generality. Thus the allotropic conditions of some chemical substances, and even perhaps the crystalline or amorphous states of many, may be regarded as varieties of this kind. These species are remarkable, not only from the generality of their nature, but from their immobility. The only possible change in a chemical species is its conversion into other species, or transformation, in which the relations become entirely changed, and the name altered. There is nothing like development here,—the gradual unfolding by assimilation and transformation of material received from without.

In the organic kingdoms the idea of the species is an abstraction from very different facts. The objects to which it refers have a separate individuality, dependant upon characters non-existent in inorganic bodies. They are incapable of transformation, but susceptible of change according to certain laws; and while the chemical individual is homogeneous, and can only be divided into parts, of which each equally well represents the species, the biological individual is divisible in parts of different kinds, which have relations of harmony and continuity, but by no means of homogeneity, these parts making up together what constitutes the organism. Thus we see a distinct gradation between chemistry and biology, in reference to the generality of the notion which forms the basis of all classification in each.

In biology itself we find that the notion of the individual is modified in an analogous manner, when we carry it up from the vegetable into the animal kingdom; at all events, in those subjects of the latter, in which animality is most clearly manifest.

In regard to taxonomy, then, or classification, botany stands between chemistry and zoology.

In reference to the qualities of form which make their first appearance in minerals, plants show an advance upon the inorganic world, since the angular solid figures, bounded by plane surfaces subject to the simplest laws of geometry, soon become complicated with figures bounded by curves; and in the plants which produce a stem the form is dependant upon the properties of spiral curves. In the animal kingdom the bilateral symmetry, which is only traceable in the appendages of the trunk in plants, becomes the general rule in all, except certain of the larger groups; this is manifestly a further departure from the geometrical forms of crystals, and indicates a gradation in advance of the forms of plants; the more especially when we remember that the. appendages of the trunk are the organs of nutrition and reproduction, therefore of life in plants; while in animals, where the vegetative life is subordinate to a higher, these organs are progressively more and more completely hidden and inclosed, and the variations of outward form depend upon a new set of developments of the trunk or central axis, forming the organs of sense and volition, or animal life.

The examination of the outward relations of natural objects leads to the same co-ordination. Mineral or lifeless bodies can only retain their specific identity while at rest, that is to say, chemically; they change in accordance with general laws, when brought into contact with each other; and in the change they become transformed into other species. Animal or vegetable, organized or living bodies, constantly manifest action and change; it is in this especially that their life consists; but in so doing they do not lose their specific identity, but rather unfold and complete the characters of this. The actions performed in the organization are partly of physical and chemical nature, depending upon the laws of these sciences, but are subject to the regulation of a superior power which guides and directs them, maintaining itself among and through these, but distinct from them. We may compare the position of this vital force of organization to an architect employing a band of workmen to construct a building, he only designing the forms, and leaving them to find the materials and mechanical appliances. When the whole is finished, or at any time when the architect is away, the whole might seem, to an ignorant observer, solely the result of the labours of the workmen; so we can only see the results of the operations of the organic force in the material products, originating under physical laws. But when we have ascertained the extent of the domains of these physical laws, we find that they do not reach far enough to account for all. In vegetable life, absorption, evaporation, diffusion of juices, &c., are physical phenomena: assimilation, respiration, and the like, purely chemical: but no physical, no chemical law, throws any light upon the process of reproduction, upon the regeneration, distribution, and subdivision of the organic force, upon which the maintenance of the living creation especially depends, since the physical forces are unceasingly striving to destroy it. Vital action must be regarded, therefore, as something superadded to chemical or other physical action.

In vital phenomena themselves, the same subdivision holds as in the forms. In animals, as a whole, we have a striking increase of complexity, by the addition of the animal or affective life to the simple organic or vegetable life. In vegetables, the existence is characterized by phenomena of nutrition and reproduction alone. In this there is a relation of servitude to the animal kingdom, the latter being wholly dependent on plants for food, since these are exclusively capable of assimilating inorganic substances; while animals require these elements to be already combined into proximate principles, or organic substances. In animals, nutrition and reproduction constitute merely the basis for phenomena of sense and will. It is obviously unnecessary to pursue this relation any further.

The relation of botany to the other natural sciences may be now regarded as sufficiently ascertained in reference to its objects and methods, taken as a whole. But it is necessary, for the proper illustration of the relations of this science to the other branches of knowledge, to enter more minutely than has yet been done, into the characteristics of the science itself. And I may premise that the explanations to which we are now about to proceed, may be taken generally as equally applicable to both branches of biological science, Botany and Zoology.

In the abstract part of botany we have to lay down three divisions, viz:—

1. Morphology (or anatomy), treating of the generalizations, laws, or principles relating to the form or organization of plants.

2. Physiology, treating of the generalizations, laws, or principles relating to the acts, or vital processes of plants.

3. Taxonomy, treating of the principles of classification of plants.

The concrete part of the science consists of the natural history of plants, in which we study the entire set of phenomena presented by individual plants or groups of plants, or even parts of plants, with a view to practical applications.

Abstract botany, phytology proper, or, as the Germans call it, scientific botany, forms the basis upon which the concrete study, or natural history of plants, must rest; and this latter will be rational and fruitful in application, in proportion to the guiding lights furnished by abstract science. But it does not follow from this, that it is indispensable for every prosecutor of natural history to verify or repeat the propositions of the abstract science; in fact, the enunciation and demonstration of them, which form the great business of the philosophical botanist, would scarcely come within the sphere of possibility for the generality of mankind, busied with other matters. At the same time, it is an almost indispensable condition of success to those who prosecute natural history in a concrete form, that they should study and adopt the principles which have been ascertained in the abstract part of the science; since otherwise, only chance, or a superhuman amount of labour, can ensure their disentangling the essentials from the mass of complicated phenomena which present themselves in every observation upon living nature.

Morphology, or the philosophical anatomy of plants, is the branch of science which is devoted to the investigation of the principles which underlie all the multitudinous conditions of form presented by the organized beings of this kingdom. It proceeds by two paths—an analytical and a synthetical—by the analysis or dissection of full-grown plants and their structures (including their teratological or abnormal conditions), and by observation of the gradual development of these from the embryonal condition. By the pursuit of these paths we arrive at a double series of the forms of paths; one half resting on the different orders of characters in the same species, the other on the different characters of the same order in different species. In arranging the parts in the first series, we advance progressively from the organic elements to the tissues, from these to the organs, and thence to the entire organism; in arranging them in the second series, we trace the progressive complexity of the elements, tissues, organs, and organisms, in the different ranks of beings, or in the different stages of development of the same being.

In the first process—simple anatomy—we perform the first operation for the investigation of laws, the separation of the particular parts; in the second—in comparative anatomy, teratology, and embryogeny—we are able to make use of analogical reasoning, or tentative induction, in two distinct ways, whereby the agreement of results gives a degree of certainty to our generalisations, which the nature of the objects would prevent our acquiring by any other means.

The same characteristics apply to the modes of investigation in physiology (including pathology, or the study of abnormal deviations from vital laws), which is pursued in a precisely similar manner, but is directed, not to the ascertainment of the laws of development of form, but the laws of vitality, on which depend the manifestations of activity in those forms of organization.

In each department of the science, morphology and physiology, we are led to the recognition of a series which must serve as the basis of a natural classification of the objects of study. The inductions of these two branches lay the foundation of the third, namely, taxonomy; and the classification established upon these grounds has a pre-eminent claim to the title of a natural classification, since it is found that the conclusions derived from morphology and physiology coincide in pointing out the rank to be assigned to any organic beings, or group of such beings. The form corresponds to the function, in the degree of complexity of the laws upon which each depends.

Taxonomy, therefore, rests upon principles obtained by induction from morphology and physiology, as these rest, each upon the basis of comparative anatomy, teratology, and embryology, and thus a well-established classification of organic beings enables us to study any one, or any group of them, in its proper order as regards complication of organization, and allows of our placing any kind previously unknown in its proper situation; while the situation which the object or group of objects occupies in the classification, affords us at once a general idea of its organization, its mode of life, and with what other objects it is to be compared.

In Botany, the facts of physiology are very general, and, in regard to the comparison of different plants, would seem scarcely to aid us in the establishment of a classification, beyond the constitution of the great groups of plants; but as applied in the co-ordination of the different kinds of organs in the same plants, they form a most important element in the institution of groups, founded on the difference of form of these organs in different plants. In other words, the diversity of physiological phenomena in vegetables is comparatively slight, but the diversity of forms of homologous organs is very great, and the rank which the diversified forms shall hold as characters in a natural classification, depends upon the physiological value of the organs in which they occur.

It is upon organography that the greater part of the details of classification depend; accurate descriptions of the organs whose homologies are ascertained by morphological and physiological inductions, constituting the materials upon which all the generalizations of taxonomy are finally based. By organography we obtain accurate descriptions of the phenomena of form, that is to say, representations, in fixed and unequivocal language, of the appearances of the objects with which the science deals; and when these are studied in their connexion in individual organisms, we obtain such descriptions of living beings as enable us to compare them scientifically with one another. These comparisons lead to the discrimination of resemblances and differences. Under the guidance of ascertained laws of physiology and morphology, we are enabled to separate in these the essential from the inessential: then, by abstraction of the essential resemblances, and dropping out of consideration the inessential differences, we obtain the notion of a *type.* This notion of a type, abstracted from the actual individual representations of the species, forms the unit of all natural history classifications; and the groups into which the species are subsequently successively collected are all founded upon a similar principle of abstraction, under this condition—that the essentiality of the resemblances becomes progressively limited to characters which are more general in a morphological or physiological point of view.

As the taxonomy, or the classification of plants, is that department of botany which gives it a special utility as a means of mental training; as it is on this ground, above all, that it founds a claim to form a part of general education, it may be permitted me to enter into some technical details here, to illustrate and enforce the propositions just laid down. In the first place, the terminology of botany demands attention. It is a fundamental condition of the existence of organography, that the botanist should possess a rigidly defined technical language, a store of descriptive terms, sufficiently copious to denote every part and every quality of the parts of plants by a distinct name, fixed, and unalterable in the sense in which it is employed. The technical language of botany, as elaborated by Linnæus and his school, has long been the admiration of logical and philosophical writers, and has indeed been carried to great perfection. Every word has its definition, and can convey but one notion to those who have once mastered the language. The technicalities, therefore, of botanical language, which are vulgarly regarded as imperfections, and as repulsive to the inquirer, are in reality the very marks of its completeness, and far from offering a reason for withholding the science from ordinary education, constitute its great recommendation, as a method of training in accuracy of expression and habits of describing definitely and unequivocally the observations made by the use of the senses. The acquisition of the terms applied to the different parts of plants exercises the memory, while the mastery of the use of the adjectives of terminology cultivates, in a most beneficial manner, a habit of accuracy and perspicuity in the use of language. What is called the nomenclature of botany refers to the names given to the abstract notions of the kinds of beings dealt with in classification—to the species, genera, families, and so on. These refer not merely to the possession of particular attributes, but carry with them the idea of those attributes being distinctive of a *kind* of things; that is, they carry with them not only their definition founded upon qualities, but the idea, superadded to their definition, that these qualities are characteristic of an abstraction. On this ground, it has been assumed that they differ in their logical value from the names used in terminology, but there does not appear to be sufficient evidence of this. The names of plants or animals represent in classification those used in organography to denote organs or parts, homologous organs standing in the same logical relations as the individuals of a species.

The principles of nomenclature in botany and zoology, since the time of Linnæus, have proceeded essentially upon abstract grounds as regards species, the names not necessarily conveying in themselves any notion but that of *kind*. The nomenclature of chemistry differs greatly in this respect, since the names of the kinds or species generally represent their composition. The names of plants or animals are analogous to the proper names of men, used in civilized nations to economize words and assist the memory. The different kinds have not independent names, but are designated as members of groups of kinds, distinguished from each other by an adjective term, either indicating a distinctive quality or not, but in any case only necessarily connoting a certain abstract definition of the kind. This abstract definition is not arbitrary, derived from a given type, but constructed by the collection of the most general characters from all those individuals which we conceive to agree in kind. With regard to the organic species, we have certain other resorts, besides direct characters, by which we are enabled to judge as to the agreement in kind, as, for example, in the physiological phenomena of reproduction. The notion of a type which comes in here is not used in the sense of a typical individual, but as an abstract standard of reference.* Species are combined into groups according to the principle of

* This natural-history signification of a *type* seems to correspond with the notion of a type or ideal image as used in the fine arts, formed by combining all the characteristic perfections, and omitting all the inessential or accidental imperfections of a *kind*.

agreement; but these groups, called genera, have not the same biological isolation, at all events in plants, as the collections of individuals constituting a species. They are constituted, however, practically by the same method—by bringing together those species which agree with each other more than they do with any other species, in the greatest number of important characteristics. These groups, in biological language as in common life, are the first which receive substantive names, and the species which they include are distinguished by adjectives appended; thus, the botanical name *rosa*, like the common word rose, indicates a genus, including many species, which are distinguished by such appended terms as *canina*, the dog-rose, *centifolia*, the hundred-leaved rose, &c. The mental types of genera are more abstract than those of species, and they become less and less definite as our groups rise in the scale of generality, presenting more and more clearly the universal character of such types, so that they are embodiments of a certain definite character which we admit to be associated with others unknown or undefined.

The genera are gathered into groups called orders, or families, founded upon similar considerations. In this way we bring the vast mass of existing species into a smaller and more manageable number of collections, represented by abstractions, in which are contained all their essential characters of resemblance or agreement. There, however, we see the groups composed of smaller groups, which have a collateral agreement or equality of taxonomic characters among themselves; but we find these groups coming into a new relation—a relation of gradation or serial progression. This is the case even with the orders as included in the classes, and still more when we examine the plan of the classes or grand divisions of the vegetable kingdom.

Taking as a guide the same principles which lead us in the estimation of the value of differences and agreement in the characters of species, we find that the types of the orders are susceptible of co-ordination in a series which shall represent the degree of complexity of the phenomena in which they exhibit the characteristics of vegetable life. Vegetation or organic growth, and reproduction, are the two principal phenomena of vegetable life, growth being the lowest attribute, least raised above inorganic accretion—reproduction, the higher, related to, and indeed identical in its characters with, the reproduction of animals. The gradual specialization of vegetable structures, their distribution into distinct organs, the gradual elimination of the reproductive organs from the vegetative, until they become quite organically independent—these give the order in which the series of the vegetable families must stand, this co-ordination being not merely the only one which can be rationally derived from morphology and physiology, in the view of exhibiting the natural affininities of plants, but becoming, like all natural classifications, an instrument of discovery in the intermediate particulars by analogical reasoning.*

The following table will illustrate these points. In it are laid down the principal classes into which the vegetable kingdom is divided, according to the laws of classification here enforced.

* On the method of concomitant variations.

VEGETABLE KINGDOM.

THALLOPHYTA:—
- Fungales.
- Lichenales.
- Algales.

CORMOPHYTA:—
- Sporocarpia.
  - AXOGAMIA:—
    - Hepaticales.
    - Muscales.
  - THALLOGAMIA—
    - Filicales.
    - Equisetales.
  - SPOROGAMIA:—
    - Lycopodiales.
    - Marsileales.
- SPERMOCARPIA:—
  - Gymnospermia.
  - Angiospermia.
    - Monocotyledones.
    - Dicotyledones.

The large groups succeeding each other in this table exhibit a progression of morphological and physiological complexity, while collateral relations of the same nature exist in proportionate complexity in the particular groups.

The length to which I have dwelt upon this subject of classification may be justified by the following quotation from an eminent writer of the present day:* "Although the scientific arrangements of organic nature afford as yet the only complete example of rational classification, whether as to the formation of groups or series, these principles are applicable to all cases in which mankind are called upon to bring the various parts of any extensive subject into mental co-ordination. They are as

* John S. Mill, Logic, 2d ed. ii. 334.

much to the point when objects are to be classed for purposes of art or business as for those of science. The proper arrangement, for example, of a code of laws depends upon the same scientific conditions as the classifications in natural history; nor could there be a better preparatory discipline for that important function, than a study of the principles of a natural arrangement, not only in the abstract, but in their actual application to the class of phenomena for which they were first elaborated, and which are still the best school for learning their use."

It remains now to direct attention briefly to the relations of botanical science to various applied and abstract sciences, which are partly or wholly dependent upon it.

In the first place, it must be evident to every one that the general physiology of plants (which presupposes a knowledge of the physical and chemical laws influencing them), together with the concrete natural history of the species dealt with, must form the only secure basis of scientific agriculture; that it has not been fully recognised as such hitherto, depends upon its inevitable imperfections, which, however, will be the sooner removed, in proportion as agriculturists devote themselves to the study of physiological laws.

Secondly, botany finds a place in the two cosmological sciences studying the past and present conditions of the globe—Geology and Geography.

The perishable nature of vegetable structures does, indeed, render fossil remains of plants less valuable as objects for palæontological reasonings, than the better-preserved hard parts of animals, especially as the latter afford safer grounds for estimating how much has been lost, how much preserved, of ancient forms of organization. But botanical reasonings form an essential link in geological inductions, although it is requisite to be very careful in applying the analogical method, derived from classification, to the history of the development of the organic creation.

In geography, that is, physical geography, the concrete natural history of plants becomes a portion of the concrete natural history of the globe; the physiological laws are involved with physical laws of climate, soil, &c., in the explanations of possible distributions, either in an abstract point of view, or for the purpose of practical application; while the systematic classifications, and the natural history of particular species, become the only guide by which we can attempt to trace back the existing conditions of distribution towards their origin, and thus perform the share due from botany; in the historical connexion of physical geography with geology, of which it is properly only the statical part.

In conclusion, I have one remark to make regarding the discourse I have just addressed to you. It will be observed that the subject which I was called upon to expound, was the relations of botanical science to the other branches of knowledge, and not the science of botany itself, the special facts and laws of which, consequently, and especially in addressing an audience gathered together for educational purposes, have been kept back beyond what was absolutely necessary to its proper characterization; and I have dwelt upon the study as a means of mental discipline, and on its practical application, rather than as a branch of science pursuing knowledge for its own sake. Let it not be supposed that I do not prize it for its last attribute, for indeed I regard this as the highest and best; and I might express my own feelings in the well-known words of the wise king: "It is the glory of God to conceal a thing, but the glory of a king to search it out."

If any ask still, to what end? I would quote to him the assurance of the great restorer of science—"Only let mankind regain their rights over nature, assigned to them by the gift of God; that power obtained, its exercise will be governed by right reason and true religion."

ON THE METHOD OF STUDYING ZOOLOGY.

A LECTURE DELIVERED BEFORE THE SCIENCE CLASSES AT THE SOUTH KENSINGTON MUSEUM.

BY

THOMAS H. HUXLEY, F.R.S., LL.D.

ON THE STUDY OF ZOOLOGY.

NATURAL HISTORY is the name familiarly applied to the study of the properties of such natural bodies as minerals, plants, and animals; the sciences which embody the knowledge man has acquired upon these subjects are commonly termed Natural Sciences, in contradistinction to other, so called "physical," sciences; and those who devote themselves especially to the pursuit of such sciences have been, and are, commonly termed "Naturalists."

Linnæus was a naturalist in this wide sense, and his "Systema Naturæ" was a work upon natural history, in the broadest acceptation of the term; in it, that great methodizing spirit embodied all that was known in his time of the distinctive characters of minerals, animals, and plants. But the enormous stimulus which Linnæus gave to the investigation of nature soon rendered it impossible that any one man should write another "Systema Naturæ," and extremely difficult for any one to become a naturalist such as Linnæus was.

Great as have been the advances made by all the three branches of science, of old included under the title of natural history, there can be no doubt that zoology and botany have grown in an enormously greater ratio than mineralogy; and hence, as I suppose, the name of "natural history" has gradually become more and more definitely attached to these prominent divisions of the subject, and by "naturalist" people have meant more and more distinctly to imply a student of the structure and functions of living beings.

However this may be, it is certain that the advance of knowledge has gradually widened the distance between mineralogy and its old associates, while it has drawn zoology and botany closer together; so that of late years it has been found convenient (and indeed necessary) to associate the sciences which deal with vitality and all its phenomena under the common head of "biology;" and the biologists have come to repudiate any blood-relationship with their foster-brothers, the mineralogists.

Certain broad laws have a general application throughout both the animal and the vegetable worlds, but the ground common to these kingdoms of nature is not of very wide extent, and the multiplicity of details is so great, that the student of living beings finds himself obliged to devote his attention exclusively either to the one or the other. If he elects to study plants, under any aspect, we know at once what to call him; he is a botanist, and his science is botany. But if the investigation of animal life be his choice, the name generally applied to him will vary, according to the kind of animals he studies, or the particular phenomena of animal life to which he confines his attention. If the study of man is his object, he is called an anatomist, or a physiologist, or an ethnologist; but if he dissects animals, or examines into the mode in which their functions are performed, he is a comparative anatomist or comparative physiologist. If he turns his attention to fossil animals, he is a palæontologist. If his mind is more particularly directed to the description, specific discrimination, classification, and distribution of animals, he is termed a zoologist.

For the purposes of the present discourse, however, I shall recognise none of these titles save the last, which I shall employ as the equivalent of botanist, and I shall use the term zoology as denoting the whole doctrine of animal life, in contradistinction from botany, which signifies the whole doctrine of vegetable life.

Employed in this sense, zoology, like botany, is divisible into three great but subordinate sciences, morphology, physiology, and distribution, each of which may, to a very great extent, be studied independently of the other.

Zoological morphology is the doctrine of animal form or structure. Anatomy is one of its branches, development is another; while classification is the expression of the relations which different animals bear to one another, in respect of their anatomy and their development.

Zoological distribution is the study of animals in relation to the terrestrial conditions which obtain now, or have obtained at any previous epoch of the earth's history.

Zoological physiology, lastly, is the doctrine of the functions or actions of animals. It regards animal bodies as machines impelled by certain forces, and performing an amount of work, which can be expressed in terms of the ordinary forces of nature. The final object of physiology is to deduce the facts of morphology on the one hand, and those of distribution on the other, from the laws of the molecular forces of matter.

Such is the scope of zoology. But if I were to content myself with the enunciation of these dry definitions, I should ill exemplify that method of teaching this branch of physical science, which it is my chief business to-night to recommend. Let us turn away then from abstract definitions. Let us take some concrete living thing, some animal, the commoner the better, and let us see how the application of common sense and common logic to the obvious facts it presents, inevitably leads us into all these branches of zoological science.

I have before me a lobster. When I examine it, what appears to be the most striking character it presents? Why, I observe that this part which we call the tail of the lobster, is made up of six distinct hard rings and a seventh terminal piece. If I separate one of the middle rings, say the third, I find it carries upon its under surface a pair of limbs or appendages, each of which consists of a stalk and two terminal pieces. So that I can represent a transverse section of the ring and its appendages upon the diagram board in this way.

If I now take the fourth ring I find it has the same structure, and so have the fifth and the second; so that in each of these divisions of the tail I find parts which correspond with one another, a ring and two appendages; and in each appendage a stalk and two end pieces. These corresponding parts are called, in the technical language of anatomy, "homologous parts." The ring of the third division is the "homologue" of the ring of the fifth, the appendage of the former is the homologue of the appendage of the latter. And as each division exhibits corresponding parts in corresponding places, we say that all the divisions are constructed upon the same plan. But now let us consider the sixth division. It is similar to, and yet different from, the others. The ring is essentially the same as in the other divisions; but the appendages look at first as if they were very different; and yet when we regard them closely, what do we find? A stalk and two terminal divisions, exactly as in the others, but the stalk is very short and very thick, the terminal divisions are very broad and flat, and one of them is divided into two pieces.

I may say, therefore, that the sixth segment is like the others in plan, but that it is modified in its details.

The first segment is like the others, so far as its ring is concerned, and though its appendages differ from any of those yet examined in the simplicity of their structure parts corresponding with the stem and one of the divisions of the appendages of the other segments can be readily discerned in them.

Thus it appears that the lobster's tail is composed of a series of segments which are fundamentally similar, though each presents peculiar modifications of the plan common to all. But when I turn to the fore part of the body I see, at first, nothing but a great shield-like shell, called technically the "carapace," ending in front in a sharp spine, on either side of which are the curious compound eyes, set upon the ends of stout moveable stalks. Behind these, on the under side of the body, are two pairs of long feelers or antennæ, followed by six pairs of jaws, folded against one another over the mouth, and five pairs of legs, the foremost of these being the great pinchers, or claws, of the lobster.

It looks, at first, a little hopeless to attempt to find in this complex mass a series of rings, each with its pair of appendages, such as I have shown you in the abdomen, and yet it is not difficult to demonstrate their existence.

Strip off the legs, and you will find that each pair is attached to a very definite segment of the under wall of the body; but these segments, instead of being the lower parts of free rings, as in the tail, are such parts of rings which are all solidly united and bound together; and the like is true of the jaws, the feelers, and the eye-stalks, every pair of which is borne upon its own special segment. Thus the conclusion is gradually forced upon us, that the body of the lobster is composed of as many rings as there are pairs of appendages, namely, twenty in all, but that the six hindmost rings remain free and moveable, while the fourteen front rings become firmly soldered together, their backs forming one continuous shield—the carapace.

Unity of plan, diversity in execution, is the lesson taught by the study of the rings of the body, and the same instruction is given still more emphatically by the appendages. If I examine the outermost jaw I find it consists of three distinct portions, an inner, a middle, and an outer, mounted upon a common stem; and if I compare this jaw with the legs behind it, or the jaws in front of it, I find it quite easy to see, that, in the legs, it is the part of the appendage which corresponds with the inner division, which becomes modified into what we know familiarly as the "leg," while the middle division disappears, and the outer division is hidden under the carapace. Nor is it more difficult to discern that, in the appendages of the tail, the middle division appears again and the outer vanishes; while, on the other hand, in the foremost jaw, the so-called mandible, the inner division only is left; and, in the same way, the parts of the feelers and of the eye-stalks can be identified with those of the legs and jaws.

But whither does all this tend? To the very remarkable conclusion that a unity of plan, of the same kind as that discoverable in the tail or abdomen of the lobster, pervades the whole organization of its skeleton, so that I can return to the diagram representing any one of the rings of the tail, which I drew upon the board, and by adding a third division to each appendage, I can use it as a sort of scheme or plan of any ring of the body. I can give names to all the parts of that figure, and then if I take any segment of the body of the lobster, I can point out to you exactly, what modification the general plan has undergone in that particular segment; what part has remained moveable, and what has become fixed to another; what has been excessively developed and metamorphosed, and what has been suppressed.

But I imagine I hear the question, How is all this to be tested? No doubt it is a pretty and ingenious way of looking at the structure of any animal, but is it anything more? Does Nature acknowledge, in any deeper way, this unity of plan we seem to trace?

The objection suggested by these questions is a very valid and important one, and morphology was in an unsound state, so long as it rested upon the mere perception of the analogies which obtain between fully formed parts. The unchecked ingenuity of speculative anatomists proved itself fully competent to spin any number of contradictory hypotheses out of the same facts, and endless morphological dreams threatened to supplant scientific theory.

Happily, however, there is a criterion of morphological truth, and a sure test of all homologies. Our lobster has not always been what we see it; it was once an egg, a semifluid mass of yolk, not so big as a pin's head, contained in a transparent membrane, and exhibiting not the least trace of any one of those organs, whose multiplicity and complexity, in the adult, are so surprising. After a time a delicate patch of cellular membrane appeared upon one face of this yolk, and that patch was the foundation of the whole creature, the clay out of which it would be moulded. Gradually investing the yolk, it became subdivided by transverse constrictions into segments, the forerunners of the rings of the body. Upon the ventral surface of each of the rings thus sketched out, a pair of bud-like prominences made their appearance—the rudiments of the appendages of the ring. At first, all the appendages were alike, but, as they grew, most of them became distinguished with a stem and two terminal divisions, to which, in the middle part of the body, was added a third outer division; and it was only at a later period, that by the modification, or abortion, of certain of these primitive constituents, the limbs acquired their perfect form.

Thus the study of development proves that the doctrine of unity of plan is not merely a fancy, that it is not merely one way of looking at the matter, but that it is the expression of deep-seated natural facts. The legs and jaws of the lobster may not merely be regarded as modifications of a common type,—in fact and in nature they are so,—the leg and the jaw of the young animal being, at first, indistinguishable.

These are wonderful truths, the more so because the zoologist finds them to be of universal application. The investigation of a polype, of a snail, of a fish, of a horse, or of a man, would have led us, though by a less easy path, perhaps, to exactly the same point. Unity of plan everywhere lies hidden under the mask of diversity of structure—the complex is everywhere evolved out of the simple. Every animal has at first the form of an egg, and every animal and every organic part, in reaching its adult state, passes through conditions common to other animals and other adult parts; and this leads me to another point. I have hitherto spoken as if the lobster were alone in the world, but, as I need hardly remind you, there are myriads of other animal organisms. Of these, some, such as men, horses, birds, fishes, snails, slugs, oysters, corals, and sponges, are not in the least like the lobster. But other animals, though they may differ a good deal from the lobster, are yet either very like it, or are like something that is like it. The cray fish, the rock lobster, and the prawn, and the shrimp, for example, however different, are yet so like lobsters, that a child would group them as of the lobster kind, in contradistinction to snails and slugs; and these last again would form a kind by themselves, in contradistinction to cows, horses, and sheep, the cattle kind.

But this spontaneous grouping into "kinds" is the first essay of the human mind at classification, or the calling by a common name of those things that are alike, and the arranging them in such a manner as best to suggest the sum of their likenesses and unlikenesses to other things.

Those kinds which include no other subdivisions than the sexes, or various breeds, are called, in technical language, species. The English lobster is a species, our cray fish is another, our prawn is another. In other countries, however, there are lobsters, cray fish, and prawns, very like ours, and yet presenting sufficient differences to deserve distinction. Naturalists, therefore, express this resemblance and this diversity by grouping them as distinct species of the same "genus." But the lobster and the cray fish, though belonging to distinct genera, have many features in common, and hence are grouped together in an assemblage which is called a family. More distant resemblances connect the lobster with the prawn and the crab, which are expressed by putting all these into the same order. Again, more remote, but still very definite, resemblances unite the lobster with the woodlouse, the king crab, the water-flea, and the barnacle, and separate them from all other animals; whence they collectively constitute the larger group, or class, *Crustacea*. But the *Crustacea* exhibit many peculiar features in common with insects, spiders, and centipedes, so that these are grouped into the still larger assemblage or "province" *Articulata;* and, finally, the relations which these have to worms and other lower animals, are expressed by combining the whole vast aggregate into the sub-kingdom of *Annulosa*.

If I had worked my way from a sponge instead of a lobster, I should have found it associated, by like ties, with a great number of other animals into the sub-kingdom *Protozoa;* if I had selected a fresh-water polype or a coral, the members of what naturalists term the sub-kingdom *Cœlenterata* would have grouped themselves around my type; had a snail been chosen, the inhabitants of all univalve and bivalve, land and water shells, the lamp shells, the squids, and the sea-mat would have gradually linked themselves on to it as members of the same sub-kingdom of *Mollusca;* and finally, starting from man, I should have been compelled to admit first, the ape, the rat, the horse, the dog, into the same class; and then the bird, the crocodile, the turtle, the frog, and the fish, into the same sub-kingdom of *Vertebrata*.

And if I had followed out all these various lines of classification fully, I should discover in the end that there was no animal, either recent or fossil, which did not at once fall into one or other of these sub-kingdoms. In other words, every animal is organized upon one or other of the five, or more, plans, whose existence renders our classification possible. And so definitely and precisely marked is the structure of each animal, that, in the present state of our knowledge, there is not the least evidence to prove that a form, in the slightest degree transitional between any two of the groups *Vertebrata*, *Annulosa*, *Mollusca*, and *Cœlenterata*, either exists, or has existed, during that period of the earth's history which is recorded by the geologist. Nevertheless, you must not for a moment suppose, because no such transitional forms are known, that the members of the sub-kingdoms are disconnected from, or independent of, one another. On the contrary, in their earliest condition they are all alike, and the primordial germs of a man, a dog, a bird, a fish, a beetle, a snail, and a polype are, in no essential structural respects, distinguishable.

In this broad sense, it may with truth be said, that all living animals, and all those dead creations which geology reveals, are bound together by an all-pervading unity of organization, of the same character, though not equal in degree, to that which enables us to discern one and the same plan amidst the twenty different segments of a lobster's body. Truly it has been said, that to a clear eye the smallest fact is a window through which the Infinite may be seen.

Turning from these purely morphological considerations, let us now examine into the manner in which the attentive study of the lobster impels us into other lines of research.

Lobsters are found in all the European seas; but on the opposite shores of the Atlantic and in the seas of the southern hemisphere they do not exist. They are, however, represented in these regions by very closely allied, but distinct forms—the *Homarus Americanus* and the *Homarus Capensis:* so that we may say that the European has one species of *Homarus;* the American, another; the African, another; and thus the remarkable facts of geographical distribution begin to dawn upon us.

Again, if we examine the contents of the earth's crust, we shall find in the later of those deposits, which have served as the great burying grounds of past ages, numberless lobster-like animals, but none so similar to our living lobster as to make zoologists sure that they belonged even to the same genus. If we go still further back in time, we discover, in the oldest rocks of all, the remains of animals, constructed on the same general plan as the lobster, and belonging to the same great group of *Crustacea;* but for the most part totally different from the lobster, and indeed from any other living form of crustacean; and thus we gain a notion of that successive change of the animal population of the globe, in past ages, which is the most striking fact revealed by geology.

Consider, now, where our inquiries have led us. We studied our type morphologically, when we determined its anatomy and its development, and when comparing it, in these respects, with other animals, we made out its place in a system of classification. If we were to examine every animal in a similar manner, we should establish a complete body of zoological morphology.

Again, we investigated the distribution of our type in space and in time, and, if the like had been done with every animal, the sciences of geographical and geological distribution would have attained their limit.

But you will observe one remarkable circumstance, that, up to this point, the question of the life of these organisms has not come under consideration. Morphology and distribution might be studied almost as well, if animals and plants were a peculiar kind of crystals, and possessed none of those functions which distinguish living beings so remarkably. But the facts of morphology and distribution have to be accounted for, and the science, whose aim it is to account for them, is physiology.

Let us return to our lobster once more. If we watched the creature in its native element, we should see it climbing actively the submerged rocks, among which it delights to live, by means of its strong legs; or swimming by powerful strokes of its great tail, the appendages of whose sixth joint are spread out into a broad fan-like propeller: seize it, and it will show you that its great claws are no mean weapons of offence; suspend a piece of carrion among its haunts, and it will greedily devour it, tearing and crushing the flesh by means of its multitudinous jaws.

Suppose that we had known nothing of the lobster but as an inert mass, an organic crystal, if I may use the phrase, and that we could suddenly see it exerting all these powers, what wonderful new ideas and new questions would arise in our minds! The great new question would be, "How does all this take place?" the chief new idea would be, the idea of adaptation to purpose,—the notion, that the constituents of animal bodies are not mere unconnected parts, but organs working together to an end. Let us consider the tail of the lobster again from this point of view. Morphology has taught us that it is a series of segments composed of homologous parts, which undergo various modifications—beneath and through which a common plan of formation is discernible. But if I look at the same part physiologically, I see that it is a most beautifully constructed organ of locomotion, by means of which the animal can swiftly propel itself either backwards or forwards.

But how is this remarkable propulsive machine made to perform its functions? If I were suddenly to kill one of these animals and to take out all the soft parts, I should find the shell to be perfectly inert, to have no more power of moving itself than is possessed by the machinery of a mill, when disconnected from its steam-engine or water-wheel. But if I were to open it, and take out the viscera only, leaving the white flesh, I should perceive that the lobster could bend and extend its tail as well as before. If I were to cut off the tail, I should cease to find any spontaneous motion in it; but on pinching any portion of the flesh, I should observe that it underwent a very curious change—each fibre becoming shorter and thicker. By this act of contraction, as it is termed, the parts to which the ends of the fibre are attached are, of course, approximated; and according to the relations of their points of attachment to the centres of motion of the different rings, the bending or the extension of the tail results. Close observation of the newly opened lobster would soon show that all its movements are due to the same cause—the shortening and thickening of these fleshy fibres, which are technically called muscles.

Here, then, is a capital fact. The movements of the lobster are due to muscular contractility. But why does a muscle contract at one time and not at another? Why does one whole group of muscles contract when the lobster wishes to extend his tail, and another group, when he desires to bend it? What is it originates, directs, and controls the motive power?

Experiment, the great instrument for the ascertainment of truth in physical science, answers this question for us. In the head of the lobster there lies a small mass of that peculiar tissue which is known as nervous substance. Cords of similar matter connect this brain of the lobster, directly or indirectly, with the muscles. Now, if these communicating cords are cut, the brain remaining entire, the power of exerting what we call voluntary motion in the parts below the section is destroyed; and on the other hand, if, the cords remaining entire, the brain mass be destroyed, the same voluntary mobility is equally lost. Whence the inevitable conclusion is, that the power of originating these motions resides in the brain, and is propagated along the nervous cords.

In the higher animals the phenomena which attend this transmission have been investigated, and the exertion of the peculiar energy which resides in the nerves has been found to be accompanied by a disturbance of the electrical state of their molecules.

If we could exactly estimate the signification of this disturbance; if we could obtain the value of a given exertion of nerve force by determining the quantity of electricity, or of heat, of which it is the equivalent; if we could ascertain upon what arrangement, or other condition of the molecules of matter, the manifestation of the nervous and muscular energies depends, (and doubtless science will some day or other ascertain these points,) physiologists would have attained their ultimate goal in this direction; they would have determined the relation of the motive force of animals to the other forms of force found in nature; and if the same process had been successfully performed for all the operations which are carried on, in, and by the animal frame, physiology would be perfect, and the facts of morphology and distribution would be deducible from the laws which physiologists had established, combined with those determining the condition of the surrounding universe.

There is not a fragment of the organism of this humble animal, whose study would not lead us into regions of thought as large as those which I have briefly opened up to you; but what I have been saying, I trust, has not only enabled you to form a conception of the scope and purport of zoology, but has given you an imperfect example of the manner in which, in my opinion, that science, or indeed any physical science, may be best taught. The great matter is, to make teaching real and practical, by fixing the attention of the student on particular facts; but at the same time it should be rendered broad and comprehensive, by constant reference to the generalizations of which all particular facts are illustrations. The lobster has served as a type of the whole animal kingdom, and its anatomy and physiology have illustrated for us some of the greatest truths of biology. The student who has once seen for himself the facts which I have described, has had their relations explained to him, and has clearly comprehended them, has so far a knowledge of zoology, which is real and genuine, however limited it may be, and which is worth more than all the mere reading knowledge of the science he could ever acquire. His zoological information is, so far, knowledge and not mere hearsay.

And if it were my business to fit you for the certificate in zoological science granted by this department, I should pursue a course precisely similar in principle to that which I have taken to-night. I should select a fresh-water sponge, a fresh-water polype or a *Cyanæa*, a fresh-water mussel, a lobster, a fowl, as types of the five primary divisions of the animal kingdom. I should explain their structure very fully, and show how each illustrated the great principles of zoology. Having gone very carefully and fully over this ground, I should feel that you had a safe foundation, and I should then take you in the same way, but less minutely, over similarly selected illustrative types of the classes; and then I should direct your attention to the special forms enumerated under the head of types, in this syllabus, and to the other facts there mentioned.

That would, speaking generally, be my plan. But I have undertaken to explain to you the best mode of acquiring and communicating a knowledge of zoology, and you may therefore fairly ask me for a more detailed and precise account of the manner in which I should propose to furnish you with the information I refer to.

My own impression is, that the best model for all kinds of training in physical science is that afforded by the method of teaching anatomy, in use in the medical schools. This method consists of three elements—lectures, demonstrations, and examinations.

The object of lectures is, in the first place, to awaken the attention and excite the enthusiasm of the student; and this, I am sure, may be effected to a far greater extent by the oral discourse and by the personal influence of a respected teacher, than in any other way. Secondly, lectures have the double use of guiding the student to the salient points of a subject, and at the same time forcing him to attend to the whole of it, and not merely to that part which takes his fancy. And lastly, lectures afford the student the opportunity of seeking explanations of those difficulties which will, and indeed ought to, arise in the course of his studies.

But for a student to derive the utmost possible value from lectures, several precautions are needful.

I have a strong impression that the better a discourse is, as an oration, the worse it is as a lecture. The flow of the discourse carries you on without proper atttention to its sense; you drop a word or a phrase, you lose the exact meaning for a moment, and while you strive to recover yourself, the speaker has passed on to something else.

The practice I have adopted of late years, in lecturing to students, is to condense the substance of the hour's discourse into a few dry propositions, which are read slowly and taken down from dictation; the reading of each being followed by a free commentary, expanding and illustrating the proposition, explaining terms, and removing any difficulties that may be attackable in that way, by diagrams made roughly, and seen to grow under the lecturer's hand. In this manner you, at any rate, insure the co-operation of the student to a certain extent. He cannot leave the lecture-room entirely empty if the taking of notes is enforced; and a student must be preternaturally dull and mechanical, if he can take notes and hear them properly explained, and yet learn nothing.

What books shall I read? is a question constantly put by the student to the teacher. My reply usually is, "None: write your notes out carefully and fully; strive to understand them thoroughly; come to me for the explanation of anything you cannot understand; and I would rather you did not distract your mind by reading." A properly composed course of lectures ought to contain fully as much matter as a student can assimilate in the time occupied by its delivery; and the teacher should always recollect that his business is to feed, and not to cram, the intellect. Indeed, I believe that a student who gains from a course of lectures the simple habit of concentrating his attention upon a definitely limited series of facts, until they are thoroughly mastered, has made a step of immeasurable importance.

But, however good lectures may be, and however extensive the course of reading by which they are followed up, they are but accessories to the great instrument of scientific teaching—demonstration. If I insist unweariedly, nay fanatically, upon the importance of physical science as an educational agent, it is because the study of any branch of science, if properly conducted, appears to me to fill up a void left by all other means of education. I have the greatest respect and love for literature; nothing would grieve me more than to see literary training other than a very prominent branch of education: indeed, I wish that real literary discipline were far more attended to than it is; but I cannot shut my eyes to the fact, that there is a vast difference between men who have had a purely literary, and those who have had a sound scientific, training.

Seeking for the cause of this difference, I imagine I

can find it in the fact, that, in the world of letters, learning and knowledge are one, and books are the source of both; whereas in science, as in life, learning and knowledge are distinct, and the study of things, and not of books, is the source of the latter.

All that literature has to bestow may be obtained by reading and by practical exercise in writing and in speaking; but I do not exaggerate when I say, that none of the best gifts of science are to be won by these means. On the contrary, the great benefit which a scientific education bestows, whether as training or as knowledge, is dependent upon the extent to which the mind of the student is brought into immediate contact with facts—upon the degree to which he learns the habit of appealing directly to Nature, and of acquiring through his senses concrete images of those properties of things, which are, and always will be, but approximatively expressed in human language. Our way of looking at Nature, and of speaking about her, varies from year to year; but a fact once seen, a relation of cause and effect, once demonstratively apprehended, are possessions which neither change nor pass away, but, on the contrary, form fixed centres, about which other truths aggregate by natural affinity.

Therefore, the great business of the scientific teacher is, to imprint the fundamental, irrefragable facts of his science, not only by words upon the mind, but by sensible impressions upon the eye, and ear, and touch of the student, in so complete a manner, that every term used, or law enunciated, should afterwards call up vivid images of the particular structural, or other, facts which furnished the demonstration of the law, or the illustration of the term.

Now this important operation can only be achieved by constant demonstration, which may take place to a certain imperfect extent during a lecture, but which ought also to be carried on independently, and which should be addressed to each individual student, the teacher endeavouring, not so much to show a thing to the learner, as to make him see it for himself.

I am well aware that there are great practical difficulties in the way of effectual zoological demonstrations. The dissection of animals is not altogether pleasant, and requires much time; nor is it easy to secure an adequate supply of the needful specimens. The botanist has here a great advantage; his specimens are easily obtained, are clean and wholesome, and can be dissected in a private house as well as anywhere else; and hence, I believe, the fact, that botany is so much more readily and better taught than its sister science. But, be it difficult or be it easy, if zoological science is to be properly studied, demonstration, and, consequently, dissection, must be had. Without it, no man can have a really sound knowledge of animal organization.

A good deal may be done, however, without actual dissection on the student's part, by demonstration upon specimens and preparations; and in all probability it would not be very difficult, were the demand sufficient, to organize collections of such objects, sufficient for all the purposes of elementary teaching, at a comparatively cheap rate. Even without these, much might be effected, if the zoological collections, which are open to the public, were arranged according to what has been termed the "typical principle;" that is to say, if the specimens exposed to public view were so selected, that the public could learn something from them, instead of being, as at present, merely confused by their multiplicity. For example, the grand ornithological gallery at the British Museum contains between two and three thousand species of birds, and sometimes five or six specimens of a species. They are very pretty to look at, and some of the cases are, indeed, splendid; but I will undertake to say, that no man but a professed ornithologist has ever gathered much information from the collection. Certainly, no one of the tens of thousands of the general public who have walked through that gallery ever knew more about the essential peculiarities of birds when he left the gallery, than when he entered it. But if, somewhere in that vast hall, there were a few preparations, exemplifying the leading structural peculiarities and the mode of development of a common fowl; if the types of the genera, the leading modifications in the skeleton, in the plumage at various ages, in the mode of nidification, and the like, among birds, were displayed; and if the other specimens were put away in a place where the men of science, to whom they are alone useful, could have free access to them, I can conceive that this collection might become a great instrument of scientific education.

The last implement of the teacher to which I have adverted is examination—a means of education now so thoroughly understood that I need hardly enlarge upon it. I hold that both written and oral examinations are indispensable, and, by requiring the description of specimens, they may be made to supplement demonstration.

Such is the fullest reply the time at my disposal will allow me to give to the question—how may a knowledge of zoology be best acquired and communicated?

But there is a previous question which may be moved,

and which, in fact, I know many are inclined to move. It is the question, why should training masters be encouraged to acquire a knowledge of this, or any other branch of physical science? What is the use, it is said, of attempting to make physical science a branch of primary education? Is it not probable that teachers, in pursuing such studies, will be led astray from the acquirement of more important but less attractive knowledge? And, even if they can learn something of science without prejudice to their usefulness, what is the good of their attempting to instil that knowledge into boys whose real business is the acquisition of reading, writing, and arithmetic?

These questions are, and will be, very commonly asked, for they arise from that profound ignorance of the value and true position of physical science, which infests the minds of the most highly educated and intelligent classes of the community. But if I did not feel well assured that they are capable of being easily and satisfactorily answered; that they have been answered over and over again; and that the time will come when men of liberal education will blush to raise such questions,—I should be ashamed of my position here to-night. Without doubt, it is your great and very important function to carry out elementary education; without question, anything that should interfere with the faithful fulfilment of that duty on your part would be a great evil; and if I thought that your acquirement of the elements of physical science, and your communication of those elements to your pupils, involved any sort of interference with your proper duties, I should be the first person to protest against your being encouraged to do anything of the kind.

But is it true that the acquisition of such a knowledge of science as is proposed, and the communication of that knowledge, are calculated to weaken your usefulness? Or may I not rather ask, is it possible for you to discharge your functions properly without these aids?

What is the purpose of primary intellectual education? I apprehend that its first object is to train the young in the use of those tools wherewith men extract knowledge from the ever-shifting succession of phenomena which pass before their eyes; and that its second object is to inform them of the fundamental laws which have been found by experience to govern the course of things, so that they may not be turned out into the world naked, defenceless, and a prey to the events they might control.

A boy is taught to read his own and other languages, in order that he may have access to infinitely wider stores of knowledge than could ever be opened to him by oral intercourse with his fellow men; he learns to write, that his means of communication with the rest of mankind may be indefinitely enlarged, and that he may record and store up the knowledge he acquires. He is taught elementary mathematics, that he may understand all those relations of number and form, upon which the transactions of men, associated in complicated societies, are built, and that he may have some practice in deductive reasoning.

All these operations of reading, writing, and ciphering, are intellectual tools, whose use should, before all things, be learned, and learned thoroughly; so that the youth may be enabled to make his life that which it ought to be, a continual progress in learning and in wisdom.

But, in addition, primary education endeavours to fit a boy out with a certain equipment of positive knowledge. He is taught the great laws of morality; the religion of his sect; so much history and geography as will tell him where the great countries of the world are, what they are, and how they have become what they are.

Without doubt all these are most fitting and excellent things to teach a boy; I should be very sorry to omit any of them from any scheme of primary intellectual education. The system is excellent, so far as it goes.

But if I regard it closely, a curious reflection arises. I suppose that, fifteen hundred years ago, the child of any well-to-do Roman citizen was taught just these same things; reading and writing in his own, and, perhaps, the Greek tongue; the elements of mathematics; and the religion, morality, history, and geography current in his time. Furthermore, I do not think I err in affirming, that, if such a Christian Roman boy, who had finished his education, could be transplanted into one of our public schools, and pass through its course of instruction, he would not meet with a single unfamiliar line of thought; amidst all the new facts he would have to learn, not one would suggest a different mode of regarding the universe from that current in his own time.

And yet surely there is some great difference between the civilization of the fourth century and that of the nineteenth, and still more between the intellectual habits and tone of thought of that day and of this?

And what has made this difference? I answer fearlessly,—The prodigious development of physical science within the last two centuries.

Modern civilization rests upon physical science; take away her gifts to our own country, and our position among the leading nations of the world is gone to-morrow; for it is physical science only, that makes intelligence and moral energy stronger than brute force.

The whole of modern thought is steeped in sçience; it has made its way into the works of our best poets, and even the mere man of letters, who affects to ignore and despise science, is unconsciously impregnated with her spirit, and indebted for his best products to her methods. I believe that the greatest intellectual revolution mankind has yet seen is now slowly taking place by her agency. She is teaching the world that the ultimate court of appeal is observation and experiment, and not authority; she is teaching it to estimate the value of evidence; she is creating a firm and living faith in the existence of immutable moral and physical laws, perfect obedience to which is the highest possible aim of an intelligent being.

But of all this your old stereotyped system of education takes no note. Physical science, its methods, its problems, and its difficulties, will meet the poorest boy at every turn, and yet we educate him in such a manner that he shall enter the world as ignorant of the existence of the methods and facts of science as the day he was born. The modern world is full of artillery; and we turn out our children to do battle in it, equipped with the shield and sword of an ancient gladiator.

Posterity will cry shame on us if we do not remedy this deplorable state of things. Nay, if we live twenty years longer, our own consciences will cry shame on us.

It is my firm conviction that the only way to remedy

it is, to make the elements of physical science an integral part of primary education. I have endeavoured to show you how that may be done for that branch of science which it is my business to pursue; and I can but add, that I should look upon the day when every schoolmaster throughout this land was a centre of genuine, however rudimentary, scientific knowledge, as an epoch in the history of the country.

But let me entreat you to remember my last words. Addressing myself to you, as teachers, I would say, mere book learning in physical science is a sham and a delusion—what you teach, unless you wish to be impostors, that you must first know; and real knowledge in science means personal acquaintance with the facts, be they few or many.

Note.—It has been suggested to me that these words may be taken to imply a discouragement on my part of any sort of scientific instruction which does not give an acquaintance with the facts at first hand. But this is not my meaning. The ideal of scientific teaching is, no doubt, a system by which the scholar sees every fact for himself, and the teacher supplies only the explanations. Circumstances, however, do not often allow of the attainment of that ideal, and we must put up with the next best system—one in which the scholar takes a good deal on trust from a teacher, who, knowing the facts by his own knowledge, can describe them with so much vividness as to enable his audience to form competent ideas concerning them. The system which I repudiate is that which allows teachers who have not come into direct contact with the leading facts of a science to pass their second-hand information on. The scientific virus, like vaccine lymph, if passed through too long a succession of organisms, will lose all its effect in protecting the young against the intellectual epidemics to which they are exposed.

ON THE IMPORTANCE OF THE STUDY OF PHYSIOLOGY.

A LECTURE DELIVERED AT THE ROYAL INSTITUTION OF GREAT BRITAIN.

BY

JAMES PAGET, M.D., F.R.S.

ON THE STUDY OF PHYSIOLOGY.

It is my office to submit to you the importance of the study of Physiology, as a branch of education for all classes; to state the grounds on which it seems desirable that every one should learn somewhat of the structure of the human body, and of the processes that are carried on within it, and the laws according to which they are governed.

The advantages to be expected from the general teaching of physiology may be grouped in two classes: the first, including such as would tend to the promotion of the science; the second, such as would belong to the students.

By a wider diffusion of the knowledge of physiology its progress would be accelerated, as that of any other science would, by the increased number of the competent observers of its facts.

But a larger advantage, and one which, I think, physiology needs more than any other science does, would arise in this,—that the communication would be easier, which is now so difficult, between those who are engaged in it, and those who specially devote themselves to other sciences that might assist it. Almost every process in the living body involves the exercise of mechanical and chemical—perhaps, also, of electrical—

forces, whose effects are mingled with those of the more proper vital force; and although this special force may modify, and in some sort veil, the effects of the others, yet must their influence be reckoned and allowed for in nearly every case we have to study. Therefore, the complete solution of any new physiological problem must require such a master of all these sciences of dead and living matter as cannot now, I believe, be found, or else it must have the co-operation of many workers, each skilled in some single science, and able to communicate with all the rest. Such co-operation is, through the present narrowness of teaching, almost impossible. The mere chemist, or mechanical, or electrical philosopher, and the mere physiologist (one, I mean, who studies it, chiefly, by anatomy or by direct experiment), can scarcely so much as understand each other's language: they work apart at the same subject; and sometimes even confuse each other, by showing the same facts in different lights, and explained in different and mutually unintelligible terms. I know well that it requires nearly all the power of a strong mind so to master any of the physical sciences, as to be able to investigate its applications in the living body; and that, therefore, few could hope to be at once excellent in physiology, and in any science of dead matter; but the co-operation that I speak of would not need more than that the skilled workman in each science should understand the language, and the chief principles, and modes of working, of the rest. I am sure that it is, in great measure, through the want of help, such as it might hence derive, that the onward steps of physiology are so slow, so retarded by backslidings, and by the consciousness of insecurity.

And in yet another way, I believe that the general teaching of physiology would insure its more rapid progress—namely, by finding out those who are especially fit for its study.

If we mark the peculiar fitness of certain men for special callings, who are even below an average ability in the common business of life, one might imagine some natural design of mutual adaptation between things to be done and men to do them; and certainly, it were to be wished that a wider scheme of education should leave it less to chance whether a man will fall, or fail to fall, in the way of that special work for which he seems designed. Really, it has seemed like a chance that has led nearly every one of our best physiologists to his appropriate work; like a chance, the loss of which might have consigned him to a life of failures, or of mediocrity, in some occupation for which he had neither capacity nor love.

Such are some of the chief benefits that might result to physiology if it were more generally studied. I might tell of more; but I will not do so, nor enlarge on these; for, it might be argued, that it would be unjust to tax every one with intellectual labour for the advancement of one science, even though that science be the foundation of the healing art, in whose improvement every one is interested. I will rather try to show that, through such labour in the study of physiology, every one would gain for himself some more direct advantage.

I believe that even a moderate acquaintance with the principles of physiology, acquired in early life, would benefit a man, with regard to both his body and his mind; and that it would do this by guiding him in the maintenance and improvement of health, by teaching him the true economy of his powers, whether mental or corporeal, by providing worthy materials for thought, and by cultivating peculiar modes, and suggesting peculiar ends, of thinking.

But before I attempt to illustrate these things, let me meet an objection which is likely to be made against any proposal that physiology should be a subject of general education,—namely, that it cannot be generally taught, because (it is supposed) its objects are difficult to show, and it requires dissections and painful experiments for its illustration.

To such objections, the answer is easy: that the rudiments of physiology are taught already, largely and efficiently, in several schools of both England and Scotland. For such instruction, no general practice of dissection or of experiments is at all necessary. For most of the illustrations, drawings would suffice; especially such as those which have been constructed with admirable art, and published for the use of schools, under the direction of Mr. Marshall, of University College, for the Board of Trade Department of Science. Other things could be well taught with models.* The organs of animals might, in some instances, be used; and dried specimens. Only let there be a demand for the materials of such teaching, and I will venture to promise, that modern art, such as these examples display, will soon supply them at no great cost, and without offence to the most refined feelings.

But while I speak of what modern art would do, I am bound to add that the teaching of physiology, not by

* Specimens were shown of models of the development of the chick, very accurately executed in wax, from nature, by Mr. Tuson.

representations, but by the very objects of its study, was long ago sanctioned by the highest and most venerated authority in the land. For, in the Museum of the College of Surgeons, there are now several beautiful specimens of the chief organs of the human body, prepared by John Hunter, which formed part of a collection, made at Kew, by his Majesty King George III., for the instruction of the princes, his sons.

But if it be admitted that physiology can be generally taught, yet some may say that, so far as the improvement of health and the economy of power are concerned, such teaching is unnecessary; for that, to these ends, a man need only follow the guidance of nature and of instinct. And, indeed, at first thought, it may seem very strange that we should want instruction for keeping ourselves in health; strange that man should be left with no natural true guidance to so great a good: that man alone, for whom the earth seems made, should need mental labour to preserve or recover bodily health. Yet so it is: for none of our untaught faculties, neither our senses nor our instincts, are sufficient guides to good or guards from evil, in even the ordinary conditions of civilized life.

The acuteness of our senses is not at all proportionate to the vital importance of the things that we observe with them. They are unable to discern the properties, or even the presence, of some of the most deadly agents. For example, we have a far keener sense of the temperature of the atmosphere than of its composition, or fitness for breathing: yet the ordinary changes in its temperature concern little more than our comfort; those in its composition may affect our life.

And thus it is that, seeking only the comfort of warmth, which their senses can discern, men will breathe atmospheres laden with noxious gases, which they can scarcely detect till they have accumulated to the peril of their lives.

So with food: we have a keener sense of hunger and thirst than of the sufficiency or fitness of our foods. We can at once appreciate their flavour, but not their nutritive value; and those we most affect are not always the most appropriate to our state.

Our instincts avail us scarcely more. After childhood, in civilized life, the instincts are almost in abeyance, and the intellect and instruction have a share in the most ordinary acts of life. The sensations of thirst and hunger impel us instinctively to seek their satisfaction, and by instinct we know how to do so; but in doing it, we drink in adaptation to instruments of intellectual invention; and we eat things intellectually cooked, with apparatus of intellectual art: yes, intellectual, for the meanest piece of cookery requires that control and management of fire, which no mind lower than the human intellect has ever reached, and the possession of which might alone suffice to prove man's primacy among all the creatures of the earth.

But I need not multiply instances (I will not say of the inutility, but) of the insufficiency of our untaught powers for our guidance, in the commonest things of civilized life, relating to our health. Every one has suffered from following what has seemed some natural guidance, and has learned that we only gradually attain some knowledge of these things by experience or education; *i.e.* by the exercise of the understanding as well as of the senses.

If it be asked whether a state of ignorance regarding his own health be natural to man, I must answer that I suppose Providence has taken ample care for his good, in all those things which are of natural ordinance and independent of his will; but that, for those conditions which he generates or incurs by his own power and free-will, he is left by the same power to provide. I suppose that men may, generally, be, like other creatures, aware, by sense or instinct, of those things which are for their good, when the simplest conditions of their existence are undisturbed. But these are not the conditions in which we live. Men have disturbed, in successive generations, almost every simple and original condition of their existence. In every generation, they have been striving, with intellectual labour, to add to the comforts and luxuries of life, to their control of the forces, and their independence of the ordinary course, of nature. And many of their successes in this strife, being achieved by the disturbance of some natural and fit condition of mere subsistence, have almost necessarily incurred some consequent evils, which have marred, though they may not have neutralized, the good, and have gradually accumulated to our damage.

If, indeed, in all the improvements of our means of life, only half the trouble had been taken to prevent or remedy the future evil, that was taken to attain the present good, our state might have been far different. If, for examples, men had been as anxious to invent the means of destroying coal-smoke, as to gain the myriad benefits of coal-fires; if they had thought as much and as soon of constructing drains below the ground, as of building above it; as much even of clearing out the refuse of our gas-lights, as of tempering and diffusing their brilliancy for comfortable use;—then we might have gained unalloyed benefits from every such disturbance of the natural conditions of life: the vast catalogue of diseases appertaining to our social state might have been unwritten; and that which one age hailed as a national blessing might not have entailed upon the next a national calamity. But this has not been done; and thus, from age to age, the evil residues of good things have accumulated; the good still, happily, preponderating, but the evils such as every man, and every society of men, have now to guard against, and such as can be averted or counteracted with no other human power than that of the intellect instructed in the science of health.

Perhaps, now, the only question is, whether this instruction need be given to all, or whether it had not better be still left, as it is by present custom, to a few, to exercise it in a special profession. I cannot doubt that here, as in other cases, for all ordinary care, for all habitual management, each man should be fit to be his own guardian; while for emergencies, and the more unusual events, he should accept and be able to choose some more instructed guidance. It is not necessary, or likely, that every one who has learnt somewhat of the structure of his own body, and of the processes carried on in it, should seek to be his own doctor; not more so than that every one who has learnt the construction and principle of a steam-engine, should be restless unless he be his own engineer. We need not fear a misuse, through excessive use, of such physiology as can be generally taught. Certainly, if I may speak as one of the medical profession, we see greater injury sustained through ignorance, than is likely to accrue to imperfect knowledge, whether it be the most timid or the most rash.

And here, when I speak of ignorance, I am obliged to say that I do not mean only the state of those who are wholly uneducated, but include the state of nearly all who have not received some special teaching. For, really, in regard to all that concerns our life and health, it seems as if no amount of general education, no clearness of apprehension for science or for the general business of life, were sufficient for security against the grossest errors. I will not speak of the follies (as I believe them to be) that are now regarded as truths, and even useful truths, by generally well-instructed, shrewd, and accomplished persons. I will only say that, at all times, such persons have been as ready as the most uneducated to believe and submit themselves to practices, which the physiology even of their own times could prove to be gross and mischievous fallacies. In every age, it has been true that "the desire of health, like the desire of wealth, brings all intellects to the same level;" that is, all that have not some special wisdom in the art of health or of wealth.

If now it may be received that physiology should be generally studied for the sake of health, it may be asked what parts of it should be chiefly taught, and in what method? I might leave this to those who are occupied with general education, and with younger students than I have had to teach. But considering that the large majority of those to whom it would be taught are to be engaged, in after life, in pursuits alien from science, and that we therefore could not hope to do much more than leave general impressions such as might abide for general guidance, I feel nearly sure that the mere facts of physiology, and much more those of anatomy, should be taught in subordination to their general principles.

If I try to illustrate this by an example, I fear lest to some I seem almost unintelligible; for I have never before this time lectured to others than students or members of my own profession, to whom I could use technical terms, and whom I could suppose to be, in some measure, already acquainted with my subject.

But, for an example,—in relation to the economy of power, suppose of muscular power, and thereby in regard to the maintenance of health, it would have to be taught, that, in the living body, the apparent stability and persistence of its structures is due, not to their being literally indestructible, but to the constant operation of a process in them, by which the materials that decay, or are outworn in the exercise of their offices, are constantly removed, and replaced by new ones like themselves. We know that in all the actions of the body, there is waste and impairment of the active parts. But though, day after day, we exert, even in the common acts of life, in walking, feeding, breathing, thinking, talking, great amounts of force, and though, with the use of force, there is always a proportionate consumption of the material of our bodies, yet, year after year (at least for many years), we appear to be and feel the same: because the consumption, the wear and tear, of material, that occur in the action of our several parts, is constantly repaired in the intervals of rest.

Then, following out this principle, it might be shown, that an economy of vital power is commonly maintained in the body by the just regulation of alternate periods of action and repose; and this might be taken as a principle for useful illustration.

The climax of the exercise of muscular power seems to be attained in the heart. Perhaps there is nothing, of equal weight, that exerts in the same time so large an amount of force as a heart does. In every second, or oftener, discharging blood from its cavities with a force equal to the lifting of a weight of from ten to fifteen pounds, it goes on hour after hour, and year after year, untired and almost unchanged. Now, by the similarity between the structure and mode of contraction of the muscular fibres of the heart, and those of the muscles over which we have control, we may be sure that its fibres are subject to the same impairment in action as theirs are known to be; and that they must need the same repair in rest, as the voluntary muscles obtain in sleep. But the heart seems never to sleep; and we explain the secret of its apparently unceasing exercise of power, by referring to its exact rhythm of alternating contractions and dilatations; by the fact, that every contraction by which it forces blood into the vessels, *i.e.* every act which we can feel as a beat or throb, is succeeded by an interval of rest, or inaction, of the same length; and by the probability, that in each period of inaction (brief as it is), the changes that occurred during the contraction are repaired.

It is the same with the muscles for breathing, in their ordinary and involuntary exercise. The alternation of their action and repose is constant; and they too, though exerting forces that are truly enormous, neither waste nor weary themselves; because (we may hold) in every period of inaction they repair the changes wrought in them by their action.

Now the principle which is thus illustrated may probably be applied to nearly all muscular exertion.

Whatever work is to be done, the largest amount of force may be utilized with the least injury, when rest and action are made to be alternate. And this is to be observed, not only in that long rest which our voluntary muscles have in sleep, but, equally, in more active life; wherein more force is always obtained by the alternate action of certain groups of muscles, than by the sustained action of any single group. Thus, I think, it can be proved that there are no voluntary actions in which the human body can exercise larger amounts of force than in ordinary progression, as in walking or in running. And it is because of the alternation of the similar acts done by the two halves of the body, and especially by the two lower extremities. For if you watch a man walking, you will see that each of his limbs is doing exactly the opposite to what the other is doing, and to what itself has just finished doing; and the corresponding muscles are never in the same action upon both sides at once: and so if one step have been made, say, chiefly, with the muscular effort of the right limb, the next will be made with a similar effort of the left, while those of the right will have an interval of comparative inaction.

In some measure, therefore, the principle of alternate action and repose, typified in the case of the heart, is applied here. But it is not so completely observed; for we tire in walking, even while our hearts may be growing more active. This, however, is not only because of the motion, but because many muscles must be in almost constant exercise for the maintenance of the erect posture, and because, probably, in these voluntary exercises the rest of a muscle is never quite perfect, even in its relaxing state.

This same principle, of the economy of force in the alternation of action and repose, is doubtless true of the nervous as of the muscular system; and on it we explain the need of repose, prolonged and deep, in direct proportion to the length and intensity of mental exercise. On the same principle, we explain the refreshment of the mind by change of occupation or of the train of thought: so that, while one part of the brain is occupied, another may be at rest after its work is done. And many like things may be thus explained, which it would be well for all to know, but chiefly for those who have to teach, and who need to regulate their pupils' mental exercises with the best economy they can.

There is another class of organs in which the alternations of action and rest, of waste and repair, appear essential to the full exercise and economy of power. The stomach is one of these; and a knowledge of the method of its office of digestion might prevent somewhat of its almost universal misuse.

Its chief office in digestion is to produce a peculiar fluid which, mingling with the food, may, by a process similar to fermentation, reduce it to solution or to a state of extremely minute division. This fluid, the gastric or digestive fluid, does not merely ooze from the blood; but is so formed in minute cells, that, for each minutest microscopic drop of it, a cell, of complex structure, must be developed, grow, and burst or be dissolved.

A diagram would very well show how the lining membrane of the stomach is formed, almost entirely, of minute tubes, set vertically in its thickness, like little flasks or test-tubes, close packed and upright. The outer walls of these are webbed over with net-works of most delicate blood-vessels, carrying streams of blood

Within, the same tubes contain cells, and those among them which chiefly secrete the digestive fluid are nearly filled with cells, which have taken materials from the blood, and from those materials have formed themselves and their contents. In what way they have done this, we cannot tell: but we can tell that the process is one of complicate though speedy development and growth; even such a process as that by which, more slowly, the body grows, or any of its parts,—the hair or the nails, or any other that we can best watch. The act of secretion or production of this fluid is, literally, the growth and dissolution of the minute cells which, though they be very short-lived, yet must need a certain time for their complete elaboration.

If this be so, it must follow, that we cannot, with impunity, interfere with that which seems a natural rule, of allowing certain intervals between the several times of feeding. Every act of digestion involves the consumption of some of these cells: on every contact of food, some must quickly perfect themselves, and yield up their contents; and without doubt, the design of that periodical taking of food, which is natural to our race, is that, in the intervals, there may be time for the production of the cells that are to be consumed in the next succeeding acts of digestion. We can, indeed, state no constant rule as to the time required for such constructions: it probably varies according to age, and the kind of food, and the general activity or indolence of life, and, above all, according to habit; but it may be certainly held, that when the times are set, they cannot, with impunity, be often interfered with; and, as certainly, that continual or irregular feeding is wholly contrary to the economy of the human stomach. And yet such constant feeding is a frequent custom—not infrequent among the adult rich, but most frequent among the infants of the poor, for whom food is the solace of every grief.

I would thus try to teach general principles of physiology; and with such principles there might easily be combined some useful rules for prudence in the ordinary management of personal or social health, and in the habitual exercise of power.

I will not venture to say that it is only by teaching physiology that prudence can be taught; for even in the cases I have cited, physiology teaches no other rule than Nature and experience had already indicated. Still, even in regard to those rules, when it shows their reason and their meaning, it gives them strength, and it enlists the power of the understanding against the overbearing of inclination and bad habit. And so, though it might be impossible to teach more than a small part of the whole body of physiology, yet one who had learned even this part would have a better apprehension of the rest than one untaught could have. One who had learned the general mode of study, and the labour which is spent in ascertaining physiological truths, and the great probability that what is generally accepted is at least nearly true, would, more than an untaught man, act on the advice of those who are instructed. Thus acting, he would, as a citizen, be no hinderer of improvements, no block of utter ignorance in the way of amending the sanitary condition of his fellows: with belief, if not with knowledge, he would give his help to good. And for his own guidance, such an one, though only partially instructed, would be a far better judge than most men are of the probable value of professed discoveries in medicine: he would be doubtful of all unreserved assertions; wisely incredulous of all results supposed to flow from apparently incompetent sources. Even the desire of health would bear frequent disappointment, before it would induce him to commit himself to the daring promises of ignorance.

I have said that we might anticipate advantages to the mind, as well as to the bodily health, from making physiology a branch of general education. And some of these advantages must not be widely separated from those of which I have been speaking; for they are, in truth, closely correspondent, derived from the same source and by the same method. The health of the mind, so far as it is within our own control, is subject to the same laws as is the health of the body. For the brain, the organ of the mind, grows and is maintained according to the same method of nutrition as every other part of the body: it is supplied by the same blood; and through the blood, like every other part, may be affected for good or ill by the various physical influences to which it is exposed. But I will not dwell on this, more than to assert, as safely deducible from physiology, that no scheme of instruction, or of legislation, can avail for the improvement of the human mind, which does not provide with equal care for the well-being of the human body. Deprive men of fresh air, and pure water, of the light of heaven, and of sufficient food and rest, and as surely as their bodies will become dwarfish, and pallid, and diseased, so surely will their minds degenerate in intellectual and moral power.

But let me suppose that these needs of the body may be happily within men's reach; and then I may speak of the advantages that would accrue, from the general study of physiology, in the mental culture it would provide.

I again remind myself that the cases to be kept in view are not only those of men who are to be chiefly occupied with science, but those of persons who are to pursue the various common businesses of life; and upon whose minds we cannot expect that those studies of their school-time, which would be widely different from the occupations of their later life, will do more than leave general impressions, and impart an habitual method and tone of thought. To such persons, I believe that the study of physiology would be useful, first, on the general ground, that they who can, with most force, apply themselves to any business in life (be it what it may), are those whose minds are disciplined and informed in all their parts, so as to be not only full and strong, but pliant, liberal, and adaptive.

Now, there are some characters in physiology by means of which its study might affect the mind, or certain parts of it, differently from any portions of even that enlarged education which it is the object of this whole course of lectures to recommend.

One of these is, that it is occupied with things of admitted incompleteness and uncertainty. In other, and especially in the physical, sciences, I think it is only the master, or the advanced student, who is impressed with their uncertainty. In them, speaking generally, that which is taught admits of clear proof; and imperfection is not spoken of, except, as it were, at the distant boundaries of a vast body of truth. But, in physiology, the teacher would need everywhere to mark the imperfections of his knowledge; in the very rudiments, he must speak of things as only, in various degrees, probable.

Some of my predecessors in this course have shown how much the value of the physical sciences lies in the possibility of proving what is held in them, and in the precision of the mental exercises which they thus demand and cultivate; and no one can be more conscious than I am that, on this account, they are indispensable elements of sound education. But I believe, also, that it would be right to mingle with this study that of a much more incomplete and uncertain science. I think it would be good, at least for some minds, to know in early life how much has yet to be done in science; so that some, through ambition of discovery, some through love of enterprise, some through mere curiosity, might be excited to work among the stores of unexplored knowledge that would be pointed out to them. It is strange how early, and how strong in early life, these ambitions of discovery and invention arise; and I suppose that, in all later life, there are no enjoyments more keen, or more invigorating to the mind, than those felt in boyhood, when such an ambition is gratified;—whether by the finding of some plant unknown before in the home-district, or by the invention of some new appliance to a toy, imitating what men deal with, or,—it matters not by how trivial a thing. I would not venture to say how large a part such ambition should be allowed to have among the motives to study, but I think it should not be quite suppressed, or starved, as it is by teaching only such things as are already proved, or decided by authority.

And, perhaps, yet another advantage would flow from the teaching of physiology, honestly and expressly, as a very incomplete and uncertain science. It is a great hindrance to the progress of truth, that some men will hold, with equal tenacity, things that are, and things that are not, proved; and even things that, from their very nature, do not admit of proof. They seem to think (and ordinary education might be pleaded as justifying the thought) that a plain "yes" or "no" can be answered to every question that can be plainly asked; and that everything thus answered is a settled thing, and to be maintained as a point of conscience. I need not adduce instances of this error, while its mischiefs are manifest everywhere in the wrongs done by premature and tenacious judgments.

I am aware that these are faults of the temper, not less than of the judgment; but we know how much the temper is influenced by the character of our studies; and I think if any one were to be free from this over-zeal of opinion, it should be one who is early instructed in an uncertain science, such as physiology. He might receive, with reverent submission, all revealed truth; he might bend unquestioning to the declarations of teachers authorized to promulgate positive commandments; but his habit of thinking how soon all inquiries concerning living things end in uncertainty, his experience of the exceeding difficulty of settling for ever even a small matter, would make him very scrupulous in accepting as completely proved, very slow in making a point of conscience of, anything that may be made a matter of reasonable discussion or of further study.

Let me repeat, that I do not hold that it is beneficial to study only or chiefly such a science as this, whose principles scarcely admit of full proof. I know too well the danger of resting satisfied with error, when truth cannot be quite attained. But I lecture only as one of many, advocating the importance of as many different branches of study; and I think that the early study of uncertainties might well be mingled with that of things which may be proved beyond all doubt.

But I have yet to speak of that through which, I believe, the general teaching of physiology would exercise the greatest influence upon the mind; namely, its being, essentially, a science of designs and final causes. In this (if we regard it in its full meaning, as the science concerning living things) it is chiefly in contrast with the physical sciences, and, so far as I know, with nearly all the other studies of even the widest scheme of education.

I do not say that it is only in living things that we can discern the evidences of design. Doubtless, things that are dead—things that we call inorganic, when we would distinguish them from living organisms—are yet purposive, and mutually adapted to co-operate in the fulfilment of design. We cannot doubt, for example, that all the parts of this dead earth, and all the members of our planetary system, are adapted to one another with mutual influence; balanced and laid out in appropriate weight and measure; fitted each to do its part, and serve its purpose, in some vast design. And thus the whole universe might be called an organism; constructed in parts and systems, almost infinite in number and variety, but adjusted with an all-pervading purpose. Still, there is a striking difference between dead and living things, in the degree and manner in which their laws and their designs are manifest to us. In the inorganic world, in the studies of the physical sciences, we seem to come nearer to the efficient, than to the final, causes of events. We discern, it may be, both the most general laws, and the most minute details of the events: but these rarely shadow forth their purpose or design; or, if they do, it is a design in adaptation to organic life, as where we may trace the fitness of the earth and air for their living occupants. But in the organic world, the reverse is true: purpose, design, and mutual fitness are manifest wherever we can discern the structure or the actions of a part; utility and mutual dependence are implied in all the language, and sought in all the studies, of physiology. The efficient causes and the general laws of the vital actions may be hidden from the keenest search; but their final causes are often nearly certain. In the sciences of the inorganic world, we can learn *how* changes are accomplished, but we can rarely tell *why* they are: in those of the organic world, the question "why" can be often answered, the question "how" is generally an enigma that we cannot solve.

Now, were there no other argument for the general teaching of physiology, I would be content with this: that an education which does not include the teaching of some science of natural designs, does not provide for the instruction of one of the best powers and aspirations of the mind.

The askings of children seem to indicate a natural desire after the knowledge of the purposes fulfilled in nature. "Why?" and "Of what use?" are the ends of half their untutored questions; and we may be sure they have not the wish for such knowledge without the power of attaining it, if the needful help be given them. And yet, in the usual subjects of education, nothing addresses itself to this desire, and so there is not only a neglect of the teaching of the peculiar modes of reasoning required, or admitted, in physiological research; but the natural love and capacity for studying design are left to spend themselves, untrained, upon unworthy objects; and so they fade or degenerate—degenerate, perhaps, into some such baseness as an impertinent curiosity about other men's matters.

I would therefore have physiology taught to all, as a study of God's designs and purposes achieved; as a science for which our natural desire after the knowledge of final causes seems to have been destined; a science in which that desire, though it were infinite, might be satisfied; and in which, as with perfect models of beneficence and wisdom, our own faculties of design may be instructed. I would not have its teaching limited to a bare declaration of the use and exact fitness of each part or organ of the body. This, indeed, should not be omitted; for there are noble truths in the simplest demonstrations of the fitness of parts for their simplest purposes, and no study has been made more attractive than this by the ingenuity, the acuteness, and eloquence of its teachers. But I would go beyond this, and, striving, as I said before, to teach general truths as well as the details of science, I would try to lead the mind to the contemplation of those *general* designs, from which it might gather the best lessons for its own guidance.

If I may presume to speak as I would to boys or girls, I would say, let us learn frugality from some of the designs that we can study in the living body; and surely the lesson may be the more impressive, if we remember that we are studying the frugality of One whose power and materials are infinite.

Observe, for example, what happens during active exercise; how the heart beats quicker and harder than it did before, and the skin grows warmer and ruddier, and the blood moves faster, and the breathing is quicker. The main design of this seems to be that the active muscles may be the more abundantly supplied with blood. But the beginning in the series of changes is an instance of that designed frugality of which I have been speaking. Veins, carrying blood to the heart, lie, as you see, branching and communicating under the skin; and there are others, like them, deeper set among the muscles of both the limbs and the trunk. Now, muscles, when they act, shorten and swell up; and in so doing (as in active exercise), they compress the veins that lie between them, or upon them underneath the skin. The effect of such compression must be to press the blood in every vein, equally in both directions,—both onwards towards the heart, and backwards from it. All that part of this pressure which is effective in propelling the blood towards the heart is so much added to the forces of the circulation; it is so much direct gain of force. But it may seem as if this gain were balanced by an equal loss, through the influence of the same pressure driving other portions of the blood backwards. And so it would be, but for the arrangement of valves in the veins, which are the instruments of this saving of force. Wherever there are muscles that in their action can compress the veins, there also the veins have valves; and a diagram and a model would show that these are little pocket-shaped membranes, which project into the canals of the veins, in such a manner that they will allow the streams of blood to pass onwards to the heart, but will close at once and hinder any stream that would flow backwards. Thus, therefore, the effect of muscular pressure on the veins is (let us say), with a certain force, to propel some blood towards the heart, and with the same force to press back other blood upon the valves and close them. You will say, then, here is still the same hindrance: if the valves be closed, the stream behind them must be stopped, and there is as much loss as gain. It would be so, if there were not this other provision; that wherever there can be muscular pressure upon veins, those veins not only have valves, but have abundant channels of communication with one another. The back-pressure of the blood, and the closure of the valves, is therefore no hindrance to the circulation; for the blood, that might be stopped in one vein, makes its way at once into another by some communicating branch. The general result, therefore, is, that all muscular pressure upon veins is an almost unalloyed advantage to the circulation. And now mark the frugality of the design. Veins *must* lie in or near these places, and the muscles *must* act (suppose for some design of our own); and if they are to be in very active exercise, they will need swifter streams of blood than will suffice in their repose. The streams could be made swifter by a greater force of the heart; but heart-force is a thing to be economized; and the muscles themselves may, without harm, contribute to accelerate the blood; for in the fulfilment of their primary purpose, of moving and sustaining the limbs and trunk, they *must* swell up, and compress the veins that are about them; and this compression can be made effective for the circulation of the blood by the mechanism of valves. So then, in the necessary fulfilment of their primary use, and without the least hindrance or damage to it, the muscles are made to serve this secondary purpose; and all that they do herein is so much saved to the forces of the heart.

Scarcely a lesson in physiology could be given but it might illustrate some such design as this. Everywhere we see examples of parts thus made to serve bye-purposes while fulfilling their primary designs.

I will mention but one more. All know that the air we have once breathed is less fit for breathing than it was before, and that if we breathe the same air often it becomes poisonous, through the mixture of the carbonic acid and other exhalations from the lungs. We must breathe out the air, therefore, as so much refuse; and ample provision is made that we may do so; and it might seem design enough fulfilled when we are thus freed from our own poison. But is it not an admirable secondary design, an admirable frugality, a true wisdom by the way, that, with this same air, we speak; that this, which we must cast out lest it destroy us, should be used for one of the noblest powers of man? Surely, one might have supposed, for so great a purpose as the communion of human thoughts, and for all that speech and vocal melody can achieve, there would be contrived some matchless instrument, some rare material. But no: the instruments of human speech are scarcely more complex organs than those which dumb creatures have to breathe and feed with; and the material for human speech carries out the refuse of blood; the very dross of the body is used for the coinage of the mind.

Such might be some lessons in that Divine frugality which is ever "gathering up the fragments that remain, that nothing be lost." The moral of such lessons is very plain.

Not less significant are those which may be studied in the designs of the body during its development. All these are instances of present things having their true purpose in some future state.

Let me endeavour to illustrate some of them.

I have here models of the changes that the chick undergoes in its development; and what they show might suffice for teaching the development of higher creatures. Now, nearly all we see here is the working out of a design, which cannot have its full end till some future time. These wings and legs—of what avail are they to the prisoner in the shell? Their purpose is not yet fulfilled; they are for the future. But if these be too plain to be impressive, let us look at more particular things.

Observe the changes through which the heart passes, from its first appearance as a little pulsating bag, to its being nearly fit for the time when the hatched bird will breathe in the open air. The changes are not merely a growth from a little heart to a big one; but are a series of acquirements of more complex shapes; so that the heart, which at first is a simple bag, then becomes very curved, and then divides into two, and then into three and four, cavities. Now, doubtless, in each of these conditions, the heart is exactly appropriate to the contemporary state of the other organs, and the circumstances of the time of life; but each of them is, besides, a necessary stage of transition towards that more perfect state, that fitness for more complex duties, which the heart attains when the bird is born to breathe with lungs in the open air.

But I would descend yet lower, and, magnifying the wonders of these plans for the future, by diminishing (as it may seem to some) the importance of the objects in which they are displayed, would trace the development of a single blood-cell in a tadpole—*i. e.* in the young fish-like embryo of a frog, such as nearly every pool would supply in the spring-time, and such as magnified sketches would fully illustrate.

By a blood-cell, I mean one of those microscopic particles by which the blood is coloured red: particles so minute that, in our own blood, about ten millions might lie on a square inch of surface.

In the earliest period of active life of these tadpoles, the little black and fish-like body is composed almost wholly of minute cells; among which you can trace, with even powerful microscopes, scarce any difference. You could not tell the future destiny of any of them by their present characters; they look all alike. But presently, as they increase in number, a differencing begins among them, and a sorting of them; and some arrange themselves for a spinal column, and some for muscles; and some are seen to be placed where the first streams of blood are to run; and some are clustered where the heart will be. At first, those that are to be blood-cells are round, and darkly shaded, and contain yellowish particles, many of which are like four-sided crystals of some fatty substance. But, in a day or two, the cells begin to move and circulate in the channels in which they were arranged; and then, as we watch them day by day, they gradually change. The particles within them become smaller and less numerous, and collect near to their borders; while their centres, clearing up, show an enclosed smaller body or nucleus. Moreover, as these changes proceed, the cells which were before colourless, acquire gradually a deeper and deeper blood-tint, and exchange their round for an oval shape; till, by the time that all the particles they first contained are cleared away, as if by solution, they have become perfect blood-cells, nearly like those which colour the blood of the completely developed frog.

The time required for these changes depends much on the temperature and degree of light to which the creature is exposed. It may vary from one to three or more weeks; and we can thus deliberately watch the development of a blood-cell, day by day, until it reaches that which we may call its perfection. In this state the cells abide for a time, unchanging; and then decline and give place to another set of blood-cells, each of which is developed through a series of changes different, indeed, from those that I have described, but not less numerous or complex.

Now, such is the life, up to the period of perfection, of every blood-cell in this trivial creature. And so it is in ourselves. Of the millions of those cells thát colour our blood, not one reaches its perfection but through changes as numerous and great as these.

Perhaps the wonder is augmented if we think that, in the embryo, the changes proceed, with equal steps, in all the cells at once: there is exact concert among them; if I may so speak, they all keep time. Nor is the harmony limited to them; for their development is exactly adjusted to that of every other part: successive changes are exactly concurrent in every part at once; so that, though all are continually changing, they never lose their mutual fitness.

I might cite more instances of these plans for futurity; but they are nearly infinite; for in truth, (and what a moral there is in such a truth!) in the living world, nothing is made at once fit for the highest purposes of which it may be capable. In all the countless crowds of living beings,—in all the countless particles of each,—there is not one but in the history of its life we may read a gradual attainment of its highest destiny; not one but has a time in which its true purpose is yet future, its true design yet unfulfilled; and, although, even in its rudiment, it is not useless, yet there will be a time when, with higher powers, it will take part in the designs of some more perfect state. So wide is that law, which has its highest instance in the history and future destiny of man himself.

But the evidence of the design of living bodies for conditions that are yet future, seems to culminate in the proofs of their capacity to repair injuries, and to recover from diseases.

It is surely only because it is so familiar, that we think lightly, if at all, of the fact that living bodies are capable of repairing most of the injuries they may sustain; and that, in this capacity, they show that provision has been made, in them, for events of which it is not certain whether they will ever occur to them or not. When we contemplate the perfect living body, the exact fitness of every part for its office, not as an independent agent, but as one whose work must be done in due proportion with that of many others, is a very marvellous thing; but it seems much more marvellous that, in the embryo, each of these parts was made fit for offices and relations that were then future: but surely more marvellous than all it is, that each of these, when perfect, should still have capacity for right action in events that are not only future, but unlikely; that are indeed possible, but are in only so low a degree probable, that if ever they happen, they will be called accidents—as things not to be expected or provided for.

Let me describe a process of repair, and describe it so simply, as it might be to school-boys.

All know, or can feel, their Achilles-tendons behind their ancles, and that these, strong as they are, are sometimes broken by a violent contraction of their muscles. I know not how small—how almost infinitely small—the chance is, that any given man, or quadruped, would ever break this or any other part; but, small as the chance may be, ample provision is made for its repair. How this is accomplished may be again illustrated by diagrams.

When the tendon in such an animal as a rabbit is divided, its pieces separate to nearly an inch apart, the upper piece being drawn up by the unrestricted action of its muscles. The muscles, no longer fastened by the tendon to the heel-bone, are thus rendered useless; and the object of the reparative process must be to form a bond of connexion between the separated pieces of the tendon.

In the two days following such an injury, all the structures between and around the ends of the divided tendon appear soaked with a half-liquid substance, the product of inflammation. And thus far we see no plan for uniting the separated pieces; there is no more of this new substance in the line between them than there is around them; and all the new substance appears alike. But in the course of two days more, we find that fresh material is deposited between the separated pieces of the tendons, and that it is firmer than that around, and has firm hold on the ends of the separated pieces, and connects them, though as yet (if I may so say) only clumsily. After this, however, each day finds the connecting substance becoming firmer, tougher, and more like the texture of the tendon itself. Each day, too, it becomes more defined from the surrounding parts; and this it does, not only because itself becomes more exactly shaped, but because they regain their natural texture. And observe the distinct design which is shown in this contrast. At first, all the parts at and about the seat of injury were soaked with a similar material; but now, that portion of this material which lay in the place for the formation of the connecting bond, has remained and contributed to the repair; but that portion of it which was more remote, and could serve no useful purpose, has been cleared away.

At the end of a week, in the rabbit, a complete cord-like bond of union is formed, and the muscles can act again. By this time, too, the bond has gained nearly the perfect texture and the toughness of the original tendon. I once tried the strength of such a bond of connexion, which had been forming for ten days after the division of the Achilles-tendon of a young rabbit. Having removed it from the dead body, I suspended weights upon it, and, after bearing weights of twenty, thirty, forty, and fifty pounds, it was at length broken by a weight of fifty-six pounds. But surely the strength it showed was very wonderful, if we remember that it was not more than the sixth of an inch in its greatest thickness, and that it was wholly formed in ten days, in the leg of a rabbit scarcely more than a pound in weight.

I might illustrate the process of repair by instances as perfect as these, observed after injuries of many, almost of any, parts. And I might, as in the instance of development, magnify its excellence by showing it in what we are apt to call trivial creatures, or even by showing that, in general, those lower species of animals that have the least means of escape or defence from mutilation, appear to be endowed with the most ample powers of repair. But time will not permit this, nor yet that I should show how many lessons of practical utility might be engrafted on the teaching of a process such as this, or how the main principles of the surgery of injuries are based on the recognition of the natural power of recovery. Nearly its whole practice consists in the prevention of any interference with that to which there is, in the very nature of the body, as great a tendency, as there is for the embryo to be developed into the perfect creature. Using the facts of the reparative process only for the present purpose of showing how physiology might be taught as the chief science of designs, I would say that the arguments of design, which are here displayed, are such as cannot be impugned by the suspicion, that the events among which each living thing is cast have determined its adaptation to them; because the adaptations here noted prove capacities for things that are future, and only not impossible.

I will mention but one more instance of general design, which I think should not be omitted in the teaching of physiology to whatever class of students—that, namely, of the adaptation of animals in their decay; how, as they do not live, so neither do they decay or die, for themselves alone, but ministering to others' good.

The chief evidence of this is in the provision, that the decaying parts of animals yield the materials from which the vegetable kingdom derives its chief supply of food. In the ordinary decomposition of the dead body, many of the products are the very materials from which, as they are mingled with the earth and atmosphere, each plant takes its food. But it is not alone through this decay in death, that animals restore to the vegetable world the materials which they have, for their own food, derived from it. The same rule is fulfilled in the decay of life; *i.e.* in those changes which occur when the particles of the animal body, having served their purpose, or lived their full time in it, are then to be cast out as refuse. For in all these changes, which are a part of that constant mutation of particles through which the body remains, through all the time of vigorous life, the same, though continually changing,—in all these, the material which is passing out, as refuse, gradually approximates, in its transition, to the inorganic state of matter. It is so with the carbonic acid and other exhalations from the lungs and skin, and with all the class of substances excreted. And thus, every form of degeneration or decay, whether in life or after death, may be described as a series of changes, through which the elements of organic bodies, instead of being on a sudden and with violence dispersed, are gradually collected into those lower combinations in which they may best rejöin the inorganic world: they are such changes, that every creature may be said to decay and die and cast out its refuse in the form which may best fit it to discharge its share in the economy of the world,—either by supplying nutriment to other organisms, or by taking its right part in the adjustment of the balance held between the organic and inorganic masses.

I have thus endeavoured to fulfil my office, and to show how the general teaching of physiology might do good among its students. I think its advantages are such as might be apprehended by students of all classes in society. I suppose, too, that, for all that part of it which can be applied in the maintenance of health the merit of utility would be admitted; and that, in general terms, it would be allowed that the study of designs and final causes should be mingled with other studies in any scheme of education by which it is proposed that the whole mind should be disciplined, and all modes of reasoning should be taught.

But still, the question may be asked, Is it possible that knowledge such as this, of the methods of design, will rest, with any influence, in a mind that must be engrossed in urgent business, or in household cares; harassed, perhaps, in struggles against poverty, or dissipated in the luxuries of wealth? It may be very well (some will say) to teach these things to the young, but men and women have other works and other pleasures to pursue.

I know all this; and I have overshot my mark if I have urged any teaching of which the effects would interfere with devotion to the necessary works of later life. But I suppose that, if any one will watch his thoughts for a few days, or even a few hours, he will find that, however engrossing may be his cares or his pleasures, however earnest his attention to what seems his most urgent need, there are yet intermingling trains of thought quite alien from these:—trains into which the mind falls, it knows not how, but in which it will wander as if resolute to refresh itself. Now these must be provided for; and so it must be an object of all education to supply, in early life, those studies from which, in later years, may arise reflections that may mingle happily with the business-thoughts of common days; that may suggest to the reason, or even to the imagination, some hidden meaning, some future purpose, some noble end, in the things about us. Reflections such as these, being interwoven with our common thoughts, may often bring to our life a tone of joy, which its general aspect would not wear; like brilliant threads shot through the texture of some sombre fabric, giving lustre to its darkness.

But besides this happy influence of the general impressions that might remain in the mind from the early teaching of physiology, I claim for it the hope that its principles might read to some minds lessons of the truest wisdom.

The student of Nature's purposes should surely be averse from leading a purposeless existence. Watching design in everything around him, he could not fail, one would think, to reflect often on the purpose of his own existence. And doing so, if his mind were imbued with the knowledge of the mutual fitness in which all the members of his body, and all the parts of the whole organic world, subsist, and minister to each other's good, he could not conclude that he exists for his own sake alone, or that happiness would be found separate from the offices of mutual help and of universal good-will. One who is conversant with things that have a purpose in the future, higher than that which they have yet fulfilled, would never think that his own highest destiny is yet achieved. Though his place among men might be only like that of a single particle—like that of a single blood-cell of the body—yet would he strive to concur, and take his share, in all progressive good. Nor would he count that, with this life ended, his purpose would be attained; but by teaching, or by record, or by some other of those means, through which, in the history of our race, things that in their rudiments seemed trivial have been developed into great results, he would strive to "achieve at least some useful work, the fruit whereof might abide." Conscious of an immortal nature, and of desires and capacities for knowledge, which cannot be satisfied in this world, he would be sure that the great law of progress, from a lower to a higher state, would not be abrogated in the Divine government of that part of him which cannot perish, and is not yet perfect. In him, even the understanding would be assured that, "as we have borne the image of the earthy, we shall also bear the image of the heavenly;" for that is the true lesson of development.

And because it abounds in lessons such as these, I claim for physiology the pre-eminence among all sciences, for the clear and full analogies which it displays between truths natural and revealed: and I would teach it everywhere; looking to its help, by these analogies, to prove the concord between knowledge and belief, and to mediate in the ever-pending conflict of intellect and faith.

OBSERVATIONS ON THE EDUCATION OF THE JUDGMENT.

A LECTURE DELIVERED AT THE ROYAL INSTITUTION OF GREAT BRITAIN.

BY

PROFESSOR FARADAY, F.R.S.

ON THE EDUCATION OF THE JUDGMENT.

I TAKE courage, Sir,* from your presence here this day, to speak boldly that which is upon my mind. I feared that it might be unpleasant to some of my audience, but as I know that your Royal Highness is a champion for and desires the truth, I will believe that all here are united in the same cause, and therefore will give utterance, without hesitation, to what I have to say regarding the present condition of Mental Education.

If the term education may be understood in so large a sense as to include all that belongs to the improvement of the mind, either by the acquisition of the knowledge of others, or by increase of it through its own exertions, then I may hope to be justified for bringing forward a few desultory observations respecting the exercise of the mental powers in a particular direction, which otherwise might seem out of place. The points I have in view are general, but they are manifest in a striking manner, among the physical matters which have occupied my life; and as the latter afford a field for exercise in which cogitations and conclusions can be subjected to the rigid tests of fact and experiment,—as all classes employ themselves more or less in the consideration of physical matters, and may do so with great advantage, if inclined in the least degree to profit by educational practices, so

* Prince Albert occupied the chair.

I hope that what I may say will find its application in every condition of life.

Before entering upon the subject, I must make one distinction which, however it may appear to others, is to me of the utmost importance. High as man is placed above the creatures around him, there is a higher and far more exalted position within his view; and the ways are infinite in which he occupies his thoughts about the fears, or hopes, or expectations of a future life. I believe that the truth of that future cannot be brought to his knowledge by any exertion of his mental powers, however exalted they may be; that it is made known to him by other teaching than his own, and is received through simple belief of the testimony given. Let no one suppose for a moment that the self-education I am about to commend in respect of the things of this life, extends to any considerations of the hope set before us, as if man by reasoning could find out God. It would be improper here to enter upon this subject further than to claim an absolute distinction between religious and ordinary belief. I shall be reproached with the weakness of refusing to apply those mental operations which I think good in respect of high things to the very highest. I am content to bear the reproach. Yet, even in earthly matters, I believe that the invisible things of Him from the creation of the world are clearly seen, being understood by the things that are made, even His eternal power and Godhead; and I have never seen anything incompatible between those things of man which can be known by the spirit of man which is within him, and those higher things concerning his future which he cannot know by that spirit.

Claiming, then, the use of the ordinary faculties of the

mind in ordinary things, let me next endeavour to point out what appears to me to be a great deficiency in the exercise of the mental powers in every direction: three words will express this great want, *deficiency of judgment.* I do not wish to make any startling assertion, but I know that in physical matters multitudes are ready to draw conclusions who have little or no power of judgment in the cases; that the same is true of other departments of knowledge; and that, generally, mankind is willing to leave the faculties which relate to judgment almost entirely uneducated, and their decisions at the mercy of ignorance, prepossessions, the passions, or even accident.

Do not suppose, because I stand here and speak thus, making no exceptions, that I except myself. I have learned to know that I fall infinitely short of that efficacious exercise of the judgment which may be attained. There are exceptions to my general conclusion, numerous and high; but if we desire to know how far education is required, we do not consider the few who need it not, but the many who have it not; and in respect of judgment, the number of the latter is almost infinite. I am moreover persuaded, that the clear and powerful minds which have realized in some degree the intellectual preparation I am about to refer to, will admit its importance, and indeed its necessity; and that they will not except themselves, nor think that I have made my statement too extensive.

As I believe that a very large proportion of the errors we make in judgment is a simple and direct result of our perfectly unconscious state, and think that a demonstration of the liabilities we are subject to would aid greatly in providing a remedy, I will proceed first to a few illustrations of a physical nature. Nothing can better supply them than the intimations we derive from our senses: to them we trust directly; by them we become acquainted with external things, and gain the power of increasing and varying facts upon which we entirely depend. Our sense perceptions are wonderful. Even in the observant, but unreflective infant, they soon produce a result which looks like intuition, because of its perfection. Coming to the mind as so many data, they are stored up, and, without our being conscious of it, are ever after used in like circumstances in forming our judgment; and it is not wonderful that man is accustomed to trust them without examination. Nevertheless, the result is the effect of education: the mind has to be instructed with regard to the senses and their intimations through every step of life; and where the instruction is imperfect, it is astonishing how soon and how much their evidence fails us. Yet, in the latter years of life, we do not consider this matter, but, having obtained the ordinary teaching sufficient for ordinary purposes, we venture to judge of things which are extraordinary for the time, and almost always with the more assurance as our powers of observation are less educated. Consider the following case of a physical impression, derived from the sense of touch, which can be examined and verified at pleasure:—If the hands be brought towards each other so that the tips of the corresponding fingers touch, the end of any finger may be considered as an object to be felt by the opposed finger; thus, the two middle fingers may for the present be so viewed. If the attention be directed to them, no difficulty will be experienced in moving each lightly in a circle round the tip of the other, so that they shall each feel the opposite, and the motion may be either in one direction or the other—looking at the fingers, or with eyes employed elsewhere—or with the remaining fingers touching quiescently, or moving in a like direction; all is easy, because each finger is employed in the ordinary or educated manner whilst obeying the will, and whilst communicating through the sentient organ with the brain. But turn the hands half way round, so that their backs shall be towards each other, and then, crossing them at the wrists, again bring the like fingers into contact at the tips. If it be now desired to move the extremities of the middle fingers round each other, or to follow the contour of one finger by the tip of the opposed one, all sorts of confusion in the motion will ensue; and as the finger of one hand tries, under the instruction of the will, to move in one course, the touched finger will convey an intimation that it is moving in another. If all the fingers move at once, all will be in confusion, the ease and simplicity of the first case having entirely disappeared. If, after some considerable trial, familiarity with the new circumstances have removed part of the uncertainty, then, crossing the hands at the opposite sides of the wrists will renew it. These contrary results are dependent not on any change in the nature of the sentient indication, or of the surfaces or substances which the sense has to deal with, but upon the trifling circumstance of a little variation from the direction in which the sentient organs of these parts are usually exerted, and they show to what an extraordinary extent our interpretations of the sense impressions depend upon the experience, *i.e.* the education which they have previously received, and their great inability to aid us at once in circumstances which are entirely new.

At other times they fail us because we cannot keep a true remembrance of former impresssions. Thus, on the evening of the eleventh of March last, I and many others were persuaded that at one period the moon had a real green colour, and though I knew that the prevailing red tints of the general sky were competent to produce an effect of such a kind, yet there was so little of that in the neighbourhood of the planet, that I was doubtful whether the green tint was not produced on the moon by some aërial medium spread before it, until, by holding up white cards in a proper position, and comparing them with our satellite, I had determined experimentally that the effect was only one of contrast. In the midst of the surrounding tints, my memory could not recall the true sentient impression which the white of the moon most surely had before made upon the eye.

At other times the failure is because one impression is overpowered by another; for as the morning star disappears when the sun is risen, though still above the horizon and shining brightly as ever, so do stronger phenomena obscure weaker, even when both are of the same kind; till an uninstructed person is apt to pass the weaker unobserved, and even deny their existence.

So, error results occasionally from believing our senses: it ought to be considered, rather, as an *error of the judgment* than of the sense, for the latter has performed its duty; the indication is always correct, and in harmony with the great truth of nature. Where, then, is the mistake?—almost entirely with our judgment. We have not had that sufficient instruction by the senses which would justify our making a conclusion; we have to contrive extra and special means, by which their first impressions shall be corrected, or rather enlarged; and it is because our procedure was hasty, our data too few, and our judgment untaught, that we fell into mistake; not because the data were wrong. How frequently may each one of us perceive, in our neighbours, at least, that a result like this derived from the observation of physical things, happens in the ordinary affairs of common life.

When I become convicted of such haste, which is not unfrequently the case, I look back upon the error as one of "presumptuous judgment." Under that form it is easily presentable to the mind, and has a useful corrective action. I do not think the expression too strong; for if we are led, either by simplicity or vanity, to give an opinion upon matters respecting which we are not instructed, either by the knowledge of others, or our own intimate observation; if we are induced to ascribe an effect to one force, or deny its relation to another, knowing little or nothing of the laws of the forces, or the necessary conditions of the effect to be considered; surely our judgment must be qualified as "presumptuous."

There are multitudes who think themselves competent to decide, after the most cursory observation, upon the cause of this or that event (and they may be really very acute and correct in things familiar to them):—a not unusual phrase with them is, that "it stands to reason," that the effect they expect should result from the cause they assign to it, and yet it is *very difficult*, in numerous cases that appear plain, to show this reason, or to deduce the true and only rational relation of cause and effect. In matters connected with natural philosophy, we have wonderful aid in the progress and assurance in the character, of our final judgment, afforded us by the facts which supply our data, and the experience which multiplies their number and varies their testimony. A fundamental fact, like an elementary principle, never fails us, its evidence is always true; but, on the other hand, we frequently have to ask what is the fact?—often fail in distinguishing it,—often fail in the very statement of it,—and mostly overpass or come short of its true recognition.

If we are subject to mistake in the interpretation of our mere sense impressions, we are much more liable to error when we proceed to deduce from these impressions (as supplied to us by our ordinary experience), the relation of cause and effect; and the accuracy of our judgment, consequently, is more endangered. Then our dependence should be upon carefully observed facts, and the laws of nature; and I shall proceed to a further illustration of the mental deficiency I speak of, by a brief reference to one of these.

The *laws of nature*, as we understand them, are the foundation of our knowledge in natural things. So much as we know of them has been developed by the successive energies of the highest intellects, exerted through many ages. After a most rigid and scrutinizing examination upon principle and trial, a definite expression has been given to them; they have become, as it were, our belief or trust. From day to day we still examine and test our expressions of them. We have no interest in their retention if erroneous; on the contrary, the greatest discovery a man could make would be to prove that one of these accepted laws was erroneous, and his greatest honour would be the discovery. Neither would there be any desire to retain the former expression; for we know that the new or the amended law would be far more productive in results, would greatly increase our intellectual acquisitions, and would prove an abundant source of fresh delight to the mind.

These laws are numerous, and are more or less comprehensive. They are also precise; for a law may present an apparent exception, and yet not be less a law to us, when the exception is included in the expression. Thus, that elevation of temperature expands all bodies is a well-defined law, though there be an exception in water for a limited temperature; because we are careful, whilst stating the law, to state the exception and its limits. Pre-eminent among these laws, because of its simplicity, its universality, and its undeviating truth, stands that enunciated by Newton (commonly called the *law of gravitation*), that matter attracts matter with a force inversely as the square of the distance. Newton showed that, by this law, the general condition of things on the surface of the earth is governed; and the globe itself, with all upon it, kept together as a whole. He demonstrated that the motions of the planets round the sun, and of the satellites about the planets, were subject to it. During and since his time, certain variations in the movements of the planets, which were called irregularities, and might, for aught that was then known, be due to some cause other than the attraction of gravitation, were found to be its necessary consequences. By the close and scrutinizing attention of minds the most persevering and careful, it was ascertained that even the distant stars were subject to this law; and, at last, to place as it were the seal of assurance to its never-failing truth, it became, in the minds of Leverrier and Addams (1845), the foreteller and the discoverer of an orb rolling in the depths of space, so large as to equal nearly sixty earths, yet so far away as to be invisible to the unassisted eye. What truth, beneath that of revelation, can have an assurance stronger than this!

Yet this law is often cast aside as of no value or authority, because of the unconscious ignorance amidst which we dwell. You hear at the present day, that some persons can place their fingers on a table, and then elevating their hands, the table will rise up and follow them; that the piece of furniture, though heavy, will ascend, and that their hands bear no weight, or are not drawn down to the wood: you do not hear of this as a conjuring manœuvre, to be shown for your amusement, but are expected seriously to believe it; and are told that it is an important fact, a great discovery amongst the truths of nature. Your neighbour, a well-meaning, conscientious person, believes it; and the assertion finds acceptance in every rank of society, and amongst classes which are esteemed to be educated. Now, what can this imply but that society, speaking generally, is not only ignorant as respects education of the judgment, but is also ignorant of its ignorance? The parties who are thus persuaded, and those who are inclined to think and to hope that they are right, throw up Newton's law at once, and *that* in a case which of all others is fitted to be tested by it; or if the law be erroneous, to test the law. I will not say they oppose the law, though I *have* heard the supposed fact quoted triumphantly against it; but as far as my observation has gone, they will not apply it. The law affords the simplest means of testing the fact; and if there be, indeed, anything in the latter new to our knowledge (and who shall say that new matter is not presented to us daily, passing away unrecognised), it also affords the means of placing *that* before us separately in its simplicity and truth. Then why not consent to apply the knowledge we have to that which is under development? Shall we educate ourselves in what is known, and then, casting away all we have acquired, turn to our ignorance for aid to guide us among the unknown? If so, instruct a man to write, but employ one who is unacquainted with letters to read that which is written; the end will be just as unsatisfactory, though not so injurious, for the book of nature, which we have to read, is written by the finger of God. Why should not one who can thus lift a table, proceed to verify and simplify his fact, and bring it into relation with the law of Newton? Why should he not take the top of his table (it may be a small one), and placing it in a balance, or on a lever, proceed to ascertain how much weight he can raise by the draught of his fingers upwards; and of this weight, so ascertained, how much is unrepresented by any pull upon the fingers downward? He will then be able to investigate the further question, whether electricity, or any new force of matter, is made manifest in his operations; or whether action and reaction being unequal, he has at his command the source of a perpetual motion. Such a man, furnished with a nicely constructed carriage on a railway, ought to travel by the mere draught of his own fingers. A far less prize than this would gain him the attention of the whole scientific and commercial world; and he may rest assured, that if he can make the most delicate balance incline or decline by attraction, though it be only with the force of an ounce, or even a grain, he will not fail to gain universal respect and most honourable reward.

When we think of the laws of nature (which by continued observation have become known to us), as the proper tests to which any new fact, or our theoretical representation of it, should, in the first place, be subjected, let us contemplate their assured and large character. Let us go out into the field and look at the heavens, with their solar, starry, and planetary glories; the sky with its clouds; the waters descending from above, or wandering at our feet; the animals, the trees, the plants; and consider the permanency of their actions and conditions under the government of these laws. The most delicate flower, the tenderest insect, continues in its species through countless years; always varying, yet ever the same. When we think we have discovered a departure, as in the *Aphides*, *Medusæ*, *Distomæ*, &c., the law concerned is itself the best means of instituting an investigation, and hitherto we have always found the witness to return to its original testimony. These frail things are never ceasing, never changing, evidence of the law's immutability. It would be well for a man who has an anomalous case before him, to contemplate a blade of grass, and when he has considered the numerous ceaseless, yet certain, actions there located, and his inability to change the character of the least among them, to recur to his new subject; and, in place of accepting unwatched and unchecked results, to search for a like certainty and recurrence in the appearances and actions which belong to it.

Perhaps it may be said, the delusion of table-moving is past, and need not be recalled before an audience like the present;—even granting this, let us endeavour to make the subject leave one useful result; let it serve for an example, not to pass into forgetfulness. It is so recent, and was received by the public in a manner so strange, as to justify a reference to it, in proof of the uneducated condition of the general mind. I do not object to table-moving, for *itself;* for being once stated it becomes a fit, though a very unpromising subject for experiment: but I am opposed to the unwillingness of its advocates to investigate; their boldness to assert; the credulity of the lookers-on; their desire that the reserved and cautious objector should be in error; and I wish, by calling attention to these things, to make the general want of mental discipline and education manifest.

Having endeavoured to point out this great deficiency in the exercise of the intellect, I will offer a few remarks upon the means of subjecting it to the improving processes of instruction. Perhaps many who watch over the interests of the community, and are anxious for its welfare, will conclude, that the development of the judgment cannot properly be included in the general idea of education; that as the education proposed must, to a very large degree, be of *self*, it is so far incommunicable; that the master and the scholar merge into one, and both disappear; that the instructor is no wiser than the one to be instructed, and thus the usual relations of the two lose their power. Still, I believe that the judgment may be educated to a very large extent, and might refer to the fine arts, as giving proof in the affirmative; and though, as respects the community and its improvement in relation to common things, any useful education must be of *self*, I think that society, as a body, may act powerfully in the cause. Or it may still be objected that my experience is imperfect, is chiefly derived from exercise of the mind within the precincts of natural philosophy, and has not that generality of application which can make it of any value to society at large. I can only repeat my conviction, that society occupies itself now-a-days about physical matters, and judges them as common things. Failing in relation to them, it is equally liable to carry such failures into other matters of life. The proof of deficient judgment in one department shows the habit of mind, and the general want, in relation to others. I am persuaded that all persons may find in natural things an admirable school for self-instruction, and a field for the necessary mental exercise; that they may easily apply their habits of thought, thus formed, to a social use; and that they ought to do this, as a duty to themselves and their generation.

Let me first try to illustrate the former part of the case, and at the same time state what I think a man may and ought to do for himself.

The *self-education* to which he should be stimulated by the desire to improve his judgment, requires no blind dependance upon the dogmas of others, but is commended to him by the suggestions and dictates of his own common sense. The first part of it is founded in mental discipline: happily, it requires no unpleasant avowals; appearances are preserved, and vanity remains unhurt; but it is necessary that a man *examine himself*, and *that* not carelessly. On the contrary, as he advances, he should become more and more strict, till he ultimately prove a sharper critic to himself than any one else can be; and he ought to intend this, for, so far as he consciously falls short of it, he acknowledges that others may have reason on their side when they criticise him. A first result of this habit of mind will be an internal conviction of *ignorance in many things respecting which his neighbours are taught*, and that his opinions and conclusions on such matters ought to be advanced with reservation. A mind so disciplined will be *open to correction, upon good grounds, in all things*, even in those it is best acquainted with; and should familiarize itself with the idea of such being the case: for though it sees no reason to suppose itself in error, yet the possibility exists. The mind is not enfeebled by this internal admission, but strengthened; for, if it cannot distinguish proportionately between the probable right and wrong of things known imperfectly, it will tend either to be rash or to hesitate; whilst that which admits the due amount of probability is likely to be justified in the end. It is right that we should stand by and act on our principles; but not right to hold them in obstinate blindness, or retain them when proved to be erroneous. I remember the time when I believed a spark was produced between voltaic metals as they approached to contact (and the reasons why it might be possible yet remain); but others doubted the fact and denied the proofs, and on re-examination I found reason to admit their corrections were well founded. Years ago I believed that electrolytes could conduct electricity by a conduction proper; that has also been denied by many through long time: though I believed myself right, yet circumstances have induced me to pay such respect to criticism as to reinvestigate the subject, and I have the pleasure of thinking that nature confirms my original conclusions. So, though evidence may appear to preponderate extremely in favour of a certain decision, it is wise and proper to hear a counter-statement. You can have no idea how often and how much, under such an impression, I have desired that the marvellous descriptions which have reached me might prove, in some points, correct; and how frequently I have submitted myself to hot fires, to friction with magnets, to the passes of hands, &c. lest I should be shutting out discovery; encouraging the strong desire that something might be true, and that I might aid in the development of a new force of nature.

Among those points of self-education which take up the form of *mental discipline*, there is one of great importance, and, moreover, difficult to deal with, because it involves an internal conflict, and equally touches our vanity and our ease. It consists in the *tendency to deceive ourselves* regarding all we wish for, and the necessity of *resistance to these desires.* It is impossible for any one who has not been constrained, by the course of his occupation and thoughts, to a habit of continual self-correction, to be aware of the amount of error in relation to judgment arising from this tendency. The force of the temptation which urges us to seek for such evidence and appearances as are in favour of our desires, and to disregard those which oppose them, is wonderfully great. In this respect we are all, more or less, active promoters of error. In place of practising wholesome self-abnegation, we ever make the wish the father to the thought: we receive as friendly that which agrees with, we resist with dislike that which opposes us; whereas the very reverse is required by every dictate of common sense. Let me illustrate my meaning by a case where the proof being easy, the rejection of it under the temptation is the more striking. In old times, a ring or button mould be tied by a boy to one end of a long piece of thread, which he would then hold at the other end, letting the button hang within a glass, or over a piece of slate-pencil, or sealing-wax, or a nail; he would wait and observe whether the button swung, and whether in swinging it tapped the glass as many times as the clock struck last, or moved along or across the slate-pencil, or in a circle or oval. In late times, parties in all ranks of life have renewed and repeated the boy's experiment. They have sought to ascertain a very simple fact—namely, whether the effect was as reported; but how many were unable to do this? They were sure they could keep their hands immoveable,—were sure they could do so whilst watching the result,—were sure that accordance of swing with an expected direction was not the result of their desires or involuntary motions. How easily all these points could be put to the proof by *not looking at the objects*, yet how difficult for the experimenter to deny himself that privilege. I have rarely found one who would freely permit the substance experimented with to be screened from his sight, and then its position changed.

When engaged in the investigation of table-turning, I constructed a very simple apparatus, serving as an index, to show the unconscious motions of the hands upon the table. The results were either that the index moved before the table, or that neither index nor table moved; and in numerous cases all moving power was annihilated. A universal objection was made to it by the table-turners. It was said to paralyze the powers of the mind; but the experimenters need not see the index; they may leave their friends to watch that, and their minds may revel in any power that their expectation or their imagination can confer. So restrained, a *dislike* to the trial arises; but what is that, except a proof that whilst they trust themselves they doubt themselves, and are not willing to proceed to the decision, lest the trust which they like should fail them, and the doubt which they dislike rise to the authority of truth?

Again, in respect of the action of magnets on the body, it is almost imposible for an uninstructed person to enter profitably upon such an inquiry. He may observe *any* symptom which his expectation has been accidentally directed to; yet be unconscious of any, if unaware of his subjection to the magnetic force, or of the conditions and manner of its application.

As a proof of the extent of this influence, even on the minds of those well aware of its force, and desirous under every circumstance to escape from it, I will mention the practice of the chemist, who, dealing with the balance, that impartial decider which never fails in its indication, but offers its evidence with all simplicity, durability, and truth, still remembers he should doubt himself; and, with the desire of rendering himself inaccessible to temptation, takes a counterpoised but unknown quantity of the substance for analysis, that he may remain ignorant of the proportions which he ought to obtain, and only at last compares the sum of his products with his counterpoise.

The *inclination* we exhibit in respect of any report or opinion that harmonises with our preconceived notions, can only be compared in degree with the *incredulity* we entertain towards everything that opposes them; and these opposite and apparently incompatible, or at least inconsistent, conditions are accepted simultaneously in the most extraordinary manner. At one moment a departure from the laws of nature is admitted without the pretence of a careful examination of the proof; and at the next, the whole force of these laws, acting undeviatingly through all time, is denied, because the testimony they give is disliked.

It is my firm persuasion, that no man can examine himself in the most common things, having any reference to him personally, or to any person, thought, or matter related to him, without being soon made aware of *the temptation* and the difficulty of opposing it. I could give you many illustrations personal to myself, about atmospheric magnetism, lines of force, attraction, repulsion, unity of power, nature of matter, &c.; or in things more general to our common nature, about likes and dislikes, wishes, hopes, and fears; but it would be unsuitable, and also unnecessary, for each must be conscious of a large field sadly uncultivated in this respect. *I will simply express my strong belief, that that point of self-education which consists in teaching the mind to resist its desires and inclinations, until they are proved to be right, is the most important of all, not only in things of natural philosophy, but in every department of daily life.*

There are numerous precepts, resulting more or less from the principles of mental discipline already insisted on as essential, which are very useful in forming a judgment about matters of fact, whether among natural things or between man and man. Such a precept, and one that should recur to the mind early in every new case is, to *know the conditions* of the matter, respecting which we are called upon to make a judgment. To suppose that any would judge before they professed to know the conditions, would seem to be absurd; on the other hand, to assume that the community *does wait* to know the conditions before it judges, is an assumption so large that I cannot accept it. Very few search out the conditions; most are anxious to sink those which oppose their preconceptions; yet none can be left out if a right judgment is to be formed. It is true that many conditions must ever remain unknown to us, even in regard to the simplest things in nature: thus, as to the wonderful action of gravity, whose law never fails us, we cannot say whether the bodies are acting truly at a distance, or by a physical line of force as a connecting link between them. The great majority think the former is the case; Newton's judgment is for the latter. But of the conditions which are within our reach we should search out all; for in relation to those which remain unknown or unsuspected, we are in that very ignorance (regarding judgment) which it is our present object, first to make manifest, and then to remove.

One exercise of the mind, which largely influences the power and character of the judgment, is the habit of forming *clear and precise ideas.* If, after considering a subject in our ordinary manner, we return upon it with the special purpose of noticing the condition of our thoughts, we shall be astonished to find how little precise they remain. On recalling the phenomena relating to a matter of fact, the circumstances modifying them, the kind and amount of action presented, the real or probable result, we shall find that the first impressions are scarcely fit for the foundation of a judgment, and that the second thoughts will be best. For the acquirement of a good condition of mind in this respect, the thoughts should be trained to a habit of clear and precise formation, so that vivid and distinct impressions of the matter in hand, its circumstances and consequences, may remain.

Before we proceed to consider any question involving physical principles, we should set out with *clear ideas* of the naturally possible and impossible. There are many subjects uniting more or less of the most sure and valuable investigations of science with the most imaginary and unprofitable speculation, that are continually passing through their various phases of intellectual, experimental, or commercial development: some to be established, some to disappear, and some to recur again and again, like ill weeds that cannot be extirpated, yet can be cultivated to no result as wholesome food for the mind. Such, for instance, in different degrees, are the caloric engine, the electric light, the Pasilalinic sympathetic compass,* mesmerism, homœopathy, odylism, the magneto-electric engine, the perpetual motion, &c. All hear and talk of these things; all use their judgment more or less upon them, and all might do that effectively, if they were to instruct themselves to the extent which is within their reach. I am persuaded that natural things offer an admirable school for self-instruction, a most varied field for the necessary mental practice, and that those who exercise themselves therein may easily apply the habits of thought thus formed to a social use. As a first step in such practice, clear ideas should be obtained of what is possible and what is impossible. Thus, it is impossible to *create* force. We may employ it; we may evoke it in one form by its consumption in another; we may hide it for a period; but we can neither *create* nor *destroy* it. We may cast it away; but where we dismiss it, there it will do its work. If, therefore, we desire to consider a proposition respecting the employment or evolution of power, let us carry our judgment,

* See "Chambers's Journal," 1851, Feb. 15, p. 105.

educated on this point, with us. If the proposal include the double use of a force with only one excitement, it implies a creation of power, and that *cannot be.* If we could by the fingers draw a heavy piece of wood or stone upward without effort, and then, letting it sink, could produce by its gravity an effort equal to its weight, that would be a creation of power, and *cannot be.*

So again we cannot *annihilate* matter, nor can we *create* it. But if we are satisfied to rest upon that dogma, what are we to think of table-lifting? If we could make the table to cease from acting by gravity upon the earth beneath it, or by reaction upon the hand supposed to draw it upwards, we *should annihilate it,* in respect of that very property which characterises it as matter.

Considerations of this nature are very important aids to the judgment; and when a statement is made claiming our assent, we should endeavour to reduce it to some consequence which can be immediately compared with, and tried by, these or like compact and never failing truths. If incompatibility appears, then we have reason to suspend our conclusion, however attractive to the imagination the proposition may be, and pursue the inquiry further, until accordance is obtained; it must be a most uneducated and presumptuous mind that can at once consent to cast off the tried truth and accept in its place the mere loud assertion. We should endeavour to separate the points before us, and concentrate each, so as to evolve a clear type idea of the ruling fact and its consequences; looking at the matter on every side, with the great purpose of distinguishing the constituent reality, and recognising it under every variety of aspect.

In like manner we should accustom ourselves to clear and definite language, especially in physical matters, giving to a word its true and full, but measured meaning, that we may be able to convey our ideas clearly to the minds of others. Two persons cannot mutually impart their knowledge, or compare and rectify their conclusions, unless both attend to the true intent and force of language. If by such words as attraction, electricity, polarity, or atom, they imply different things, they may discuss facts, deny results, and doubt consequences for an indefinite time without any advantageous progress. I hold it as a great point in self-education, that the student should be continually engaged in forming exact ideas, and in expressing them clearly by language. Such practice insensibly opposes any tendency to exaggeration or mistake, and increases the sense and love of truth in every part of life.

I should be sorry, however, if what I have said were understood as meaning that education for the improvement and strengthening of the judgment is to be altogether repressive of the imagination, or confine the exercise of the mind to processes of a mathematical or mechanical character. I believe that, in the pursuit of physical science, the imagination should be taught to present the subject investigated in all possible, and even in impossible views; to search for analogies of likeness and (if I may say so) of opposition—inverse or contrasted analogies; to present the fundamental idea in every form, proportion, and condition; to clothe it with suppositions and probabilities, that all cases may pass in review, and be touched, if needful, by the Ithuriel spear of experiment. But all this must be *under government*, and the result must not be given to society until the judgment, educated by the process itself, has been exercised upon it. Let us construct our hypotheses for an hour, or a day, or for years; they are of the utmost value in the elimination of truth, "which is evolved more freely from error than from confusion;" but, above all things, let us not cease to be aware of the temptation they offer, or, because they gradually become familiar to us, accept them as established. We could not reason about electricity without thinking of it as a fluid, or a vibration, or some other existent state or form. We should give up half our advantage in the consideration of heat if we refused to consider it as a principle, or a state of motion. We could scarcely touch such subjects by experiment, and we should make no progress in their practical application, without hypothesis; still it is absolutely necessary that we should learn to doubt the conditions we assume, and acknowledge we are uncertain, whether heat and electricity are vibrations or substances, or either.

When the different data required are in our possession, and we have succeeded in forming a clear idea of each, the mind should be instructed to *balance them* one against another, and not suffered carelessly to hasten to a conclusion. This reserve is most essential; and it is especially needful that the reasons which are adverse to our expectations or our desires should be carefully attended to. We often receive truth from unpleasant sources; we often have reason to accept unpalatable truths. We are never freely willing to admit information having this unpleasant character, and it requires much self-control in this respect, to preserve us, even in a moderate degree, from errors. I suppose there is scarcely one investigator in original research who has not felt the temptation to disregard the reasons and results which are against his views. I acknowledge that I have experienced it very often, and will not pretend to say that I have yet learned on all occasions to avoid the error. When a bar of bismuth or phosphorus is placed between the poles of a powerful magnet, it is drawn into a position across the line joining the poles; when only one pole is near the bar, the latter recedes; this and the former effect is due to repulsion, and is strikingly in contrast with the attraction shown by iron. To account for it, I at one time suggested the idea that a polarity was induced in the phosphorus or bismuth the reverse of the polarity induced in iron, and that opinion is still sustained by eminent philosophers. But observe a necessary result of such a supposition, which appears to follow when the phenomena are referred to elementary principles. *Time* is shown, by every result bearing on the subject, to be concerned in the coming on and passing away of the inductive condition produced by magnetic force; and the consequence, as Thomson pointed out, is, that if a ball of bismuth could be suspended between the poles of a magnet, so as to encounter no resistance from the surrounding medium, or from friction or torsion, and were once put in motion round a vertical axis, it would, because of the assumed polar state, go on for ever revolving, the parts which at any moment are axial moving like the bar, so as to become the next moment equatorial. Now, as we believe the mechanical forces of nature tend to bring things into a stable, and not into an unstable condition; as we believe that a perpetual motion is impossible; so, because both these points are involved in the notion of the reverse polarity, which itself is not supposed to be dependent on any consumption of power, I feel bound to hold the judgment balanced, and therefore hesitate to accept a conclusion founded on such a notion of the physical action; the more especially as the peculiar test facts* which prove the polarity of iron are not reproduced in the case of diamagnetic bodies.

As a result of this wholesome mental condition, we should be able to form a *proportionate judgment.* The mind naturally desires to settle upon one thing or another; to rest upon an affirmative or a negative; and that with a degree of absolutism which is irrational and improper. In drawing a conclusion, it is very difficult, but not the less necessary, to make it *proportionate* to the evidence: except where certainty exists (a case of rare occurrence), we should consider our decisions as probable only. The probability may appear very great, so that in affairs of the world we often accept such as certainty, and trust our welfare or our lives upon it. Still, only an uneducated mind will confound probability with certainty, especially when it encounters a contrary conclusion drawn by another from like data. This suspension in degree of judgment will not make a man less active in life, or his conclusions less certain as truths; on the contrary, I believe him to be the more ready for the right amount and direction of action on any emergency; and am sure his conclusions and statements will carry more weight in the world than those of the incautious man.

When I was young, I received from one well able to aid a learner in his endeavours towards self-improvement, a curious lesson in the mode of estimating the amount of belief one might be induced to attach to our conclusions. The person was Dr. Wollaston, who, upon a given point, was induced to offer me a wager of two to one on the affirmative. I rather impertinently quoted

* Experimental Researches in Electricity, paragraphs 2,657—2,681.

Butler's well-known lines* about the kind of persons who use wagers for argument, and he gently explained to me, that he considered such a wager not as a thoughtless thing, but as an expression of the amount of belief in the mind of the person offering it; combining this curious application of the wager, as a *meter*, with the necessity that ever existed of drawing conclusions, not absolute, but proportionate to the evidence.

Occasionally and frequently the exercise of the judgment ought to end in *absolute reservation.* It may be very distasteful, and great fatigue, to suspend a conclusion; but as we are not infallible, so we ought to be cautious: we shall eventually find our advantage, for the man who rests in his position is not so far from right as he who, proceeding in a wrong direction, is ever increasing his distance. In the year 1824, Arago discovered that copper and other bodies placed in the vicinity of a magnet, and having no direct action of attraction or repulsion upon it, did affect it when moved, and were affected by it. A copper plate revolving near a magnet carried the magnet with it; or if the magnet revolved, and not the copper, it carried the copper with it. A magnetic needle vibrating freely over a disc of glass or wood, was exceedingly retarded in its motion when these were replaced by a disc of copper. Arago stated most clearly all the conditions, and resolved the forces into three directions, but not perceiving the physical cause of the action, exercised a most wise and instructive reservation as to his conclusion. Others, as Haldat, considered it as the proof of the universality of a magnetism of the ordinary kind, and held to that

* "Quoth she, 'I've heard old cunning stagers,
Say fools for arguments use wagers.'"

notion though it was contradicted by the further facts; and it was only at a future period that the true physical cause, namely, magneto-electric currents induced in the copper, became known to us. What an education Arago's mind must have received in relation to philosophical reservation; what an antithesis he forms with the mass of table-turners; and what a fine example he has left us of that condition of judgment to which we should strive to attain!

If I may give another illustration of the needful reservation of judgment, I will quote the case of oxygen and hydrogen gases, which, being mixed, will remain together uncombined for years in contact with glass, but in contact with spongy platinum combine at once. We have the same fact in many forms, and many suggestions have been made as to the mode of action, but as yet we do not know *clearly* how the result comes to pass. We cannot tell whether electricity acts or not. Then we should suspend our conclusions. Our knowledge of the fact itself, and the many varieties of it, is not the less abundant or sure; and when the truth shall hereafter emerge from the mist, we ought to have no opposing prejudice, but be prepared to receive it.

The education which I advocate will require *patience* and *labour of thought* in every exercise tending to improve the judgment. It matters not on what subject a person's mind is occupied, he should engage in it with the conviction that it will require mental labour. A powerful mind will be able to draw a conclusion more readily and more correctly than one of moderate character, but both will surpass themselves if they make an earnest, careful investigation, instead of a careless or prejudiced one; and education for this purpose is the more necessary for the latter, because the man of less ability may, through it, raise his rank and amend his position. I earnestly urge this point of self-education, for I believe it to be more or less in the power of every man greatly to improve his judgment. I do not think that one has the complete capacity for judgment which another is naturally without. I am of opinion that all may judge, and that we only need to declare on every side the conviction that mental education is wanting, and lead men to see that through it they hold, in a large degree, their welfare and their character in their own hands, to cause in future years an abundant development of right judgment in every class.

This education has for its first and its last step *humility*. It can commence only because of a conviction of deficiency; and if we are not disheartened under the growing revelations which it will make, that conviction will become stronger unto the end. But the humility will be founded, not on comparison of ourselves with the imperfect standards around us, but on the increase of that internal knowledge which alone can make us aware of our internal wants. The first step in correction is to learn our deficiencies, and having learned them, the next step is almost complete: for no man who has discovered that his judgment is hasty, or illogical, or imperfect, would go on with the same degree of haste, or irrationality, or presumption as before. I do not mean that all would at once be cured of bad mental habits, but I think better of human nature than to believe, that a man, in any rank of life, who has arrived at the consciousness of such a condition, would deny his common sense, and still judge and act as before. And though such self-schooling must continue to the end of life to supply an experience of deficiency rather than of attainment, still there is abundant stimulus to excite any man to perseverance. What he has lost are things imaginary, not real; what he gains are riches before unknown to him, yet invaluable; and though he may think more humbly of his own character, he will find himself at every step of his progress more sought for than before, more trusted with responsibility and held in pre-eminence by his equals, and more highly valued by those whom he himself will esteem worthy of approbation.

And now a few words upon the mutual relation of two classes, namely, *those* who decline to educate their judgments in regard to the matters on which they decide, and those who, by self-education, have endeavoured to improve themselves; and upon the remarkable and somewhat unreasonable manner in which the latter are called upon, and occasionally taunted, by the former. A man who makes assertions, or draws conclusions, regarding any given case, ought to be competent to investigate it. He has no right to throw the onus on others, declaring it their duty to prove him right or wrong. His duty is to demonstrate the truth of that which he asserts, or to cease from asserting. The men he calls upon to consider and judge have enough to do with themselves, in the examination, correction, or verification of their own views. The world little knows how many of the thoughts and theories which have passed through the mind of a scientific investigator have been crushed in silence and secrecy by his own severe criticism and adverse examination; that in the most successful instances not a tenth of the suggestions, the hopes, the wishes, the preliminary conclusions have been realized. And is a man so occupied to be taken from his search after truth in the path he hopes may lead to its attainment, and occupied in vain upon nothing but a broad assertion?

Neither has the assertor of any new thing a right to claim an answer in the form of *Yes* or *No;* or think, because none is forthcoming, that he is to be considered as having established his assertion. So much is unknown to the wisest man, that he may often be without an answer; as frequently he is so, because the subject is in the region of hypothesis, and not of facts. In either case he has the right to refuse to speak. I cannot tell whether there are two fluids of electricity or any fluid at all. I am not bound to explain how a table tilts any more than to indicate how, under the conjuror's hands, a pudding appears in a hat. The means are not known to me. I am persuaded that the results, however strange they may appear, are in accordance with that which is truly known, and if carefully investigated would justify the well-tried laws of nature; but, as life is limited, I am not disposed to occupy the time it is made of in the investigation of matters which, in what is known to me of them, offer no reasonable prospect of any useful progress, or anything but negative results. We deny the right of those who call upon us to answer their speculations "*if we can,*" whilst we have so many of our own to develop and correct; and claim the right for ourselves of withholding either our conclusions or the reasons for them, without in the least degree admitting that their affirmations are unanswerable. We are not even called upon to give an answer to the best of our belief: nor bound to admit a bold assertion because we do not *know* to the contrary. No one is justified in claiming our assent to the spontaneous generation of insects, because we cannot circumstantially explain how a mite or the egg of a mite has entered into a particular bottle. Let those who affirm the exception to the general law of nature, or those others who upon the affirmation accept the result, work out the experimental proof. It has been done in this case by Schulze, and is in the negative; but how few among the many who make, or repeat, the assertion, would have the requisite self-abnegation, the subjected judgment, the perseverance, and the precision which has been displayed in that research.

When men, more or less marked by their advance, are led by circumstances to give an opinion adverse to any popular notion, or to the assertions of any sanguine inventor, nothing is more usual than the attempt to neutralize the force of such an opinion by reference to the mistakes which like educated men have made; and their occasional misjudgments and erroneous conclusions are quoted, as if they were less competent than others to give an opinion, being even disabled from judging like matters to those which are included in their pursuits by the very exercise of their minds upon them. How frequently has the reported judgment of Davy, upon the impossibility of gas-lighting on a large scale, been quoted by speculators engaged in tempting monied men into companies, or in the pages of journals occupied with the popular fancies of the day; as if an argument were derivable from that in favour of some special object to be commended. Why should not men taught in the matter of judgment far beyond their neighbours, be expected to err sometimes, since the very education in which they are advanced can only terminate with their lives? What is there about them, derived from *this education*, which sets up the shadow of a pretence to perfection? Such men cannot learn all things, and may often be ignorant. The very progress which science makes amongst them as a body is a continual correction of ignorance—*i.e.* of a state which is ignorance in relation to the future, though wisdom and knowledge in relation to the past. In 1823, Wollaston discovered that beautiful substance which he called Titanium, believing it to be a simple metal: and it was so accepted by all philosophers. Yet this was a mistake, for Wöhler, in 1850, showed the substance was a very compound body. This is no reproach to Wollaston or to those who trusted in him; he made a step in metallurgy which advanced knowledge, and perhaps we may hereafter, through it, learn to know that metals are compound bodies. Who, then, has a right to quote his mistake as a reproach against him? Who could correct him but men intellectually educated as he himself was? Who does not feel that the investigation remains a bright gem in the circlet that memory offers to his honour?

If we are to estimate the utility of an educated judgment, do not let us hear merely of the errors of scientific men, which have been corrected by others taught in the same careful school; but let us see what, as a body, they have produced, compared with that supplied by their reproachers. Where are the established truths and triumphs of ring-swingers, table-turners, table-speakers? What one result in the numerous divisions of science or its applications can be traced to their exertions? Where is the investigation completed, so that, as in gas-lighting, all may admit that the principles are established and a good end obtained, without the shadow of a doubt?

If we look to electricity, it, in the hands of the careful investigator, has advanced to the most extraordinary results: it approaches at the motion of his hand; bursts from the metal; descends from the atmosphere; surrounds the globe: it talks, it writes, it records, it appears to him (cautious as he has learned to become) as a universal spirit in nature. If we look to photography, whose origin is of our own day, and see what it has become in the hands of its discoverers and their successors, how wonderful are the results! The light is made to yield impressions upon the dead silver or the coarse paper, beautiful as those it produced upon the living and sentient retina: its most transient impression is rendered durable for years; it is made to leave a visible or an invisible trace; to give a result to be seen now or a year hence; made to paint all natural forms and even colours; it serves the offices of war, of peace, of art, science, and economy: it replaces even the mind of the human being in some of its lower services; for a little camphine lamp is set down and left to itself, to perform the duty of watching the changes of magnetism, heat, and other forces of nature, and to record the results, in pictorial curves, which supply an enduring record of their most transitory actions.

What has clairvoyance, or mesmerism, or table-rapping done in comparison with results like these? What have the snails at Paris told us from the snails at New York? What have any of these intelligences done in *aiding* such developments? Why did they not inform us of the possibility of photography; or, when that became known, why did they not favour us with some instructions for its improvement? They all profess to deal with agencies far more exalted in character than an electric current or a ray of light: they also deal with mechanical forces; they employ both the bodily organs and the mental; they profess to lift a table, to turn a hat, to see into a box, or into the next room, or a town:—why should they not move a balance, and so give us the element of a new mechanical power? take cognizance of a bottle and its contents, and tell us how they will act upon those of a neighbouring bottle? either see or feel into a crystal, and inform us of what it is composed? Why have they not added one metal to the fifty known to mankind, or one planet to the number daily increasing under the observant eye of the astronomer? Why have they not corrected one of the *mistakes* of the philosophers? There are no doubt very many that require it. There has been plenty of time for the development and maturation of some of the numerous public pretences that have risen up in connexion with these supposed agencies; how is it that not one new power has been added to the means of investigation employed by the philosophers, or one valuable utilitarian application presented to society?

In conclusion, I will freely acknowledge that all I have said regarding the great want of judgment manifested by society as a body, and the high value of any means which would tend to supply the deficiency, have been developed and declared on numerous occasions, by authority far above any I possess. The deficiency is known hypothetically, but I doubt if in reality; the individual acknowledges the state in respect of others, but is unconscious of it in regard to himself. As to the world at large, the condition is accepted as a necessary fact; and so it is left untouched, almost ignored. I think that education in a large sense should be applied to this state of the subject, and that society, though it can do little in the way of communicated experience, can do much, by a declaration of the evil that exists and of its remediable character; by keeping alive a sense of the deficiency to be supplied; and by directing the minds of men to the practice and enlargement of that self-education which every one pursues more or less, but which, under conviction and method, would produce a tenfold amount of good. I know that the multitude will always be behindhand in this education, and to a far greater extent than in respect of the education which is founded on book learning. Whatever advance books make, they retain; but each new being comes on to the stage of life, with the same average amount of conceit, desires, and passions, as his predecessors, and in respect of self-education has all to learn. Does the circumstance that we can do little more than proclaim the necessity of instruction justify the ignorance? or our silence? or make the plea for this education less strong? Should it not, on the contrary, gain its strength from the fact that all are wanting more or less? I desire we should admit that, as a body, we are universally deficient in judgment. I do not mean that we are utterly ignorant, but that we have advanced only a little way in the requisite education, compared with what is within our power.

If the necessity of the education of the judgment were a familiar and habitual idea with the public, it would often afford a sufficient answer to the statement of an ill-informed or incompetent person; if quoted to recall to his remembrance the necessity of a mind instructed in a matter, and accustomed to balance evidence, it might frequently be in answer to the individual himself.

Adverse influence might, and would, arise from the careless, the confident, the presumptuous, the hasty, and the dilatory man, perhaps extreme opposition; but I believe that the mere acknowledgment and proclamation of the ignorance, by society at large, would, through its moral influence, destroy the opposition, and be a great means to the attainment of the good end desired: for if no more be done than to lead such to turn their thoughts inwards, a step in education is gained: if they are *convinced* in any degree, an important advance is made; if they learn only to *suspend* their judgment, the improvement will be one above price.

It is an extraordinary thing that man, with a mind so wonderful that there is nothing to compare with it elsewhere in the known creation, should leave it to run wild in respect of its highest elements and qualities. He has a power of comparison and judgment, by which his final resolves, and all those acts of his material system which distinguish him from the brutes, are guided: shall he omit to educate and improve them when education can do much? Is it towards the very principles and privileges that distinguish him above other creatures, he should feel indifference? Because the education is internal, it is not the less needful; nor is it more the duty of a man that he should cause his child to be taught than that he should teach himself. Indolence may tempt him to neglect the self-examination and experience which form his school, and weariness may induce the evasion of the necessary practices; but surely a thought of the prize should suffice to stimulate him to the requisite exertion: and to those who reflect upon the many hours and days, devoted by a lover of sweet sounds, to gain a moderate facility upon a mere mechanical instrument, it ought to bring a correcting blush of shame, if they feel convicted of neglecting the beautiful living instrument, wherein play all the powers of the mind.

I will conclude this subject;—believe me when I say I have been speaking from self-conviction. I did not think this an occasion on which I ought to seek for flattering words regarding our common nature; if so, I should have felt unfaithful to the trust I had taken up; so I have spoken from experience. In thought I hear the voice, which judges me by the precepts I have uttered. I know that I fail frequently in that very exercise of judgment to which I call others; and have abundant reason to believe that much more frequently I stand manifest to those around me as one who errs, without being corrected by knowing it. I would willingly have evaded appearing before you on this subject, for I shall probably do but little good, and may well think it was an error of judgment to consent: having consented, my thoughts would flow back amongst the events and reflections of my past life, until I found nothing present itself but an open declaration, almost a confession, as the means of performing the duty due to the subject and to you.

ON THE INFLUENCE OF THE HISTORY OF SCIENCE UPON INTELLECTUAL EDUCATION.

A LECTURE DELIVERED AT THE ROYAL INSTITUTION OF GREAT BRITAIN.

BY

WILLIAM WHEWELL, D.D., F.R.S.

ON THE

SCIENTIFIC HISTORY OF EDUCATION.

THE managers of the Royal Institution having determined to provide for their members and others a series of Lectures upon Education, and having expressed their wish that I should offer to the audience here assembled any views which may appear to me suited to such a purpose, I venture to do so, relying upon an indulgence which I have more than once experienced here on similar occasions. Of such indulgence I strongly feel the need, on various accounts, but especially on these *two*—first, that being so unfrequently in this metropolis, I do not know what trains of thought are passing in the minds of the greater part of my audience, who live in the midst of a stimulation produced by the lively interchange of opinion and discussion on the prominent questions of the day, to one of which what I have now to say in a great degree refers; and next, that in this hall, where you are accustomed to listen to the most lively explanations of scientific discoveries, illustrated by the most skilful and striking experiments, *I* have to present to you a series of remarks on subjects more or less abstract and vague, without being able to aid my exposition by anything addressed to the eye. The pictures which words can give of abstruse and general mental conceptions, when they alone form a diorama on which the mental eye of an assembly is to be directed for a whole hour, always appear to me to be in great danger of fading away into a dream of cloudland or a vacant blank. However, as to that point, I have an advantage in speaking on the History of Science, which is my present subject, in this room. To those of you who are in the habit of coming here, the walls must appear, from their customary aspect, to be hung with pictures which illustrate my theme. The striking facts in the history of science which you have presented to you in this place, week after week, are illustrations, in particular cases, of the general views which I have to offer to you; and if such expressions as *experience* and *theory, discovery* and *generalization*, *Baconian ascents* to comprehensive *axioms*, and *descents* thence to wonderful *works*—if such expressions be in danger of being *to others* vague and empty sounds, to *you* they will be, I may trust, all enlivened and embodied by what you have again and again seen here.

The subject on which I am desirous of making a few remarks to you at present is this: *The Influence of Scientific Discovery upon Intellectual Education*:—the influence of the scientific discoveries of any period upon the intellectual education of the succeeding period: the influence, that is, of the intellectual achievements of one or two gifted men, at various epochs of the world's history, upon all those persons, in the next succeeding generations, who have aimed to obtain, for themselves or for their children, the highest culture, the best discipline, of which man's intellectual faculties are capable. I wish to show that there has been such an influence, and that it has been great at all periods; that is, at all those periods of intellectual energy and activity which come within the conditions of the terms;—all periods which have been periods of *discovery*. I wish to show that this influence has been so great, that its results constitute, at this day, the whole of our intellectual education;—that in virtue of this influence, intellectual education has been, for those who avail themselves of the means which time has accumulated, progressive;—that our intellectual education now, to be worthy of the time, ought to include in its compass elements contributed to it in every one of the great epochs of mental energy which the world has seen;—that in this respect, most especially, we are, if we know how to use our advantages, inheritors of the wealth of all the richest times; strong in the power of the giants of all ages; placed on the summit of an edifice which thirty centuries have been employed in building.

Perhaps I shall most simply make myself intelligible by stating plainly and frankly a proposition which I wish to illustrate by various examples, as it has been exemplified in various ages and countries. The proposition is this: That every great advance in intellectual education has been the effect of some considerable scientific discovery, or group of discoveries. Every improvement of the mental discipline of those who stand in the forefront of humanity has followed some signal victory of their leaders; every addition to the means of intellectual culture has been the result of some extraordinary harvest, some more than ordinary bounty of the intellectual soil, bestowed on the preceding years.

Without further preface, let us proceed to examples. The first great attempt made for the improvement of intellectual education, so far as history tells us, was that undertaken and prosecuted with persevering vigour by Socrates and Plato. The aim of those philosophers was, I say, mainly and peculiarly, an improvement of the *intellectual education* of their countrymen. The Athenians of that time,—I mean, the more eminent and affluent classes of them,—had already an education in a very considerable degree elaborate, and large and elevated in its promises. The persons by whom this education was, in its higher departments, conducted—the teachers whom Socrates and Plato perseveringly opposed—have been habitually called *the Sophists;* because, though at the time their ascendancy was immense, in the course of ages Plato's writings have superseded theirs, and he so describes them. But it has been shown recently, in the most luminous and striking manner, by one among ourselves, that the education which these teachers professed to give, and frequently gave, was precisely what we commonly mean by *a good education.* It was an education enabling a young man to write well, speak well, and act efficiently, on all ordinary occasions, public and private. The moral doctrines which they taught, even according to the most unfavourable representation of them, were no worse than the moral doctrines which are most commonly taught among ourselves at the present day,—the morality founded upon *utility;* but many of them repudiated this doctrine as sordid and narrow, and professed higher principles, which they delivered in graceful literary forms, some of which are still extant in the books which we put in the hands of the young.

Such were the Sophists, against whom Socrates and Plato carried on their warfare. And why did Socrates and Plato contend against these teachers; and how was it that they contended so successfully, that the sympathy of all posterity has been with them in their opposition? It was because Socrates and Plato sought for solid principles in this specious teaching, and found none. It was because, while these professors of speaking well and acting well imparted their precepts to their pupils, and exemplified them by their practice, they could not bear the keen cross-questioning of Socrates, when he tried to make them tell what it was *to speak* WELL, and *to act* WELL; they could not tell Plato what was that "First Good, First Perfect, and First Fair," from which everything else derived goodness, beauty, and perfection. Socrates and Plato were not content with illustrations, they asked for principles; they were not content with rhetoric, they wanted demonstration: it was not enough for them that these men taught the young Athenian to *persuade* others, they wanted to have him *know*, and to know *what* he *knew*. These were the demands, as you will many of you recollect, that recur again and again in the Platonic Dialogues. This is the tendency of all the trains of irresistible logic which are put in the mouth of Plato's imaginary Socrates. *What* do we know? *How* do we know it? *By* what *reasoning? From* what *principles?* These questions are perpetually asked. They are never completely answered. The respondent always breaks down at some point or other; and then Socrates says, with his calm irony, "How disappointing! How vexatious! We are where we were! We must begin again. We have not yet found what we were seeking. We have not yet got hold of the real and essential truth."

And what was it that had put Socrates and Plato upon this eager and obstinate search of a real and essential truth? How was it they could not be satisfied without it? Why might not that which had been taught by the wise and eloquent men of previous generations suffice for *their* generation? Why must their inquiries go further than the inquiries of their ancestors had done? This real and essential truth which they sought, what had put the notion of it into their heads? What had made them think that such a thing could be found? Had they seen any example of such truth; had they seen any specimen of this treasure, which they sought for with so vehement and persevering a quest?

Yes: for this is the point to which I wish to draw your attention; they *had* seen specimens of this treasure. They had had placed before them examples of real and certain truth; they had been admitted to contemplate clear and indisputable truths; truths which they could demonstrate to be true; truths which they could trace to principles of intuitive evidence; truths which it did not appear to be speaking too highly of, if they called them necessary and eternal.

Such truths they had already seen and known; for they had known some of the truths of *geometry*. No doubt some of these truths,—the truths of geometry,—some casual and happy guesses—had been known at a much earlier period. Pythagoras had known that the squares on the two sides of a right-angled triangle are equal to the square on the third. But the lore of Pythagoras, imparted in a mysterious manner to an initiated few, had long crept stealthily among the secret societies of the Italian coast, and hardly made its way, in any considerable degree, into Greece, till it was introduced by Plato and his friends. But the age of Plato was an age of great geometrical discovery in Greece.

The general body of geometry, such as it exists to this day, was then constructed. Plato himself was an eminent geometer, not only by geometrical discoveries which he made, but still more by his clear and strong perception of the importance of the study. He repeatedly exhorts his fellow-countrymen to pursue this study; he promises that it shall lead them to a true view of the heavens; he discerns how this is to be done; he points out new branches of mathematical science which must be constructed for this purpose; he repeatedly refers to the Definitions, the Axioms, the Proofs of Geometrical Propositions; he writes over the gate of the gardens of Academus, where his disciples meet to listen to his teaching—*Οὐδεὶς ἀγεομέτρητος εἰσίτω*. "Let no one enter who is destitute of Geometry."

And why this requirement? Why this prohibition? What was the need of Geometry for his disciples? What use was he to make of it? What inference was he to draw from it when they had it?

Precisely the inference which I have mentioned;—that there was a certain and solid truth; a knowledge which was not mere opinion; science which was more than seeming: that man has powers by which such truth, such knowledge, such science, may be acquired; that therefore it ought to be sought, not in geometry alone, but in other subjects also; that since man can know, certainly and clearly, about straight and curved in the world of space, he ought to know,—he ought not to be content without knowing,—no less clearly and certainly, about right and wrong in the world of human action. That man has such powers, was the beginning of Plato's philosophy. To use them for such purposes was the constant aim of his mental activity. The impression which had been left upon his mind by the geometrical achievements of his contemporaries, and by those which he himself began, was, that the powers by which such discoveries are made are evidences of the exalted nature of the human mind; of its vast profundity; of its lofty destiny. He repeatedly, and with obvious gratification, refers to geometrical truths as evidences of the nature of the human mind, and even of its hope of immortality. Since the mind can thus reason *to certain truths*, it must have in it the principles *of truth;* and whence did it derive them? Since it can know what it has not learned from the *senses*, it must have some *other* source of knowledge; and how much is implied in this! Since it can conceive and bring forth eternal truths, how can it be the child of a day, a transient creature, born one moment and perishing the next?

Perhaps it may serve to add distinctness to the account I am trying to give you of Plato's teaching, if I give you, in his own way, an example of this teaching of his. It shall be very brief. In Plato's Dialogue, called *Meno*, Socrates, in discourse with Meno the Thessalian, is trying to discover what Virtue is: and pressing his inquiry from point to point, and finding the truth perpetually escape him, he is led to ask, at last, "What is meant by *discovering* anything? Can we do it? If so, how?" And on this, with more of direct assertion than he commonly ventures upon, he declares that we *can* do it, and that he will show how we do it. He calls up a young and intelligent boy, an attendant of Meno, and he propounds to him a geometrical problem, simple, yet not quite obvious. He draws a diagram in the sand, and asks him various questions as to the lines which serve to illustrate this problem; and the boy, though at first he says he does not know, is soon led to answer rightly to these interrogations, by his natural apprehension of the relations of space. At every step, Socrates says, "You see I tell him nothing. He goes on towards the truth, but I do not teach him. He finds it in his own mind. He does not learn from another, he recollects what he has already known. His knowledge is recollection. His science is reminiscence."

This doctrine—that knowledge is recollection, that science is reminiscence—is the main result deduced in the *Meno* from this geometrical investigation. In that Dialogue, as I have said, the doctrine is applied to illustrate the nature of the discovery of truth in general. In the *Phædo*—that Dialogue which has so deeply moved thoughtful men in every age, in which Socrates, standing before the gates of death, reasons with his weeping friends as to what he shall find beyond them—this same doctrine is employed to warm their hopes and elevate their thoughts. Since, it is argued, the soul thus contains in itself the principles of eternal truth, it must be itself eternal. But it is not with this purpose that I here refer to the use thus made of geometrical reasoning. My object is to establish this view:—that the great step in pure scientific discovery, made by the Greeks of Plato's time,—the construction of a connected and comprehensive body of geometrical truths, led to the conviction that geometry was an immensely valuable element in intellectual education. The apprehensions of such truths threw a new light upon the nature of all truth, and the means of attaining to it. It was seen that, thenceforth, they who were altogether ignorant of geometry, were destitute of the best means then known, of showing them what is the genuine aspect of essential truth,—

what is the nature of the intellectual vision by which it is seen,—what is the consciousness of intuitive power on which its foundations rest. And thus, in virtue of the geometrical discoveries of the Platonic epoch, geometry became a part of the discipline of the Platonic school;—became the starting point of the Platonic reformation of the intellectual education of Athens;—became an element of a liberal education. And not only became so then, but has continued so to this day: so that among ourselves, and in every other country of high cultivation, no education is held to be raised on good foundations which does not include geometry,—*elementary* geometry, at least,—among its component portions. And thus, in our Education, as in our Science, the completest form, in the latest time, includes and assumes the earliest steps of real progress: and this is so, in the one case as in the other, because the one must always depend on the other; because the progress of Education is affected, at every great and principal step, by the progress of Science.

You will not be surprised to be thus told that our modern education has derived something from the ancient Greek education, because you know that our modern science has derived much from the ancient Greek science. You know that our science, in the ordinary sense of the term, has derived little from the ancient Romans;—little, that is, which is original; and therefore you will not be surprised, if our education have derived little from the Roman education. If the fact were so, it would still be a negative illustration of the doctrine which I am trying to elucidate; the dependence of the progress of education on the progress of science. But if we take the term *science* in a somewhat wider acceptation, we shall derive from the Roman history, not a *negative*, but a *positive* exemplification of our proposition. For in that wider sense, there *is* a science of which Rome was the mother, as Greece was of geometry and mathematics. The term *Science* may be extended so widely, as to allow us to speak of the Science of Law—meaning the doctrine of Rights and Obligations, in its most definite and yet most comprehensive form;—in short, the Science of Jurisprudence. In this science, the Romans were really great discoverers; or rather, it was they who made the subject a science,—who gave it the precision of a science, the generality of a science, the method of a science. And how effectually they did this we may judge, from the fact that the jurisprudence of Rome is still the basis, the model, the guide, the core of the jurisprudence of every civilized country; of our own less than most, but still, in no small degree, of our own. The imitators and pupils of the Greeks in every other department of human speculation, in jurisprudence the Romans felt themselves their masters. Cicero says, proudly, but not too proudly, that a single page of a Roman jurist contained more solid and exact matter than a whole library of Greek philosophers. The labours of jurists deserving this character, which thus began before Cicero, continued through the empire, to its fall; —continued even beyond its fall. As Horace tells us that captive Greece captived the conqueror and taught him arts; so Rome subdued, subdued the victor hordes, and taught them law. The laws of Rome gave method to the codes of the northern nations, and are the origin of much that is most scientific in the more recent systems of legislation. That general law is a science, we owe to the Romans; and we in England may be reminded of this, by our inability to translate the Roman word by which this science is described: for though the term, *Jus*, is the root of *jurist*, and *jurisprudence*, and the like, it is, as yet, hardly naturalized in its technical sense, as designating the general Doctrine of Rights and Obligations; nor have we any word which has that meaning, as *Droit* has in French, and *Recht* in German.

Here is a great science, then, of which the discoverers were the Romans: can we trace, as according to our view we ought to be able to trace, any corresponding great step in intellectual discipline? Was *jus* a prominent part of Roman education? Is Roman jurisprudence a prominent part in the liberal education in modern times? To both these questions we must answer most emphatically, *Yes*. The law of Rome was the main part of the education of the Roman youth. Cicero reminds his brother Quintius, that they had learnt the old laws, and the formulæ of legal proceedings, by heart, as a sort of domestic catechism or nursery rhyme. Every Roman of eminence spent the early part of his morning in giving legal opinions to his clients:—not like our Justice of the Peace, when appealed to as a magistrate, but as an adviser and protector; and every young member of the aristocracy had to fit himself for this office. Every young Roman of condition was a Roman jurist. And the study of the law, thus made a leading branch of a liberal education, continued so through the middle ages—continues so still. It occupied the great Italian universities—Bologna, Pisa, Padua, and the like—in the darkest part of the dark ages. It occupies most of the universities of Europe to this day. The Roman law is still the main element of the liberal education of Italy, of Germany, of Greece, and, in some degree, even of France and Spain. In Germany its prevalence has been such, that in recent times all the great moral controversies have been debated in the most strenuous and searching manner *in terms* of the *Civil Law*, as the Roman law is still called all over Europe. And we shall hardly doubt, if we look into the matter, that these legal studies have given to the well-educated men of those countries a precision of thought, and an exactness of logic on moral subjects, which, without such a study, would not have been likely to prevail. To define a Right or Obligation, to use proper terms in framing a law, in delivering a judicial sentence, in giving a legal opinion, is precisely the merit of an accomplished jurist; as is emphatically asserted by Cicero. And even our own law, fragmentary and unscientific as it is, is not without a value of the same kind, as an instrument of a liberal education. It may be a means of giving exactness to the thoughts, method and clearness to the reasoning, precision to the expressions of men, on the general interests of man and of society; and is *so* recommended, and often so employed, by those who are preparing for active life. Of the moral sciences, without some study of which no education can be complete, the science of jurisprudence is most truly a science, and most effectually a means of intellectual discipline. And, as you see, the use of such discipline in education dates from the period of that great advance in speculation on moral subjects and social relations, by which jurisprudence became a science.

And thus two of the great elements of a thorough intellectual culture, Mathematics and Jurisprudence, are an inheritance which we derive from ages long gone by from two great nations—from *the* two great nations of antiquity. They are the results of ancient triumphs of man's spirit over the confusion and obscurity of the aspects of the external world; and even over the waywardness and unregulated impulses of his own nature, and the entanglements and conflicts of human society. And being true sciences, they were well fitted to become, as they became, and were fitted to continue, as they have hitherto continued, to be main elements in that discipline by which man is to raise himself above himself; is to raise—since that is especially what we have now to consider—his intellect into an habitual condition, superior to the rudeness, dimness, confusion, laxity, insecurity, to which the *undisciplined* impulses of human thought in all ages and nations commonly lead..

And before we proceed any further, let us consider, for an instant, that such an education, consisting of the elements which I have mentioned, might be, and would be, in well conducted cases, an education of no common excellence, even according to our present standard of a good intellectual education. A mind well disciplined in elementary geometry and in general jurisprudence, would be as well prepared as mere discipline can make a mind, for most trains of human speculation and reasoning. The mathematical portion of such an education would give clear habits of logical deduction, and a perception of the delight of demonstration; while the *moral* portion of the education, as we may call jurisprudence, would guard the mind from the defect, sometimes ascribed to mere mathematicians, of seeing none but mathematical proofs, and applying to all cases mathematical processes. A young man well imbued with these, the leading elements of Athenian and Roman culture, would, we need not fear to say, be superior in intellectual discipline to three-fourths of the young men of our own day, on whom all the ordinary appliances of what is called *a good education* have been bestowed. Geometer and jurist, the pupil formed by this culture of the old world might make no bad figure among the men of letters or of science, the lawyers and the politicians, of our own times.

But there is another remark which I must make, tending to show the *defect* of this education of antiquity, as compared with the intellectual education of our own times; or rather, as compared with what the education of our own times ought to be. The subjects which I have mentioned, geometry and jurisprudence, are both *deductive* sciences;—sciences in which, from certain first principles, by chains of proof, conclusions are deduced which constitute the doctrines of the science. In the one case, geometry, these first principles are given by intuition; in the other, jurisprudence, they are either rules instituted by authority and consent, or general principles of human nature and human society, obtained from experience interpreted by our own human consciousness. We deduce properties of diagrams from geometrical axioms; we deduce decisions of cases from legal maxims. Jurisprudence, no less than geometry, is a deductive science; and has been compared with geometry, by its admirers, for the exactness of its deductive processes. They have said (Leibnitz and others) that jural demonstrations are as fine examples of logic as mathematical; and that pure reason alone determines every expression of a good jurist, no less than of a good mathematician; so that there is no room for that play of individual character, which shows itself in the difference of style of different authors. But however perfectly the habits of *deduction* may be taught by these studies, such teaching cannot, according to the enlarged views of modern times, compose a complete intellectual culture. Induction, rather than deduction, is the source of the great scientific truths which form the glory, and fasten on them the admiration of modern times; and a modern education cannot be regarded as giving to the intellect that culture, which the fulness of time, and the treasures of knowledge now accumulated, render suitable and necessary, except it convey to the mind an adequate appreciation of and familiarity with the *inductive* process, by which those treasures of knowledge have been obtained. As the best sciences which the ancient world framed supplied the best elements of intellectual education up to modern times; so the grand step by which, in modern times, science has sprung up into a magnitude and majesty far superior to her ancient dimensions, should exercise its influence upon modern education, and contribute its proper result to modern intellectual culture.

Who is to be taken as the representative of the great epoch of the progress of science in modern times; that is, beginning from the sixteenth century? In different ways, Galileo, Descartes, Bacon, Newton, may seem best suited to occupy that position. But Galileo's immediate influence was limited, both as to subjects and as to the number of admirers. It was when Descartes summed up into a *system* the discoveries of Galileo and his disciples, and added to them inventions of his own, some true, many captivating, that the new physical philosophy acquired a large and vigorous hold upon Europe north of the Alps. In France especially, always eager in its admiration of intellectual greatness, Descartes was unhesitatingly regarded as the great man who brought in a new and more enlightened age of philosophy. Indeed, for a large portion of philosophy, he is still so regarded by French philosophers; and though his influence in metaphysics is to be distinguished from his authority in physics, still the ascendancy of his more abstract and general philosophical opinions was closely connected with his recognised eminence as a physical philosopher, and with the admiration which his system of the universe obtained. The Cartesian philosophy was the proclaimed and acknowledged antagonist of the Aristotelian philosophy; it was the new truth of which the standard was raised against the old falsehood. Any one acquainted with the French literature of the seventeenth century will recollect innumerable illustrations of this view of the matter. You remember, perhaps (as an example), the noted passage in Fontenelle's lively dialogues on *The Plurality of Worlds.* There, the sages of antiquity, the Pythagorases, Platos, Aristotles, are represented as looking at the spectacle of the universe, like so many spectators in the pit of the Opera House looking at the ballet. The subject of the ballet is supposed to be, Phaëton carried away by the winds: and to represent this, the dancer who enacts the part of Phaëton, is made to fly away through the upper part of the scene, to the great admiration of the gazers. The more speculative of these attempt to explain this extraordinary movement of Phaëton. One says, "Phaëton has an *occult quality,* which carries him away." This is the Aristotelian. Another says, "Phaëton is composed of certain *numbers,* which make him move upwards." This is the Pythagorean. Another says, "Phaëton has a longing for the top of the theatre. He is not easy till he gets there." This is the philosophy which explains the universe by Love and Hate. Another says, "Phaëton has not naturally a tendency to fly; but he prefers flying to leaving the top of the scene empty." This is the doctrine of the *fuga vacui*, nature's horror of a vacuum. And after all this, says the speaker, comes Descartes, and some other moderns; and they say, Phaëton goes up, because he is drawn by certain cords, and a weight, heavier than he is, goes down behind the scenes. And in truth, the physical philosophy of Descartes did contain the greater part of the true explanation of the phenomena of the universe, which was known up to this time. It contained the principles of Mechanics, with few errors; the principles of Optics, and the beautiful explanation of the rainbow, in the discovery of which Descartes had so large a share; and a true system of Astronomy, so far as the mere motions are concerned. And Descartes' peculiar invention, the hypothesis of *tourbillons*,—vortices or whirlpools of celestial fluid, by which these motions are produced,—though false, was not only separable from the other parts of the system, but was capable, by modifications, of expressing many mechanical truths, as the Bernoullis, and other mathematicians who retained it for a century, often showed. In England, as in France, the Cartesian philosophy meant the Mechanical Philosophy, as opposed to the philosophy of sympathies and antipathies, occult qualities, arbitrary notions of Nature, and the like. The Cartesian philosophy, in this sense, was introduced into England; but I doubt whether the doctrine of vortices was ever accepted here to any considerable extent. It has been made, I may be allowed to say, ignorantly and absurdly made, an accusation against the University of Cambridge, that the Cartesian system found acceptance there. Such an event showed a promptitude in accepting new scientific views, which has repeatedly been exemplified there. But I much doubt whether the Cartesian system was *ever* presented to Cambridge students, without a refutation of the vortices being put in the notes on the same page. Assuredly it was not taught for more than a few years in any other form; but I believe, not at all. And in like manner in other places, the new mechanical philosophy, Cartesian in France, Newtonian in England, rapidly superseded the verbal dogmatism of the middle ages.

And with this triumph of the new opinions, as a revolution in science, came the introduction of the new doctrines as a revolution, or extension, in education. The Cartesian philosophy,—instantly, in England transformed into the Newtonian philosophy, on the publication of Newton's mighty discoveries,—was eagerly received, from its very first appearance, and incorporated with the elements of a liberal education, both in Newton's own university, and elsewhere. And not only were the new theories of the solar system rapidly diffused, by means of lectures, books, and in other ways; but the principles by which such theories are collected from observation,—the principles of that induction on which this great fabric of science rests,—became objects of attention, respect, and praise. Bacon, with his majestic voice,—the trumpeter who stirred up the battle, as he himself calls himself,—had already prepared men's minds for this feeling of respect and admiration for inductive discovery, even while the movement was only beginning: and in this country at least, many persons, Gilbert, Cowley, and others, had re-echoed the sentiment which he expressed. He had declared that knowledge, far more ample and complete than had yet been obtained by man, was to be gained by the use of new methods of investigation; and the succeeding time, having produced noble examples of such knowledge, had made men see that they had entered upon a new epoch of science. And it was natural and desirable that in this, as in other cases, the possession of a body of new truths, and the admiration of the method by which these had been acquired, should operate upon the culture of the intellect, among those who sought the best means of such culture; should introduce new elements into liberal education;—should make it a part of the mental discipline of the best-taught classes, that they should learn to feel the force and see the beauty of *inductive* reasoning; as the older elements of a liberal education, mathematics and jurisprudence, had been employed, among other uses, to make men feel the force, and see the beauty, of deductive reasoning.

And thus we are naturally led to ask, Has this been done? Has education in its most advanced form been thus extended? Is there, in the habitual culture of the intellect, in the best system of education, this cultivation of the habit, or at least of the appreciation, of inductive teaching in science? How is such culture to be effected? How are we to judge whether it has been affected?

These are very large questions, and yet the time admonishes me, if nothing else did, that I must be very brief in any answers that I may give to them. I must content myself with a hint or two bearing upon the subject. And first, of the mode in which this culture of the inductive habit of mind, or at least appreciation of the method and its results, is to be promoted; if I might presume to give an opinion, I should say that one obvious mode of effecting this discipline of the mind in induction is, the exact and solid study of some portion of inductive knowledge. I do not mean the mechanical sciences alone, Physical Astronomy and the like; though these undoubtedly have a prerogative value as the instruments of such a culture; but the like effect will be promoted by the exact and solid study of any portion of the circle of natural sciences; Botany, Comparative Anatomy, Geology, Chemistry, for instance. But I say, the *exact* and *solid* knowledge; not a mere verbal knowledge, but a knowledge which is real in its character, though it may be elementary and limited in its extent. The knowledge of which I speak must be a knowledge of things, and not merely of names of things; an acquaintance with the operations and productions of nature, as they appear to the eye, not merely an acquaintance with what has been said about them; a knowledge of the laws of nature, seen in special experiments and observations, before they are conceived in general terms; a knowledge of the types of natural forms, gathered from individual cases already made familiar. By such study of one or more departments of inductive knowledge, the mind may escape from the thraldom and illusion which reigns in the world of mere words.

But there is another study which I may venture to mention, of a more general and literary kind, also eminently fitted to promote an appreciation of the nature and value of inductive treatment of nature. I mean, the History of the Natural Sciences; for in such history we see how, in the study of every portion of the universe, the human mind has ascended from particular facts to general laws; and yet in every different class of phenomena, by processes very *different*, at first sight at least.

And I mention this study, of the history of science, and especially recommend it, the rather, because it supplies, as I conceive, a remedy for some of the evils which, along with great advantages, may result from *another* study which has long been, and at present is, extensively employed as an element of a liberal education—I mean, the study of *Logic.* The study of Logic is of great value, as fixing attention upon the conditions of deductive proof, and giving a systematic and technical view of the forms which such proof may assume. But by doing this for all subjects alike, it produces the impression that there is a close likeness in the process of investigation of truth in different subjects;—closer than there really is. The examples of reasoning given in books of Logic are generally so trifling as to seem a mockery of truth-seeking, and so monotonous as to seem idle variations of the same theme. But in the History of Science, we see the infinite variety of nature; of mental, no less than bodily nature; of the intellectual as well as of the sensible world. The modes of generalization of particulars,—of ascent from the most actual things to the most abstract ideas,—how different are they in botany, in chemistry, in geology, in physiology! Yet all most true and real; all most certain and solid; all of them genuine and indisputable lines of union and connexion, by which the mind of man and the facts of the universe are bound together; by which the universe becomes a sphere with intellect for its centre; by which intellect becomes in no small degree able to bend to its purposes the powers of the universe.

The history of science, showing us how this takes place in various forms,—ever and ever new, when they seem to have been exhausted,—*may* do, and carefully studied, *must* do, much to promote that due apprehension and appreciation of inductive discovery: and inductive discovery, now that the process has been going on with immense vigour in the nations of Europe for the last three hundred years, ought, we venture to say, to form a distinct and prominent part of the intellectual education of the youth of those nations. And having said this, I have given you the ultimate result of the reflections which have occurred to me on this subject of intellectual education, on which I have ventured to address you. And here, therefore, I might conclude. But if it did not weary you, I should wish to make a remark on the other of the two questions which I asked a little while ago. I then asked, How is such a culture to be effected? and also, How are we to judge whether it has been effected?

With regard to the latter question, the remark which I have to make is briefly this.—In the inductive sciences, every step of generalization is usually marked by some *word*, which, adopted to mark that step, acquires thenceforth a fixed and definite meaning; and is always to be used in the sense so given it, not in any other way in which other resemblances or incidents may suggest. And the definition of *technical words* in inductive science, is contained in the history of the science; is given by the course of previous research and discovery. "The history of science is our dictionary; the steps of scientific induction are our definitions." Now this being so, we may remark, that when we hear a man, in the course of an argument, asking for Definitions, as something by which error is to be avoided and truth learned, such a demand is evidence that his intellectual training has been deductive, not inductive—logical, not scientific.

In geometry, and in other demonstrative sciences, Definitions are the beginning of the science—the fountains of truth. But it is not so in the inductive sciences. In such sciences, a Definition and a Proposition commonly enter side by side—the definition giving exactness to the proposition; the proposition giving reality to the definition.

But further: as technical terms, appropriate to a precise and steady sense, mark every step of inductive ascent in science, the exact and correct use of the technical terms of science is evidence of good inductive culture of the mind; and a vague and improper use of such terms, is evidence of the absence of such culture. When we hear men speak, as we often do, of *impetus* and *momentum*, of *gravity* and *inertia*, of *centripetal* and *centrifugal force*, and the like, using the terms mostly by guess, and assuming oppositions and relations among them which do not exist; as, for instance, when they oppose the centrifugal and centripetal force, as if they were *forces* in the same sense,—we cannot help saying that such persons, however ingenious and quick they may be in picking a possible meaning out of current words, by means of their etymology, or any other casual light, have not the habit of gathering the meaning of scientific words from the only true light, the light of induction.

And this remark may not be without a special use, if we recollect that there are at present a number of scientific words current among us, which are applied with the most fantastical and wanton vagueness of meaning, or of no meaning. At all periods of science, probably, scientific terms are liable to this abuse, after scientific discoveries have brought them into notoriety, and before the diffusion of science has made their true meaning to be generally apprehended. The names, indeed, of *attraction, gravitation,* and the like, have probably now risen, in a great degree, out of this sphere of confusion and obscurity, in which any word may mean anything. But there are words—belonging to sciences which have more recently reached scientific dignity—which words every one pursuing fancies which are utterly out of the sphere of science, seems to think he may use just as he pleases. *Magnetism* and *Electricity*, and the terms which belong to these sciences, are especially taken possession of for such purposes, and applied in cases in which we know that the sciences from which the names are "*conveyed*" have not the smallest application. Is Animal Magnetism anything? Let those answer who think they can: but *we* know that it is not *Magnetism.* When I say *we*, I mean those who are in the habit of seeing in this place the admirable exhibitions of what Magnetism is, with which you have long been familiar. And assuredly, on the same ground, I may say that you have been shown, and know, what Electricity is, and what it can do, and what it cannot do, and what is not Electricity. And having had the opportunity of seeing this, you, at least, have so much of the culture of the intellect which inductive science supplies, as not to suppose that your words would have any meaning, if you were to say of any freak of fancy or will, shown in bodily motion or muscular action, that it is *a kind of Electricity.*

ON THE IMPORTANCE OF THE STUDY OF ECONOMIC SCIENCE.

A LECTURE DELIVERED AT THE ROYAL INSTITUTION OF GREAT BRITAIN.

BY

W. B. HODGSON, LL.D.

"Ignorance does not simply deprive us of advantages; it leads us to work our own misery; it is not merely a vacuum, void of knowledge, but a *plenum* of positive errors, continually productive of unhappiness. This remark was never more apposite than in the case of Political Economy."—Samuel Bailey's *Discourses*, &c. p. 121. 1852.

"If a man begins to forget that he is a social being, a member of a body, and that the only truths which can avail him anything, the only truths which are worthy objects of his philosophical search, are those which are equally true for every man, which will equally avail every man, which he must proclaim, as far as he can, to every man, from the proudest sage to the meanest outcast, he enters, I believe, into a lie, and helps forward the dissolution of that society of which he is a member."—Rev. C. Kingsley's *Alexandria and her Schools*. L. ii. p. 66. 1854.

"A man will never be just to others who is not just to himself, and the first requisite of that justice is, that he should look every obligation, every engagement, every duty in the face. This applies as much to money as to more serious affairs, and as much to nations as to men."—*Times*, June 6, 1854.

ON THE
STUDY OF ECONOMIC SCIENCE.

It was truly said in this room, some weeks ago, by one whose departure from London we must all regret —Professor Edward Forbes—that "*It is the nature of the human mind to desire and seek a law.*" The higher desires of man have not been left, any more than his lower, without their object and their fulfilment; and just as the bodily appetite desires food, while the earth yields stores of nourishment,—as the imagination craves for beauty, and beauty is on every side,—so, responding to man's desire for law, does all Nature bear the impress of law. Not to the ignorant or careless eye, however, does LAW anywhere reveal itself. The discovery of its traces is the student's rich and ever fresh reward. To men in general, the outward sense reports only a number of detached phenomena; their relations become gradually apparent to him only whose mental vision is acute enough, and whose gaze is steady enough, to behold them. SCIENCE, therefore, consists not in the accumulation of heterogeneous facts, any more than the random up-piling of stones is architecture, but in the detection of the principles which co-relate facts even the most dissimilar and anomalous, and of the order which binds the parts into a whole. SCIENCE is, in brief, the pursuit of LAW; and the history of science is the record of the steps by which man in this pursuit rises through classifications, of which the last is ever more comprehensive than its predecessors, from the complexity of countless individuals to the simplicity of the group, and from the diversity of the many, at least towards the oneness of the universal.

The discoveries, however, which it needed a Newton or a Cuvier to make, may be rendered intelligible in their results, if not always in their processes, to ordinary understandings; and whether our knowledge be superficial or profound, the belief in the omnipresence of law, in at least the physical world, has long ago taken its place in the convictions of the least instructed man. Let any one, then, who can realize mentally the difference between the aspect which the starry heavens bear to the quite ignorant beholder, and that which those same heavens present to the man most slightly acquainted with the discoveries of astronomy, or between the appearances of the vegetable world before and after some acquaintance with Vegetable Physiology, but who has never thoughtfully considered the phenomena of industrial life,—let such a one station himself, say on London Bridge, at high tide, and in the busy hour of day; let him watch the ever-flowing streams of human beings, each bound on his several errand,—the seemingly endless succession of vehicles, with their freight, animate and inanimate; let him look down the river, and observe the number and variety of shipping, coming and departing from and to all parts of the world, remote or near; let him observe, as he strolls onwards, the shops, and warehouses, and wharfs, and arsenals, and docks, with their overflowing stores; the almost interminable lines of streets with houses of every size and kind, each tenanted by its respective occupants; the railway stations from which and to which go and come, hourly, thousands of human beings, and the produce of the industry of millions of human beings; the electric telegraph, transmitting from town to town—nay, from land to land—the outward symbols of thought, with almost the proverbial speed of the inward thought itself; let him consider, that within the range of a few miles of ground that produces, *directly*, none of the necessaries of life, are gathered together more than 2,000,000 of men, women, and children, at the rate, in some parts, of 186,000 to the square mile; let him ponder how it is that all these people are daily fed, and clothed, and lodged,—how it is that all these things have been produced and are maintained; let him further consider that this stupendous spectacle is but a sample of what is going on, with great varieties, in so many other regions of the world; that people, separated by thousands of miles of land and sea, who never saw each other, who, it may be, scarcely know of each other's existence, are busily providing for each other's wants, and each procuring his own sustenance by ministering to others' necessities or desires; and then let him, without at all losing sight of the too obvious evil mixed up with all this, seriously ask himself, Is this vast field of contemplation the theatre also of LAW, which binds the several parts together; or is it a mere giddy and fortuitous dance of discordant and jostling atoms,—in a word, a huge weltering chaos, waiting the fiat of some Monsieur Cabet or Babœuf to reduce it to order, and convert it into a cosmos, by persuading or compelling the several atoms to adopt some cunningly devised principle of so-called "organization of labour?" To this question Economic Science professes, at least, to supply the answer; and if *science* be the pursuit of law, and deserve the title in proportion to its success in that pursuit, the claims of Economic Science must be tested by the nature of the reply it gives.

It may occur to some who hear me, that the term LAW is not applicable in the same sense or way to the various classes of phenomena which I have casually indicated. In the first,—the region of astronomy,—LAW suggests the idea of some mighty force which irresistibly compels motions on the grandest scale; in the second,—the vegetable world,—it suggests rather a mere principle of arrangement, according to which certain unresisting bodies are distributed; while in the third,—the Economic World of Man,—a vast difference appears between it and the other two, inasmuch as we have here a multitude of independent intelligences and wills, acting consciously and voluntarily from within, in every variety of direction, and often in seeming opposition to each other. This difficulty merits a consideration, serious if brief. Between the first and second the difference is not real, but only apparent. The growth of a plant is as wonderful,—as grand an exercise of power, as the revolution of a planet; and gravitation, as we call it, no more than growth, is in itself a power; both are alike expressions and results of that WILL which is in the universe the only real power—the only true cause. Our very word *order* has a double sense—*arrangement* and *command;* so natural is it for us to identify the one with the other, and to believe that arrangement or system exists only by command or LAW. And, in truth, throughout all things, however diverse the special phenomena, whether it be the sweep of a comet, or the budding of a flower, we can recognise still only a principle or method of arrangement as the result of WILL; and it is because these are so closely and invariably connected in our minds, that we are so apt to use the word LAW sometimes for the one, and sometimes for the other, personifying Law, just as we do Providence in ordinary speech.

The real difficulty, however, lies in the third case, that is, the subject immediately before us. Having seen the *primâ facie* and analogical improbability of the notion that the economic world is *lawless*, the question arises —In what way does LAW operate amid so many seemingly independent and conflicting individualities? I have no desire, and there is happily no need, for long or subtle disquisition. I would merely submit a consideration in itself quite simple, but fraught, if I mistake not, with the most important practical results. In the purely inorganic world, law operates irresistibly, and command and obedience are strictly coincident, co-extensive, and identical. In the motions of the heavenly bodies, for example, there is no *eccentricity* in the popular sense of the term; even the orbit of a comet, between whose successive re-appearances many decades of years and whole generations of men pass away, is absolutely known—eclipses with the longest intervals are certainly foretold. The same fact holds in the organized but inanimate world, as in the world both inanimate and unorganized. As we ascend in the scale, and enter on the animate creation, we find a like fixity and uniformity provided for *to a very large extent* by that most marvellous faculty—*Instinct*, which guides almost infallibly the lower orders of animals, which maintains an almost precise sameness among the most distant generations and conducts all surely and unconsciously to the end of their being. But MAN is a being vastly more complex in his nature; he, too, has instincts, but these form a much smaller proportion of his whole faculty; with all that the lower orders of being have, he has much more besides—moral faculties, reason, and will, both the latter differing vastly in degree, if not in kind, from those of any other creature. The part which he has to play in creation is proportionally complex; and here it is that perplexity, and discord, and confusion begin to appear, or at least chiefly manifest themselves. It is this surface confusion which hides from us the central and pervading LAW, and makes it difficult to trace its operation. The laws or conditions, however, which determine human well-being, are really as fixed and absolute as are the laws of planetary motion; but man, though so constituted as to desire and seek his well-being, has not an infallible perception of that in which it consists, or of the means by which this end is to be attained. We find, throughout, this distinction between man and the lower animals. Thus other animals are gifted by nature with the clothing suitable to their condition, and it even varies in colour and thickness according to the seasons. Man alone has with effort to construct what clothing he requires; so, more or less, is it with food; so is it with shelter. Is this an inferiority on the part of man? Surely not; for it is by this very discipline that his higher faculties are called into play, and enlarged, and strengthened. What appears a penalty is, in reality, a blessing. Nature's very provision for the comfort of bird or beast seems, at the same time, the sentence of incapacity for improvement. Man, however (I speak now of the individual), is progressive, being capable of improvement; and he is stimulated to improvement because his wants are not supplied for him, but he is compelled to supply them for himself, and his desires ever grow with the means of their gratification. The whole universe is thus, in truth, a great educational organization—a great school,—for the calling out and the direction, of what powers are in man latent. But his progress is not a smooth advance from good to better; his way lies through evils of many kinds—evils attendant inseparably on defective knowledge, and ill-regulated desires. LAW, which in the physical universe operates UNI-*formly*, here operates, so to speak, BI-*formly*: the law wears, Janus-like, two faces; but it is one law nevertheless. It assumes, however, a twofold sanction, reward for obedience, punishment for disobedience, each being but the complement and corollary of the other. Thus the pallid face and irritable nerves of the sedentary student, the ruddy cheek and iron muscles of the ploughman,—the trembling hand and blood-shot eyes of the drunkard, the steady pulse and clear open countenance of the temperate man,—are the results not of two antagonistic laws, but of one law, vindicating its majestic universality in the one case not less than in the other. So is it with the stagnant and pestilential swamp as contrasted with the cultivated plain; the ruined village with the thriving town; the land of inhabitants few but poor, with the land of inhabitants many and rich. It is this difference, accordingly, which in the human sphere translates LAW into DUTY, and the MUST of the Physical World into the OUGHT of the Moral. Wordsworth, the most philosophical of poets, has not failed to detect their kinship, however, when, in his noble "Ode to Duty," he says:—

> "Flowers laugh before thee on their beds,
> And fragrance in thy footing treads :
> Thou dost preserve the stars from wrong,
> And the most ancient heavens through Thee are fresh and strong."

Good, then, being the great end of all the established conditions of our life, evil is, and must ever be, the result of their violation. As Paley has said that no nerve has ever been discovered whose function lies in the giving of pain, so, in all things, pain or evil follows the breach, not the observance, of a law. But this very pain or evil is not in its end vindictive, or simply punitive; its aim is reformation for the future, not merely punishment for the past. The child burns its finger in the candle flame, cuts its hand with a knife, makes a false step and falls, and profits all its life through by the lessons it has gained. And so the exhaustion of mind or body from over-exertion, the headache from intemperance, are Nature's solemn warnings, tending powerfully to prevent future transgression. Man's successes and his failures are both, in different ways, instructive; both help him in his career.

But Man is progressive not only as an individual, but as a race. Here, still more, is his superiority to all other animals apparent. He is, in some measure, the heir of the discoveries, the inventions, the thoughts, and the labours, of all foregoing time; and each man has, in some measure, for his helper, the results of the accumulated knowledge of the world. But the transmission of experience and knowledge from generation to generation is the fundamental condition of progress throughout the successive ages of the life of mankind. To a large extent, of course, we cannot but profit from the labour of our predecessors; all those products, and instruments, and agencies, which we style "civilization," our roads, our railways, our canals, our courts of law, our houses of legislature, and a thousand other embodiments of the combined and successive efforts of many generations, are our inheritance by birth; but the very guidance and employment of these for their improvement, or even for their maintenance, require ever increased knowledge and intelligence. The higher the civilization that a community has attained, the more, not the less, necessary is it that its members, as one race succeeds another, should be enlightened and informed. No inheritance of industrial progress can dispense with individual intelligence and judgment, any more than the accumulation of books can save from the need of learning to read and write. But thousands of human beings, born ignorant, are left to repeat unguided the same experiments, and to incur the same failures and penalties as their parents,—as their ancestors. Where these stumbled, or slipped, and fell, they too stumble, or slip, and fall, rising again perhaps, but not uninjured by the fall. Nature teaches, it is true, by penalty as well as by reward; but it is surely wise, as far as may be, to anticipate in each case this rough teaching, to aid it by rational explanation, and to confine it within safe bounds. The world, doubtless, advances, in spite of all. That industrial progress is what it is, proves that the amount of observance of law is, on the whole, largely in excess of its violation; were it otherwise, society would retrograde, and humanity would perish. This predominance of good results from the very constitution of human nature and of the world, by which the individual, working even unconsciously and for his own ends, and learning even by failure, achieves a good wider than that he contemplates, and by which progress, in spite of delay and fluctuation, is maintained alike in the individual and the race. But how shall the evil which yet mars and deforms our civilization be abated, if not removed, while progress is made more rapid, and sure, and equable? Both depend alike on increased observance of law; and it is by diffusing knowledge of its existence and operation that observance of law is rendered more general and less precarious. If, then, we would convert not only disobedience into obedience, but obedience blind, unconscious, and precarious, into obedience conscious, intelligent, and habitual, we must teach all to understand the nature of the laws on which the universal wellbeing depends, and train all in those habits which facilitate and secure the observance of those laws.

Assuming, then, that in the industrial or economic sphere the laws of human wellbeing are as fixed as in any other, and that what measure of wellbeing we anywhere behold is the result of obedience, conscious or unconscious, to those laws, we ought next to inquire what those LAWS are. As a preliminary, let us take a hasty survey of the steps by which any people ascends from barbarism to civilization, from destitution to comfort, from poverty to wealth. From the review alike of good and of evil, we shall be able to extract the principles which run throughout, and which both good and evil concur to attest. In barbarous countries we find men scattered in small numbers over a wide extent of territory, living by hunting or fishing, or both combined; every man supplies his own wants directly; he makes his own bow and arrows; he kills a buffalo for himself; with hides stripped and dressed by himself, he constructs his own robe or tent; he lives from hand to mouth, feasting voraciously to-day, then starving till another supply of food can be obtained; ever on the verge of famine, and eking out a precarious subsistence by robbery and murder, which he calls war. All but the strong perish in early years, and the average duration of life is low. If we contemplate the pastoral life instead of that of hunting and fishing, still we find that large tracts of country are needed for the maintenance of few people. If the earth be at all cultivated, it is with the rudest implements, and the produce is proportionally scanty. So long as each man is entirely occupied in providing for his own wants, progress is impossible. So soon, however, as by the gradual and slow introduction of better implements, and the acquirement of greater skill, agriculture becomes more productive, and the labour of one man becomes sufficient for the support of more than one, of some, of many; the first condition of progress is realized, and the labour of some or many is now set free for other occupations. Food and clothing, fuel and shelter, are the first necessaries of life. But instead of every man preparing all these for himself directly, instead of every man making for himself all that he requires, gradually one man begins to construct one article, or set of articles only, while another devotes himself to another, with a consequent great increase of productiveness in each case, from increased skill and economy of time; in other words, the *division of labour* is begun. But so soon as the industry of the community is thus divided, and that of each thus restricted, as each still requires all the articles which before he constructed for himself, he can obtain them only from those who employ themselves in their production; and this he can do only by giving some of his own product as an equivalent, in other words, by *exchange*. This transaction gives meaning to the term *value*, which denotes simply the amount of commodities that can be procured in exchange for any other commodity. Division of labour and exchange are thus simultaneous in their origin. From the introduction of exchange, industrial progress gains a fresh life. Industry having been thus rendered more productive than before, subsistence is now provided for a larger number of persons than before. The reward of industry increasing with its productiveness, ingenuity is stimulated to the invention of improved methods, and of improved instruments called *tools*, or, as they become more complicated and powerful, *machines*, though a machine is in principle only a tool; and the very argument which is good, if good at all, against a steam-plough, is good against the common plough, or a hoe, or a spade, or a stake hardened in the fire.

Population having meantime increased, the land available for production becomes more and more fully appropriated; and as one portion is more fertile, or more advantageously situated than another, it becomes more advantageous to pay a portion of the produce for the right to cultivate a more productive soil, than to cultivate an inferior soil even for nothing; *e.g.* to pay ten measures of grain for a soil which produces fifty measures, than nothing for a soil which produces, say thirty or thirty-five; and hence arises what we call *rent*. But, meantime also, the productiveness of industry having become ever greater in proportion to the consumption of its produce, the process of accumulation goes on, and the unconsumed results of previous labour, which, however various their kinds, we term WEALTH, swell to larger proportions. But this wealth is not equally possessed by all; one man, from superior skill, or intelligence, or economy, or other causes, coming to possess more than others, while some, it may be, possess none at all. Mere labour, however, without the results of foregone labour, embodied in some form, can accomplish little; while the results of foregone labour, in whatever form embodied, need fresh labour in order to become still more productive. Thus, *e.g.* a spade is a result of past labour; without it the labourer could accomplish little; and, on the other hand, the spade, without the labourer to wield it, would be unproductive. Now, the spade here represents that portion of wealth which is devoted to further production, and which is called CAPITAL. Capital and labour are thus indispensable to each other. They may exist in different hands, or in the same; but they must co-exist, and co-operate. Thus—if we suppose them to be in different hands—the owner of the spade, whom we may call the *capitalist*, may undertake to give the *labourer* a fixed compensation for his labour aided by the spade (an amount which will more or less exceed, and can in no case fall below, what the labourer without the spade can earn), reserving for himself any surplus that may arise after that labour is paid. In this case, the labourer's reward is called WAGES; the capitalist's reward is called PROFIT. Or the *capitalist* may lend the spade to the *labourer* for a fixed return (which will be somewhat less than, and which cannot exceed, the difference in the labourer's productiveness, caused by the spade), the labourer claiming as his own all that he can realize over and above what he pays. In this case, the labourer's return, whatever it may be called, is partly wages and partly profit, while the capitalist's return is termed *interest*, or much better, *usance,* an obsolete English word, for it is really what is paid for the *use* of capital in any form. If the capital and labour be in the same hands, *e.g.* if the labourer own the spade he uses, the joint return ever consists of the two items here discriminated.

As industry extends and wealth increases, it is early found necessary to provide for the security of property; for the suppression of violence and fraud; and for the settlement of disputes that will here and there arise, even without evil intention on either side. Hence all the machinery of courts of justice, and of government, from its highest to its lowest functionary. As these, though not in themselves directly producers, are indispensable to production, and exist for the welfare of all, they must be maintained at the expense of all; hence comes TAXATION of various kinds, which it is the business of the legislature to impose justly, and in the way least likely to fetter industry, and prevent increase of wealth.

So far as we have hitherto seen, exchanges have as yet been effected by direct giving and taking of commodity for commodity, or, as it is termed, *barter;* but great and serious difficulties attend this system, difficulties ever more deeply felt as exchanges multiply, and become more various; the baker may not want the shoemaker's shoes, if the latter want his bread; but the latter may not want as much bread as equals the value of a pair of shoes; and payment by a half or a third of a pair of shoes is impossible. A medium of exchange, accordingly, is introduced; usually the *precious* metals, as they are called, the very word implying one of their fitnesses for the task—viz., that in a small bulk they contain great value. The non-liability to decay; capability of division without loss; comparative exemption from fluctuations of supply; and facility of recognition, are among their other claims. Exchange, thus facilitated by the adoption of a medium which all are ready to receive, and by which most minute proportions of value may be easily represented, proceeds with vastly increased rapidity; and value being thus measured habitually in money, we have the new element of PRICE. Though money in itself is but a very small portion of the capital, and still less of the total wealth, of a nation, it so habitually represents every kind of capital and wealth, that it conveniently becomes a synonyme for both, not, however, without some risk of mental confusion and error as the result.

Exchanges becoming thus continually more frequent and complicated, it is found convenient and advantageous, on the principle of the division of labour, that a class of men should devote themselves to conduct the business of exchange solely, the work of production being left to others. By the introduction of *merchants*, who do not themselves produce, a greater amount of production is attained, on the whole, than would be possible if all both produced and exchanged without their intervention.

But, for facility and frequency of exchange, even at home, rapidity, and ease, and safety of communication, are indispensable; good roads, swift conveyances, canals, and ultimately railways arise, with their adjuncts of carriers and couriers, and post-establishments, and telegraphs of ever greater ingenuity and efficiency.

Exchange, which was at first confined within the limits of one country, soon extends to other countries, with an immense advantage to all, for all are thus made partakers in the productions of each, which are more and more diverse according to their diversity of climate. Foreign commerce, with all that it involves of ships, and docks, and warehouses, is the most powerful stimulus to home industry. But exchange, whether at home or abroad, is, in all cases, when analyzed, simply each man's giving something that he wants less, for something else that he wants more.

As geographical knowledge and means of transit are increased, numbers pass from one country to another; from countries densely to those less densely peopled; from countries where land is all appropriated, to those where it is still unclaimed; from countries where capital and labour are comparatively unproductive, to those where both are more amply rewarded; new fields being thus perpetually opened up for human industry, and increased enjoyment provided by fresh and ever augmented interchange, both for those who go and for those who stay.

But long ere this, as yet the highest, stage of progress has been reached, the precious metals themselves have been found incompetent to discharge the full duty of exchange; and paper money, or duly vouched promises to pay money, is introduced, with an ever more complicated machinery of bank-notes and bills of exchange, for the management of which class of transactions a still further division of labour is introduced by means of bankers, bill-brokers, and the other agents by whom what we call comprehensively CREDIT is carried on.

But life and property are subject to contingencies which involve serious loss, and which it is impossible always to prevent. It is discovered that the evil results to individuals, which would be ruinous to one, may, by combination, be distributed over many. Hence insurances against fire, against death, against disaster at sea, against hail-storms and diseases among cattle, against railway accidents, and even against fraud on the part of clerks or other assistants, all of which are based on calculation of averages, this again being based on the conviction that a certain regularity prevails among events even the most anomalous and irregular.

And thus, step by step, by a strictly natural course, does the work of industrial progress go on, till we witness its gigantic results in our own time and our own land—results of which the great Crystal Palace (the opening of which was not inaptly coincident with the day fixed for this exposition of the principles whose triumph it exemplifies) may be justly regarded as the crowning and most various illustration—raised, as it has been, by voluntary combination, on strictly economic grounds, and embracing within itself, in one vast space, examples of the productions of the labour, the ingenuity, the fancy, the skill, the science of all ages and of every land.

In this inevitably brief and incomplete sketch of the industrial progress of the world, not only has much been omitted, but it is to be observed that the steps do not always follow each other in precisely the same order, and that much that is here recorded, perforce, successively, takes place simultaneously. It is not possible here or now to extract from even this most hasty sketch the merely *theoretic* principles which it involves. This is the business of a long course of lectures, and it is not, besides, my purpose to expound Economic Science itself, any further than may be indispensable to show its importance as a branch of general instruction. Let us rather look at some of the great *practical* lessons that may be deduced from it for the guidance of individual conduct.

Everything, then, that we or others possess, is more or less the result of human, that is, of individual, industry. It is observable that not where Nature itself is most prolific is human labour the most productive; so true is it that necessity is the mother of invention and of industry as well. Truly has Rousseau remarked, "In the south, men consume little" (he might have said *produce* little) "on a grateful soil; in the north, men consume much," (and of course *produce* much) "on a soil ungrateful." * Where man has most done for him, he often does least for himself; and though his labours must be seconded by the productiveness of Nature, the latter is really more dependent on the former than the former on the latter. Now this law holds true of the future as well as of the present or the past. Every human being must subsist on the produce of his own industry, or on that of some one else. *Industry*, then, is the first duty of him who would be honourably independent.

But it is not by present labour, any more than by future, that any man is really sustained. While the crop is growing, for example, the labourer is fed by the grain of former harvests. Now, if the produce of labour were consumed as fast as it is produced, not only would progress be impossible, but life itself would be endangered, and would ere long cease. Hence the duty of what is called, in its narrower sense, *economy*, or the frugal and prudent consumption of what has been produced. Disasters, too, will arise, which no human wisdom can prevent, but against whose consequences it may provide.

* Emile. Liv. I.

The very progress of industry involves *displacement* of labour, though it is not true that labour is so *superseded,* as the phrase is. The invention of printing threw *amanuenses* out of their old employment, though it soon employed a thousand men instead of one. During all such transitions, it is only by previous savings that those thus affected can be maintained till they can adapt themselves to the change. Again, the early years of every human being are incapable of industrial effort, and the child must be maintained by the previous labour of others. Upon whom this duty fairly falls, whether on some abstraction that we call the State, or society, or on the parents of the child to whom his being is due, is a question which needs less to be asked than merely to be suggested here. Again, the years of labour are limited; the evening of that night approaches in which no man can work, and here is another call on the proceeds of past industry. The very old, as well as the very young, must be supported alike by foregone labour; in the case of the young, it must be by the labour of others; in the case of the old, it must be either by their own previous labour, or by that of their children now grown up, or by that of society at large—which way is best is surely not doubtful. During the years of active life itself, sickness will sometimes invade, throwing men often for long periods on the resources of the past. Hence the necessity of *forethought,* as regards equally the future of others whom affection and duty alike commend to our care, and our own, when the days of decay and weakness shall arrive. Now, *forethought* involves *judgment,* and *diligence,* and *self-denial.* 1. As to judgment. Earnings may be saved, but if injudiciously invested, they may be lost. To take a simple case,—hoarded potatoes are a more precarious economy than hoarded grain; and so throughour, where savings are invested through banks, or building societies, or railway shares, or in any other way. The division of labour itself calls for ever fresh exercise of judgment. So long as each man produces all that he wants for himself, he knows precisely what he wants, and how much; but so soon as labour is divided, each man produces not what he wants himself, but what others want, or are supposed to want. If, then, any one produce by mistake articles which others do not want, or of a quality, or to an extent at variance with the demand, he suffers serious loss, it may be ruin. 2. As to diligence. Without this, labour is little different from idleness. But mere labour, however diligent, can accomplish little unless guided by *intelligence*, for which, as the demands of society increase, there is an ever louder call. *Knowledge*, then, is indispensable to the attainment of any beyond the lowest results of industry. The more we know of the nature of that on which, and by which, and in which, and for which, we work, the more likely, nay certain, is our work to turn to good account. This knowledge, when embodied in practice and confirmed by it, becomes *skill*. The very tools and machines which some fancy supersede human labour and skill, are the results of both, and they render the former infinitely more productive, and call for ever more of the latter for their improvement, if not for their actual guidance. 3. As regards self-denial. One of its most important forms is *temperance*, without which labour, especially of the higher kinds, is precarious; it may be, impossible. As society advances, the relations of man to his fellows become more and more numerous and complex. *Credit*, as it is well called, holds a larger and larger place, and reliance on each other's faith becomes more and more important. *Honesty*, accordingly, whether in its lower forms, such as *punctuality*, or in its higher, to which we give the name *integrity*, is thus an indispensable condition of human progress. Were the exceptions to this condition to become much more frequent, the bonds of human society would be proportionally loosened, and civilization would go backward. In scarcely a subordinate degree are civility, courtesy, mutual forbearance, and willingness to oblige, necessary to oil the wheels of the social machine, which, without these, would move but slowly and creakingly along. These things we all need in our own case; and to be received, they must be given.

It is only in so far as all these qualities of diligence, and economy, and skill, and forethought, and intelligence, and temperance, and integrity, and courtesy, have been manifested, that wealth has been created, and that society in any age or country has advanced. It is just in so far as these have been neglected that poverty, and misery, and evil, of every kind, abound. Such are some of the chief practical lessons of Economic Science when rightly studied.

And will any one ask, "Are these mere truisms the boasted results of economic teaching?" In reply, much may be said. What is a truism to one mind, say to all here, may be *really* unknown to thousands beyond these walls. In such subjects, again, the profoundest truth is ever the simplest. It is its very simplicity that blinds us to its value and comprehensiveness. Further, we are so easily familiarized with the mere names of duties, and so accustomed to assent with the lips to their obligation, that we neglect to consider either their basis or their practical working. We go on daily assenting to truths we daily violate; it is not uncommon to lecture on ventilation in rooms whose atmosphere is stifling; to eulogize economy in the midst of reckless expenditure; and health is sometimes injured by very diligence in the study of its laws. What men all want, is not merely the discovery and promulgation of new truth, however useful, but the freshening up of old truths long ago admitted. The coins which we carry about with us, and which pass continually from hand to hand, have had the sharpness of their edges worn off, their legend all but effaced. We need to have them cast anew into the mint of thought, and re-stamped with their original "image and superscription." Rote-teaching is pernicious in morals not less than in merely intellectual matters. The explanation of a law, its demonstration, should ever go hand in hand with its inculcation. For the sake of those who may say, or at least think, "All this we knew long ago," let me use an illustration from the quite parallel case of *Physiology*. In my younger days I was accustomed to hear much vague talk about air and exercise; on all hands I heard that nothing was so good as exercise and fresh air. Well, so long as the restless activity of boyhood lasted, there was less need for instruction on this head; boys take fresh air and exercise in blind obedience to a blessed law of their nature. But when youth came on, and intellect became more mature, and books began to push cricket from its throne, all the rumour about air and exercise was quite inoperative to prevent long days and late nights of sedentary position, of confinement in close rooms, of hard work of the brain, while the circulation of the blood was impeded, the lungs laboured, the muscles lost their energy, and the skin its freedom of transpiration and its vigour to resist agencies from without. When, like most of you, I listened in delight to the beautiful expositions of my immediate predecessor, perhaps I was not alone in thinking that, had we all been taught in early life the economy of the lungs, and heart, and blood-vessels, and brain,—had we been shown that the blood which nourishes the body must be purified by frequent contact with the outer air; that for this purpose it passes frequently through the lungs, receiving from the air fresh life, while its impurities are thrown off; that in the process of breathing, the air is rapidly deteriorated and rendered unfit to sustain life, constant renovation being thus required; that by muscular compression consequent on exercise, the circulation is quickened, as well as the breathing, so that the blood is thus more rapidly purified, the effete particles of matter are more quickly removed, and our bodies in truth more frequently and healthfully renewed,—we should many of us have been spared much suffering and much loss of power arising necessarily from violation of the vital laws. And so with Economic Science. It is of no avail to repeat by rote phrases about industry, and temperance, and frugality, &c. The results of the observance and of the violation of those duties, as exemplified in the actual working of social life, must be clearly shown, and so enforced that the knowledge shall be wrought into the very tissue and substance of the mind, never to perish while life lasts, so that all things shall be brought to the test of the principles thus incorporated with the intellect itself. Further, in the case of both sciences alike, mere teaching, or addressing of the intellect, even if that be convinced, is not all, or enough. *Training* must accompany *teaching;* the formation of habits must go on with the clearing of the intellectual vision. I speak not of schools alone, or of homes alone; in both must the embryo man be accustomed, as well as told, to do what is right. He who has once learned by habit the delight and the advantage of daily ablution of the whole body, or of daily exercise in all weathers, in the open air, will not easily abandon or interrupt either of these habits. And so with industry and the rest. Every fresh act of obedience is no longer, as it were, the effort of a distinct volition, but an almost automatic repetition of an act first commanded by reason. This conversion of the *voluntary* into the *spontaneous* is the true guarantee for perseverance in any line of conduct, the excellence of which has been already recognised by the understanding.

The analogy between the Physiological and the Economic Sciences, both in their nature and in their present position, seems to me to hold throughout. Thus ignorance does not in either confer any exemption from the evils attending the breach of any law, however it may be admitted in extenuation at the bar of human justice. The child who takes arsenic for sugar, dies as surely as the wilful suicide. The youth launched on this busy world without any of the knowledge here indicated, finds Greek iambics, and even conic sections, of no guidance in its industrial relations, and he suffers and fails accordingly. What is the inference? That ignorance should be removed, and evil prevented, by early teaching, rather than left to the bitter regimen of experience. Coleridge has finely compared experience to the *stern* lights of a vessel, which illuminate only the track over which it has passed. It is for us rather to fix the light of knowledge on the *prow*, to illumine the course which the ship has yet to take. It would surely be a great gain, were all offences against economic law reduced to the category of wilful disobedience, in spite of knowledge; for such, I firmly believe, are, especially at the outset, vastly the minority.

Again: Health, much as it depends on individual observance of its laws, is greatly dependent on their observance by others also. The profligate parent transmits a feeble and sickly organization to his child; just as opposite conduct tends to the opposite result. The pestilence which foulness in one part of a city has bred, extends to other parts; and the consequences of the offence spread far beyond the original offender. So, economically, does each man suffer for others' transgressions besides his own. The idleness, and wastefulness, and intemperance of parents entail hunger, and raggedness, and every form of misery, on the unhappy children. The industrious, and provident, and honest members of the community are stinted in their means for the support of the idle, and improvident, and dishonest, and for their own protection against the depredations of those who seek to live by others' labour rather than their own. No law of our existence is more sure than this. It is idle to cavil or complain. Let us rather see how the recognition of this law should affect us. What is the practical inference? It is that the interests of humanity are one; that throughout mankind there is, in French phrase, a *solidarity*, which renders each responsible, in some measure, for the rest. The policy of selfish isolation is, therefore, vain, as well as sinful. We suffer from our neglect of the well-being of our fellowmen. The gaol fever, which the gross negligence of prison authorities produced in former days, slew the juryman in the box, and even the judge upon the bench. And it is not in purse alone, or even chiefly, that we suffer from the existence of the destitute, or the depraved. The great mountain of human evil throws its dark, cold shadow on every one of us; in such an atmosphere our own moral nature droops and pines; and just proportioned to the mental elasticity which attends every successful effort to spread good around us, is the numbing and hardening pressure of that great mass of vice and misery which we feel ourselves impotent to relieve.

One more analogy I would briefly note. We know how common quack medicines are. Why is this? Because, through ignorance of physiological laws, people are silly enough to believe that any nostrum can exist potent to repair, as by a magic spell or incantation, the evil results of their own neglect of health and its conditions. To such people, talk about air and exercise, and washing, and regular diet, and early hours, and temperance, and alternation of labour and rest, is very uninteresting and commonplace. To a similar class of persons, discourse on diligence and economy, and forethought and integrity, is very dull. "What is the use of all your chemistry," said the old lady, "if you cannot take the stain out of my silk gown?" And by tests not less narrow and erroneous are the teachings of science, whether economical or physiological, often tried. But a change is coming over the public estimate of the latter, at least in this respect. *Prevention* is being ever more thought of than *cure;* or, in technical phrase, the *prophylactic* claims, and now receives, more attention than the *therapeutic* portion of the physician's art. Pure water, and fresh air and light are now, almost for the first time, really recognised as the fundamental and indispensable conditions of health; and baths, and drains, and ventilators, and wash-houses, are fast encroaching on the domain of the blister and the lancet, the pill and the black draught. Now, what systems of the treatment of disease are to Sanitary Physiology, Poor-laws and Charitable Institutions and Criminal Legislation are to Economic Science. It aims at preventing the evils which those seek to deal with as they arise. The attempt may never quite succeed; but its success will be exactly proportioned to the vigour and unanimity with which it is made. It seeks to treat the source of the disease, rather than the mere symptoms. It is only as the former is removed that the latter will disappear. By all means let no palliative be neglected in the meantime, but let no cure be expected therefrom. Efforts to *perfect* systems of poor-laws, or criminal laws, however excellent or useful, must be abortive, because the very existence of the evils which these address is abnormal; and it is for the removal of these wens and blotches on the social system that we must strive, not for their mere abatement by topical applications, or the rendering of them symmetrical and trim. Wisdom and Benevolence here meet, and are at one.

Yet persons are not wanting who meet our desire that Economic Science should be taught to all, and especially to the young, by the cry that "it tends to make men selfish." In reply, I will not content myself with saying, in the words of Shakspere, "Self-love is not so vile a sin as self-neglecting." I go much further, and assert that this teaching, if properly conducted, has precisely the opposite tendency. Its great purpose is, to show

how the community is enriched by the industry of the individual, and how the value of individual industry is measured by its result in enriching the community. It wholly disowns and condemns every mode of enriching the individual at the general expense, or even without the general advantage. Thus, the merchant who brings a commodity, say tea, from a country where it is cheap to one where it is dear, and gains a profit by the transaction, fulfils the conditions of Economic Science. He serves at once the community in which he lives by bringing an article from a place where it is less, to a place where it is more, wanted ; and the community with which he trades by giving them in exchange for the article they sell something that they value more. But the man who enriches himself at the gaming-table, or by other means more or less resembling the picking of pockets, does injury, not service, to the community. He is wholly out of the pale of Economic Science ; he may be a *chevalier d'industrie*, in the French sense, but Economic Science disowns his industry, and condemns him as a wasteful consumer of what others have produced. It teaches every man to look on himself as a portion of society, and widens, not narrows, his views of his own calling.

And here I cannot but express my deep regret that one to whom we all owe, and to whom we all pay, so much gratitude, and affection, and admiration, for all he has written and done in the cause of good—I mean Mr. Charles Dickens—should have lent his great genius and name to the discrediting of the subject whose claims I now advocate. Much as I am grieved, however, I am not much surprised, for men of purely literary culture, with keen and kindly sympathies which range them on what seems the side of the poor and weak, against the rich and strong, and, on the other hand, with refined tastes, which are shocked by the insolence of success and the ostentation incident to newly-acquired wealth, are ever most apt to fall into the mistaken estimate of this subject which marks most that has yet appeared of his new tale, *Hard Times*. Of wilful misrepresentation we know him to be incapable; not the less is the misrepresentation to be deplored. We have heard of a young lady who compromised between her desire to have a portrait of her lover, and her fear lest her parents should discover her attachment, by having the portrait painted very unlike. What love did in the case of this young lady, aversion has done in the case of Mr. Dickens, who has made the portrait so unlike, that the best friends of the original cannot detect the resemblance. His descriptions are just as like to real Economic Science as "statistics" are to "stutterings," two words which he makes one of his characters not very naturally confound. He who misrepresents what he ridicules, does, in truth, not ridicule what he misrepresents. Of the lad Bitzer, he says, in No. 218 of *Household Words*:—

"Having satisfied himself, on his father's death, that his mother had a right of settlement in Coketown, this excellent young economist had asserted that right for her with such a stedfast adherence to the principle of the case, that she had been shut up in the workhouse ever since. It must be admitted that he allowed her half a pound of tea a year, which was weak in him: first, because all gifts have an inevitable tendency to pauperize the recipient; and, secondly, because his only reasonable transaction in that commodity would have been to buy it for as little as he could possibly give, and to sell it for as much as he could possibly get; it having been clearly ascertained by philosophers that in this is comprised the whole duty of man—not a part of man's duty, but the whole."—P. 335.

Here Economic Science, which so strongly enforces *parental* duty, is given out as discouraging its moral, if not economic correlative—*filial* duty. But where do economists represent this maxim as the whole duty of man? Their business is to treat of man in his industrial capacity and relations; they do not presume to deal with his other capacities and relations, except by showing what must be done in their sphere to enable any duties whatever to be discharged. Thus it shows simply that without the exercise of qualities that need not be here named again, man cannot support those dependent on him, or even himself. If it do not establish the obligation, it shows how only the obligation can be fulfilled.

Let me once more recur to physiology for an illustration. The duty of preserving one's own life and health will not be gainsaid. Physiology enforces this duty by showing how it must be fulfilled. But, if one's mother were to fall into the sea, are we to be told that physiology forbids the son to leap into the waves, and even peril his own health and life in the effort to save her who gave him birth? Physiology does not command this, it is true; this is not its sphere; but this, at least, it does,—it teaches and trains to the fullest development of strength and activity, that so they may be equal for every exigency—even one so terrible as this; and so precisely with Economic Science.

Again, we are told it discourages marriage:—

"'Look at me, ma'am,' says Mr. Bitzer. 'I don't want a wife and family. Why should they?'

'Because they are improvident,' said Mrs. Sparsit.

'Yes, ma'am, that's where it is. If they were more provident, and less perverse, ma'am, what would they do? They would say, "While my hat covers my family," or, "While my bonnet covers my family," as the case might be, ma'am, "I have only one to feed, and that's the person I most like to feed."'"—P. 336.

Does this mean that men or women ought to rush blindly into the position of parents, without thinking or caring whether their children can be supported by their industry, or must be a burden on that of society at large? If not, on what ground is prudent hesitation, in assuming the most solemn of all human responsibilities, a subject for ridicule and censure? Is the condition of the people to be improved by greater or by less laxity in this respect?

But not merely are we told that this teaching (which, by the way, scarcely exists in any but a very few schools), tends to selfishness, and the merging of the community in the individual; it has, it seems, also, a quite opposite tendency to merge the individual in the community, by accustoming the mind to dwell wholly on *averages*. Thus, if in a city of a million of inhabitants, twenty-five are starved to death annually in the streets, or if of 100,000 persons who go to sea, 500 are drowned, or burned to death, we are led to believe that Economic Science disregards these miseries, because they are exceptional, and because the average is so greatly the other way! Now, though in comparison of two countries, or two periods, such averages are indispensable, Economic Science practically teaches everywhere to analyze the collective result into its constituent elements,—in a word, to *individualize*. It teaches, for example, that every brick, and stone, and beam of this building, of this street, of this city, has been laid by some individual pair of hands; and it urges every man to work for himself, and to render his own industry ever more productive, surely not to rest in idle contemplation of the average of industry throughout the land. It is his duty to swell, not to reduce that average. So with prosperity. I am quite unable to see what tendency the knowledge of that average can have to discourage the effort to increase it. Besides, it is a fundamental error to confound mere statistics with economic science, which deals with *facts* only to establish their connections by way of cause and effect, and to interpret them by *law*.

But were it otherwise, with what justice can economic instruction be charged with destroying imagination, by the utilitarian teaching of "stubborn facts?" Why should either exclude the other? I can see no incompatibility between the two. By all means let us have poetry, but first let us have our daily bread, even though man is not fed by that alone. It is the *Poet* Rogers who says, in a note to his poem on *Italy*, "To judge at once of a nation, we have only to throw our eyes on the markets and the fields. If the markets are well supplied, and the fields well cultivated, all is right. If otherwise, we may say, and say truly, these people are barbarous or oppressed." Destitution must be removed, for the very sake of the higher culture. If we would have the tree fling its branches widely and freely into the upper air, its roots must be fixed deeply and firmly in the earth. But enough of this subject, on which I have entered with pain, and only from a strong sense of duty. The public mind, alas! is not enlightened enough to render such writing harmless.

Hitherto, I have spoken only of those great principles, and the duties flowing therefrom, which pervade the whole subject. But if these principles are the most comprehensive, there are very many others which, in the practical affairs of life, it is most important thoroughly to understand, and which it is the peculiar business of Economic Science to expound. It is an error to suppose that in matters touching men's "business and bosoms," even though of daily and hourly recurrence, instruction is not needed, and that "common sense" is a sufficient guide. Alas! *common* sense is widely different from *proper* sense. It is precisely in these subjects that error most extensively prevails, and that it is most pernicious where it does prevail. In matters far removed from ordinary life and experience, pure ignorance is possible, perhaps; and, in comparison, little mischievous. But in those which concern us all and at all times, it is alike impossible to be purely ignorant and to be ignorant with impunity. If the mind have not right notions developed at first, it will certainly have wrong ones. Hence we may say of knowledge what Sheridan Knowles says of virtue: "Plant virtue early! Give the *flower* the chance you suffer to the *weed!*"

The minds of most men are a congeries of maxims, and notions, and opinions, and rules, and theories picked up here and there, now and then, some sound, others unsound, each often quite inconsistent with the rest, but which are to them identified with the whole body of truth, and which are the standard by which they try all things. This fact explains a remark in a recent school report, that it is far easier to make this science intelligible to children than to their parents. No doubt, just as it is easier to build on an unoccupied ground, than on one overspread by ruins. And so, not only is it possible to teach this subject to the young; but it is to the young that we must teach it, if we would have this teaching most effective for good. For further evidence of the general need for this kind of instruction, it suffices to look around us, and test some of the opinions prevalent lately or even now. And here there is much of interest that might be said, did time permit, of still prevailing errors regarding strikes, and machinery, and wages, and population, and protection, and taxation, and expenditure, and competition, and much more besides. But into this field my limits forbid even me to enter.

The programme of this lecture speaks of the importance of Economic Science to all classes. It would be a serious error to suppose that its advantage is confined wholly, or even chiefly, to those who depend on daily labour for daily bread. Even were it so, in the midst of frequent and rapid changes of position, the rich man becoming poor, as well as the poor man becoming rich, this kind of teaching would still be important for all classes. But the *capitalist* not less, it may be said even more, than the *labourer*, needs instruction. He has been styled the captain of industry; it is for him to marshal, and equip, and organize, and pay its forces, and to guide their march. Any mistake on his part must be widely injurious. The wise employment of capital is a most momentous question; for it determines the direction of the industry of millions, and affects the prosperity of all coming time. From the class of the rich, too, are our legislators chiefly chosen. To them this kind of knowledge is important just in proportion as, in their case, ignorance or error is most pernicious. Of the aristocracy of our day, were old Burton living now, he would scarcely say what he said of those of his own time: "They are like our modern Frenchmen, that had rather lose a pound of blood in a single combat, than a drop of sweat in any honest labour."* The contagion of industry has spread to them; and idleness is less than ever confounded with nobility. But there is ample room for further progress. If wealth, even economically considered, involve increased responsibility, it calls the more loudly for enlightenment and guidance.

Again, on the side of expenditure, or consumption, does this subject especially concern the rich. As *supply* ever follows *demand*, it is by this that production is mainly guided. Shall it run in the direction of sensuality and self-indulgence, or shall it flow in better and more useful channels? Memorable are the words of Lord Byron in his later days in Greece:—

> "The mechanics and working classes who can maintain their families are, in my opinion, the happiest body of men. Poverty is wretchedness; but it is perhaps to be preferred to the heartless, unmeaning dissipation of the higher orders. I am thankful I am now entirely clear of this, and my resolution to remain clear of it for the rest of my life is immutable." †

At this most suggestive topic I can barely hint. Much beside I am forced wholly to omit. But I must not pass in total silence the claims of this subject on the attention of the other sex. Fortunately, little needs be said within this Institution, of whose audience at lectures on every subject ladies form perhaps not the smallest, and certainly not the least attentive portion. Surely I shall not be told that a superficial sketch, such as mine, is for

* Anatomy of Melancholy.

† Last Days of Lord Byron. By W. Parry, 1825. P. 205.

them unobjectionable, but that the serious study of the science is, in their case, to be discountenanced. If any kind of knowledge can do harm to any living being, it is just this very superficial knowledge. It is like the twilight which, holding of day on the one hand, and of night on the other, mocks the senses with distorted appearances which thicker darkness would hide, but which a broader daylight would dispel. In truth, women have a special interest in this subject. The part they play in industrial pursuits depends much on conventional circumstances, and varies in various countries; but in all, their influence in the region of expenditure is vastly great. Who shall say how deeply the welfare of families and of society at large is involved in this? Again, the domain of charity is peculiarly feminine; and the benevolent impulse, ever so ready to spring up, needs to be guided to the prevention, rather than to the relief, of what is too often, in fitter phrase, the indirect increase of misery. Well does Thomas Carlyle (no friend of *the dismal science*, as he loves to call it), in his quaint, odd way, exclaim:—

"What a reflection it is, that we cannot bestow on an unworthy man any particle of our benevolence, our patronage, or whatever resource is ours,—without withdrawing it, and all that will grow of it, from one worthy, to whom it of right belongs! We cannot, I say; impossible: it is the eternal law of things. Incompetent Duncan M'Pastehorn, the hapless incompetent mortal to whom I give the cobbling of my boots—and cannot find in my heart to refuse it, the poor drunken wretch having a wife and ten children; he *withdraws* the job from sober, plainly competent and meritorious Mr. Sparrowbill, generally short of work, too; discourages Sparrowbill; teaches him that he, too, may as well drink and loiter and bungle; that this is not a scene for merit and demerit at all, but for dupery, and whining flattery, and incompetent cobbling of every description—clearly tending to the ruin of poor Sparrowbill! What harm had Sparrowbill done me, that I should so help to ruin him? And I couldn't *save* the insalvable Mr. Pastchorn: I merely yielded him, for insufficient work, here and there a half-crown, which he oftenest drank. And now Sparrowbill also is drinking!" *

Between the Lady Bountiful of olden times, with her periodical distributions of coals and blankets, and simples and cowslip wine, who regarded the poor as her pets, her peculiar luxury, of which, did they cease to be mendicants, she would be cruelly deprived,—and the Mrs. Jellyby, whose long-ranged benevolence shoots in a parabolic curve far over what is near, to descend on what is remote, hurrying past and above St. Giles or Whitechapel, and exploding on "Borrioboola Gha;"—between these widely distinct forms of what is called in both alike CHARITY, there is room and there is need for women of judgment as clear as their sympathy is earnest, who can think for themselves, as well as feel for others; who shall not so do good that evil may come, but rather help the feeble to self-help, and, while they raise the fallen, look mainly to "forestalling" others "ere they come to fall."

Up to this point I have spoken solely of one class of advantages attending the teaching of Economic Science. But, as you have been told oftener than once during this course, the teaching of every branch of knowledge has, in different degrees, two sorts of advantage; 1st, in increasing man's outward resources; 2nd, as a means of mental discipline and inward culture. Of the second of

* Model Prisons, p. 24; Latter-Day Pamphlets, No. 2.

these advantages I can now say but little. It is wholly unimportant to discuss the comparative claims of different subjects in this respect. The difference among them is, perhaps, rather of kind than of degree. Mathematics discipline one set of powers, metaphysics another; or in so far as both exercise the same powers, it is in different ways. I claim no monopoly, I arrogate no superiority. I simply assert the *educational* value of this subject, without prejudice to any other, and all the more strongly, because it has been and is so sadly neglected. Surely, those subjects which have the most direct and powerful bearing on human wellbeing, and which treat of some of the most important relations between man and man, cannot be educationally less efficient than other studies which concern man less closely and directly. And I leave it to you who have heard even this most imperfect and hurried exposition, to judge whether it can fail to be a most improving mental exercise to sift such questions as the relations and laws of price, of capital and labour, and wages and profits, and interest and rent, and to trace to their origin, and follow to their results, the fluctuations affecting all these in our own and other countries, in our own and other times. As regards the other sex, on this ground, at least, there can be no doubt, even if the former admitted of hesitation. To women and to men, this discipline is alike valuable: for women it is even more necessary; for men are inevitably brought more into contact with the world and its affairs, and so have the defects of their early teaching in part corrected. It is well, at the same time that the understanding is exercised, to foster an interest in human welfare by an enlarged comprehension of its conditions. We hear little now of the policy or propriety of confining women's studies to superficial accomplishment. It were an error, scarcely less serious, to confine them to inquiries which leave the individual isolated from the race.

Let me not, in conclusion, be supposed to ignore, because I would not invade, other, and (by common consent) the most sacred grounds on which the moral aspects of this subject may be viewed. Let the duties on which human welfare, even industrially considered, is dependent, be enforced elsewhere, by reasons too high for discussion here. But surely this ground, at least, is in common to religious sects of every variety of creed and name. Surely it is a solemn and cogent consideration, that the very fabric of our social being is held together by moral laws, and that the man who violates them, outlaws himself, as it were, from the social domain, and rouses into armed hostility a thousand agencies which might and would otherwise fight upon his side. Not only the profligate, the gambler, the swindler, and the drunkard, but the idle, the reckless, the unpunctual, the procrastinating, find here a bitter but wholesome condemnation; and the very science which is ignorantly charged with fostering selfishness, teaches every man to estimate his labours by their tendency to promote the general good. Nor is it unimpressive, as regards even what Wordsworth so finely calls

"The *unreasoning* progress of the world,"*

to watch how the social plan is carried on by the composition of so many volitional forces, each bent on its

* "In the unreasoning progress of the world
A wiser spirit is at work for us,
A better eye than ours."—*Wordsworth.*

own aims. "The first party of painted savages," it has been well said, "who raised a few huts upon the Thames, did not dream of the London they were creating, or know that in lighting the fire on their hearth they were kindling one of the great foci of Time." . . . "All the grand agencies which the progress of mankind evolves are formed in the same unconscious way. They are the aggregate result of countless single wills, each of which, thinking merely of its own end, and perhaps fully gaining it, is at the same time enlisted by Providence in the secret service of the world." * If law be indeed the expression of an intelligent and benevolent will, reverence and obedience towards the great Lawgiver must surely be fostered (mark, I do not say *created*) by the study of His laws, and the contrasted results of their observance and their violation. And, finally, as regards that practical religion whose testing fruit is effort for the good of man,—a study which shows so clearly that human welfare is involved in obedience to fixed laws, and that obedience, to be reliable, must be based on knowledge of their existence and authority, must surely stimulate the extension of this needful knowledge among all classes of the people. In this light, it is abundantly apparent that, sacred as is the duty of acquiring knowledge, the duty of diffusing it is not less sacred; and that knowledge is no exception to the divine precept—"It is more blessed to give than to receive."

* James Martineau.

ON POLITICAL EDUCATION.

BY

HERBERT SPENCER.

FROM

ESSAYS MORAL, POLITICAL, AND ESTHETIC.

AND now let us look at the assembly of representatives thus chosen. Already we have noted the unfit composition of this assembly as respects the interests of its members; and we have just seen what the representative theory itself implies as to their intelligence. Let us now, however, consider them more nearly under this last head.

And first, what is the work they undertake? Observe, we do not say, the work which they *ought* to do; but the work which they *propose* to do, and *try* to do. This comprehends the regulation of nearly all actions going on throughout society. Besides devising measures to prevent the aggression of citizens on each other, and to secure each the quiet possession of his own; and besides assuming the further function, also needful in the present state of mankind, of defending the nation, as a whole, against invaders; they unhesitatingly take on themselves to provide for countless wants, to cure countless ills, to oversee countless affairs. Out of the many beliefs men have held respecting God, Creation, the Future, etc., they presume to decide which are true; and endow an army of priests to perpetually repeat them to the people. The distress inevitably resulting from improvidence, and the greater or less pressure of population on produce, they undertake to remove: they settle the minimum which each rate-payer shall give in charity; and how the proceeds shall be administered. Judging that emigration will not naturally go on fast enough, they provide means for carrying off some of the labouring classes to the colonies. Certain that social necessities will not cause a sufficiently rapid spread of knowledge, and confident that they know what knowledge is most required, they use public money for the building of schools and paying of teachers; they print and publish State school-books; they employ inspectors to see that their standard of education is conformed to. Playing the part of doctor, they insist that every one shall use their specific, and escape the danger of small-pox by submitting to an attack of cow-pox. Playing the part of moralist, they decide which dramas are fit to be acted, and which are not. Playing the part of artist, they prompt the setting up of drawing-schools; provide masters and models; and, at Marlborough House, enact what shall be considered good taste, and what bad. Through their lieutenants, the corporations of towns, they furnish appliances for the washing of people's skins and clothes; they, in some cases, manufacture gas, and put down water-pipes; they lay out sewers, and cover over cess-pools; they establish public libraries, and make public gardens. Moreover, they determine how houses shall be built, and what is a safe construction for a ship; they take measures for the security of railway travelling; they fix the hour after which public-houses may not be open; they regulate the prices chargeable by vehicles plying in the London streets; they inspect lodging-houses; they arrange for town burial-grounds; they fix the hours of factory hands. In short, they aim to control and direct the entire national life. If some social process does not seem to them to be going on fast enough, they stimulate it; where the growth is not in the mode or the direction which they think most desirable, they alter it; and so they seek to realize some undefined ideal community.

Such being the task undertaken, what, let us ask, are the qualifications for discharging it? Supposing it possible to achieve all this (which we do not), what must be the knowledge and capacities of those who shall achieve it? Successfully to prescribe for society, it is needful to know the structure of society—the principles on which it is organized—the natural laws underlying its progress. If there be not a true understanding of what constitutes social development, there must necessarily be grave mistakes made in checking these changes and fostering those. If there be lack of insight respecting the mutual dependence of the many functions which, taken together, make up the national life, unforeseen disasters will ensue from not perceiving how an interference with one will affect the rest. If there be no knowledge of the natural *consensus* at any time subsisting in the social organism, there will of course be bootless attempts to secure ends which do not consist with its passing phase of organization. Clearly, before any effort to regulate the myriad multiform changes going on in a community, can be rationally made, there must be an adequate comprehension of how these changes are caused, and in what way they are related to each other—how this entangled web of phenomena hangs together—how it came thus, and what it is becoming. That is to say, there must be a due acquaintance with the social science—the science involving all others; the science standing above all others in subtlety and complexity; the science which the highest intelligence alone can master.

And now, how far do our legislators possess this qualification? Do they in any moderate degree display it? Do they make even a distant approximation to it? That many of them are very good classical scholars is beyond doubt: not a few have written first-rate Latin verses, and can enjoy a Greek play; but there is no obvious relation between a memory well stocked with the words talked two thousand years ago, and an understanding disciplined to deal with modern society. That in learning the languages of the past they have learnt some of its history, is true; but considering that this history is mainly a narrative of battles and intrigues and negotiations, it does not throw much light on social philosophy—not even the simplest principles of political economy have ever been gathered from it. We do not question, either, that a moderate percentage of members of Parliament are fair mathematicians; and that mathematical discipline is valuable. As, however, political problems are not susceptible of mathematical analysis, their studies in this direction cannot much aid them in legislation.

To the large body of military officers who sit as representatives, we would not for a moment deny a competent knowledge of fortification, of strategy, of regimental discipline, but we do not see that these throw much light on the causes and cure of national evils. Indeed, considering that all war is anti-social, and that the government of soldiers is necessarily despotic, military education and habits are more likely to unfit than to fit men for regulating the doings of a free people. Extensive acquaintance with the laws, may doubtless be claimed by the many barristers and solicitors chosen by our constituencies; and this seems a kind of information having some relation to the work to be done. Unless, however, this information is more than technical—unless it is accompanied by a knowledge of the ramified consequences that laws have produced in times past, and are producing now (which nobody will assert), it cannot give much insight into Social Science. A familiarity with laws is no more a preparation for rational legislation, than would a familiarity with all the nostrums men have ever used, be a preparation for the rational practice of medicine. Nowhere, then, in our representative body, do we find appropriate culture. Here is a clever novelist, and there a successful maker of railways; this member has acquired a large fortune in trade, and that member is noted as an agricultural improver; but none of these achievements imply fitness for controlling and adjusting social processes. Among the many who have passed through the public school and university *curriculum*—including though they may a few Oxford double-firsts and one or two Cambridge wranglers—there are none who have received the discipline required by the true legislator. None have that competent knowledge of science in general, culminating in the science of life, which alone can form a basis for the science of society.

For it is one of those open secrets which seem the more secret because they are so open, that all phenomena displayed by a nation are phenomena of life, and are without exception dependent on the laws of life. There is no growth, decay, evil, improvement, or change of any kind, going on in the body politic, but what has its original cause in the actions of human beings; and there are no actions of human beings but what conform to the laws of life in general, and cannot be truly understood until those laws are understood. We do not hesitate to assert, that without a knowledge of the laws of life, and a clear comprehension of the way in which they underlie and determine social growth and organization, the attempted regulation of social life must end in perpetual failures.

See, then, the immense incongruity between the end and the means. See, on the one hand, the countless difficulties of the gigantic task; and, on the other hand, the almost total unpreparedness of those who undertake it. Need we wonder that legislation is ever breaking down? Is it not natural that complaint, amendment, and repeal, should form the staple business of every session? Is there anything more than might be expected in the absurd Jack-Cadeisms which almost nightly disgrace the debates? Even without setting up so high a standard of qualification as that above specified, the unfitness of most representatives for their duties is abundantly manifest. You need but glance over the miscellaneous list of noblemen, baronets, squires, merchants, barristers, engineers, soldiers, sailors, railway-directors, etc., and then ask what training their previous lives have given them for the intricate business of legislation, to see at once how extreme must be the incompetence. One would think that the whole system had been framed on the sayings of some political Dogberry:—"The art of healing is difficult, the art of government easy. The understanding of arithmetic comes by study, while the understanding of society comes by instinct. Watchmaking requires a long apprenticeship, but there needs none for the making of institutions. To manage a shop properly requires teaching; but the management of a people may be undertaken without preparation."

Against this danger the only safeguards appear to be, the spread of sounder views among the working classes, and the moral advance which such sounder views imply.

"That is to say, the people must be educated," responds the reader. Yes, education is the thing wanted; but not the education for which most men agitate. Ordinary school-training is not a preparation for the right exercise of political power. Conclusive proof of this is given by the fact that the artisans, from whose mistaken ideas the most danger is to be feared, are the best informed of the working classes. Far from promising to be a safeguard, the spread of such education as is commonly given, appears more likely to increase the danger. Raising the working classes in general to the artisan-level of culture, rather threatens to augment their power of working political evil. The current faith in reading, writing, and arithmetic, as fitting men for citizenship, seems to us quite unwarranted: as are, indeed, most other anticipations of the benefits to be derived from learning lessons.

There is no connexion between the ability to parse a sentence, and a clear understanding of the causes that determine the rate of wages. The multiplication-table affords no aid in seeing through the fallacy that the destruction of property is good for trade. Long practice may have produced extremely good penmanship without having given the least power to understand the paradox, that machinery eventually increases the number of persons employed in the trades into which it is introduced. Nor is it proved that smatterings of mensuration, astronomy, or geography fit men for estimating the characters and motives of Parliamentary candidates. Indeed, we have only thus to bring together the antecedents and the anticipated consequents, to see how untenable is the belief in a relation between them. When we wish a girl to become a good musician, we seat her before the piano: we do not put drawing implements into her hands, and expect music to come along with skill in the use of pencils and colour-brushes. Sending a boy to pore over law-books, would be thought an extremely irrational way of preparing him for civil engineering. And if in these and all other cases, we do not expect fitness for any function except through instruction and exercise in that function, why do we expect fitness for citizenship to be produced by a discipline which has no relation to the duties of the citizen?

Probably it will be replied, that by making the working man a good reader, we give him access to sources of information from which he may learn how to use his electoral power; and that other studies sharpen his faculties and make him a better judge of political questions. This is true, and the eventual tendency is unquestionably good. But what if, for a long time to come, he reads only to obtain confirmation of his errors? What if there exists a literature appealing to his prejudices, and supplying him with fallacious arguments for the mistaken beliefs which he naturally takes up? What if he rejects all teaching that aims to disabuse him of cherished delusions? Must we not say that the culture which thus merely helps the workman to establish himself in error, rather unfits than fits him for citizenship? And do not the trades'-unions furnish us with examples of this?

How little that which people commonly call education prepares them for the use of political power, may be judged from the incompetency of those who have received the highest education the country affords. Glance back at the blunders of our legislation, and then remember that the men who committed them had mostly taken University degrees, and you must admit that the profoundest ignorance of social science may accompany intimate acquaintance with all that our cultivated classes regard as valuable knowledge. Do but take a young member of Parliament fresh from Oxford or Cambridge, and ask him what he thinks Law should do, and why? or what it should not do, and why? and it will become manifest, that neither his familiarity with Aristotle, nor his readings in Thucydides, have prepared him to answer the very first question a legislator ought to solve. A single illustration will suffice to show how different an education from that usually given, is required by legislators, and consequently by those who elect them; we mean the illustration which the Free-trade agitation supplies. By kings, peers, and members of Parliament mostly brought up at universities, trade had been hampered by protections, prohibitions, and bounties. For centuries had been maintained these legislative appliances, which a very moderate insight shows to be detrimental. Yet, of all the highly-educated throughout the nation during these centuries, scarcely a man saw how mischievous such appliances were. Not from one who devoted himself to the most approved studies, came the work which set politicians right on these points; but from one who left college without a degree, and prosecuted inquiries which the established education ignored. Adam Smith examined for himself the industrial phenomena of societies; contemplated the productive and distributive activities going on around him; traced out their complicated mutual dependencies; and thus reached general principles for political guidance. In recent days, those who have most clearly understood the truths he enunciated, and by persevering exposition have converted the nation to their views, have not been graduates of universities. While, contrariwise, those who have passed through the prescribed *curriculum*, have commonly been the most bitter and obstinate opponents of the changes dictated by politico-economical science. In this all-important direction, right legislation was urged by men deficient in the so-called best education; and was resisted by the great majority of men who had received this so-called best education!

The truth for which we contend, and which is so strangely overlooked, is, indeed, almost a truism. Does not our whole theory of training imply that the right preparation for political power is political cultivation? Must not that teaching which can alone guide the citizen in the fulfilment of his public actions be a teaching that acquaints him with the effects of public actions?

The second chief safeguard to which we must trust is, then, the spread, not of that mere technical and miscellaneous knowledge which men are so eagerly propagating, but of political knowledge; or, to speak more accurately, knowledge of social science. Above all, the essential thing is, the establishment of a true theory of government—a true conception of what legislation is for, and what are its proper limits. This question, which our political discussions habitually ignore, is a question of greater moment than any other. Inquiries which statesmen deride as speculative and unpractical, will one day be found infinitely more practical than those which they wade through Blue Books to master, and nightly spend many hours in debating. The considerations that every morning fill a dozen columns of *The Times*, are mere frivolities when compared with the fundamental consideration—What is the proper sphere of government? Before discussing the way in which law should regulate some particular thing, would it not be wise to put the previous question, whether law ought, or ought not, to meddle with that thing? and before answering this, to put the more general question—What law should do, and what it should leave undone? Surely, if there are any limits at all to legislation, the settlement of these limits must have effects far more profound than any particular Act of Parliament can have; and must be by so much the more momentous. Surely, if there is danger that the people may misuse political power, it is of supreme importance that they should be taught for what purpose political power ought alone to be used.

Did the upper classes understand their position, they would, we think, see that the diffusion of sound views on this matter more nearly concerns their own welfare, and that of the nation at large, than any other thing whatever. Popular influence will inevitably go on increasing. Should the masses gain a predominent power while their ideas of social arrangements and legislative action remain as crude as at present, there will certainly result disastrous meddlings with the relations of capital and labour, as well as a disastrous extension of State-administrations. Immense damage will be inflicted: primarily on employers; secondarily on the employed; and eventually on the nation as a whole. These evils can be prevented, only by establishing in the public mind a profound conviction that there are certain comparatively narrow limits to the functions of the State; and that these limits ought on no account to be transgressed. Having first learned what these limits are, the upper classes ought energetically to use all means of teaching them to the people.

ON EARLY MENTAL TRAINING AND THE STUDIES BEST FITTED FOR IT.

BY

F. A. P. BARNARD, LL. D.,

PRESIDENT OF COLUMBIA COLLEGE.

READ BEFORE THE UNIVERSITY CONVOCATION FOR 1866

EARLY MENTAL TRAINING, AND THE STUDIES FITTEST FOR IT.

WHENEVER it happens that any subject interesting to man becomes matter of protracted controversy, the zeal of opposing parties often carries them so far, as to make both of them equally intolerant of one who is not wholly with themselves, though at the same time he may be by no means with their adversaries. The task, therefore, of one who undertakes to show—what is usually true—that to a certain extent both parties are in the right, while neither is wholly so, is by no means an easy one. He is very likely to incur the disapproval of both, while he is not sure to conciliate the favor of either.

This consideration embarrasses me in the attempt I am about to make, to exhibit certain views connected with our system of higher education, founded upon convictions which have long been gradually growing upon me, but which I apprehend are not likely to be in full accordance with those of any considerable number of the experienced educators whom I have the pleasure of addressing.

In the discussions which have taken place in our time with respect to the merits of our system of collegiate education, the field has been occupied almost exclusively by two parties holding opinions widely discordant; so much so, indeed, as hardly to admit of any description of compromise. One of these parties, which may properly be styled the conservative, has made classical learning its watchword, and has steadily resisted the encroachments upon our time-honored course of modern science in all its branches. It has regarded every slight recognition which has been made of the value of this knowledge, as an unwise concession to popular clamor and a wrong done to the cause of education; and has maintained, or if it spoke its full thought would doubtless maintain, that the collegiate education of this country was vastly better at the close of the eighteenth century than it is now, in the middle of the nineteenth. The other, which styles itself the progressive, and is styled by its opponents the destructive party, denounces with contempt a system which rests, as it asserts, upon a literature and a history which have long since ceased to have any living interest for the human race; and occupies itself with the painful study of languages which exist only as literary curiosities, and which will never more be either spoken or written; while, shutting its eyes to the condition of the living world of to-day, it treats as unworthy of notice the great discoveries which in recent times have revolutionized the aspect of society and transformed the whole surface of the planet, is indifferent to the great lessons of political and social science to be drawn from the fruitful pages of modern history, and finally flings its *élèves* into the midst of the world's conflicts, as little prepared to deal with the real problems of life as if they had dropped from the moon.

It is hardly necessary to say that the actual state of our educational system satisfies neither of these extreme classes. The former are chagrined that so much has been already lost; the latter are discontented that so little has yet been won. But there has gradually been growing up a third class, limited as yet perhaps in numbers, who, without falling in the least behind the first of those just described in their esteem for the ancient learning, have perceived that the time has come when that learning must abandon its claims to an absolute monopoly of the educational field, and are now earnestly inquiring whereabouts in the educational course and to what extent it may profitably be superseded. It is to this class, small perhaps as yet in numbers and inconsiderable in weight of influence, to which I avow myself to belong. Hitherto the attention of this class has been principally occupied with the teaching of colleges—taking it apparently for granted that the course of preparatory study, which is substantially the same everywhere, is susceptible of no material improvement and needs no essential modification. But it is precisely at this point, as it seems to me, that modification is most necessary; and it is here that I desire to suggest that a suitable modification may be at once the means of accomplishing more efficiently the general ends of education (which is of course the matter to be first looked after), and of rendering at the same time instruction in classical learning more productive than it is at present of tangible results.

More productive, I say, of tangible results. For what are, in fact, the results which we do actually reach in the teaching of the classics at this time? Are they in truth any thing like what we claim for them? We hear, for instance, a great deal said of the intellectual treasures locked up in the languages of Greece and Rome, which it is asserted that our system of education throws open to the student freely to enjoy. And yet we know that practically this claim is without foundation. It will not, I presume, be affirmed of the graduates of American colleges generally, that they become familiar with any portions of the literature of Rome and Greece, which do not form part of their compulsory reading. It will hardly be affirmed that one in ten of them does so. And why not? The reason is twofold. First, there is hardly one in ten, in whose mind the classics ever cease to be associated with notions of painful labor. Reading is not therefore pursued beyond the limit of what is required, because it is not agreeable. But secondly and chiefly, there is hardly one in ten whose knowledge of the Latin or the Greek is ever sufficiently familiar to give him the command of the ancient literature which it is asserted for him that he enjoys. I suppose that to read with any satisfaction any work in any language, we should be able to give our attention to the *ideas* that it conveys, without being embarrassed or confused by want of familiarity with the machinery through which they are imparted. It will not be for mere pleasure that we shall pursue our task, if every sentence brings us a new necessity to turn over our lexicons, or to reason out a probable meaning by the application of the laws of syntax. And yet, if there are any of our graduates who are able, without such embarrassments, to read a classical author, never attempted before, the number must be very few. If there are any who can read even such books of Latin or Greek as they have read before, with any thing like the fluency with which they read their mother tongue, the number cannot be large; and if there are any who can read, with similar facility, classic works which they take up for the first time, it is so small that I have never seen one.

It appears to me, then, that the results actually attained under our present system of instruction are neither very flattering nor very encouraging. We should certainly not have been so content with them as we seem, if we had not all along kept up before us the fiction that they are not what they are, but what they ought to be. For a period varying from seven to ten years (four years in college and from three to six in preparation), we keep young men under a course of instruction in Latin and Greek, and, at the end of that time, they are unable, in any proper sense, to read either the one or the other. Can a person be said to know a language which he cannot read? And is it a result worth the time and labor expended upon it to attain such a doubtful acquaintance with a language or any thing else, as that which the majority of our graduates carry away with them of these, at the close of their educational career? Might not the same amount of time and labor differently employed have produced at last something having a value at least appreciable? And is not the immense disproportion between labor expended and results obtained, itself the best evidence that this labor has not been expended most wisely for the accomplishment of its own avowed end? For surely there cannot be any language, dead or living, in the known world, which any intelligent person ought not to be able to acquire, so as at least to read it, in a course of ten years' study.*

I know that we are continually informed, when we complain of the meagreness of the actual results reached in the classical teaching of our colleges, that it is not after all so much on account of the knowledge acquired that

* It need hardly be said that there is no intention, in these remarks, to question the fact of the existence among us of accomplished and thorough classical scholars. That we have such, and not a few of them, I am proud to believe. But how many of them became so in school or in college? That is the question immediately before us. Our scholars, as a rule, are self-made. Their scholarship is the growth of their maturer life. The observations of the text are to be understood of American students at their graduation as Bachelors of Arts—not later.

these studies are useful—it is because of the admirable intellectual discipline which they furnish, and which it is claimed for them that they only can furnish so well. This question we will waive for the moment; but in the mean time we may take occasion to note that the educationist who falls back upon this ground, admits in so doing, that the other is untenable, and that the value of these languages which has been so much insisted on, in opening up to the student all the choicest literary treasures of the world of antiquity, is for the majority of our graduates practically zero. And the admission may as well be made, though in making it we shall reduce to the form of empty pretence, and rate as no better than so much idle wind, a vast proportion of what has been written in eulogy of the educational uses of the classics. We may as well admit it, I say, because it is true; and until we recognize the truth in regard to the condition of our educational instrumentalities or methods, we can never proceed intelligently to make them better. Nor will it render the truth I insist on any the less positive, or the admission any the less necessary, that there may be here and there exceptions to the general rule, that now and then there may be found a student whose eight or ten years' study of the ancient languages may have really enabled him to read them. No one who claims this can claim that such cases are any thing but exceptions. Even in the British universities, where the preference given to classical study is greatly more decided than with us, and where its prosecution is stimulated by the promise of the most brilliant rewards, even there such cases, though naturally more numerous than here, are only exceptional still. In fact, their system would almost seem to have been expressly made for the production of these exceptions, and nothing else, without the slightest thought of or regard for the greatest good of the greatest number; for certainly it could not have accomplished the thing better, if it had been really devised with that deliberate intent. No system of performing the work of education, or for performing any other work, can be called a good system, which fails with the great majority and succeeds only with the few.

But then, if the argument so often used in defence of our system, derived from the great value of the classical knowledge it is presumed to impart, be fallacious, is not at least that which rests upon the disciplinary efficacy of classical study more substantial? Upon this point, again, there is some reason to believe that our educationists accept too readily what might be for what is. If mental discipline consists in invigorating the mental faculties by wholesome exercise, and in training them to habits of method in exercise, it is indeed certain that the study of language, undertaken at the suitable stage in the process of culture, must prove a most efficacious instrumentality—perhaps the most efficacious of all—for accomplishing this object. But to place before the immature mind a subject which might possibly later call into exercise certain of its powers, say for instance comparison, judgment, reasoning, is not by any means to insure that, under the actual circumstances, it will do so. It may hardly awaken an active faculty at all, and may remain merely matter of consciousness and memory. And especially is it probable that in early life the higher faculties, the reflective and reasoning powers, will fail to respond to the provocatives addressed to them, when those provocatives consist of abstractions which are not themselves conceived without effort.

The first step, for instance, in the process of reasoning,

is comparison. The easiest efforts of comparison are made when the objects are objects of simple perception; and if Nature dictates any thing on the subject of education too plainly to admit of mistake, it is that children should first be taught to compare by the help of visible things. But if this plain dictate of Nature is disregarded, and we present to immature minds, as subjects of thought, definitions (for instance) of the parts of speech, or the distinctions between the dative and ablative case, the probability is that no comparison or discrimination will be exercised at all, and that the only faculty which will come into play will be the memory. I say the probability is, but I might better say the certainty; and if personal experience is worth any thing in the case, I may add that in one instance, at least, this certainty has been to me matter of knowledge.

Valuable then as is the study of language for its educational uses, it does not follow that it is so for the earliest stages of education. Still less, at that early period, will that language be found useful, of which the structure is the most complicated, the inflections the most numerous, the syntax the most artificial, and the order of words and clauses in a sentence the most widely contrasted with that which prevails in the learner's own vernacular. And yet such a language possesses in the highest degree the properties which make of language a useful educational instrumentality, provided the proper place be assigned to it in the educational course.

There is a professor of physical training in New York who promises a wonderful development of the muscles of the arms and chest, to such as choose to practise under his direction for a few months in wielding certain ponderous clubs—thirty pounds, more or less, I believe, in weight.

He can point to some striking living examples of the success which has attended his method; but I have never heard that he had placed his clubs in the hands of boys of ten years old. And so, when we impose on the intellects of boys, at the same tender age, a burden like that of the grammar of the Latin or the Greek language, we overtask them as much as we should overtask their bodily strength by requiring them to go through a gymnastic exercise with a club of thirty pounds' weight. They can lift the burden no more in the one case than in the other. They do not lift it, though we may persuade ourselves that they do, because we tie them to it and leave them there. And by this I mean to say that the study of Latin and Greek, between the ages of eight and twelve (I have heard of cases in which the study began at six), does not really serve the educational purpose that it is supposed to do; does not really occupy the reflective and reasoning powers of the mind, but exercises almost exclusively the memory. But then, if it does not do this, it does something worse. It blinds us to the fact that the educational process is not going on at all, at the very most important and critical time in the youthful learner's life. It prevents us from perceiving that the mind which we are endeavoring to train, refusing a task to which it is unequal, remains inactive, except in the very humblest of its faculties. It conceals from us the unhappy truth that the perceptive powers remain dormant or sluggish; that the powers of comparison, analysis, judgment, and reasoning, are never called into action; and that the period of life when habits of careful observation are most easily formed, when in fact they must be formed, or never formed at all, is passing away unimproved.

To me, therefore, it seems to be an error of very serious gravity to suppose that the study of the ancient languages at a very early period of life is a means of valuable and wholesome mental discipline. That study seems to me rather, at that time, to act as a sedative, repressing the activity of the higher mental powers, than as a stimulant awakening them to exertion. And no stronger corroboration of the justice of this view could be presented than is to be found in the very moderate amount of attainment which appears in the end to be acquired, as the result of all this labor. The object of education, considered as a formative process, is not indeed directly the increase of knowledge. It is to form and not to inform the mind. But there is no process of formation which does not imply information. There is no species of mental exercise in which the understanding is not employed in the acquisition of new truths, or in forming new combinations of familiar truths, in such a manner as to enlarge the scope of our ideas. And in so far as the processes we call educational fail to increase knowledge, although not planned with that express intent, in precisely so far they fail to accomplish their proper end. There is then no impropriety in judging of the educational value of any study by considering how much it has contributed to the learner's stock of positive knowledge, and what proportion this addition bears to the time which has been devoted to securing it. Now, imperfect as is the acquaintance of our college graduates with the languages which occupy so largely their attention throughout their whole educational course, there is no doubt that the greater part of what they know of them is acquired after they become members of college. And yet, considering the exclusiveness with which, in the preparatory schools, they are confined to these subjects of study, there is as little doubt that the time they expend on them in those schools exceeds in most cases, and very much exceeds in many, all that they can give to them afterward. That is to say, in the earlier years the study is comparatively barren of results; it fails to impart an amount of knowledge bearing any fair proportion to the amount of time expended on it. And this fact is sufficient proof in itself that the disciplinary value of the study, at that period of the education, cannot be what has been claimed for it.

I shall be very much misunderstood if I am supposed, because of what I have said, to undervalue classical learning. I shall be misunderstood if I am supposed to desire to exclude the classics from our course of liberal education. No one places a higher estimate upon the ancient learning than I do.* No one feels more sensibly than I the force of all the arguments which have been urged in its favor. The influence which the perusal of the many

* It seems worth while to insist a little upon this point. There is a great deal that is sensible and well worth attention uttered by the class of educational controversialists who take the greatest pains to display their contempt of classical learning; but this fails to impress their opponents, because their heterodoxy upon the point esteemed most vitally important discredits them with these upon every other. The writer is not to be confounded with such. He has labored as earnestly as any man in vindication of the claims of classical learning to the prominent place which it holds in our system of higher education—a place which he hopes to see it still maintain. But there is certainly danger, and a daily increasing danger, that it will lose this pre-eminence; and this appears to the writer to be inevitable, unless some such reform as is recommended above shall be introduced into the earlier periods of the educational course. So far, therefore, is the writer in what he has said from meditating any assault upon the classics, that he honestly believes that the prevalence of the views here advocated, and the practical consequences which would follow, would do more than any thing else to fortify them against assault, and to quiet the growing disposition to assail them. This belief may be a mistaken one; but however that may be, its existence is an evidence that the foregoing remarks and reasonings are dictated by a friendly and not by a hostile spirit.

models of literary excellence which it furnishes upon the formation of a correct taste in letters, the pleasure which the perusal of such affords to those who are able to read them freely in their original tongues, the importance of an acquaintance with the ancient languages to the correct understanding and scholarly use of our own, the many modes in which the history of ancient polity and ancient thought has affected the course of events in more recent times, in the political no less than in the intellectual world —these considerations, and others like them, will ever secure for the ancient learning a large space in any judicious system of liberal mental culture. Nor do I in the least question that the disciplinary value of these studies, considered as furnishing a wholesome mental gymnastics, is, when introduced at the right time and in the right place, all that has been claimed for them. What I maintain is that the right time is not, as the prevailing practice assumes, the period of emergence from childhood, and the right place is not at the very beginning of the educational course. By giving them the false position which they at present occupy, we seem to me to accomplish three evils at the same time. First, we fail to secure any thing like such a degree of attainment in the classics themselves, as the labor bestowed upon them ought to produce; secondly, we prevent the learner from acquiring much substantially useful knowledge, for which no opportunity so fitting will again occur; and thirdly—which is most important of all —we display a singular disregard of the plain indications of Nature, who herself points out the order in which the faculties should be drawn out into action.

Curiosity is the most marked mental characteristic of childhood. This trait manifests itself in the thousand questions with which the child assails and often annoys all those who surround him. It manifests itself in the exuberant and enthusiastic delight with which he overflows at the sight of every new thing. It manifests itself in the eagerness with which he lays hold of and scrutinizes every object within his reach which he does not understand. It manifests itself in the interest with which he traces the simplest effects to their immediate causes. It manifests itself in his lively sensibility to all the impressions of sense. It manifests itself in the activity of his observation of all the minute particulars of every new scene.

All these things serve to show how remarkably at this period of life the perceptive faculties are in advance of the others in the order of development. They furnish proof, if proof were needed, of what is Nature's educational plan. And as it is sometimes permitted us to discover the wisdom of the order which the Supreme Creator has established to govern the works of His hands, so here we perceive of how inappreciable importance to the welfare of the race is the fact that the predominant characteristic of the infant mind is the instinctive desire to know, and how favorable to the rapid multiplication of ideas is the restless activity of the perceptive powers which accompanies this desire. For the child comes into the world totally ignorant. Even the simplest facts which it concerns his immediate personal safety to know, are to be acquired by him by observation and experience. That fire is hot and that ice is cold, that the moon is more distant than the candle, and that the candle is more agreeable to look at than to touch; these are rudimentary truths which it is useless to tell him—he must learn them for himself. And in the same way all his elementary knowledge, of whatever description, must be acquired. Much of this is an acquisition earlier than language. It must be so, for language is but symbolic of ideas, and signs will not be used until there is something to be signified. In the earliest period of life, therefore, oral teaching is impossible. No medium exists through which it can be conveyed. The instructions of the parent or the nurse must be limited to the endeavor to enlarge the child's vocabulary by associating in his mind visible objects or recognizable expressions of emotion in the countenance or gesture, with the sounds by which these are recalled in language. To attempt to expound to him one word by the help of others, is an absurdity never thought of. And even after language has been acquired, sufficient for the ordinary purposes of life, it holds for a long time but a subordinate place as an instrument of instruction. It may be employed with great effect to direct and assist the powers of observation, but if relied on solely as a means of conveying new ideas, the result cannot fail to be unsatisfactory. Objects, facts, phenomena, must themselves be directly presented to the learner, or there will be no substantial growth in knowledge. Seeing thus the absolute dependency of the child upon his own unaided perceptive powers for all his earliest knowledge, and seeing to how very great a degree he continues long to be dependent upon the exercise of the same powers for his subsequent advancement, we easily recognize the admirable wisdom of that provision of the Creator by which these powers, first of all and in the very dawn of life, spontaneously awaken, and manifest afterward through all the earlier years of existence, an activity which never tires and which will not be repressed.

Now, I hold it to be the first principle of a sound educational philosophy, that the powers of the mind should be subjected to culture in the most natural order; and what I understand by natural order, is the order in which the powers unfold themselves when they are subjected to no artificial control at all. If this is not the test of what is natural, then we have no test. And I suppose that the reason why we should follow Nature, is because Nature will thus most willingly follow us. The tasks we impose will be pleasing, because they will be adapted to the strength. The learner will easily submit himself to our guidance, because we take him in the direction in which he is already inclined to go. He will understand what we require of him, and he will be encouraged because he understands.

I do not mean to assert that any judicious course of instruction can be devised which shall present nothing but a series of unmingled delights. I am not of the visionary class who believe that continuous mental effort will ever, under any system, be attended, for the majority of individuals, with the same exhilaration and eagerness of spirit with which the same individuals are found to pursue the athletic sports by which their physical powers may be developed. They who, like Herbert Spencer, take such a ground as this, only injure the cause they would befriend, and weaken the force of their otherwise unanswerable arguments. The effort which is useful, whether it be physical or mental, must always partake of the character of labor, and labor brings with it sometimes weariness and pain. But what I do say is, that the labor need not be made a repulsive labor, as it always must be when it brings with it no recognizable, or at least no adequate profit; but may be made so richly productive as actually to become positively attractive.

Now, in what I have just said, I believe there is nothing which is not, in the abstract, perfectly orthodox—nothing which will not meet the approval of every educationist who hears me. I wish to inquire, therefore, to what extent it is practically true, that in our established system of liberal culture, we conform to the order which Nature points out to us? Is it true that we make the development and training of the perceptive faculties the first object of our attention? Is it, as it ought to be, our first great aim to improve the powers of observation, of analysis, of induction, of classification? Are all the studies which we prescribe to boys, as preparatory to their introduction to the abstruser subjects of grammar, and logic, and ethics, and rhetoric, and metaphysics, directed to this end? Is there even a single one of them that is? We know that it is not so. Beyond those most elementary branches of knowledge which are indispensable as furnishing the implements by which all other knowledge is to be acquired—beyond orthography and reading and writing, the simplest rules of arithmetic, and perhaps some imperfect outlines of geography—to the great majority of the youth of this country destined for college, nothing at all is taught of any description, before they are required to devote themselves exclusively to the study of the most difficult languages ever spoken by man, and this by the most difficult of processes—the purely synthetic. They follow up this species of study for several years. Few follow it cheerfully, for few follow it intelligently. Their progress is slow. The average attainment at the end of three, four, or more years is far from being what it should be—far from what it might be could they have entered upon it with a proper preliminary training. Yet we do not appreciate the insignificance of the result, because the system itself has created a mean standard, according to which our expectations are justified.

They are then advanced to the college. The same

subjects occupy them here as before, with the addition mainly of mathematics, logic, and rhetoric, for two years longer; and then finally, as they approach the close of their educational career, they are for the first time introduced to the sciences of observation and experiment. That is to say, we have inverted the natural order just as completely as possible, placing those subjects which address themselves to the faculties earliest awake, at the very conclusion of the course. And this inversion of the order of Nature, carries with it the unfortunate consequence that no satisfactory knowledge is acquired at last, either of the sciences or of the languages. A large portion of my own life has been devoted to the teaching of physics. During all this time it has been manifest to me that my classes have come to this part of their course totally unpractised how to observe. And it has seemed to me that their perceptive faculties have been actually dwarfed by the forced inaction to which they have been constrained during the period most favorable to their cultivation. Thus it has happened that the brief time which can only be given to these subjects in the college course has been exhausted in the attempt to convey such elementary notions as should have been familiar long before. And the same observation has been made to me by other gentlemen who are among the most skilled instructors in science that I have ever known. If, then, I am asked if I would displace these subjects from the position they occupy in the course of collegiate instruction, I would answer, by no means. What I would desire would be to secure such an early culture, and such an acquaintance with the elements of science, that it might be permitted us to give, at this more advanced period, such larger views and such profounder applications of the principles of these sciences, that the student might feel, in the end, that he had acquired some mastery over them, and might be qualified to prosecute inquiry independently and profitably after he had mastered them.

Probably the faults of our present system of liberal education result to a great degree from the fact that our young men are in too great haste to be educated. It does not seem to me that the system can be radically reformed until our colleges shall decline to receive students below the age of seventeen or eighteen years. Some of them, perhaps a majority, have placed their minimum age at fourteen. Some of them have no provision of law upon the subject at all; but all receive candidates who give evidence of having read a certain limited amount of Latin and Greek. The other qualifications required are exceedingly moderate and are not very severely insisted on. Nor, though there are some who enter later in life, is it possible to secure to such the advantage this fact should bring with it. The course of study prescribed must be the same for all, and must not be beyond the capacity of the youngest. In the British universities, the average age of students at admission is, according to the reports of the royal commissioners, about eighteen years and a half. Were it the same with us, or were it a year less, there would be ample time in the earlier years for such a course of preliminary training as to insure, what we by no means now insure, a thorough education. But even without any such modification of our exactions as to age, there is still room for a sensible improvement of the existing state of things. And having said this, I shall probably be expected to state specifically what are the improvements which I consider practicable.

First, then, I would say that I believe that boys should

not, as a rule, be required to take up the study of Latin before the age of fourteen or fifteen years. The earlier years may be much more profitably employed in other things; and if so employed, the study of the ancient languages may afterward be pursued much more rapidly and much more intelligently. It is a fact which has been frequently observed, which every teacher has probably observed for himself, that youths who have even not had the advantage of early systematic training, but possess only the greater maturity of the faculties which comes with advancing years, and who, at a period much later than the average, have resolved to fit themselves for admission to college, have been able to accomplish all that is required in a singularly short space of time, often within the compass of a single year. And such students, when of ordinary native ability, have usually approved themselves among the most thorough linguists of the classes to which they belonged. There is no doubt that two years is as good as two dozen for the acquisition of all that our colleges require of preparation in the classics, provided violence be not done to Nature by forcing the study upon minds unprepared to receive it.

During the earlier period, now occupied with weary, and to a great degree profitless, labor over uncongenial studies, I would introduce, first, the sciences of classification, embraced under the general name of Natural History—as botany, zoology, mineralogy. No subjects are better suited than these to gratify the eager curiosity of the growing mind; to satisfy its cravings after positive knowledge; to keep alive the activity of the perceptive powers; to illustrate the beauty and value of method, and to lead to the formation of methodical habits of thought. That these subjects will interest children of very early years, and that such children will require no painful constraint to secure their attention to them, I have myself seen experimentally verified ; and the testimony of Professor Hooker, before the royal commissioners appointed to inquire into the condition of the public schools of England, in regard to the success of his distinguished relative, Prof. Henslow, in giving instruction in the same subjects in one of the humblest schools of England, is conclusive to the same effect. The lessons of Professor Henslow were given to children between the ages of eight and fifteen. The attendance was altogether voluntary. The children became deeply interested in the subject of botany, learned to analyze and classify plants, to distinguish the relations of the parts of plants to each other, and of one plant to another. The result was a very obvious improvement in the powers of observation and of reasoning, and an increase of general intelligence. These effects were so sensibly manifest, that some of the inspectors of the schools remarked that these children were decidedly more intelligent than those of other parishes, and attributed the fact to the training which their observant and reasoning powers had received from this instruction.

Along with these sciences, I would teach those which depend on observation and experiment, embracing chemistry and the various branches of physics. As in natural history we have classification of individuals referred to form, so here we have classification of facts and phenomena referred to law. These sciences present the happiest examples of reasoning in both the inductive and deductive forms. They lead to the formation of habits of arranging premises and deducing conclusions which accord most with the daily exigencies of human life, and thus promote that soundness of judgment which is among the most striking characteristics of practical men. Of course, it is not to be expected or desired that, in the early period of education, these sciences should be pursued into their abstruser developments. The deductive part of physics involves, in many portions, the application of the higher mathematics, and opens up branches of inquiry which must be left to be supplied at a more advanced period; but that which is simply inductive addresses itself to the senses, and not only may be easily understood, but never fails to prove intensely interesting even to very young learners.

So much as is here suggested, is actually required as a qualification for admission to King's College, London, or for matriculation in the London University. The eminent physiologist, Dr. Carpenter, who is one of the examiners for the London University, in his evidence before the commission already referred to, speaks of the requisition as most important and useful. And the opinions expressed by him are supported by the unanimous voice of all the other witnesses of the same class who speak to the point, embracing some of the most distinguished physicists of England, and presenting a weight of authority entitled to the highest respect. Among these we find the names of Lyell, Hooker, Faraday, Owen, Airy, and Ackland. We have these names, because these gentlemen were summoned before the commission. But it is assuming very little to say that we might have had along with them those of every eminent physicist in England, had they all been in like manner called upon for their evidence.

The adaptedness of this class of subjects to the mental wants of boys in the earlier period of their education, and its fitness, therefore, to fasten their attention and keep alive their mental activity, is manifested in the earnest interest they display in any description of physical or chemical experiments, and in the eagerness with which they will endeavor to imitate such and contrive new ones. It is manifest in the curiosity they exhibit to witness the action and to understand the *rationale* of every new machine which falls in their way, and in the efforts to invent or to construct for themselves, which form a part of the early history of almost every youth. It is interesting to any one to be introduced at any time of life into a great cotton-mill or foundery, or manufactory of any description which he has never seen before, but to a young lad, whose observant powers are in the morning of their development, and who possesses the lively impressibility belonging to that early age, such a visit is a source of delight beyond all measure, and it is often found almost impossible to tear him away from objects which so fill him with admiration and gratify his desire to know.

If it were proper here to refer to matters of personal history, in illustration of what I have asserted of the fitness of the sciences of Nature to occupy the place of precedence in an educational system founded upon that sound philosophy which consults first the demands of Nature, I would say that the point of my own life to which, at a distance of more than forty years, I look back as that in which my education truly began, was that at which, while engaged in the irksome study of the dead languages, which for the seven years preceding my admission to college, crushed me down like an incubus, I had an opportunity to attend a course of lectures on chemistry, magnetism, and electricity by an itinerant lecturer. It seemed to me that a new world had suddenly been revealed to me. From that time forward I could think of nothing else. It was my constant amusement, with such rude materials as I could gather, to repeat the experiments which I had seen, and to endeavor to devise new ones. Cut off from books of my own on those subjects, I improved my time during the holidays which permitted me to visit home, in devouring the text-books of a sister, who, being superior to me in age, was pursuing in her own school, subjects which, according to the received theory, are more advanced than those then allowed to me—that is to say, the dead languages. In assuming, therefore, that those subjects are the subjects best suited to early mental culture, I do not merely put forth opinions founded on considerations *a priori*, I speak with the conviction which results from actual experience.

But these subjects are recommended not only on educational grounds, but because they embody in themselves a vast amount of substantial knowledge, such as cannot fail to be of the highest practical usefulness in life. They relate to the real and material world by which man is surrounded, and in the midst of which he lives. Whatever may be the value of the study of the classics in a subjective point of view, nothing could possibly more thoroughly unfit a man for any immediate usefulness in this matter-of-fact world, or make him more completely a stranger in his own home, than the purely classical education which used recently to be given, and which with some slight improvement is believed to be still given, by the universities of England. This proposition is very happily enforced by a British writer, whose strictures on the system appeared in the London *Times* some twelve or thirteen years ago :

" Common things are quite as much neglected and despised in the education of the rich as in that of the poor. It is wonderful how little a young gentleman may know when he has taken his university degrees, *especially if he has been industrious, and has stuck to his studies.* He may really spend a long time in looking for somebody more ignorant than himself. If he talks with the driver of the stage-coach, that lands him at his father's door, he finds he knows nothing of horses. If he falls into conversation with a gardener, he knows nothing of plants or flowers. If he walks into the fields, he does not know the difference between barley, rye, and wheat; between rape and turnips; between lucerne and saintfoin; between natural and artificial grass. If he goes into a carpenter's yard, he does not know one wood from another. If he comes across an attorney, he has no idea of the difference between common and statute law, and is wholly in the dark as to those securities of personal and political liberty on which we pride ourselves. If he talks with a county magistrate, he finds his only idea of the office is, that the gentleman is a sort of English sheik, as the mayor of the neighboring borough is a sort of cadi. If he strolls into any workshop, or place of manufacture, it is always to find his level, and that a level far below the present company. If he dines out, and as a youth of proved talents, and perhaps university honors, is expected to be literary, his literature is confined to a few popular novels—the novels of the last century, or even of the last generation, history, and poetry, having been almost studiously omitted in his education. The girl who has never stirred from home, and whose education has been economized, not to say neglected, in order to send her own brother to college, knows vastly more of those things than he does. The same exposure awaits him wherever he goes, and whenever he has the audacity to open his mouth. *At sea he is a landlubber, in the country a cockney, in town a greenhorn, in science an ignoramus, in business a simpleton, in pleasure a milksop*—everywhere out of his element, everywhere at sea, in the clouds, adrift, or by whatever word utter ignorance and incapacity are to be described. In society and in the work of life, he finds himself beaten by the youth whom at college he despised as frivolous or abhorred as profligate. He is ordained, and takes charge of a parish, only to be laughed at by the farmers, the tradespeople, and even the old women, for he can hardly talk of religion without betraying a want of common sense."

I know that with a pretty large class of educational philosophers, when methods of education are under discussion, the word *usefulness* has long been tabooed. I know that with such, to speak of a subject of study as likely to be productive of direct and practical and tangible benefit to the learner in the real business of life, is to bring that subject immediately under suspicion, if not to insure its summary condemnation without any examination of its claims. I cannot but hold, on the contrary, that if we can find any subject which, while it is capable of affording the most salutary intellectual exercise, is also certain to enrich the student with a store of knowledge of that very kind of which he is going to feel the need every day of his life, then this subject should have a place in our educational schemes in preference to any which can only claim the first of these advantages without possessing the second at all.

The kind of lofty contempt or aversion to subjects recommended for their practical utility, which is manifested by the class of educators to which I have referred, appears to be founded upon an assumption which has been so long taken for granted, that for them it has passed into a kind of axiom, and that is, that a subject of knowledge which is adapted to educational uses cannot be, or at least is extremely unlikely to be, of any other direct use in the world; and conversely, that a subject which is self-evidently practically useful can by no possibility have any educational use whatever. According to them, therefore, as it has been very well remarked before, Nature seems in respect to this particular matter to have deviated from that rule of severe economy which distinguishes her everywhere else, and to have ordained a necessity for two sets of machinery where one might have sufficed—ordained, that is, that the mind shall require one class of studies for subjective culture, and another class for its furniture—one class to make it fit for work, and another class to provide for it material to work upon. The fallacy of this doctrine has been so well exposed by abler hands—notably by Dr. Hodgson, of England, and by Mr. Atkinson in our own country—that I will not dwell upon it here. I mention it only for the purpose of entering my protest against any disparagement of the studies which I would recommend as preparatory to college, to be deduced from the consideration that they have upon them the taint of possible usefulness.

I have dwelt somewhat at length upon the subjects of study which have occupied us thus far, because of their pre-eminent importance and their adaptation to a special culture now wholly neglected, and not because I consider them, in themselves, sufficient in the business of preparation for college. There is no period in a course of education in which it is not important to vary the labor, and to relieve the tension upon one class of faculties by calling another into action. There are certain subjects which are now professedly required, although seldom made subjects of any searching examination—hardly, perhaps, examined upon at all—but of which, in the language of one of the resolutions of Convocation adopted at the last annual meeting, the knowledge is rather "presupposed." Among these are "arithmetic, English grammar, descriptive geography, and the history of the United States." To presuppose a knowledge of these things, without employing pretty thorough measures to ascertain that the presumption is justified, implies a tolerably strong exercise of faith, and requires that, like the marchioness in the "Curiosity Shop," one should "make believe a great deal." The experience of every college officer will, I think, bear me out in the assertion that, notwithstanding the length of time spent by most lads in preparatory study, there is always a large proportion who struggle to secure admission into college on the very minimum of attainment allowable; so that, when they know so little of the subjects on which they are sure of being examined, it is not quite safe to "presuppose" that they will know any thing at all of those on which they hope to escape examination. These subjects I would still insist on, and would insist also that we should adopt effectual means of insuring that they receive proper attention. And to these I would add plane geometry, so much of algebra as includes equations of the second degree, and finally the French and German languages. Time admonishes me not to attempt here the discussion of the propriety of all these suggestions. I will limit myself to assigning briefly my reasons for the last.

And here I would observe that the popular idea which limits the educational growth of the man to the period of scholastic discipline, is one which will not be entertained by any member of this Convocation. What the school and the college accomplish for the individual who enjoys their advantages, is to fit him to take his education into his own hands. No man who remains stationary at the point where the college leaves him can ever be distinguished in any vocation, or prove a successful laborer in any part of the intellectual field. When in the view of the world the education of the youth is completed, we must regard it, in its highest and most appropriate sense, as only just begun. In order, therefore, that it may proceed successfully, the student must be in possession of certain instrumentalities, which he will henceforth find indispensable to every effective step of progress. And among these instrumentalities, none is more essentially important than a knowledge of those languages in which, along with his own, is embodied the richest literature of modern times upon all subjects of interest to man. As the commonest education exacts, as a condition antecedent, the power to read at least one language, so the highest demands a similar power for more than one; and the student whose tastes, or whose ambition, or whose sense of duty impels him to aim unceasingly at progress, should he have neglected the study of the modern languages till the close of his collegiate career, will find himself arrested or seriously embarrassed, at the very outset of his independent labors, by the impossibility of consulting authorities, or of keeping himself advised of the simultaneous labors of others. Neglects, I say, to the *close of his collegiate career*, for if he neglects these subjects *before* he becomes a member of college, that is what he is practically pretty sure to do; since there is no college known to me in which the modern languages form, much more than in name, a part of the regular teaching. It should not be forgotten that the knowledge of French and German which the scholar or the scientific man of this day needs, is not such a knowledge as that which our graduates usually possess of Latin and Greek—a knowledge, that is to say, which does not permit them to read those languages with fluency—a fluency something like that with which they read their mother tongue. It must be a real knowledge, such a knowledge as frees them effectually from slavery to grammars and lexicons. Surely the acquisition of such a knowledge, which to the man who is to be really educated is absolutely a *sine qua non*, may much better be commenced in early life, when the other implements essential to mental progress are acquired, than deferred to the period to which, unfortunately, so many defer it, when it forms an obstruction to mental progress in mid career—an obstruction which must be removed with much annoying and impatient labor before the student is ready to make a single further step of advance.

But it may be inquired, if foreign languages are to be made part of the early discipline, what becomes of the objection to Latin and Greek, as unsuited to the powers of the juvenile learner? The reply is twofold—first, these languages by no means present the difficulties to the learner which are characteristic of Latin and Greek. They are less complicated in structure, and, at least in the case of the French, far less different in their usages from our own. But secondly and chiefly, the objection to the Latin and Greek is to be found quite as much in the stereotyped modes of presenting them—modes which it is probably vain to expect to alter, and which need not be altered, if we defer the teaching to a period a little later—as to the nature of the languages themselves. The modes of teaching which I believe are universally prevalent, are after the severest fashion synthetic. They are as totally unsuited to the state of mental development of the juvenile learner as they could by any possibility be made. And this fact, apart from the difficulties inherent in the languages themselves, is, in my mind, quite decisive of the question.

The prevalent modes of teaching the modern languages are not synthetic, or are so to a much less degree. Those employed with young learners ought not to be so, and certainly need not be.

To this it may be added, that if there were no difference between the two classes of languages in the respects which have just been indicated, and were the modern languages in this part of the course just as objectionable in their subjective relations as the ancient, there is this, at least, to be said in favor of the former, which is not at all true of the others, that they will probably be really mastered before they are done with, and will certainly be of some practical use after they are mastered.

If up to the age of fourteen, fifteen, or sixteen years—preferably the last—a lad shall have been subjected to the training indicated in the foregoing remarks, he will then be in condition to take up, profitably, along with the studies above enumerated, the Latin, and somewhat later, the Greek language. I am not quite sure that it might not be well to drop from the preparatory course the Greek altogether, and to leave that study wholly to the college. That is a question at which I will merely hint without discussing it. In such a case, the omission would be with a view to make the preparation in Latin more thorough. And considering the great help which may be derived, in the study of this language, from the knowledge of the languages (especially of the French) already acquired, there can be no doubt that a single additional year of study would result in a more satisfactory preparation for college than is now obtained in three, or four, or five. Thus there could be secured, along with a vast and valuable fund of real knowledge, an immense economy of time.

Furthermore, I cannot but be convinced that such a preparatory training would render the *collegiate* course greatly more profitable than it is at present; and still further, that classical scholarship itself, whose peculiar friends and champions may be disposed to see in all that has been said, nothing but a tissue of dangerous heresies, would be improved to that extent that it might become no very uncommon thing among us to find a graduate who should really be able to *read* Latin and Greek.

In conclusion, I have to advert to one serious fact which is always a subject of discouragement to me when I think of the possibility of a reform of the higher education in our country. It is this. There are between two hundred and two hundred and fifty institutions in the United States which are chartered as colleges. Any movement which any one of these, or any limited number of these may make, in the direction of larger exactions as qualifications for admission, is likely to result, not in the hoped-for improvement of the system, but in driving students from their own doors to those of their more accommodating neighbors. The colleges of New York, bound together in a kind of federal league, with the advantage of a common supervisory board, might act unitedly; and if New York were isolated in the world—cut off by an ocean from other States, or severed by difference of language and political institutions from the peoples on its borders—they might act with effect. As we are actually situated, it would be no very difficult thing to improve our system of education at the expense of our existence.

It is unfortunately true of a very large proportion of our young men that they desire not so much an education as the name of being educated. All these, where other things are equal, will naturally prefer those institutions which will furnish them the coveted certificate on the easiest terms. Nothing short of an effort in which all of the leading colleges of the country should act simultaneously and in concert, could probably avail to change materially the system which at present exists. Whether it is owing to the faults of this system, or to some deeper lying cause, it is a fact which cannot be controverted, that our colleges are gradually losing ground in the public estimation. Though the creation of new ones is an every-day occurrence, the ratio to the entire population of the aggregate annual number of their graduates is steadily, though slowly, diminishing. In England, also, a similar change seems to be simultaneously going on. Conclusive proof of this is presented by Mr. Atkinson, in his able address before the Massachusetts Institute of Technology; and among his citations is the remarkable testimony of Lord Lyndhurst, who expressed in Parliament, in 1855, the opinion that the universities had evidently a far weaker hold upon the public feeling of the country than they had possessed at no very distant previous period. "When I first entered public life," said he, "I found in the other House of Parliament that a majority of the members of that assembly had been educated at one or the other of the universities. Now, however, as I understand, not more than one-sixth, or, at most, one-fifth of the representatives of the people have been educated at either of those great institutions."

I cannot but regard these results as owing, in some degree, to the faults of the preparatory system in both countries; faults which the subsequent teaching in the colleges does not and cannot correct, and which entail educational deficiencies—deficiencies of practical knowledge on subjects held in the highest esteem by the public—upon all their graduates.

If we take up the reports of the regents of the university of this State, we shall see that in every academy under their control, without exception I believe, instruction is given on all those subjects which I have named as proper to be placed upon the list of preparatory studies. These subjects are not taught to those who are in process of preparation for college in those schools. They are undoubtedly taught to others no more advanced in age than they. When the public see these things, how is it possible that they should fail occasionally to draw unfavorable comparisons? How is it possible that they should not sometimes imagine that perhaps the education which a youth may acquire in the academy may better fit him for success in life, than all that can be done for him by a system which carries him professedly a great deal higher, yet lays its first foundation in a manner of which common sense fails to discover the wisdom?

Permit me, finally, to remark that I have not submitted these observations with any expectation that they will affect the action of this Convocation. If the views which I have expressed have any foundation in reason, I am aware that they too widely differ from those which are generally entertained, to justify me in anticipating that they will be immediately approved. If they serve to awaken attention to the subject, and lead to its more deliberate examination, all the end which I have proposed to myself in presenting them will have been answered.

THE DEVELOPMENT OF IDEAS IN PHYSICAL SCIENCE.

AN ADDRESS DELIVERED BEFORE THE ROYAL ACADEMY OF SCIENCES, IN MUNICH, 25TH JULY, 1866.

BY

JUSTUS VON LIEBIG.

ON THE

DEVELOPMENT OF SCIENTIFIC IDEAS.

THE history of physical science teaches us that our knowledge of things and of natural phenomena has, for its starting-point, the material and intellectual wants of man, and is conditioned by both. Nature has denied to man the means of withstanding injuries from without, which constantly imperil his existence; and it is, first of all, the pressure of the external world upon him, which arouses his dormant intellectual energies to resist it. All that he needs for shelter against the weather and against his enemies, for subsistence, and for the restoring of his health, he wins from nature; whence results an acquaintance with innumerable objects and their properties, and with the events which make them suitable for his ends.

In a former discourse I had occasion to speak of the peculiar power of the imagination, of bringing the images awakened in it by sensual impressions into mutual relation, and thence of framing conclusions standing in a dependence on each other, similar to that of the conceptions which lead the intellect in its combinations; with this difference, however, that the conclusions of the imaginative faculty are themselves images. What, for the intellect, a word is, as mark of a conception, that for the phantasy is an impression of sense. The word "tar" might produce no effect at all on the imagination of most men, whereas the smell of tar might perchance awaken, in the fancy of an individual, the image of a ship or harbor which he had visited years before.

The husbandman, herdsman, hunter, live in immediate intercourse with nature: the first learns, through mere sensual perception, how sunshine and rain affect the growth of his vegetables, how the seed germinates and is developed into a plant, how the plant blossoms and bears fruit; so, too, the herdsman gathers a mass of experiences concerning the nutrition and propagation of the animals he guards, he becomes acquainted with their diseases, thence with nutritive and poisonous plants; he forms for himself a clock in the starry sky, and learns the course of the heavenly bodies, and how they change with the seasons. The priest, who dissects the victim, comes to know its internal parts and their connection. A multitude of such facts enables the observers of them to draw inferences as to the existence of others. The shepherd seeks medicinal herbs for his animals, and afterward applies them to men. From the changes caused by disease in the organs of beasts, the sacrificing priest forms judgments as to the nature of human maladies. Thus the shepherd becomes the earliest therapeutist, the priest the first pathologist. The methods of preparing leather, soap, glass, wine, oil, bread, cheese, were devised through conclusions of a like kind; they were primitive; even so the converting of wool and vegetable fibres into textures, the process of dyeing, that of extracting many metals, as copper, tin, iron, silver, and gold, from their ores.

Man's superiority to the beast depends essentially on his faculty of devising inventions for the gratification of his wants, and it is the sum of them amongst a people which embraces the conception of their "civilization." Through inventions in the industrial arts, in medicine, mechanics, astronomy, facts are acquired indispensable to the subsequent development of science: they lead to an acquaintance with the phenomena of motion in the heavens and on the earth's surface, with the component parts of terrestrial bodies, animals, and plants; to the discovery of the effects of fire and of natural forces: but the experimental procedure, which conducts to inventions, seeks no explications of the nature and essence of things and phenomena, for this lies wholly beside its aim.

The scientific knowledge of nature has a different problem; it springs out of man's intellectual wants, out of an impulse of his soul to interpret the world wherein he lives, and the objects and appearances which daily engross his senses. But, in the beginning of his inquiry, he knows nothing of the nature of his senses, nor that the ground of things is inaccessible to them; those senses, which are to help him understand the outward world, are, for him, instruments with the handling of which he is unacquainted; he sees and hears, yet knows nothing of light or sound, knows not whether he sees in his eyes or out of them, nor that the temperature he feels is his own.

History informs us that mankind's representations of outward objects have been developed in like manner as with the child, which learns to cognize the indications of its senses only by degrees. Through repeated examination of objects with hand, eye, tongue, the child comes to ascertain their figure, color, and quality, and to distinguish the tangible, resisting solid from the fluid, cold from warm, dry from moist; and his further development depends essentially on his power of reproducing to himself his perceptions, without further aid from sense. Gradually the remembered images accumulate, and the intellect begins, unconsciously, to ask questions of the senses; it compares, and discovers resemblances and differences; learns that the cold object sometimes becomes warm; the fluid, solid; the solid, fluid. It is long, however, before man marks the peculiar and essential in each thing; his conception of motion is connected with that of a hand, which lifts, draws, or pushes a body.

With notions of this sort the investigation of nature began, and its subsequent development proceeded as in an individual, only that the senses and intellect of many were concerned in it; each, in his contact with objects and his contemplation of events, assumes a standing-point of his own, each sees a different face and profile in the thing or the phenomenon, which is thus gradually studied on all its sides; subsequently, when the individualities become better defined, it is found that many phenomena are composed of parts, and that things co-operate which elude ordinary perception; the earlier confidence in the indications of sense is lost, and tests for their examination are sought.

Thus are gradually formed determinate conceptions of things and events, conceptions serviceable in intellectual operations; with the increase of them, the number of their combinations is of course augmented, as also the command of the intellect over the senses; instead of questions merely spontaneous, it now frames them with definite purpose, and instead of single questions, a multitude. The perceptions thus become conscious observations.

Nobody will affirm that in the senses of men there lay an obstacle, in earlier times, to perceiving things as we now perceive them. Nor again, is the difference between our perceptions and earlier ones, as to many phenomena, due to the want of facts in those times. True, we know more facts than formerly; nevertheless, those relative to the most frequently recurring phenomena, e. g., to air and fire, evaporation and freezing, rain and vapor, heat and cold, were as well known a thousand years ago as now; and nobody will believe that before the discovery of oxygen, people had any doubt about the necessity of air in combustion and respiration, or that of a strong draught to the production of greater heat.

Our superior intelligence rests not on our senses, nor on our larger intellectual faculties; for, as to the latter, the great philosophers of antiquity, who occupied themselves in seeking explications of the nature of things and of phenomena, stand to this day unsurpassed. The real ground is, that we are become richer in conceptions. But man is not born with notions of things; that is, he is not born acquainted with sensible objects, their properties and effects; those notions must be gained by experience, and become developed in his mind; far otherwise than with the animal, whose faculties expand to their attainable perfection, without his own effort, by means of natural laws acting in him.

All these conceptions have sprung or been derived from sensible marks, and as natural phenomena are always composite, and their conditions or parts are likewise things having determinable and invariable marks, it is clear that the conception of an object or phenomenon must involve all these marks. We speak of *carbon* as an element of plants or of the animal body, without, however, thinking under that name, of diamond, charcoal, sea-coal or lampblack; similarly, of phosphorus and iodine, which do not occur at all in nature as such. These are simply abstract conceptions, which, once fixed, excite, in all cases where their marks are perceived, the idea of carbon, phosphorus, iodine.

Since, now, natural phenomena are interconnected like the knots of a net, the investigation of particular phenomena evinces that they have certain conditions (which, as remarked, are active things) in common; and, as the whole number of the conditions or parts of all natural phenomena is limited and proportionally small, all these phenomena must come at last to be resolved into conceptions. This is the problem of science. Scientific progress depends on the accumulation of facts, though this progress stands not in relation to their number, but to the sum of the materials of thought derived from them. A thousand facts change not of themselves the standing-point of science, and a single one, which has become comprehensible, outweighs, in time, the value of all the others. These remarks concerning the development of our empirical conception, are perhaps fitted to lead to a juster estimate, than hitherto, of the different periods in the knowledge of natural phenomena.

As the explication of a natural phenomenon is a logical process, the intellect is able to fix beforehand the principles, that is, the logical conditions, conjointly requisite to such explication. This was done by Aristotle. "The procedure of philosophy," he remarks, "is that of all the other sciences; we must first collect facts, and get a knowledge of the things which are the subject of them: not the mass of facts at once, but each for itself is to be first examined, and conclusions thence drawn. Having the facts, it is our subsequent business to establish their connection. The facts themselves are obtained through sensual perceptions; when these are imperfect, so will be the knowledge reared upon them We can have no general theoretical propositions, except by means of induction, and inductions can be framed only through sensual perceptions, for these are concerned with the particular."

Such are the principles of investigation bequeathed us by the greatest of the ancient thinkers. They are as valid now as they were two thousand years ago.

Comparing Aristotle's explanations of natural phenomena, as well as those of the whole following series of investigators, down to our day, we find at all times the opinion prevalent that the conceptions were in harmony with the facts, and indeed the explications always corresponded to the laws of logic, but the later ones are constantly in contradiction with the earlier; what was deemed true is afterward found to be false, and thus the following explanations always annul the preceding, which procedure goes on for centuries. Manifestly, therefore, the truth of explications does not depend on the principles of logic alone. If, however, we consider the empirical conceptions of Aristotle and of subsequent investigators, we at once perceive the ground wherefore the most highly developed intellect and the subtlest logic are not sufficient, of themselves, to the framing of a just explication, for this depends on the *contents* of the empirical conceptions.

At the outset the facts embraced in a conception are indeterminate, being not fixed either in their number or extension, whence the first explications can, manifestly, be neither definite nor limited, and they must change just in proportion as the facts are more distinctly ascertained, and as the unknown ones belonging to the conception are discovered and are incorporated in it. The earlier explanations are therefore only relatively false, and the later only therein truer that the contents of the conceptions of things are more comprehensive, determinate, and distinct. This takes place in a certain succession.

No later developed conception can precede in time an earlier, and if this happens the conception is without effect, because deficient in comprehension. On the earlier conception is grounded the development of all the following ones. The explications of natural phenomena by the Greek philosophers, and by subsequent investigators, manifest the extent and comprehension of their empirical ideas, and nothing further; in which respect those explications are of special interest for the history of the evolution of ideas in natural science, containing, as they do, the beginnings and bases of our own conceptions.

Aristotle distinguishes the solid from the fluid and aëriform. All solid things are with him varieties of something solid; we can understand that transparent bodies have something in common with water; but language is inadequate to the limiting of the other differences of solid bodies in figure, color, hardness; that alone is determinable which can be formed from those bodies, or which proceeds from them. A white stone, in the fire, yields lime; another white stone melts into glass; a red stone gives iron; another red stone gives quicksilver; a gray stone, tin; a black, lead. "The essential of things," remarks Aristotle, "lies in the form." *Here is the first conception of chemical analysis.*

"Daily experience shows that solids cannot float in air or in space, unless sustained by something, and as we see the stars behind the moon, and the moon is nearer the earth than the sun is, these bodies must, as solids, be fixed on transparent rings or spherical shells, which revolve about the earth, bearing those bodies with them.

"A stone, falling freely, descends to the earth with accelerated velocity; the senses and understanding are wholly incapable of perceiving that the earth has any connection with the fall; evidently there must exist an impulse in the stone itself to seek that place which Nature has assigned to it." *Here is the beginning of the conception of gravity, or of an attractive force.*

These notions of the Greeks were entirely in accordance with their experience, and so far right, as no others were then possible. The conception of time, which belongs to the composite notion of velocity, was first developed fifteen hundred years after Aristotle, and became incorporated in it. Clocks, or time-measurers for short intervals, the Greeks had not.

In the beginning of physical investigation, the complex phenomena of rain, rainbows, combustion, and respiration, are of course looked upon as simple, for nothing is then known of their parts; later it is found that cloud must precede rain, that without the sun there is no rainbow, and without air no combustion or respiration. The subsequently observed part of the phenomenon is constantly regarded as its cause, the sun as cause of the rainbow, the air as cause of respiration and combustion, entirely in the sense that we consider the moon's revolution as causing the ebb and flow.

So the detecting and establishing by Thales of the manifold relations of water, of those of air by Anaximenes, of those of fire by Heraclitus, belong to the greatest discoveries, for these philosophers thus cleared the way for all the questions relating to the most important phenomena on the earth's surface, to the life of animals and men—questions which engrossed attention up to the most recent period.

From the acute verbal analyses of the Greek thinkers, we learn with great definiteness the sum of the conceptions, which the words, that occupied them in their intellectual operations, involve, and it would suffice to compare the comprehension of one of these words, *e. g.*, "air," in its several periods, with our own, in order to obtain a clear view of the character of the empirical conceptions in those periods, and of their mode of development.

The Greeks knew that air in a bladder resists pressure, and that the water in which an empty glass is inverted will not fill the glass; air was regarded as a resisting, space-filling thing, as an element, and, next to fire (*i. e.*, smoke which ascends in the atmosphere), as the lightest element. Down to the beginning of the sixteenth century, it was supposed to be transformable into water, in the middle of that century, as not transformable into water—it was found to contain water in the form of air; in 1630 it was ascertained to be heavy, *i. e.*, ponderable; 1643, to be something which presses with its whole weight upon all bodies on the earth's surface; 1647, it was discovered that its invisible molecules press upon each other and are elastic, whence the lower atmospheric strata are denser than the higher; 1660, that kinds of air, elastic like common air, can be produced artificially in chemical processes; 1727, that there are such kinds of air in plants, animal matters, stones, and metallic calxes; not products, but educts, many combustible, others extinguishing fire; 1774, amongst them a kind wherein combustible bodies burn more freely than in common air; 1775, that the mass of the atmosphere consists of two sorts of air, one of which supports combustion, the other not, moreover of a variable amount of watery vapor; at the close of the eighteenth century, that it contains also carbonic acid; in the nineteenth century, ammonia and nitric acid, and, lastly, that fungous spores of all sorts float in it.

Our standing-point relatively to the conception of air

has been gained in consequence of the efforts of hundreds of the acutest of minds, during a space of more than two thousand years, through a continual extending, purging, and limiting of the original conception, and therein lies the difference between former notions of things and events, and those of our own day. I shall afterward have occasion to show that, to the discovery of the facts which were connected with the conception of air, and which gradually gave to its comprehension more largeness and definiteness, the "idea" of the facts was anterior, *i. e.*, that they were first "thought" and then discovered.

It is readily perceived that most of our conceptions in philosophy, and especially in jurisprudence, have been obtained and evolved in a way wholly similar, so that, for instance, the notions now embraced in the word "state" or "church" differ from those of a century ago. The conception of "God" undergoes change and development with that of "force."

Each of our present notions is the fruit of time, and of infinite toil and intellectual effort, and if our speculations are less bold than those of the Greeks, it is because we have learned, from their example, that the highest soaring of imagination and the subtlest logic change not our standing-point, and are without effect on the regular course of the evolution of our empirical conceptions. Euclid, with all his great mathematical talent, believed that vision takes place by means of rays issuing *from* the eyes; and Descartes, one of the most powerful of all thinkers, could not rise, in his day, to the notion of an attractive force.

The opinion prevails widely that there was a gap in the investigation of nature between the days of the Greeks and our modern times down to the fifteenth century. Accordingly, the middle ages are characterized by historians as a period of pause and stagnation, and the fifteenth century as that of the renascence of the sciences. As regards Europe this opinion is not absolutely true, and does not hold of Western Europe (Germany, England, and the present France), in which Grecian and Roman culture could not have become extinct in the middle ages, seeing it was not introduced there until much later. It should be remembered that, in the times of the academies of Athens, Western Europe was inhabited by half-savage populations, who clothed themselves in skins; that under Charlemagne most of the dignitaries and greatest barons of the empire could not write their own names; that in the thirteenth century Rome was still the focus of the traffic in Christian slaves, and that there were great slave-markets in Lyons, and in the cities lying on the east and north seas.

Charlemagne's endeavors, by the establishment of schools, to elevate the intelligence of the rude and ignorant priesthood of the age, could have no result; the soil on which culture thrives being not yet prepared. The development of culture, *i. e.*, the extending of man's spiritual domain, depends on the growth of the inventions which condition the progress of civilization; for, through these, new facts are obtained, indispensable to the increase of empirical conceptions or material of thought.

The development of science, the mother of which is culture, requires still other conditions; it depends on the formation of a class who shall devote their powers to the cultivation of the intellectual domain, exclusive of every other end. As the men who consecrate themselves to this labor produce no marketable commodities which they can exchange for the necessaries of life, such a class cannot arise until a certain surplus amount of riches has been accumulated, not needed by its possessors for the satisfaction of their material wants. Such accumulation once realized, men's spiritual wants presently assert their claims, and the wealthy class becomes ready to exchange a portion of its riches for the means of mental culture.

Although, during the middle ages, there was uninterrupted intercourse between the Eastern empire and Italy, and no obstacle existed to the diffusion of Byzantine learning, this learning did not, however, pass into the West until the fourteenth century, because here an intellectual class being not yet formed, the conditions necessary to the encouragement and advancement of it were wanting. Manifestly, Grecian culture could spread in Western Europe only in proportion as the civilization of the peoples became approximate to that of Greek antiquity. It is easily shown that the civilization of the European populations constantly advanced from the decline of the old Greek states, but, through peculiar relations presently to be noticed, it remained for some time without influence on the progress of culture, *i. e.*, of its intellectual department, whence a seeming break.

As to the influence of inventions upon the development of conceptions and ideas in physical science, it is enough to mention that, *e. g.*, the true view of the motion of the earth and other planets became established through the invention of the telescope; as, also, all the advances of astronomy were dependent on the improvement of optical instruments. The invention of colorless glass preceded that of the telescope. The further improvement of optical instruments rested upon the fabrication of flint-glass, and on that of achromatic lenses, which Newton deemed impossible. With Galileo's telescope, Uranus and Saturn's satellites could not have been discovered. Copernicus regarded his own view, not as "true," but as "simpler" and "fairer," just as we consider the notions of the psychologist not true in the same sense as $2 \times 2 = 4$ is so, but as "appropriate," "profound," or "exhaustive."

Chemical analysis issued from the art of assaying; mineral chemistry from the technico-chemical trades; organic chemistry from medicine. The theory of heat has received extension through the steam-engine, that of light through photography.

In astronomy, the Greeks did the utmost that the command of a single unaided sense permitted; they discovered the law of the reflection of light, the arithmetical relations of tones, the centre of gravity, the law of the lever and that of hydrostatic pressure, and also whatever, by the aid of mathematics, could be deduced from these laws and from astronomical observations; but all further progress was restricted through the degree of their civilization. The source of the trade, wealth, and power of the Grecian states in their prime, was a very highly developed and varied industry: Corinth furnished what might be styled the Birmingham and Sheffield wares; Athens was the centre of such manufactures as are now distributed between Leeds, Staffordshire, and London (woollen cloths, dyeing, earthenwares, gold and silver utensils, ship-building). The citizens were in largest measure manufacturers, ship-owners, merchants, having their counting-houses and factories on all the coasts of the Black Sea and Mediterranean; the men of science were burghers' sons, and initiated in industrial pursuits. Socrates was a stone-cutter, Aristotle an apothecary (preparer of medicines and physician), Plato and Solon not unfamiliar with trade.

The learned, in ancient Greece, spoke and wrote the same language as the industrial class; in their education, the last stood on the same level with the philosophers;

they differed only in the direction of their knowledges. Democratic institutions united both in a close personal intercourse. Indeed, the thirty-eight chapters of the "Problems" seem to be nothing else but questions by masters of trades, artificers, musicians, architects, engineers, which Aristotle sought to answer, so far as his empirical conceptions enabled him.

No other country of the ancient world united (down to the time of Pericles), in its social state, in the intimate conjunction of the productive with the intellectual class, the conditions necessary to the origination of science, so well as Greece did. But Greece was a slave country, and in slavery lay the ban which enclosed her civilization in narrow limits and rendered them impassable. All the products of Greek manufactories were the work of slaves. Athens, in her prime, contained nearly two thousand slaves to every hundred citizens, a number which indicates the extraordinary development of her industry.

It is plain that a workman, *e.g.*, an artisan, is not, of himself alone, in a condition to produce more exchangeable commodities than will suffice to purchase for him and his family the merest necessaries; he must be able to command the labor of twenty men and upward, before he can manufacture a surplus adequate to satisfy the wants of a portion of his countrymen; and the entire industrial classes of a country must produce a very much greater surplus, before their commodities can become objects of foreign commerce. This last condition is realized in all industrio-commercial states, and was realized in Greece; for the wealth existing there in the precious metals was not obtained by pillage, but by exchanging the products of Grecian industry, in other countries, where they were more wanted than gold and silver.

The progress of Greek civilization was dependent essentially on the change of slave-labor into free, a transfor mation not supposable without the employment of natural forces, applied to labor-saving machines.

It is evident that, with the invention of a machine which shall convert a given natural force (*e. g.*, a falling weight of water) into an industrial force, performing the labor of twenty men, the inventor could grow rich and twenty slaves be set free; moreover, that the natural effect of the introduction of machines is an augmentation of the productive class, whence a greater number of inventors and increased production. But, in a slave-state, the application of natural forces and the substitution of machine-labor for servile, is mainly impossible, for as, in such a state, the profits of the capitalist rest upon his slaves, he sees that the introduction of machines must imperil his resources, and when, as in Greece, the capitalists belong to the ruling class, the government and people will combine to perpetuate the existing system, *i. e.*, slavery;—the government with the seemingly-wise purpose of assuring subsistence to the laborers.

Only the freeman, not the slave, has a disposition and interest to improve implements or to invent them; accordingly, in the devising of a complicated machine, the workmen employed upon it are generally co-inventors. The eccentric and the governor, most important parts of the steam-engine, were devised by laborers. The improvement of established industrial methods by slaves, themselves industrial machines, is out of the question.

Freedom, that is, the absence of all restrictions which can prevent men from using to their advantage the powers which God has given them, is the weightiest of all the conditions of progress in civilization and culture.

A glance at China enables us to understand the effect produced upon a gifted people, simply by excluding the application of natural forces to labor-saving machines. Its high civilization has been thus rendered stationary for the past two thousand years.

In England, however, and especially in the United States of North America, where free action is not restricted by antiquated regulations and laws, the product of ignorance, we see a perpetual growth of wealth, power, and civilization, and it can hardly be doubted that amongst the peoples of the North American Free States, all the conditions exist for their development to the highest point of culture and civilization attainable by men.

A modern state, wherein there is no liberty of industry, where the management and extension of a business depends on the will of ignorant officials, where the freeman is hindered from choosing the place which he finds most suitable for the employment of his powers, and cannot marry without permission of his superiors, this is the old slave-condition, in which the pith and marrow of the people is poor and without susceptibility for intellectual and moral culture, and of which the wealth and power are an allusive varnish that a little friction rubs away.

The effect of riches on the spirit of the productive classes is visible in the commercial states whose trade rests on industry. The sons of the opulent manufacturers and merchants abandon their fathers' business, which was the source of their wealth; being rich to superfluity, they transfer their ambition to the pursuit of rank and reputation, devoting themselves to science, to politics, to the army, or church, and in this wise the intellectual class grows out of the productive.

In modern Europe a manufacturer is not transmitted to

the third generation; so, too, most commercial houses pass to other hands in the second. Hence, in a free country, the renewal of the producing class with each generation, and the constant resuscitation of industry. The industrials, grown rich, give place to energetic, inventive poor men, and thus a circulation is established in the state, through which its power and wealth increase continually.

In Greece, the course of things was quite different. There, as everywhere, riches generated the intellectual order, whose maintenance, of course, depended on the productive class; but this last was not renewed and rejuvenated; the poor freeman was obliged to emigrate; he could, perhaps, fabricate a machine, but not slaves, and, without slaves, the acquisition of wealth, through industry, was impossible. Commerce alone remained open to a minority.

With the ceasing of that circulation in the state, which maintains industry and the power of production, and is the condition of their progress, Greece had reached the bounds of her civilization. There were no more inventions by the people grown rich, and, in the absence of new facts won from nature, the source of the empirical conceptions indispensable to the extension of the intellectual domain, *i. e.*, of culture, became exhausted. The trade in Grecian products necessarily passed, by degrees, into a trade in foreign commodities; the accumulated capital, therefore, could not long remain undiminished, though, indeed, the vital nerve of the slave-state was withered centuries before there were any outward marks of decline.

Greek civilization travelled through the Roman empire and the Arabians into every European country, and its continuous evolution is manifested throughout the middle ages in the increase of inventions. At the close of the fifteenth century we find already an advanced algebra and trigonometry, the decimal notation, an improved calendar, and a complete revolution prepared in medicine; we remark extraordinary progress in mining and smelting, in dyeing, weaving, tanning, in glass-making, architecture, and especially in the department of chemistry. Paper, telescopes, guns, clocks, knitting with needles, table-forks, horse-shoes, bells, chimneys, wood-engraving, copperplate-engraving, wiredrawing, preparing of steel, table-glass, lead-foiling and tin-foiling of mirrors, windmills, stamping-mills, saw-mills, were all invented; the corn-mill and the loom improved.

These facts give a notion of the progress of civilization in Western Europe, and, on these and on the geographical discoveries, rest all the acquisitions in the intellectual domain during the fifteenth century: we find a flourishing commerce, which, from Genoa, Pisa, Venice, and the coast-cities of the North and East Seas, embraced all Europe, linking it with Arabia and India, and having as its basis a varied industry in the busy towns of the Netherlands, Italy, Germany, and England; we see in these towns a free, opulent burgher-class arise in advanced vigor, and naturally from this class, in consequence of the accumulated wealth, the intellectual order develops itself. From that point began the continuation of Grecian and Roman culture.

The members of the newly originated intellectual class were at first occupied in gaining possession of the treasures of ancient learning; and so long as they were themselves still learners, that is, not so thoroughly imbued with the spirit of ancient culture as to be able to advance and extend it, they could not efficiently discharge their proper office of being teachers of the public; they even turned away from the people and the popular dialect, not indeed without reason, for the vernacular literature exhibited scarce any thing worthy to attract and enchain minds disciplined by the study of antique models.

The position and employment of the learned of those times concurred in withdrawing them from contact with the productive classes. Accordingly, the literature of that age gives no indication of the degree of the popular civilization and culture; for the knowledge circulating through the masses and absorbed into their thinking, a knowledge originating in their improved acquaintance with physical laws, and proportionate to the sum of their juster ideas of things and the relations of things, was not yet stored up in books, and was wholly foreign to the learned.

The approximation of the intellectual and productive orders was hardly prevented by the exclusiveness of the former; in truth, the industrial population, down to the fourteenth century, from the rudeness and poverty of the written language, lacked the necessary means of such approximation. In place of the learned, the Meistersanger, in their singing-schools, had much influence in promoting the development and diffusion of language, oral and written, amongst the burgher-classes. These last had been previously restricted altogether to personal intercourse through travel, for the interchange and increase of their experiences; they were migratory; but, with the command of a written language, the facts and observations gathered by them were collected and made diffusible; reading and writing, arts unknown before, were recognized by the people as most important helps for the advancement and interchange of knowledge—first of all in the towns whose industry was incompatible with a migratory population. In these towns the earliest popular schools were founded.

The impulse to diffuse the lore of antiquity, by means of schools, was as strong amongst the learned as was the wish for instruction in the productive class. Both circumstances combined to stimulate the desire for books; the difficulty of satisfying it through copyists gave occasion to the invention of printing, in the middle of the fifteenth century. A century earlier, the invention would have had no influence on intellectual progress. From the time of its actual occurrence, dates a new period in the history of culture.

A survey of literature, at the end of a century after the printing of the first book with movable type, awakens our astonishment at the extent and importance of the achievements in the physical sciences and medicine, and at the extraordinary mass of facts and experiences, which the middle ages had acquired and transmitted, in astronomy, technics, engineering, and in the trades, and which were now collected by the intelligent scholars of the learned schools, who stood nearest to the producing classes, namely the physicians. In the sixteenth century the physicians were the founders of the modern natural sciences, they participated in the diffusion and extension of Greek learning, and intervened in the intellectual education of the people.

Another century and a half elapsed, however, before the knowledge, accumulated by them, was arranged and rendered comprehensive and complete enough to be employed in university instruction. Hitherto the foreign language, in which that knowledge was communicated—a language universally current amongst the learned of Europe—had had the inestimable advantage of uniting all the European thinkers devoted to the sciences, in the solution of their high problems. Without the common Latin language, this fruitful conjunction of labors had been impossible. It was not until near the end of the eighteenth century, that, with the exclusion of Latin in schools and literature, the last barrier between the intellectual and producing classes fell. Both again spoke, as in old Greece, the same language, and understood each other; for science, school, and poetry acted conjointly in diffusing an equally high grade of intellectual discipline amongst all ranks.

With the extinction of the slavery of the ancient world, and the union of *all* the conditions for the evolution of the human mind, a progress in civilization and culture is thenceforth assured, indestructible, imperishable.

In the natural course of physical inquiry a change has taken place. Most of the facts from which the investigator elaborated empirical ideas, he had long received from the metallurgists, the engineers, the apothecaries, briefly, from the industrials, and had resolved their inventions into conceptions, which the producing classes received back in the form of explications and applied to their own practical ends. The industrials thence abandoned their dislike of theory; the craftsman, technist (Techniker), agriculturist, physician, as formerly in Greece, ask counsel of the learned theorist.

A new change began when the learned physical investigator, the teacher of medicine, had acquired the technical dexterity of the practical classes, and when these had appropriated the laws and scientific principles established by the learned. In the pursuit of his ends, the scientific inquirer has thus become independent and an inventor; the craftsman, agriculturist, etc., have gained independence of inquiry, intellectual freedom. The future discloses to our view an animated picture of an endless activity, fertile in results. The past appears to us now in a different light.

We see that the warfare against physical inquiry, waged by the scholasticism and theology of the middle ages, was of no import whatsoever. The ground of it was an inability, at the time, to distinguish a dogma from a fact. The spiritual and temporal powers united could not have prevented the invention of the telescope and mariner's compass and the discovery of oxygen, nor have repressed the effect of them on the minds of men. A book can be burned, but not a fact.

With the proof that this earth is a small planet circulating about the sun, the early representation of "Heaven" became meaningless, as did the representation of "Hell" with the explanation of fire. Upon the discovery of atmospheric pressure, the belief in witchcraft and magic had no further support, for, along with her "horror vacui," Nature lost her "willing," her love and her hate. With these discoveries, mankind began to feel their strength and position in the universe.

As to the scholasticism of the middle ages, had Aristotle and Plato risen from their graves, to become teachers in its schools, they could not have furthered intellectual progress, because of the lack of advanced empirical conceptions. The logic of those ages, and the intellectual gymnastics resting upon it, best corresponded to that time and the future. The hostility against the later physical inquiry was without effect.

Physical science would not have advanced one step further than it has done, nor have developed itself earlier or otherwise, even had the entire spiritual and political power been in league with it.

A computation, were it made, of the effect produced by

Luther upon our day and our stand-point, *with* the great discoveries in nature then extant, and of the effect these would have produced *without* Luther, would lead to a correct result.

We now know that ideas develop themselves organically according to determinate laws of nature and of the human mind, and we see the tree of knowledge which the Greeks planted expand uninterruptedly on the soil of civilization and with the due culture of it, and blossom and bear fruit, under the sunshine of freedom, at the proper time. We have learned that its branches can indeed be bent by external force, but not broken, and that its fine and innumerable roots lie hidden so deep, that their silent activity is wholly withdrawn from the will of men.

The history of nations informs us of the fruitless efforts of political and theological powers to perpetuate slavery, corporeal and intellectual: future history will describe the victories of freedom which men achieved through investigation of the ground of things and of truth—victories won with bloodless weapons, and in a struggle wherein morals and religion participated only as feeble allies.

OBSERVATIONS ON THE SCIENTIFIC STUDY OF HUMAN NATURE.

A LECTURE DELIVERED BEFORE THE LONDON COLLEGE OF PRECEPTORS.

BY

EDWARD L. YOUMANS, M.D.

"No system or rule of practice in education can safely be admitted which does not associate itself with this part of science (physiology)."

Sir Henry Holland.

"If it be possible to perfect mankind, the means of doing so will be found in the medical sciences."

Descartes.

"Of old it was the fashion to try to explain nature from a very incomplete knowledge of man; but it is the certain tendency of advancing science to explain man on the basis of a perfecting knowledge of nature."

Dr. Henry Maudsley.

ON THE SCIENTIFIC STUDY OF HUMAN NATURE.

PERHAPS the most correct conception of science that has yet been formed is that which regards it as the highest stage of growing knowledge. Ideas about men, like those about other subjects, undergo development. There is a rude acquaintance with human nature among barbarians: they observe that the young can be trained, and that men are influenced by motives and passions; for without some such knowledge, their limited social relations would be impossible. These primitive notions have been gradually unfolded by time into the completer and more accurate ideas which mark the civilized state. Yet the prevailing knowledge of human nature is still imperfect and empirical—that is, it has not expanded into rational principles and general laws. That it will become still more perfect accords with all analogy; and if this process continues, as it undoubtedly must, there seems reasonable hope of the formation of something like a definite Science of Human Nature.

That the scientific method of inquiry is inadequate and inapplicable to the higher study of man, is a widely prevalent notion, and one which seems, to a great extent, to be shared alike by the ignorant and the educated. Holding the crude idea that science pertains only to the material world, they denounce all attempts to make human nature a subject of strict scientific inquiry, as an intrusion into an illegitimate sphere. Maintaining that man's position is supreme and exceptional, they insist that he is only to be comprehended, if at all, in some partial, peculiar, and transcendental way. In entire consistence with this hypothesis, is the prevailing practice; for those who by their function as teachers, preachers, and lawgivers, profess to have that knowledge of man which best qualifies for directing him in all relations, are, as a class, confessedly ignorant of science. There are, some, however, and happily their number is increasing, who hold that this idea is profoundly erroneous, that the very term "human nature," indicates man's place in that universal order which it is the proper office of science to explore; and they accordingly maintain that it is only as "the servant and interpreter of nature" that he can rise to anything like a true understanding of himself.

The past progress of knowledge, as is well known, has not been a steady and continuous growth: it has advanced by epochs. An interval of apparent rest, perhaps long protracted, is brought to a close by the introduction of some new conception, which revolutionizes a department of thought, and opens new fields of investigation, that lead to uncalculated consequences. Those who have watched the later tendencies of scientific thought can hardly fail to perceive, that we of the present age are entering upon one of those great epochs in our knowledge of man. Standing at the head of the vast system of being of which he forms a part, it is inevitable that the views entertained concerning him at any age will be but a reflex of the knowledge of nature which that age has reached. So long as little was known of the order of the universe, little could be understood of him in whom that order culminates. Those triumphs of science which are embodied in external civilization are well fitted to kindle our admiration; but they are of secondary moment when compared with the consequences which must flow from the full application of the scientific method to the study of man himself.

The method of regarding man which tradition has transmitted to us from the earliest ages, is, at the outset, to cleave him asunder, and substitute the idea of two beings for the reality of one. Having thus introduced the notion of his double nature—mind and body as separate, independent existences—there grew up a series of moral contrasts between the disjointed products. The mind was ranked as the higher, or spiritual nature, the body as the lower, or material nature. The mind was said to be pure, aspiring, immaterial; the body gross, corrupt, and perishable; and thus the feelings became enlisted to widen the breach and perpetuate the antagonism. Having divided him into two alien entities, and sought all terms of applause to celebrate the one, while exhausting the vocabulary of reproach upon the other, the fragments were given over to two parties—the body to the doctors of medicine, and the spirit to the doctors of philosophy, who seem to have agreed in but one thing, that the partition shall be eternal, and that neither shall ever intrude into the domain of the other.

As a necessary consequence of this rupture, the living reality, as a subject of study, disappeared from view, and the dignified fraction was substituted in its place.

Not *man*, but *mind*, became the object of inquiry. With the disappearance of the actual being, went also the conception of individuality, and there remained only *mind as an abstraction*, to be considered as literally out of all true relations as if the material universe had never existed. The method thus begun has been closely pursued, and for thousands of years the chief occupation of philosophic thought has been to speculate upon the nature and operations of mind as manifested in consciousness. Admitting the legitimacy of the inquiry, and that it has to a certain extent yielded valid results, it is clear that the effect of the divorce was fatally to narrow the course of investigation and to prevent all free and thorough research into the reality of the case; thus justifying the charge of emptiness and fruitlessness which is now so extensively made against metaphysical studies. From Plato to Sir William Hamilton, who inscribed upon the walls of his lecture-room, "*On earth there is nothing great but man; in man there is nothing great but mind*," a method has been pursued so confessedly vacant of valuable results, that its partizans have actually denied the attainment of truth to be their object: declaring that the supreme aim of philosophy is nothing more than to serve as a means of intellectual gymnastics.*

In pointed contrast with this view is the method of modern science. In a spirit of reverence for the order and harmony of nature where all factitious distinctions of great and small disappear; striving to dispossess herself of prejudice, and to aim only at the attainment of truth; rejecting all assumptions which can show no better warrant than that they were made in the infancy of the

* See the opening lectures of Hamilton's Metaphysics.

race, she begins with the simple examination of facts, and rises patiently and cautiously to the knowledge of principles. The study of man is entered upon in the same temper, and by the same methods, that have conducted to truth in other departments of investigation. Finding the notion of his duality, as interpreted in the past, with its resulting double series of independent inquiries, to be erroneous, science proceeds at the outset to reunite the dissevered fragments of humanity, and to reconstitute the individual in thought as he is in life, a concrete unit—the living, thinking, acting being which we encounter in daily experience. It is now established that the dependence of thought upon organic conditions is so intimate and absolute, that they can no longer be considered except as unity. Man, as a problem of study, is simply an organism of varied powers and activities; and the true office of scientific inquiry is to determine the mechanism, modes, and laws of its action.

My purpose, on the present occasion, is to show that the doctrine which has prevailed in the past, and still prevails, is doomed to complete inversion; that the bodily organism which was so long neglected as of no account, is in reality the first and fundamental thing to be considered; and that, in reaching a knowledge of mind and character through the study of the corporeal system, there has been laid the firm foundation of that Science of Human Nature, the completion of which will constitute the next and highest phase in the progress of man. Of course, so vast a subject can receive but scanty justice in the limits of a lecture: the utmost that I can hope to do will be to present some decisive illustrations of the dependence of mental action upon the bodily system, and to point out certain important results which have been already arrived at by this method of inquiry. A hasty glance, in the first place, at the several steps by which it has been reached, will help to an understanding of the present state of knowledge upon the subject.

The establishment of the modern doctrine, that the brain is the organ of the mind, naturally led to a train of researches into the conditions of the connexion. The instrument of thought, being a part of the living system, is, of course, subject to its laws, and our understanding of its action becomes dependent upon the progress of physiological knowledge. Physiology, again, depending upon the various physical sciences, the higher investigation could proceed only with the general advance of inquiry. The discovery of the circulation of the blood laid the foundation for the modern science of physiology; but that discovery did not reach its full significance until chemistry had revealed the constitution of matter, and the reciprocal action of its elements: only then was it possible to arrive at the great organic laws of waste and repair, of digestion, nutrition, and respiration. The brain, in its functional exercise, was found to depend, equally with all other living parts, upon these processes. The discovery of the minuter structure of the brain resulted from the application of the perfected microscope. Its grey matter was found to consist of cells, and the white substance of fibres of amazing minuteness —the cells being regarded as the sources of nerve-power, while the fibres serve as lines for its discharge.

When a tolerably clear conception of the structure of the nervous system had been reached, physiology immediately propounded the question of its mode of action. The first decisive response was made a number of years ago, by Sir Charles Bell, who found that there are two great systems of nerves, which perform different functions; one conveying impressions from the surface of the body to the centres, and another transmitting impulses from the centres to the muscles, and thus controlling mechanical movement. This discovery was of the gravest importance. It had been contemptuously asked, What has anatomy to do with mind? Bell silenced this cavilling for ever by showing that it first revealed a definite mental mechanism, and traced out some of the fundamental conditions of the working of mind.

A few years later, Dr. Marshall Hall made another very important step, in determining the organic conditions of mental activity, by the discovery of the independent action of the spinal cord. It had hitherto been held, that the brain was the sole seat of nervous power. All impressions were supposed to be conducted directly to it, and all mandates to the muscles to issue from it; and as the brain was the seat of consciousness and volition, these operations were thought to be essentially involved in every bodily action. But Dr. Hall demonstrated that the spinal cord is itself a chain of nerve-centres, and that impressions reaching it from the surface through the sensory nerves, may be immediately *reflected* back, through the motor nerves, upon the muscles, thus producing bodily movements, without the brain being at all involved. This is termed *reflex action.* Thus, if the foot of a sleeper be tickled, it will be jerked away—that is, the impression from the skin is conveyed to the spinal centre, and an impulse is immediately reflected back, which contracts the proper muscles of the limbs, and the foot is withdrawn. The most perfect example of it, however, is where stimulus at the surface produces movements of the limbs after division of the cord from the head, and therefore in total unconsciousness. The discovery of reflex action was the first step in the systematic elucidation of the spontaneous movements, or what is known as the *automatic system* in animal mechanisms.

But reflex action has another aspect. When an impression passes upward along the cord to the nervous masses at the base of the brain, it first flashes into consciousness and becomes a sensation. Reflex effects now take place, in which sensation and consciousness are implicated. Winking, sneezing, coughing, swallowing, are examples: we are conscious of the actions, but they are not the results of volition. The will may, indeed, exert a partial control over them, but they are usually of an automatic character. Thus far, the part of the nervous mechanism called into action is the spinal system, and the ganglionic masses at the base of the brain known as the sensorium. This apparatus is not peculiar to man; he shares it with the entire vertebrate series, and it is regarded as the source of all purely instinctive actions.

The establishment of these fundamental facts in reference to the working of the mental mechanism of our nature—the definite separation of a large part of its actions from that higher sphere of intellection and volition to which they had hitherto been assigned, was a signal event in the progress of physiological inquiry, as it quickly led to the extension of the principle of automatism, to the cerebrum itself. This portion of the brain is now regarded as the organ of all the higher mental activities;—the seat of ideas and of the complex intellectual operations, memory, imagination, reason, volition. The most obvious case of reflex cerebral action is where a remembered or suggested idea produces a spontaneous movement. Thus, the recollection of a ludicrous incident may excite an involuntary burst of laughter, the remembrance of a disgusting taste may cause vomiting. When ideas are associated with pleasure or pain, a class of powerful feelings is produced,—the emotions, which become the springs of impulsion, or reflex activity. Those bursts of movement which are peculiar to the various emotions, as anger, terror, joy, and which we term their *expressions*, are examples of cerebral spontaneity.

These facts prepare us to understand the scope and limits of voluntary activity, the function of which is to restrain the impulsive tendencies, and direct the bodily movements to various ends. In voluntary action the will does not replace or dispense with the involuntary system, but rather *uses* it. Its action is limited by the laws of the vital mechanism with which it works. Of all the numberless movements going on in the organism, volition has control only of the muscular, and of these but partially. It cannot act directly upon the muscles, but liberates nerve-force in the brain, which, in turn, produces muscular contraction. The voluntary powers determine the *end* to be accomplished; and employ the automatic system to execute the determination. I will a given action, and of the many hundred muscles in my system, a certain, and perhaps a large number, will be called into simultaneous exercise, requiring the most marvellous combinations of separate actions to accomplish it; but the will knows nothing of this, it is concerned with the *result* alone.

In the formation of habits and in the processes of education, voluntary actions are constantly becoming reflex, or, as it is termed, "secondarily automatic." Thus learning to walk at first demands voluntary effort, but at length the act of walking becomes automatic and unconscious. So with all adaptive movements, as the manipulatory exercises of the arts; they at first require an effort of will, and then gradually become "mechanical," or are performed with but slight voluntary exertion. And so it is, also, in the purely intellectual operations, where the cerebral excitement, instead of taking effect upon the motor system, expends itself in the production of new intellectual effects, one state of consciousness passing into another, according to the established laws of thought. Here, also, the agency of the will is but partial, and the mental actions are largely spontaneous. In the case of memory, we all know how little volition can directly effect. We cannot call up an idea by simply *willing* it. When we try to remember something, which is, of course, out of consciousness, the office of volition is simply to fix the attention upon various ideas which will be most likely to recall, by the law of association, the thing desired. We have all experienced this impotence of the will to recover a forgotten name, or incident which may subsequently flash into consciousness after the attention has long been withdrawn from the search. The same thing is observed in the exercise of the imagination. It is said of eminent poets, painters, and musicians, that they are born, and not made; that is, their genius is an endowment of nature,—a gifted organism which spontaneously utters itself in high achievements, and they often present cases of remarkable automatism. When Mozart was asked how he set to work to compose a symphony he replied, "If you once *think* how you are to do it, you will never write anything worth hearing; I write because I cannot help it." Jean Paul remarks of the poet's work: "The character must appear living before you, and you must hear it, not merely see it; it must, as takes place in dreams, dictate to you, not you to it. A poet who must *reflect* whether, in a given case, he will make his character say Yes, or No, to the devil with him!" An author may be as much astonished at the brilliancy of his unwilled inspirations as his most partial reader. "That's splendid!" exclaimed Thackeray, as he struck the table in admiring surprise at the utterance of one of his characters in the story he was writing. Again, the mental actions which constitute reasoning, have an undoubted spontaneous element, the office of volition being, as in the former cases, to rivet the attention to the subject of inquiry, while the gradual blending of the like in different ideas into general conceptions is the work of the involuntary faculties. You cannot will a logical conclusion, but only maintain steadily before the mind the problem to be solved. Sir Isaac Newton thus discloses the secret of his immortal discoveries: "I keep the subject constantly before me, and wait till the first dawnings open, by little and little, into a full light."

But corporeal agency in processes of thought has an aspect still more marked; the higher intellectual operations may take place, not only independent of the will, but also independent of consciousness itself. Consciousness and mind are far from being one and the same thing. The former applies only to that which is at any time present in thought; the latter comprehends all psychical activity. Not a thousandth part of our knowledge is at any time in consciousness, but it is all and always in the mind. An idea or feeling passes out of consciousness, but not into annihilation; in what state, then, is it? We cannot be satisfied with the indefinite statement, that it is stored away in the receptacle or chamber of memory. Science affirms an organ of mind, and demands an explanation, in terms of its action. As the thought passes from consciousness, something remains in the cerebral substratum, call it what you will, —trace, impression, residue. What the precise character of these *residua* may be, is perhaps questionable, but it is impossible to deny their existence in some form consistent with the nature of the cerebral structure and activity. All thoughts, feelings, and impressions, when disappearing from consciousness, leave behind them in the nerve substance, their effects or residua, and in this state they constitute what may be termed latent or statical mind. They are brought into consciousness by the laws of association, and there is much probability that, in this unconscious state, they are still capable of acting and reacting, and of working out true intellectual results.

There are few who have not had experience of this unconscious working of the mind. It often happens that we pursue a subject until arrested by difficulties which we cannot conquer, when, after dismissing it entirely from the thoughts for a considerable interval, and then taking it up again, the obscurity and confusion are found to have cleared away, the subject is opened in quite new relations, and marked intellectual progress has been made. Nor can we explain this by assuming that the arrest was simply due to weariness, and the clearer insight to the restoration of vigour by rest, as after a refreshing night's sleep. Time enters largely as an element of the case; weeks and months are often required to produce the result, while the entirely new development which the subject is found to have undergone, seems only explicable by the intermediate and unconscious activity of the cerebral centre. The brain also receives impressions and accumulates residua in partial or total unconsciousness. In reading, for example, we gather the sense of an author most perfectly while almost oblivious of the separate words. And thus, as Dr. Maudsley remarks, "the brain not only receives impressions unconsciously, registers impressions, without the co-operation of consciousness, elaborates material unconsciously, calls latent residua again into activity, without consciousness, but it responds also as an organ of organic life to the internal stimuli, which it receives unconsciously from other organs of the body." *

Science now teaches that we know nothing of mental action, except through nervous action, without which there is neither thought, recollection, nor reason. An eminent authority upon this subject, Dr. Bucknill, says, "The activity of the vesicular neurine of the brain is the occasion of all these capabilities. The little cells are the agents of all that is called mind, of all our sensations, thoughts, and desires; and the growth and renovation of these cells are the most ultimate conditions of mind with which we are acquainted." And again, "Not a thrill of sensation can occur, not a flashing thought, or a passing feeling can take place without a change in the living organism, much less can diseased sensation, thought, or feeling occur without such changes."

These facts sufficiently disclose the agency of the bodily system in carrying on mental action; but the view becomes still more impressive when we observe to

* The Physiology and Pathology of Mind, by Dr. Maudsley, p. 20.

what an extent corporeal conditions influence and determine intellectual states.

The weight of the human brain ranges from sixty-four ounces to twenty ounces, and, other things being equal, the scale of intellectual power is held to correspond with its mass. Cerebral action has thus an enormous range of limitation, due to the variable volume of the mental organ, but it is also modified in numerous ways and numberless degrees by accompanying physiological conditions. The brain is an organ of power; power depends upon change, and change upon circulation; the lungs and heart are, therefore, immediately involved. To high and sustained mental power, ample lungs and a vigorous heart are essential. And these organs, again, fall back upon the digestive apparatus, which, if feeble, may impair the capacity of a good heart, sound lungs, and a well-constituted brain. Digestion, and even the caprice of appetite, thus stand in direct dynamic relation to intellectual results.

As the brain is more largely dependent than any other organ upon the torrent of blood which pours through it, we find that even a transient variation in the supply disturbs the course of thought. If a portion of the skull is removed, and pressure be made upon the brain, consciousness disappears, and the same thing occurs in fainting, from suspension of the circulation. With invigorated action of the heart, there is a general exaltation of the mental powers, while an enfeebled circulation depresses mental activity. Apoplectic congestion produces stupor and insensibility; inflammation of the grey substance causes delirium; while inflammation of the fibrous portion produces torpor and diminishes the power of the will over the muscles. In thus saying that the state of the blood influences the mind, we do not use the term mind in any vague or abstract sense; we mean that it affects our views, opinions, feelings, judgments, actions. Change of circulation alters our mental pitch, and, with it, our relation to the universe. Dr. Laycock observes:—"In the earliest stage of general paralysis there is a feeling of energy. Everything, therefore, appears hopeful to the patient; large enterprizes, the success of which he never doubts, occupy his mind, and he rushes sometimes into the most extravagant and wasteful speculations. This is the stage of erethism of the capillaries of the part of the brain affected, when it is just sufficient to excite increased cerebral vigour. If, however, from any cause, this activity declines, so as to sink below par, a precisely opposite state of consciousness arises, and the patient may fall into a profound melancholy, and be insanely hopeless, distrustful, and anxious as to all events, past, present, and to come."* Even the variation in the quantity of blood which enters the brain, by simply taking the recumbent position, may affect mental activity in a marked degree. Persons who, through over-exertion of mind, have impaired the contractility of the cerebral vessels, often become intensely wakeful after lying down, although very drowsy before, and sometimes can only sleep in the erect position. Dendy mentions the case of an individual who, when he retired to rest, was constantly haunted by a spectre, which attempted to take his life; though, when he raised himself in bed, the phantom vanished.

Persons have had their entire character changed by an apparently trifling interference with the circulation of

* Correlations of Consciousness and Organization. Vol. ii., page 325.

blood in the head. "A person of my acquaintance," says Dr. Hammond, "was naturally of good disposition, amiable, and considerate; but after an attack of vertigo, attended with unconsciousness of but a few minutes' duration, his whole mental organization was changed; he became deceitful, morose, and overbearing." Tuke and Bucknill mention the instance of a conscientious lady, who recovered from the brain-congestion accompanying small-pox with her disposition greatly changed. The susceptibility of conscience had increased to a state of actual disease, disturbing her happiness, and disqualifying her for the duties of life.

A blow on the head may produce marked mental derangement. The memory may be dislocated, events obliterated, and whole passages from the past life expunged: the faculty of speech may be partially or wholly destroyed, the memory of words confused, or entire parts of speech lost.

Mental perversions are also caused by certain changes in the properties of the blood. A fluid of amazing complexity, holding in exquisite balance the constituents from which the whole being is elaborated, all delicacies of feeling and niceties of thought depend upon its purity. "Polished steel is not quicker dimmed by the slightest breath than is the brain affected by some abnormal conditions of the blood."

If the poisonous products of bodily waste are not constantly swept from the system, the cerebral changes are disturbed and the mind stupified. Foods, drinks, and drugs affect specifically the appetites, passions, and thoughts. To become exhilarated and joyous, man charges his blood with wine; to exalt the sensations, he takes hashish; to secure a brilliant fancy and luxurious imagination, he uses opium; to abolish consciousness of pain, he breathes vapour of chloroform. Swedenborg had a peculiar class of visions "after coffee." "A person I know," observes Dr. Laycock, "after taking morphine, in a fever, was haunted by hideously grotesque and fiend-like spectres; they then shortly changed into groups of comical human faces, and finally altered to forms of the human figure of the most classic beauty, and then disappeared." And this learned inquirer maintains that the pictorial productions of the insane vary in a definite order, the early stages of excitement enabling the artist to execute beautiful conceptions of figures and landscapes; then, as the disease advances, he passes into comic delineations, and ends with the grotesque, or hideous.

Those fluctuations of feeling with which all are more or less familiar, the alternations of hope and despondency, are vitally connected with organic states. In high health, the outlook is confident, there is joy in action, and courage in enterprise; but with a low or disturbed circulation, thin, morbid blood, and bodily exhaustion, there is depression of spirits, gloom, inaction, paralysis of will, and weariness of life. That variability of mental state which is so striking and general an experience with the literary and artistic classes, the periods when work is impossible, the moods of sluggish and unsatisfactory effort, the seasons of steady and successful accomplishment, and the moments of rare exaltation, capricious as they may seem, are but the exponents of varying constitutional conditions.

But the part played by the organism becomes still more apparent when we consider the mode of action of the nervous system in producing mental effects. It has been stated that this system is composed of fibres and cells; hence the simplest conceivable case of nervous activity is where a cell and fibre become active, producing an excitement and a discharge; the highest action of the organ being nothing more than a complex system of excitements and discharges. In sleep, for example, a fly lights upon the face, producing an impression, or change, which causes a discharge along the nerves to the grey matter of the spinal cord. Here force is again liberated, which is discharged along another set of nerves upon the appropriate muscles, which, being contracted, bring the hand to the place where the fly settled. This is the course of power in a simple reflex action. But when the brain is called into conscious exercise in the higher processes of intellection just the same thing occurs. A person may be engaged in tranquil thinking, when one idea leads on to another in a natural train of association, that is, where the excitement of one state of consciousness is discharged into another, forming a succession of cerebral changes. In this quiet course of thought, a ludicrous idea, or a witty combination may arise, when a large amount of feeling, or nerve excitement, is suddenly awakened. This may be discharged in several directions. One portion may be spent upon the muscles of the face and chest, producing laughter; another portion may pass along the nerves leading to the stomach, perhaps stimulating digestion; and a third may be expended in producing other states of consciousness, or new trains of ideas. Mental action is thus manifested as definite and limited nervous action, and when we speak of the unfolding of mind, as in education, the fact signified is the growing adaptation of the brain and nervous apparatus to produce more and more complex effects in accordance with their necessary mode of working.

The child comes into the world a little fountain of spontaneous power. For certain purposes its nervous mechanism is perfected, channels of discharge are open, connexions are ready formed, and reflex actions go on from the first. The infant also inherits the capabilities of its type; that is, the possibility of high development which belongs to man as distinguished from inferior creatures, and it also inherits the special tendencies and aptitudes of its particular ancestors. The order of the surrounding universe now begins to take effect upon it, and working within its organic limits, which of course vary widely in different cases, its education begins. Impressions pour in through the senses, and begin to open channels of discharge through the nerve centres. The child sees and desires an object, but has more or less difficulty in connecting the sensation with the movement necessary to seize it. By numberless efforts a nervous path is at length formed, and when a desirable object is seen, the sensation discharges upon the proper muscles, producing a suitable movement, and the hand grasps it. So with walking and speaking; by repeated exertions lines of nervous discharge are completed, and the sensations involved are co-ordinated with the movements of locomotion and utterance. Repetition strengthens association and facilitates action; that which is difficult at first, requiring a large expenditure of voluntary effort, at last seems "to go of itself." Upon this point Dr. Carpenter remarks, "There can be no doubt that the nerve-force is disposed to pass in special *tracks*, and it seems probable that whilst some are originally marked out for the automatic movements, others may be gradually *worn in* by the habitual action of the will, and that thus when a train of sequential actions originally directed by the will has been once set in operation, it may continue without any further influence from that source."*

Thus, in committing to memory a poem, or in learning a piece of music, voluntary effort wears a path of association, so that each word or sound automatically suggests the next, and we can either repeat the words or hum the air in silence, or link on the automatic movements of expression: but by sufficient repetition the words and sounds become so closely associated, that when the first bar of the melody, or the first stanza of the poem is awakened, it will cost an effort to prevent running through with them. In this way, as the child grows to maturity, brain connexions are established between sensations, ideas, and movements; they become automatic and powerful, and give rise to fixed habits. Peculiarities of gait, attitude, gesture, and speech, and the iteration of set phrases, become partially automatic; their paths of discharge getting so deeply worn that repetition occurs involuntarily. The same thing is seen also in the higher region of ideas and beliefs. Long-established associations and opinions survive their rejection by reason: convince a man of his life-long errors to-day and he re-asserts them to-morrow, so strong is the tendency of thought to move in its long-accustomed cerebral tracks.

Now, when we experience a feeling, or think a thought, or determine an act, that is, in every case of excitement and discharge, there is a partial decomposition of the

* Principles of Human Physiology. Fifth Edition, page 699.

nervous structure in action. In every such act there is loss of energy, or partial exhaustion, the cells and fibres fall below par, and the equilibrium is restored by the nutrition of the weakened part. Brain-repair thus takes place, *in accordance with the modes of mental action*, and, as in the blacksmith's arm muscular nutrition is commensurate with its exercise, and augments power, so in every special kind of mental exercise, cerebral nutrition co-operates to raise the standard of nervous power. As waste accompanies exercise, and repair follows waste, the nutrition of the organ is determined by the modes of mental activity—given associations and ideas become patterns, as it were, in conformity to which the brain is moulded. In this way the organic processes re-inforce mental acquisition, and assimilation tends to perpetuate states of feeling and modes of thought and action. Throughout infancy, childhood, and youth, when nutrition is in excess, the brain is thus adapted to its circumstances, and *grows* to the order of impressions and ideas which it receives.

We have seen that the office of volition is to determine the course of thought and direct bodily actions to specific ends. This capability is the noblest element of our nature, but is greatly variable in different individuals by habit and constitution, and is inexorably limited in all. The will is not an absolute Despot, with unbounded authority to do what it lists, but rather a constitutional President, exercising vast power, it may be, but strictly subject to the laws of the organic state. Its regnant prerogative, as we have seen, is that of controlling the attention, by which it is enabled to wield the entire energy of the organism to the accomplishment of its purposes. In this way the automatic system becomes a means of exalting the office of volition, and making it in an eminent degree the arbiter of individual destiny. But in the exercise of its prerogative the will is governed by the same great law which rules all the other powers, namely, the acquirement of strength by exercise. Only through that constant exertion by which energy is accumulated can the will gain command of the thoughts and mastery of the impulses. By continual practice the organism grows, as it were, into subordination, and the voluntary powers become habitually predominant. The will is thus, in an eminent degree, capable of education, but when we see how it is enfeebled in bodily debility and utterly extinguished in numerous morbid states of the system, it becomes apparent to what an extent physiological conditions must enter into the policy of its intelligent management. Even its limited freedom, as physicians well understand, is only coincident with healthy bodily action.

Sufficient, I trust, has now been said, to show that mental operations are so inextricably interwoven with corporeal actions, that to study them successfully apart is altogether impossible. The mental life and the bodily life are manifestations of the same organism, growing together, fluctuating together, declining together. They depend upon common laws, which must be investigated by a common method; and science, in unravelling the mysteries of the body, has thrown important light upon the workings of the mind. It only remains now to point out, that when subjected to the Baconian test of "fruitfulness"—of practical application to the emergencies of experience, the scientific method of regarding human nature, incomplete as it may be, already stands in marked contrast to the proverbial barrenness of the old metaphysics. I will briefly refer to two or three such applications.

One of the gloomiest chapters of man's social history is that which records the treatment of the insane. Those upon whom had fallen the heaviest calamity possible in life, were looked upon with horror, as accursed of God, and treated with a degree of cruelty which seems now incredible. Asylums were dark and dismal jails, where their inmates were left in cold, hunger, and filth, to be chained and lashed at the caprice of savage keepers. And this barbarism continued in countries claiming to be enlightened down to the middle of the present century. Let me mention a solitary instance, of which the literature of the subject is full.

Said Dr. Conolly, in a lecture in 1847: "It was in the Female Infirmary at Hanwell, exactly seven years ago, that I found, among other examples of the forgetfulness of what was due either to the sick or insane, a young woman lying in a crib, bound to the middle of it by a strap around the waist, to the sides of it by the hands, to the foot of it by the ankles, and to the head of it by the neck; she also had her hands in the hard leathern terminations of canvas sleeves. She could not turn, nor lie on her side, nor lift her hand to her face, and her appearance was miserable beyond the power of words to describe. That she was almost always wet and dirty, it is scarcely necessary to say. But the principal point I wish to illustrate by mentioning this case is, that it was a feeble and sick woman who was thus treated. At that very time her whole skin was covered with neglected scabies, and she was suffering all the torture of a large and deep-seated abscess of the breast." "Again," he remarks, "old and young, men and women, the frantic and the melancholy, were treated worse and more neglected than the beasts of the field. The cells of an asylum resembled the dens of a squalid menagerie ; the straw was raked out, and the food was thrown in through the bars, and exhibitions of madness were witnessed which are no longer to be found, because they were not the simple product of malady, but of malady aggravated by mis-management."

Now, these statements represent a condition of things as old as history, and we are called upon to account for it. Granting that the insane were dangerous, and required restraint, and granting all that may be urged concerning the barbarity of the times, we have yet to find the cause of the apparently gratuitous ferocity of which they were the victims; and this we do find in the legitimate consequences of the prevailing theory of human nature. The ancient philosophy taught that the body is to be despised, degraded, renounced. This view was adopted by theology, and thrown into a concrete and dramatic shape, which made it more capable of vivid realization by the multitude. It pronounced the body to be "a sink of iniquity," the "intrenchment of Satan," a fit residence for demons. The lunatic was one who had incurred Divine displeasure, and was given over to the powers of darkness, by whom he was "possessed." This doctrine, of which witchcraft was one of the developments, abundantly explains the attitude of society towards the victims of mental disorder. What more suitable than dungeons, scourgings, and tortures for the detested wretch, who was thus manifestly forsaken of God, and delivered over to the Devil? The merciless brute who inflicted untold sufferings upon these unhappy beings deemed himself, like the Inquisitor, but an instrument for executing the will of Heaven.

It availed nothing that, for thousands of years, there had been a broad current of intense and powerful thought in the channels of poetry, polemics, oratory, philosophy, politics, theology, and devotion. All this multifarious culture was powerless to arrest the evil consequences of a radically erroneous view of human nature, for the simple reason that the discovery of truth was not among its objects. It was only when a class of men, participating in the new spirit of modern times, and drawn to the investigation by the necessities of their profession, entered earnestly upon the study of the body, that views were reached which have revolutionized and humanized the treatment of the insane. Discovering that the mind is dependent upon the organism, and that its disordered manifestations are the results of organic derangement, they found that insanity is not a devil to be exorcised, but a disease to be cured. After a sharp struggle with popular ignorance and traditional prejudice, the better views have triumphed, and society is beginning to reap the beneficent consequences of their labours: the stern and violent measures, that served but to aggravate the malady, have given place to gentle and kindly treatment, which is found to be of itself a most potent means of restoration.

The management of the idiotic, or feeble-minded, equally illustrates the argument. Throughout the past no movement was made for the relief of this wretched class, and no one dreamed that anything could be done for them; but the progress of Physiology has made a new revelation in this field also. Dr. Edward Seguin, in his recent able work upon "The Treatment of Idiocy by the Physiological Method," observes: "Idiots could not be educated by the methods, nor cured by the treatment, practised prior to 1837; but most idiots, and children proximate to them, may be relieved, in a more or less complete measure, of their disabilities by the physiological mode of education."

These facts have a profound significance. They not only show that to be *practicable* which the world had never suspected to be *possible*, and that science is true to her beneficent mission in the higher sphere as well as in the lower; they not only show that a change of method in the study of human nature ended some of the grossest barbarisms of the past, but they involve this deeper result—that by reaching a knowledge of the true causes of insanity and imbecility, we gain command of the means of their prevention, and arrive at the principles of mental hygiene. And this leads to the consideration of those wider consequences to society at large which the modern method of inquiry is beginning to produce.

This is perhaps best illustrated in the establishment of what may be called the law of *mental limitations.* The old contrast between matter and mind led to the growth of an all-prevalent error upon this point. To matter belongs extension or limitation in space; but mind is inextended, and therefore it has been inferred to be unlimited: being indefinite, it was supposed to be unbounded in its nature. But force also is inextended, although rigorously limited and measurable; and as mind is nothing more nor less than mental power, it must be subject to the laws of power, and work within quantitative limits, like any other form of force. Power, again, is but the accompaniment of material change, and is, hence, restricted in quantity by the amount of that change; and as mind is accompanied by cerebral transformation, it must have a necessary limit in the quantity of cerebral transformation. In, therefore, considering man as a being in whom mind is conditioned by a bodily organism, the limitation of mental effects becomes a practical question of the very highest importance.

The doctrine of the conservation of energy and the mutual convertibility of the various forces, is now accepted as a fundamental truth of science. Nor is there any ground for regarding the vital forces as an exception to the principle. That the organism cannot create its own force, that its energy is entirely derived from the food ingested, and which, in this point of view, is merely stored force, is beyond question; and the source being thus limited, that its expenditure in one direction makes it impossible to use it in another, is equally evident. This principle applies, even in a more marked degree, to the cerebral system. Every one knows that hearty digestion and violent exercise lower the mental activity, that is, the forces are diverted from the brain, and thrown upon the stomach and muscles.

That the purely intellectual powers are also subject to limitation is unquestionable. All minds are fissured with incapacities in one direction or another,—clipped away on this side or on that,—all are fragmentary. There may be great mathematical ability, but no imagination; fine poetical gifts, without logical faculty; large executive power, coupled with deficient judgment. Dr. Whewell had a powerful memory for books, but a very bad one for persons; Sir William Hamilton cultivated the lore and history of philosophy, at the expense of his power of origination and organization; Prescott was so irresolute that he could only spur himself to his literary tasks by the stimulus of betting with his secretary that he would do a certain amount of work in a given time; Theodore Parker was loaded with erudition, but exclaimed on his premature death-bed, "Oh, that I had known the art of life, or found some book, or some man to tell me how to live, to study, to take exercise." The greatest men are all dunces in something: Shakspeare and Newton illustrate the law as absolutely as the veriest weakling of the asylum. The full-orbed intellect is yet to come, and will doubtless bring with it the "perpetual motion," and the Jew's "Messias."

These phenomena find no explanation in the old hypothesis of mind as a vague, spiritual entity; they throw us back immediately on the organism whose acknowledged limitations offer at once a solution of the mystery. These mental inaptitudes may be either organic deficiencies, or a result of concentrating the cerebral energy in certain directions, and its consequent withdrawal from others. Thus viewed, every attainment involves the exercise of brain-power—each acquisition is a modification of cerebral structure. All sensations of objects and words that we remember, all acquired aptitudes of movement; the associations of the perception of things with visible symbols, vocal actions and sounds, the connexions of ideas with feelings and emotions, and the formation of intellectual and moral habits, are all concomitants and consequents of the only kind of action of which the brain is capable—are all the products of organic nutrition; and the rate and limit of acquisition, as well as the capacity for retention, are conditioned upon the completeness of the nutritive processes. As each acquirement involves a growth, it is evident that acquisition may reach a point at which the whole organic force is consumed in conserving it, and further attainments can only be made at the expense of the decay and loss of old ones. Hence, if we overburden the brain, as in school-"cramming," nutrition is imperfect, adhesion feeble, and acquisition quickly lost.

The one great physiological law upon which bodily and mental health are alike dependent, is the alternation of action and repose which results from the limitation of power. The eternal equation of vital vigour is, *rest equals exercise.* That tendency to rhythmic action, which seems to mark all displays of power in the universe, is conspicuously manifested in the organic economy, allowing the muscles of respiration eight hours' repose out of twenty-four, and six hours' rest to those of the heart. The cerebral rhythm is diurnal: except that rest which parts of the brain may obtain when only other parts are in action, the organ finds its appropriate repose in sleep. "Half our days we spend in the shadow of the earth, and the brother of death extracteth a third part of our lives," says the eloquent Sir Thomas Browne; that is, the periodicities of cerebral action are defined by astronomic cycles; the brain and the solar system march together. Exercise and repose are equally indispensable to mental vigour; deficiency of exercise produces mental feebleness; deficiency of rest, disease. But there lurks in this statement a deeper and more dangerous meaning than at first appears. The equilibrium once lost is most difficult to restore,—there is a fatal persistence in the morbid state. It is a general law of the animal economy, that when the vital powers are, from any cause, depressed below a certain point, they are not easily, and sometimes are never, repaired. A large loss of blood, or a profound exhaustion, may entail effects upon the constitution which will last for years, perhaps for life. As might be expected, the brain illustrates this principle more impressively than any other portion of the system: if worked beyond its limits, there is produced a rapid exhaustion of power which renders repose impossible. The exhaustion of over-work is accompanied by excitement, which tends to perpetuate the work and accelerate the exhaustion. The will is thus swamped in the uncontrollable mobility of the automatic system, the attention becomes insanely exalted, the brain will not be ordered to rest, and words of warning are wasted. When his physicians admonished Sir Walter Scott of the impending consequences of excessive mental labour, he sadly replied: "As for bidding me not work, you might as well tell Molly to put the kettle on the fire, and then say, 'now don't boil.'"

We live in an age of intense mental activity and ever-increasing cerebral strain. Steam and electricity are tasked to bring daily tidings of what is happening all over the world, and impressions pour in upon the brain at a rate with which nothing in the past is comparable. The fierce competitions of business, fashion, study, and political ambition, are at work to sap the vigour and rack the integrity of the mental fabric, and there can be no doubt that there is, in consequence, an immense amount of latent brain disease, productive of much secret suffering and slight aberrations of conduct, and which is liable, in any sudden stress of circumstances, to break out into permanent mental derangement. The price we pay for our high-pressure civilization is a fearful increase of cerebral exhaustion and disorder, and an augmenting ratio of shattered intellects. We are startled when some conspicuous mind, strained beyond endurance, as in the cases of Hugh Miller, or Admiral Fitzroy, crashes into insanity and suicide, yet these are but symptoms of the prevailing tendencies of modern life.

And here I call attention to the deep defects of that predominant scheme of culture which not only ignores the human brain, and the sciences which illustrate it, as objects of earnest systematic study, but explodes upon it all the traditional contempt which it cherishes for material nature. "This hasty pudding within the skull," said Frederick Robertson, as he epitomized, in a single expression, the stupid prejudice of the prevailing "scholarship." Poor Robertson! smitten down in the midst of a noble career, by the consequences of over-tasking, dying of brain disease in the prime of manhood:—how cruelly did Nature avenge the insult!

Men admire the steam-engine of Watt and the calculating engine of Babbage; but how little do they care for the thinking engine of the Infinite Artificer! They venerate days, and dogmas, and ceremonials; but where is the reverence that is due to that most sacred of the things of time, the organism of the soul! We speak of the glories of the stellar universe; but is not the miniature duplicate of that universe in the living brain a more transcendent marvel? We admire the vast fabric of society and government, and that complicated scheme of duties, responsibilities, usages, and laws which constitutes social order; but how few remember that all this has its deep foundation in the measured march of cerebral transformations. We point to the inventions, arts, sciences, and literatures, which form the swelling tide of civilization; but were they not all originated in that laboratory of wonders, the human brain? Geological revelations carry us back through durations so boundless, that imagination is bewildered, and reason reels under the grandeur of the demonstration; but through the measureless series of advancing periods, we discover a stupendous plan. Infinite Power, working through infinite time, converges the mighty lines of causality to the fulfilment of an eternal design,—the birth of an intellectual and moral era through the development of the brain of man, which thus appears as the final term of an unfolding world.

The ultimate and decisive bearing of the foregoing views upon plans and processes of instruction, can hardly fail to have been perceived. The scientific method of studying human nature, important as may be its relation to the management of the insane and feeble-minded, and valuable as is its service in establishing the limits of mental effort, must find its fullest application to the broad subject of education. For, whatever questions of the proper subjects to be taught, their relative claims, or the true methods of teaching may arise, there is a prior and fundamental inquiry into the nature, capabilities, and requirements of the being to be taught, upon the elucidation of which all other questions immediately depend. A knowledge of the being to be trained, as it is the basis of all intelligent culture, must be the first necessity of the teacher.

Education is an art, like Locomotion, Mining, or Bleaching, which may be pursued empirically or rationally, as a blind habit, or under intelligent guidance; and the relations of science to it are precisely the same as to all the other arts—to ascertain their conditions, and give law to their processes. What it has done for Navigation, Telegraphy, and War, it will also do for Culture. The true method of proceeding may be regarded as established, and many important results are already reached, though its systematic application is hardly yet entered upon. Although there is undoubtedly a growing interest in the scientific aspects of the subject, yet what Mr. Wyse wrote twenty-five years ago remains still but too true. He says, "it is, unquestionably, a singular circumstance, that, of all problems, the problem of Education is that to which by far the smallest share of persevering and vigorous attention has yet been applied. The same empiricism which once reigned supreme in the domains of chemistry, astronomy, and medicine still retains possession, in many instances, of those of education. No journal is kept of the phenomena of infancy and childhood; no parent has yet registered, day after day, with the attention of an astronomer who prepares his ephemerides, the marvellous developments of his child. Until this is done, there can be no solid basis for reasoning; we must still deal with conjecture." And why has nothing been done? Because, in the prevailing system of culture, the art of observation, which is the beginning of all true science, the basis of all intellectual discrimination, and the kind of knowledge which is necessary to interpret these observations, are universally neglected. Our teachers mostly belong to the old dispensation. Their preparation is chiefly literary; if they obtain a little scientific knowledge, it is for the purpose of *communicating* it, and not as a means of tutorial guidance. Their art is a mechanical routine, and hence, very naturally, while admitting the importance of advancing views, they really cannot see what is to be done about it. When we say that education is an affair of the laws of our being, involving a wide range of considerations,—an affair of the air respired, its moisture, temperature, density, purity, and electrical state; an affair of food, digestion, and nutrition; of the quantity, quality, and speed of the blood sent to the brain; of clothing and exercise, fatigue and repose, health and disease; of variable volition, and automatic nerve action; of fluctuating feeling, redundancy and exhaustion of nerve-power; an affair of light, colour, sound, resistance; of sensuous impressibility, temperament, family history, constitutional predisposition, and unconscious influence; of material surroundings, and a host of agencies which stamp themselves upon the plastic organism, and reappear in character; in short, that it involves that complete acquaintance with corporeal conditions which science alone can give,—when we hint of these things, we seem to be talking in an unknown tongue, or, if intelligible, then very irrelevant and unpractical.

That our general education is in a deplorably chaotic state, presenting a medley of debased ideals, conflicting systems, discordant practices, and unsatisfactory results, no observing person will question; that this state of things is to last for ever, we all feel to be impossible; and that its future removal can only come through that powerful instrumentality to which we owe advancement in other departments of social activity, is equally clear to the reflecting. The imminent question is, how may the child and youth be developed healthfully and vigorously, bodily, mentally and morally; and science alone can answer it by a statement of the laws upon which that development depends. Ignorance of these laws must inevitably involve mismanagement. That there is a large amount of mental perversion, and absolute stupidity, as well as of bodily disease, produced in school, by measures which operate to the prejudice of the growing brain, is not to be doubted; that dulness, indocility, and viciousness, are frequently aggravated by teachers, incapable of discriminating between their mental and bodily causes, is also undeniable; while, that teachers often miserably fail to improve their pupils, and then report the result of their own incompetency as *failures of nature*, all may have seen, although it is now proved that the lowest imbeciles are not sunk beneath the possibility of elevation.

The purpose of the foregoing remarks has been to bring forward an aspect of man which cannot fail to have an important influence upon processes of instruction. I have endeavoured to illustrate the extent to which Nature works out her own results in the organism of man. The numerous instances of self-made men, who, with no external assistance, have risen to intellectual eminence, and the still more marked instances where students have forced their way to success in spite of the hindrances of an irrational culture, testify to the power of the spontaneous and self-determining tendencies of human character, while the general overlooking of this fact has unquestionably led to an enormous exaggeration of the potency of existing educational methods. In establishing this view, science both limits and modifies the function of the instructor. It limits it by showing that mental operations are corporeally conditioned, that large regions of our nature are beyond direct control, and that mental attainment depends in a great degree upon inherited capacity and organic growth. It limits it by showing that ancestral influences come down upon us as we enter the world, like the hand of Fate; that we are born well, or born badly, and that whoever is ushered into existence at the bottom of the scale, can never rise to the top because the weight of the universe is upon him. It shows how not to mistake the surface effects of an ostentatious system for a thorough in-forming of character; how not to mistake the current smattering of languages, the cramming for examinations, the glossing of accomplishments, the showy and superficial pedantries of literature, and the labelling of degrees, for true education.

The office of the teacher is thus narrowed but not denied. If inherited organization is a factor of destiny never to be cancelled, there is another factor in that culture which rests upon a knowledge of the laws of life and character. Science modifies the tutorial offices by disclosing the direction of its real work, and guarding against waste of effort, and specious and spurious results—by showing that education does not consist in the acquisition of knowledge to be siphoned into the intellectual receivers of the school-room, but is rather to direct the working of a mechanism over which neither its owner nor his teacher is omnipotent—a mechanism in which effects follow causes, and which always operates according to law. It shows the Instructor that he must take his pupil as he finds him; not a mental abstraction, to be classed with other "minds" and worked by a universal formula, but a personal reality—a part of the order of nature which never repeats itself in a single case; a being with individual attributes which are inexorably bound within the limits of his organization. It therefore demands of him to leave the lore which is glorified by tradition until he has thoroughly grounded himself in the elements of that knowledge of human nature—of the springs of action and the conditions and possibilities of real improvement, which alone can confer the highest skill in quickening the intellect, and moulding the character.

I have thus attempted to prove that only by inverting the rule of the past, which exalted the mind at the expense of the body, and bringing the resources of modern induction to the study of the corporeal organism, can we arrive at that higher and clearer knowledge of man, which will make possible anything like a true Science of Human Nature. I have pointed out the salutary results which have already flowed from this method in the crucial test of the treatment of the insane; and the vast benefits which society cannot fail to reap from that clearer perception of the laws of vital and mental limitations which recent research has so decisively established; and I have also endeavoured to unfold the bearing of this view upon the subject of education. But the results enumerated are far from exhausting the broad applicability of the method. The grand characteristic of science is its universality; what is it, indeed, but the latest report of the human mind on the order of nature? Its principles are far-reaching and all-inclusive, so that when a knowledge of the true constitution of man is once attained, it confers insight into all the multitudinous phases of human manifestation. The same economy of power which science confers in the material world, and by which we obtain a maximum of effect from a minimum of force, she confers also in the world of mind. When we have mastered the laws of physical education we have the essential data for dealing with questions of mental education, and these steps are the indispensable preparation for an enlightened moral education. And the same knowledge of the organism which shows how it may be best developed, gives also the clue to the understanding of its aberrant phenomena. That mysterious ground which has hitherto been the hot-bed of noxious superstitions and dangerous quackeries, is reclaimed to rational investigation, and the remarkable effects of reverie, ecstasy, hysteria, hallucinations, spectral illusions, dreaming, somnambulism, mesmerism, religious epidemics, and other kindred displays of nervous morbidity, find adequate explanation in the ascertained laws of our being. This kind of knowledge is, furthermore, not only of the highest value to all classes for practical guidance, but the philosophical students of man, whether viewing him in the moral, religious, social, æsthetic, ethnological or historic aspects, must find their equal and indispensable preparation in the mastery of the biological and psychological laws which can alone explain the nature of the subject of their research.

After what has been said, it will not be supposed that I entertain any very extravagant expectations of the immediate results to be obtained from improved methods of dealing with human nature. On the contrary, one of the most impressive lessons of science, is that permanent growths are slow, and that there are limits which cannot be overpassed. Dealing largely with causes which only work out their results in the fulness of time, it teaches patience, hope, and labour; and not the least of its salutary influences will be, through wholesome discipline of the imagination, and a rational control of the sympathies, to check the waste of power upon impossible projects, and restrain those enthusiasms which are born of the feelings rather than of the judgment. Nor do I believe that the perfectibility of the human race is at hand through the teaching of a little more physiology in schools, or that science is to apply a calculus to human actions, and thus supersede the common sense and practical judgments of mankind. That there is a vast body of valid knowledge concerning the nature of man, which is reduced to application, and serves for the management of conduct, is shown in all the multifarious aspects of social activity: I simply hold that this knowledge, valuable as it is, is yet imperfect—in many respects deplorably imperfect—and must grow to a higher state and a more scientific character; and that the organized culture of the present age is bound to help and not to hinder this tendency. The time, I think, has come for demanding that the curriculum of modern liberal education be so reconstructed that its courses of study shall have a more direct and positive bearing upon that most desirable end—a clearer understanding of the Laws of Human Nature.

APPENDIX.

APPENDIX.

ON UNIVERSITY STUDIES.

BY SIR J. F. W. HERSCHEL, BART., F.R.S.

WHEN Sir John Herschel, a few years ago, was residing at the Cape of Good Hope, to observe the stars of the southern hemisphere, he was consulted by Dr. Adamson respecting the scheme of instruction for a South African College. His views were given in a letter from which the following is an extract:—

"A good practical system of public education ought, in my opinion, to be more real than formal; I mean, should convey much of the positive knowledge, with as little attention to mere systems and conventional forms, as is consistent with avoiding solecisms. This principle carried into detail would allow much less weight to the study of the languages than is usually considered its due in our great public schools, where, in fact, the acquisition of the latter seems to be regarded as the one and only object of education, while, on the other hand, it would attach great importance to all those branches of practical and theoretical knowledge whose possession goes to constitute an idea of a well-informed gentleman; as, for example, a knowledge of the nature and constitution of the world we inhabit, its animal, vegetable, and mineral productions, and their uses and properties as subservient to human wants; its relation to the system of the universe, and its natural and political subdivisions: and, last and most important of all, the nature and propensities of man himself, as developed in the history of nations and the biography of individuals; the constructions of human society, including our responsibilities to individuals and to the social body of which we are members. In a word, as extensive a knowledge as can be grasped and conveyed in an elementary course, of the actual system and the laws of nature, both physical and moral.

"Again, in a country where free institutions prevail, and where public opinion is of consequence, every man is to a certain extent a legislator; and for this his education (especially where the Government of the country lends its aid and sanction to it) ought at least so far to prepare him, as to place him on his guard against those obvious and popular fallacies which lie across the threshold of this as well as of every other subject with which human reason has anything to do. Every man is called upon to obey the laws, and therefore it cannot be deemed superfluous that some portion of every man's education should consist in informing him what they are. On these grounds, it would seem to me that some knowledge of the principles of political economy, of jurisprudence, of trade and manufactures, is essentially involved in the notion of a sound education. A moderate acquaintance also with certain of the useful arts, such as practical mechanics or engineering, agriculture, draughtsmanship, is of obvious utility in every station in life; while, in a commercial community, the only remedy for that proverbial short-sightedness to their best ultimate interests, which is the misfortune rather than the fault of every mercantile community upon earth, seems to be to inculcate, as a part of education, those broad principles of free interchange and reciprocal profit and public justice on which the whole edifice of permanently successful enterprise must be based.

"The exercise and development of our reasoning faculties is another grand object of education, and is usually considered, and in a certain sense justly, as most likely to be obtained by a judicious course of mathematical instruction, while it stands, if not opposed to, at least in no natural connexion with, the formal and conventional departments of knowledge (such as grammar and the so-called Aristotelian logic). It must be recollected, however, that there are minds which, though not devoid of reasoning powers, yet manifest a decided inaptitude for mathematical studies—which are *estimative* not *calculating*, and which are more impressed by analogies and by apparent preponderance of general evidence in argument, than by mathematical demonstration, where all the argument is on one side and no show of reason can be exhibited on the other. The mathematician listens only to one side of a question, for this plain reason—that no strictly mathematical question *has* more than one side capable of being maintained otherwise than by simple assertion; while all the great questions that arise in busy life and agitate the world, are stoutly disputed, and often with a show of reason on both sides, which leaves the shrewdest at a loss for a decision.

"This, or something like it, has often been urged by those who contend against what they consider an undue extension of mathematical studies in our universities. But those who have urged the objection have stopped short of the remedy. It is essential, however, to fill this enormous blank in every course of education which has hitherto been acted on, by a due provision of some course of study and instruction which shall meet the difficulty by showing how valid propositions are to be drawn, not from premises which virtually contain them in their very words, as is the case with abstract propositions in mathematics, nor from the juxtaposition of other propositions assumed as true, as in the Aristotelian logic, but from the broad consideration of an assemblage of facts and circumstances brought under review. This is the scope of the inductive philosophy, applicable, and which ought to be applied (though it never yet has fairly been so), to all the complex circumstances of human life; to politics, to morals and legislation; to the guidance of individual conduct, and that of nations. I cannot too strongly recommend this to the consideration of those who are now to decide on the normal course of instruction to be adopted in your College. Let them have the glory—for glory it will really be—to have given a new impulse to public instruction by placing the Novum Organum, for the first time, in the hands of young men educating for active life, as a text-book, and as a regular part of their College course. It is strong meat, I admit, but it is manly nutriment; and though imperfectly comprehended (as it must be at that age when the College course terminates), the glimpses caught of its meaning, under a due course of collateral explanation, will fructify in after life, and, like the royal food with which the young bee is fed, will dilate the frame and transform the whole habit and economy. Of course, it should be made the highest book for the most advanced classes."

(*Extract from a Communication to the English Public School Commissioners, from* SIR J. F. W. HERSCHEL).

REGARDING as a "Public School" any considerable permanent educational establishment, in which a large number of youths go through a fixed and uniform course of school instruction, from the earliest age at which boys are usually sent to school to that in which they either enter the University, or pass in some other mode into manly life, and in which it is understood that the education is what is called a liberal one, with no special professional bias or other avowed object than to form a youth for general life and civilized society, I should consider any system radically faulty which should confine itself to the study of the classical languages, and to so much of Greek and Roman history as is necessary to understand the classical authors as its main and primary feature; and should admit, and that reluctantly, a mere *minimum* of extra-classical teaching. Such a system must necessarily, I conceive, suffer the reasoning faculty to languish and become stunted and dwarfed for want of timely exercise in those years between fourteen and twenty, when the mind has become capable of consecutive thought, and of following out a train of consecutive argument to a logical conclusion. In those years it is quite as important that youths should have placed in their hands, and be obliged to study, books which may best initiate them in this domain of human thought, as in that of classical literature. To be able to express one's self fluently in Greek or Latin, prose or verse; to have attained an extensive familiarity with ancient literature, and a perfect knowledge of the niceties of his grammar, prosody, and idiom,—all, in short, which is included in the idea of classical scholarship,—is, no doubt, very desirable; and I should be one of the last to depreciate it. But it is bought too dear, if obtained at the sacrifice of any reasonable prospect of improving the general intellectual character by acquiring habits of concentrated thought, by familiarizing the mind with the contemplation of abstract truth, and by accustoming it to the attitude of investigation, induction, and generalization, while it is yet plastic and impressible."[2]

ON THE GENERAL INFLUENCE OF SCIENTIFIC CULTURE.

BY GEORGE E. PAGET, M.D., F.R.C.P.

(*Extract from an Address before the British Medical Association, delivered at Cambridge*, 1864.)

THE general question, whether the study of natural science should become an established part of the education of the higher classes, is a subject of such interest as to need no apology for its introduction before any audience, and least of all before you. It is not only one of the great educational questions of the day, but a question, in the right solution of which no class is more interested than is our profession.

I confess that, to me, it seems high time to consider whether natural science might not be useful as part of a liberal education, when an author of great distinction and undoubted learning—one whose writings have been rewarded with the applause of the educated world and with some of the highest dignities in the gift of the Crown—states as a "well-attested fact, that a man's body is lighter when he is awake than sleeping; a fact" (he says) "which every nurse who has carried a child would be able to attest;" and concludes from these *well-attested facts*, that "the human consciousness, as an inner centre, works as an opposing force to the attraction of the earth." I quote from a *seventh* edition, *revised*.

To my mind, the *necessity* for more general instruction in natural science needs no further proof, when ladies and gentlemen appear in a court of law to vouch their belief in the supernatural powers of a crystal globe; when those who are called highly educated throng the necromancer's consulting room to hear disembodied spirits rap on his table; when they daily become the dupes of barefaced quackeries; and, while avowing their belief in what is absurd or even impossible, plume themselves on their superiority to prejudice, regard themselves with complacency as walking in the spirit of the age—as being *au courant* with its progress—and class with the persecutors of Galileo any who question the accuracy of their facts or the logic of their conclusions.

Whatever may be thought of the enlightenment of the present age, there can be no doubt of the readiness and boldness with which it forms or avows its opinions. Far be it from me to question the birthright of an Englishman, to judge of all matters, whether he understands them or not. The right of private judgment is the most precious of civil rights; but it *may* occasionally make fools of us, when exercised upon questions in which we are uninstructed. Even freedom of thought is not an unmixed good. It stirs a community in *all* directions—not always in the direction of progress. In the unwise and presumptous it is often the parent of mischievous errors, that find ready acceptance among the ignorant and indolent, and cost for their removal much time and trouble of wiser men. It is easier to refute errors than to remove them. Ignorance must be instructed, self-sufficiency must become modest, before it can be convinced.

I have sometimes fancied that the rapid succession of brilliant discoveries and inventions which has characterized the present age, and should have enlightened it, has actually enhanced its credulity for the pretensions of quackery and imposture; that the unexpected and unimagined achievements of true science have so dazzled the minds of people, as to render them more accessible to other marvels, whether true or false, and more ready to yield unquestioning belief in *whatever* is new and wonderful: as, in times of old, the heroic deeds of a Hercules or King Arthur led their admiring countrymen to ascribe to them other achievements, not only unreal, but impossible.

Or as, in the sixteenth century, when men's minds had been roused and agitated by the spiritual preaching of the Protestant Reformers, a readier credence was given, not to spiritual *truths* only, but also to spiritual and mystical *errors*. Then was the time when enthusiasts abounded, whose imagination called up before their eyes every object they desired to see; then it was that astrology was the most widely spread and most generally studied as an useful science; then it was that demons were classified, and that witches were burnt in thousands. *Then*, even self-reliant intellects that had thrown off the yoke of ancient beliefs, yielded a ready credence to almost anything which had a spiritual semblance. Melancthon was one of the chief defenders of astrology. Luther attributed diseases to the immediate agency of the devil, and was indignant with the physicians who referred them to natural causes. Paracelsus and Cardan, while shaking the popular faith in ancient physic, rested their own on cabalism and astrology.

In the old city of Aberdeen sorcery had lain undiscovered, though the holy clerks of King's College had been there for a hundred years, ready at any time to have exorcised it with bell, book, and candle; but in the fourth year after the founding of Marischal College and the spiritual teaching of its Protestant professors, twenty-four witches were burnt alive for dancing with the devil around the market cross.

As the minds of men in those days, when awakened to new and deep spiritual convictions, were opened also to mystical *errors*;—so in the present day, when startled with scientific wonders beyond their comprehension, do they gape at and swallow indiscriminately every new thing that is presented to them under the outward guise of science:—and this, while they are disposed rather to scepticism than credulity in matters of ancient belief.

Truth, it has often been said, is stranger than fiction. They that use the proverb have, commonly, in view only the events of history or of social life. But it is equally true, if we compare the established facts of science with the pretended facts of fraud or quackery. If you tell an uninstructed person that you can talk easily and fluently with a friend a thousand miles off,—can write to him at that distance in letter or in cypher, whichever he prefers, and that all the help you need is in some pieces of zinc and copper and some acid and a long piece of wire, and a thing somewhat like the face and hands of a clock; and then tell him, that by merely resting your fingers on a table, you can make it turn round and stand on one leg, and then move of itself about the room: both things may seem to him very strange, very wonder-moving; but surely the truth here must seem stranger than the fiction. To an uninstructed person table-turning must seem at least as credible as electric telegraphy. Or, again, if you were to tell him that there are rays of light which give no light; that, when separated from other rays, and admitted into a darkened room, they cannot be seen, they give no light, and the room remains dark as before, and yet that Professor Stokes has made them visible—has made these dark rays shine and give light in the room—merely by intercepting them with a solution of a salt of quinine contained in an ordinary glass; and if, then, an advocate of homœopathy were to expound to the same hearer his views of the action of medicines,—surely the dogmas of Hahnemann (unproved and unsound as we know them to be) may seem to the uninstructed person no more strange or incredible than what you had told him about the rays of light, though the latter be well-assured facts, that can be verified at any moment, and are in harmony with the whole body of optical science.

It is plain that by no instinct, no common sense, no natural power, can any man discern between truth and untruth in these matters: to the uninstructed in sciences of observation the truth must seem stranger, less credible, than the fiction. It is to this want of special scientific instruction that we must ascribe the popularity of error. For it must be admitted, that they who believe the fictions are not all, in a general sense, fools: there are among them prudent statesmen, astute lawyers, faithful ministers, discreet housewives, such as, in their several callings, we might be content to take as our guides. And yet, because of their want of scientific training, their want of that knowledge which would tell them what it takes to establish a real fact in science, they are unable to distinguish truth from its counterfeit, or to gainsay the pretensions of quackery and imposture.

How, then, can people be guided to a better judgment in these things? Chiefly by being themselves in some measure instructed in some of the sciences of observation; and then by being taught that, in such things as I have put in contrast, the one set of statements are, and the other are not, founded on careful, repeated, various inquiries by men of special training: that the one set are, and the other set are not, provable by every test to the satisfaction of all who will look on and who are too acute to be deceived; and, finally, that the truths are, and the fictions are not, parts of a system or whole body of sciences.

It is this—the value and weight of a body of science—that uneducated people cannot understand. They may perhaps form some judgment whether the reasons advanced for any new view be in themselves good or bad, but they cannot estimate the kind or amount of evidence necessary to establish its truth; nor can they appreciate the objections to it. They know not the multitude of well-assured facts which make up the body of true science, and each of which must be a standing argument against the admission of any new view that is at variance with them. To persons versed in science, this objection, in its aggregate, is well nigh conclusive. We may, in short, safely assert, that whatever cannot bear the test of other scientific inquiry, whatever cannot be incorporated with other knowledge, is probably not true.

These, unfortunately, are tests which they who are uninstructed in science cannot apply for themselves; and, as this class must always remain a large one, we may be sure that quackery and credulity, fraud and folly, will never cease while the world lasts. They are evils that can never be wholly removed.

Yet, assuredly, they may be mitigated. If some portion of the natural sciences, and in particular those which treat of the laws of life, should become an established part of the higher general education—of the education, not of medical students only, but of every English gentleman,—we may expect that society will, in course of time, become more conversant with the kind of knowledge required for distinguishing between true science and its counterfeit. We may reasonable look forward to this improvement, if the universities of Oxford and Cambridge go onwards in the course they have taken of late years, and do not rest until no one shall be called well educated who has not been trained in the knowledge of some natural science. I say expressly *some* natural science; for he that has studied even one, and has learned with what temper it must be pursued, with what labour it has been set up, with what evidence every new doctrine in it must be supported, and how that evidence must be able to bear a jealous cross-examination,—he, I say, that has learned this in any one natural science, will not lightly adopt spurious imitations of facts in any other.

And this wider diffusion of a knowledge of natural science—how much it would add to social and national happiness! Very few men pass through life without repeated occasions for the exercise of scientific knowledge in questions of their own or others' health, or property, or social relations; and according as a man guides himself, or submits to guidance, wisely or unwisely, so is the result for his life, his health, or a great portion of his happiness.

But if we would see to what a height of importance the correct appreciation of science may rise, let us look at its bearings on matters of vital interest to the whole nation. We have an instance in what Sidney Herbert accomplished for the health of the British army. Till 1857 the mortality in the infantry serving at home was nearly *double* that of the civil population of the corresponding ages. *Now* it is actually *less* than in civil life. It is *less than half* of what it was. This represents the saving of the lives of British soldiers in time of peace. The contrast is even more striking in war, if we compare the mortality from sickness in the two wars in China—the one before, the other after, the introduction of the new regulation; —and yet these were little more than well-known sanitary rules, applied intelligently by an able and earnest minister.

Then, if we turn from what has been done to what has *not* yet been done—to the report of the sanitary state of our army in India, to the facts which it discloses, and the sad reflections it suggests—we may see, in matters in which the highest political interests of the empire are concerned, how much *might have been* effected by men of station if they had been instructed in sanitary science, or had guided themselves by the advice of others who were.

But it is a *general* diffusion of such knowledge, or at least of respect for such knowledge, which is needed in a country like England; where the government is so much under the immediate influence of popular opinion, that scarcely a step can be taken for which the general public is not prepared. An autocrat, or his minister, if he be alive to the advances of science, may apply them at once to the exigencies of the state. But with us, there can be little progress without a progress of the whole nation.

After all, it is not to be maintained that the study of natural science has the peculiar merit of making men, in all respects, wiser than the study of any physical science, or of literature, might make them. I fear it must be admitted that the body medical, instructed though all of us have been in natural science, has furnished its share of victims to the quackeries of religious profession, of politics, and of speculative finance. But this only strengthens the argument for the necessity of general education in natural science. Just as scientific men err, when they engage in matters that they have not studied; so do the unscientific, when they essay to judge in scientific questions, without even knowledge enough to choose their guides.

And if some acquaintance with the natural sciences be so needful for men in general, what should be expected of *us*, the medical profession, who practise daily an art which has its only sound basis in these very sciences.

I am well aware of the difficulty of maintaining a high standard of scientific acquirements for all, without exception, that seek to enter our profession; but surely this is what should be unceasingly aimed at. Without scientific knowledge, the practice of medicine becomes mere empiricism; without scientific and general acquirements, our profession may strive in vain to uphold its social status and its influence.

Every ignorant man admitted into our profession has an injurious influence on the estimation in which the entire body is held. His demerits have a tendency to lower us throughout the circle in which he is known. The want of confidence in him—the want of respect for him—beget distrust and disrespect for the profession in general.

Contrast with this, the influence on our social status of such men as Mead, Freind, and Arbuthnot, Thomas Young, Abercrombie, and Brodie, and of the many others, whose acquirements or achievements in literature or science have raised them to eminence in the eyes of the world. Have they not elevated in some degree the whole body medical; nay, are there not some of our own associates, now living—are there not some here present—who have made us all their debtors by the lustre they have thus reflected on our common calling?

And so, likewise, must our scientific character be the measure of our social *influence;* and especially of our power of maintaining truth against error in questions that are daily exciting the attention of society, and of which we ought to be the accepted exponents.

When we consider that the sciences, with which we are, or ought to be, conversant, include subjects of which people in general are so ignorant, and in which nevertheless they take so lively and curious an interest, and which concern their well-being in almost all they do or suffer; surely it is in our power, as it certainly comes within our duty, to exercise a wide influence for good; surely it is our duty, and may be our privilege, to be in these matters the scientific "salt of the earth."

Our profession has never been backward in such work. The learned and ingenious author of "Inquiries into Vulgar Errors" was a provincial physician. It was a physician also who, in the sixteenth century, strove single-handed with the arms of reason against the barbarous hosts of witch-burners, and bore the glorious reproach of folly and presumption for putting the judgment of an insignificant physician in opposition to the dicta and decrees of emperors and kings, legislators and judges, divines and philosophers of all ages and all countries. And something has been done in our time—and well done—for the direct refutation of error. The most fashionable of modern quackeries has been ably and thoroughly exposed by Dr. Simpson.

Few have the ability for works of this kind; but there are many of us, who might do *something* to prevent the spread of mischievous errors. We might do much, if we were to aid in such instruction as would be some *safeguard* against them. We know what was effected by the late Professor Henslow; how in a few years he brought about a complete revolution, intellectual as well as moral, in a grossly ignorant village community; how even such people as those were instructed in some knowledge of science, and filled with a rational and elevating respect for it. And really the means employed were little more than might be in the power of any medical practitioner who has his home in the country. It was not the depth of Professor Henslow's knowledge, but the simplicity with which he imparted it, that gave to it so powerful an influence. Our country members are quite capable of giving short, easy lectures, as Professor Henslow did, and many of them are capable of doing it well. I am not unaware of the objections that may be urged against medical men lecturing, and of the fatally easy transition from lectures for the benefit of others, to lectures for the benefit of one's self; but I think such objections are not applicable to the case of a man instructing the poor of his own village, where he is officially charged with the care of them in sickness—in fact, though not in name, the true guardian of the poor,—and where some little instruction in such simple matters as the air they breathe, and the food they eat, may save his poor neighbours from suffering, or even death, and himself from some portion of his ill-requited labours.

I am disposed even to think, that our patients of the upper classes would have more confidence in orthodox medicine, if we were to vouchsafe more frequently to gratify their natural curiosity as to the nature of their diseases and the processes of cure. I am well aware of the opinion of shrewd "practical men," that no doctors acquire a reputation for skill, like those that hold their tongues; and, doubtless, silence is the most prudent for those, that aim to be counted wise, though they be not so; but I think, nevertheless, that an explanation of the case is as much due from the physician to his patient, as it is from the lawyer to his client; and that the confidence of the public in rational medicine would be strengthened by such explanations. I do not mean that the doctor should put on an air of profundity, and look, like Lord Thurlow, more wise than it is possible for any man to be; nor that he should impress on his patient that

"These are diseases he must know the whole on,
For he talks of the peritoneum and the colon;"

but I mean that he should be willing to give a plain explanation in words as free as may be from technicalities.

We do injustice to medicine, if we treat it as a mystery. It is a science, and entitled to rank as such; and we at least should be ready to show that its maxims are founded in truth and reason.

Let us hope that the educational changes now in progress will aid us in maintaining the dignity which is its due;—that, when people are better instructed as to the sciences on which medicine rests, when they themselves have examined into some parts of its broad and firm foundations, they will have a juster appreciation of medicine itself. Let us hope, that medicine will then receive the respect that is due to it, as the only one of the learned professions which holds its doctrines open to all inquiries, and never condescends to uphold itself on any dogma either of authority or tradition. Let us hope—as we have a right to hope—that medicine will then be honoured as the profession in which all discoveries and inventions are offered freely for the benefit of mankind, and in which their concealment for selfish purposes, or their appropriation by patent right, is held to be disgraceful.

And till then, if the world deny to our profession the full honour which we feel and know is due to it, we may be well content with the ordinary round of duties, which are at once our lot and our privilege: we may be content with the internal satisfaction that our time is spent to the best of our ability in doing good to our fellow-men; that we do not rest supinely satisfied with what is imperfect in our science, but are ever earnestly and laboriously seeking for fresh light; and when God vouchsafes it to our inquiries, we use it gladly in such works as He would have us do—in the relief of human sufferings, in healing the sick, in striving to make the lame walk and the blind see—in earnest endeavours to follow our Divine Exemplar, though it be with the limited powers and faltering steps of human infirmity.

ON THE ORDER OF DISCOVERY IN THE PROGRESS OF KNOWLEDGE.

By Herbert Spencer.

(*From "First Principles," p.* 128.)

The growing belief in the universality of Law is so conspicuous to all cultivated minds, as scarcely to need illustration. None who read these pages will ask for proof that this has been the central element of intellectual progress. But though the fact is sufficiently familiar, the philosophy of the fact is not so, and it will be desirable now to consider it. Partly because the development of our conception of Law will so be rendered more comprehensible; but chiefly because our subsequent course will thus be facilitated, I propose here to enumerate the several conditions that determine the order in which the various relations among phenomena are discovered. Seeing, as we shall, the consequent necessity of this order, and enabled, as we shall also be, to estimate the future by inference from the past, we shall perceive how inevitable is an advance towards the ultimatum that has been indicated.

The recognition of Law being the recognition of uniformity of relations among phenomena, it follows that the order in which different groups of phenomena are reduced to law, must depend on the frequency and distinctions with which the uniform relations they severally present are experienced. At any given stage of progress, those uniformities will be most recognised with which men's minds are oftener and most thoroughly impressed. In proportion partly to the number of times a relation has been presented to consciousness (not merely to the senses); and in proportion partly to the vividness with which the terms of the relation have been cognised, will be the degree in which the constancy of connexion is perceived.

The frequency and impressiveness with which different classes of relations are repeated in conscious experience, thus primarily determining the succession in which they are generalized, there result certain derivative principles to which this succession must more immediately and obviously conform. First in importance comes *the directness with which personal welfare is affected*. While, among surrounding things, many do not appreciably influence the body in any way, some act detrimentally, and some beneficially, in various degrees; and manifestly, those things whose actions on the organism are most influential, will, *cæteris paribus*, be those whose laws of action are earliest observed. Second in order is, *the consciousness of one or both the phenomena between which a relation is to be perceived*. On every side are countless phenomena so concealed as to be detected only by close observation; others not obtrusive enough to attract notice; others which moderately solicit the attention; others so imposing or vivid as to force themselves upon consciousness: and, supposing incidental conditions to be the same, these last will, of course, be among the first to have their relations generalized. In the third place, we have *the absolute frequency with which the relations occur*. There are co-existences, and sequences of all degrees of commonness, from those which are ever present, to those which are extremely rare; and it is clear that the rare co-existences and sequences, as well as the sequences which are very long in taking place, will not be reduced to law so soon as those which are familiar and rapid. Fourthly, has to be added, *the relative frequency of occurrence*. Many events and appearances are more or less limited to times and places; and as a relation which does not exist within the environment of an observer, cannot be cognised by him, however common it may be elsewhere; or in another age, we have to take account of the surrounding physical circumstances, as well as the state of society, of the arts, and of the sciences; all of which affect the frequency with which certain groups of facts are exposed to observation. The fifth corollary to be noticed is, that the succession in which different classes of phenomena are reduced to law, depends in part on their *simplicity*. Phenomena presenting great complexity of causes or conditions, have their essential relations so masked, that it requires accumulated experience to impress upon consciousness the true connexion of antecedents and consequents they involve. Hence, other things equal, the progress of generalization will be from the simple to the complex; and this it is which M. Comte has wrongly asserted to be the sole regulative principle of the progress. Sixth, and last, comes *the degree of abstractness*. Concrete relations are the earliest acquisitions. The colligation of any group of these into a general relation, which is the first step in abstraction, necessarily comes later than the discovery of the relations colligated. The union of a number of these lowest generalizations into a higher and more abstract generalization, is necessarily subsequent to the formation of such lowest generalizations. And so on continually, until the highest and most abstract generalizations have been reached.

DEFICIENCIES OF CLERICAL EDUCATION.

BY JOHN W. DRAPER, M.D., LL.D., OF THE UNIVERSITY OF NEW YORK.

(*From "Thoughts on the Future Civil Policy of America," p.* 273.)

THERE are three organs of public instruction—the School, the Pulpit, the Press.

As respects schools, the primary condition for their efficiency is a supply of well-trained and competent teachers. In former times the education of youth was too often surrendered to persons who had become superannuated in other pursuits, or had failed in them, or had been left in destitute circumstances. But little heed was given by parents or the public to the quality of the information imparted in these concerns. There was a vague notion, which, as we shall see, still unhappily prevails as regards the higher establishments of education, that the training of the mind is of more importance than the nature of the information imparted to it.

Normal schools for the preparation of teachers must necessarily be an essential part of any well-ordered public-school system. In these, young persons of both sexes may be prepared for assuming the duties of teaching. The rule under which they should not only be taught, but likewise subsequently teach—the rule that should be made to apply in every establishment, from the primary school to the university, is this—Education should represent the existing state of knowledge.

But in America this golden rule is disregarded, especially in the case of the higher establishments. What is termed classical learning arrogates to itself a space that excludes much more important things. It finds means to appropriate, practically, all collegiate honours. This evil has arisen from the circumstance that our system was imported from England. It is a remnant of the tone of thought of that country in the sixteenth century; meritorious enough and justifiable enough in that day, but obsolete in this. The vague impression to which I have above referred, that such pursuits impart a training to the mind, has long sustained this inappropriate course. It also finds an excuse in its alleged power of communicating the wisdom of past ages. The grand depositories of human knowledge are not the ancient, but the modern tongues. Few, if any, are the facts worth knowing that are to be exclusively obtained by a knowledge of Latin and Greek; and as to mental discipline, it might reasonably be inquired how much a youth will [illegible] by translating daily a few good sentences of Latin and Greek into bad and broken English. So far as a preparation is required for the subsequent struggles and conflicts of life—for discerning the intentions and meeting the rivalries of competitors—for skill to design movements and carry them out with success—for cultivating a clearness of perception into the character and motives of others, and for imparting a decision to our own actions—so far as these things are concerned, an ingenious man would have no difficulty in maintaining the amusing affirmation that more might be gained from a mastery of the game of chess than by translating all the Greek and Latin authors in the world.

The remarks I am thus making respecting the imperfections of general education apply, I think, very forcibly to the education of the clergy. The School, the Pulpit, the Press, being the three organs of public instruction, a right preparation of the clergy for their duty is of as much moment as a right preparation of teachers and journalists.

In the education of the American clergyman the classical element very largely predominates. Indeed, it may with truth be affirmed that it is to no inconsiderable degree for the sake of securing such a result that that element is so carefully fostered in the colleges, from which it would otherwise have long ago been eliminated, or, at all events, greatly reduced in prominence. The strength of this wish is manifested by the munificent endowments with which many pious and patriotic men have sustained classical professorships. Perhaps, however, they do not sufficiently reflect that the position and requirements of the clergy have of late years very much changed. Preaching must answer to the mode of thinking of the congregations. But now literary authority has to a very great degree lost its force. Elucidations of Scripture and the defence of doctrine, in modern times, require modern modes of treatment.

But, moreover, in one important respect is the education of the clergy defective. Unhappily, and, it may be added, unnecessarily, there has arisen an apparent antagonism between Theology and Science. Tradition has been made to confront discovery. Now, the discussion and correct appreciation of any new scientific fact requires a special training, a special stock of knowledge. That training, that knowledge, are not to be had in theological seminaries. The clergyman is thus constrained to view with jealous distrust the rapid advancement of practical knowledge. In the case of any new fact, his inquiry necessarily is, not whether it is absolutely true, but whether it is in accordance with conceptions he considers established. The result of this condition of things is, that many of the most important, the most powerful and exact branches of human knowledge, have been forced into a position they never would have voluntarily assumed, and have been compelled to put themselves on their defence—Astronomy, in the case of the globular form of the earth, and its position as a subordinate planet; Geology, as respects its vast antiquity; Zoology, on the problem of the origin of species; Chemistry, on the unchangeability of matter and the indestructibility of force.

In thus criticising education in the higher American establishments, I present views that have forced themselves on my attention in an experience of thirty years, and on a very extensive scale. Not unfrequently I have superintended the instruction, professional or otherwise, of nearly four hundred young men in the course of a single year, and have had unusual opportunities of observing their subsequent course of life.

The education of the clergy, I think, is not equal to that of physicians or lawyers. The provisions are sufficient, and the time is sufficient, but the direction is faulty. In the study of medicine everything is done to impart to the pupil a knowledge of the present state of the subjects or sciences with which he is concerned. The profession watches with a jealous eye its colleges, exposing without hesitation any shortcomings it detects. It will not be satisfied with erudition, it insists on knowledge.

But such modernised instruction is actually less necessary in the life of a physician than it is in the life of a clergyman. The former pursues his daily course in an unobtrusive way; the latter is compelled by his position to publicity. The congregations whom he must meet each Sabbath day, and, indeed, perhaps more frequently, are often too prone to substitute the right of criticism for a sentiment of simple devotion. Very few among them can appreciate the monotonous, the wearing strain of compulsory mental labour—labour that at a given hour must with punctuality be performed. On topics that have been thought about, and written about, and preached about for nearly twenty centuries, they are importunately and unreasonably demanding something new.

In that ordeal the clergyman spends his existence. To maintain the respect that is his due, there are but two things on which he can rely—purity of life and knowledge. Men unconsciously submit to the guidance of what they discern to be superior intelligence. Here comes into disastrous operation the defective organization of the theological seminaries. Content with such a knowledge of nature as might have answered a century ago, the imposing and ever-increasing body of modern science they decline. And yet it is that science and its practical applications which are now guiding the destinies of civilization.

In my "History of the Intellectual Development of Europe" I have had occasion to consider the consequences of the Reformation, and may perhaps be excused the following quotation: "America, in which, of all countries, the Reformation at the present moment has farthest advanced, should offer to thoughtful men much encouragement. Its cities are filled with churches, built by voluntary gifts; its clergy are voluntarily sustained, and are in all directions engaged in enterprises of piety, education, mercy. What a difference between their private life and that of ecclesiastics before the Reformation! Not, as in the old times, does the layman look upon them as the cormorants and curse of society. They are his faithful advisers, his honoured friends, under whose suggestion and supervision are instituted educational establishments, colleges, hospitals, whatever can be of benefit to men in this life, or secure for them happiness in the life to come."

No one can study the progress of modern civilization without being continually reminded of the great, it might be said, the mortal mistake committed by the Roman Church. Had it put itself forth as the promoter and protector of science, it would at this day have exerted an unquestioned dominion all over Europe. Instead of being the stumbling-block, it would have been the animating agent of human advancement. It shut the Bible only to have it opened forcibly by the Reformation; it shut the book of Nature, but has found it impossible to keep it closed. How different the result, had it abandoned the obsolete absurdities of patristicism, and become imbued with the spirit of true philosophy—had it lifted itself to a comprehension of the awful magnificence of the heavens above and the glories of the earth beneath—had it appreciated the immeasurable vastness of the universe, its infinite multitude of worlds, its inconceivable past duration! How different, if in place of for ever looking backward, it had only looked forward—bowing itself down in a world of life and light, instead of worshipping, in the charnel-house of antiquity, the skeletons of twenty centuries! How different, had it hailed with transport the discoveries and inventions of human genius, instead of scowling upon them with a malignant and baleful eye! How different, had it canonized the great men who have been the interpreters of Nature, instead of anathematizing them as Atheists!

In our national development it is for the American clergy to shun that great, that fatal mistake. It is for them to remember that the Reformation remains only half completed, until to the free reading of the Book of God there is added the free reading of the Book of Nature. It is for them to remember that there are two volumes of Revelation—the Word and the Works; and that it is the indefeasible right of every man to study and interpret them both, according to the light given him, without molestation or punishment.

Since the invention of printing, the power of the pulpit has been subordinated to the power of the press, which is continually gathering force from the increasing diffusion of education. In America the newspaper has become a necessary of life. It makes its successful appearance in villages of which the population would be considered, in other countries, inadequate for its support. Cheap reading is to be had everywhere. The consequence is, that all sides of a question are apt to be read. It is affirmed that the consumption of paper in America, for printing and writing, is more than that of England and France put together.

THE PHYSIOLOGICAL BASIS OF PRIMARY EDUCATION.

BY EDWARD SEGUIN, M.D.

(*From his recent work, "Idiocy, and its Treatment by the Physiological Method," published by William Wood and Co. New York.*)

THUS education connects a small body with all bodies, a small intellect with the general laws of the universe, through specific instruments of perception.

This being the law of perception of phenomena, it does not matter through which sense we perceive; the same operation being entirely from the mind, is always identical with itself; this law is nothing less than the principle of our physiological method of education.

Thence the law of evolution of the function of the senses ending in intellectual faculty, rules from the youngest child to the most encyclopædic nervous apparatus. A corollary law to this, is the mode of perception and idealization of the impressions according to certain conditions, conformable to the teachings of anatomy and physiology. One thing at a time, is the law of sensorial perception for inferior animals. As many things at a time as necessary to form a complete idea, is the law for the intellectual comprehension of man. In animals some senses are more perfect than in man, hence their sensations are more perfect than ours; nevertheless, theirs being received in singleness and registered without associations, cannot become ideas, because their notions acquired alone, live or die alone, incapable of fecundation; the lower animals are as far down as that.

But we cannot study the progress of sensorial and intellectual evolution without finding already animals inferior to mammalia which register their sensations and feelings in comparison with each other, and with a meaning attached to them. These animals must receive compared and comparable impressions, to be capable of combining them presently or hereafter, to form new judgments and determinations. The ant, the bee, the spider, the blue-fly and many more, give evidence of their power of idealizing notions, and of the rationality of their determinations. But for the immense majority of animals, the rule seems to be one perception at a time, whose isolated notion is incapable of entering into collections of images, parents to ideas. Though every observation points to the probable issue of this difference between man and brutes, as being only a gradation, whose lowest strata begins lower than the corals, which know in what direction to build and propagate, and ends where man does not yet dare to aspire. However, few minds are prepared for this affirmation, unless it could be supported by the following observation :—

In the nervous apparatus of animals, the sensory ganglia are larger than the hemispheres in proportion to the development of their respective functions ; sensorial perceptions being in them more extensive than the ideal products of comparison. On the contrary, in our human nervous system, the intellectual ganglia are larger than the sensorial ones in proportion to the predominance of the reflective and willed above the perceptive faculties.

The following remarks constitute the psychological corollary to this observation.

The motor of life in animals is mostly centripetal ; the motor of life in man is mostly centrifugal. But how many uneducated, or viciously educated men display none but the ferocious centripetal power of the beast : while a dog shall affront death to defend his master, that master may work the ruin of twenty families to satisfy a single brute appetite ; nevertheless, the motor in the beast is called instinct, in man soul. Well, we will say yes ; instinct, when a wild, uneducated, or uneducable stock ; soul, when engrafted by education and revelation. As a generality, however, animals have only a centripetal or individual life ; men, educated and participating in the incessant revelation, have a social and centrifugal existence also, being, feeling, thinking, in mankind, as mankind is, feels, and progresses in God. What can be done to a certain extent for brutes, may be done for idiots and their congeners ; their life may be rendered more centrifugal, that is to say more social, by education.

True, this view of our subject and of our race would not deprive animals of some kind of soul. But our mind must have already become familiar with that sort of concessions ; since women, Jews, peasants, Sudras, Parias, Indians, negroes, imbeciles, insane, idiots, are not now denied a soul, as they were once by religious or civil ordinances. Nations have perished by the over-educating of a few ; mankind can be improved only by the elevation of the lowest through education and comfort, which substitute harmony to antagonism, and make all beings feel the unity of what circulates in all, life.

Contrarily to the teachings of various mythologies of the brain, and with the disadvantage of working against the prevalent anthropological formula, we were obliged at the same time to use most of its terms ; we have developed our child, not like a duality, nor like a trinity, nor like an illimited poly-entity, but, as nearly as we could, like a unit. It is true that the unity of the physiological training could not be gone through without concessions to the language of the day, nor to necessities of analysis, quite repugnant to the principle ; it is true that we have been speaking of muscular, nervous, or sensorial functions, as of things as distinct for us as muscles, nerves, and bones are for the anatomist ; but after a long struggle with these difficulties, psycho-physiology vindicated its rights against the feebleness of our understanding, and the mincing of our vocabularies.

We looked at the rather immovable, or ungovernable mass called an idiot with the faith that where the appearance displayed nothing but ill-organized matter, there was nothing but ill-circumstanced animus. In answer to that conviction, when we educated the muscles, contractility responded to our bidding with a spark from volition; we exercised severally the senses, but an impression could not be made on their would-be material nature, without the impression taking its rank among the accumulated idealities; we were enlarging the chest, and new voices came out from it, expressing new ideas and feelings; we strengthened the hand, and it became the realizer of ideal creations and labour; we started imitation as a passive exercise, and it soon gave rise to all sorts of spontaneous actions; we caused pain and pleasure to be felt through the skin or the palate, and the idiot, in answer, tried to please by the exhibition of his new moral qualities: in fact, we could not touch a fibre of his, without receiving back the vibration of his all-souled instrument.

In opposition to this testimony of the unity of our nature given by idiots, since they receive a physiological education, might be arrayed the testimony of millions of children artificially developed by dualistic or other antagonistic systems; as millions of ox and horse teams testified to the powerlessness of steam. The fact that dualism is not in our nature but in our sufferings, is self-evident. Average men who oppose everything, were compressed from birth in some kind of swaddling bands; those who abhor study were forced to it as to punishment; those who gormandize were starved; those who lie were brought to it by fear; those who hate labour have been reduced to work for others; those who covet were deprived: everywhere oppression creates the exogenous element of dualism. Of the two terms of "the house divided against itself," one is the right owner, the other is evidently the intruder. We have done away with the last in educating idiots, not by repression, which would have created it, but by ignoring it.

One of the earliest and most fatal antagonisms taught to a child is the forbidding of using his hands to ascertain the qualities of surrounding objects, of which his sight gives him but an imperfect notion, if it be not aided by the touch; and of breaking many things as well, to acquire the proper idea of solidity. The imbecility of parents in these matters has too often favoured the growth of the evil spirit. The youngest child, when he begins to totter on his arched legs, goes about touching, handling, breaking everything. It is our duty to foster and direct that beautiful curiosity, to make it the regular channel for the acquisition of correct perceptions and tactile accuracy; as for breaking, it must be turned into the desire of preservation and the power of holding with the will; nothing is so simple, as the following example will demonstrate:—

Once a very excitable child, eighteen months old, touching, breaking, throwing everything he could, seemed really ready, if he had been once punished for it, to become possessed by the old intruder; but it was not our plan. We bought unmatched *Sèvres* cups and Bohemia glasses, really splendid to look at, and served the child in one of them, after showing him the elegance of the pattern, the richness of the colours, everything which could please and attach him to the object. But he had no sooner drunk than he threw the glass away. Not a word was said, not a piece removed from where it fell; but the next time he was thirsty, we brought him where the fragments lay, and let him feel more thirst before we could find another glass equally beautiful. Some more were broken in the same petulant spirit; but later, he slowly dropped one, when, at the same time, he looked into our eyes to catch signs of anger. But there were none there, nor in the voice; only the composure and accent of pity for the child who could willingly incur such a loss. Since then, baby took good care of his cups and glasses, finer than ours; he taught his little fingers how to embrace with security the thin neck of one, the large body, or the diminutive handle of others. In practising these so varied handlings, his mind became saving and his hands a model of accuracy.

ON MODERN COLLEGIATE STUDIES.

(*Extract from an Address delivered at Union College, Schenectady, N. Y., by* FRANCIS WAYLAND, D.D.)

IF you will allow me to commence with an elementary thought, I would remark, that every act of the mind *ends* in a knowledge, sometimes only subjective, but generally both subjective and objective. Thus I am conscious of a simple emotion; here is a mental act, a mere subjective knowledge. I perceive a tree; here is a subjective consciousness and an objective knowledge. And, on the other hand, every knowledge *presupposes* an act of mind; for were there no mind, or were the mind incapable of action, knowledge would be impossible.

From this simple and obvious fact, it has naturally come to pass that men have looked upon the subject of education in two distinct points of view, as they have contemplated either the act of mind, or the knowledge in which it results. Hence, some have considered education to consist merely in the communication of knowledge; others almost entirely in the discipline of mind. If the first be our object, it will be successfully accomplished precisely in proportion to the amount and the value of the knowledge which we communicate. If, on the other hand, we desire simply to cultivate the intellect, our success must be measured by the number of faculties which we improve, and the degree of culture which we have imparted to them.

It is, I presume, for this reason, that a division has, to a considerable degree, been established between the studies which enter into our course of higher education. Some of them, of which the results are acknowledged to be in general valueless, are prosecuted on account of the mental discipline which they are supposed to impart. That they tend to nothing practical, has sometimes been deemed their appropriate excellence. Hence, some learned men have exulted rather facetiously in the "glorious inutility" of the studies which they recommend. On the other hand, there are many studies which communicate knowledge, admitted by all men to be indispensable, which are supposed to convey no mental discipline, or, at least, only that which is of the most elementary character. Hence, you at once perceive that a wide ground for debate is afforded, which writers on education have not been backward to occupy. Hence, also, the various discussions on the best methods of education, which seem to me to approach with but slow and unequal steps to any definite conclusion. The studies which are most relied on for mental discipline, for instance, are the classics and the mathematics. While the advocates for these discard, almost contemptuously, all other methods of culture, they are by no means agreed among themselves. The mathematicians look with small favour upon the lovers of lexicons, and paradigms, and accents; and claim that nothing but exact science can invigorate the power of ratiocination, on which all certainty of knowledge depends. The philologists, on the other hand, inveigh in no measured terms against the narrow range of mathematical culture, and boldly affirm that it unfits men for all reasoning concerning matter actually existing, while it withers up every delicate sentiment and turns into an arid waste the entire field of our emotional nature. Here issue is joined, and I am compelled in truth to add, *adhuc sub judice lis est.*

But is it not possible to escape from the smoke and din of this controversy, and look upon this question from a somewhat higher point of view? It may, I think, be safely taken for granted, that the system of which we form a part, is the work of a Being of infinite wisdom and infinite benevolence. He made the world without us and the world within us, and He manifestly made each of them for the other. He has made knowledge, intellectual culture, and progress, all equally necessary to our individual and social well-being. He abhors all castes, and desires that every one of his children shall enjoy to the full all the means of happiness which have been committed to his trust. Is it then to be supposed that He has made for our brief probation two kinds of knowledge; one necessary for the attainment of our means of happiness, but incapable of nourishing and strengthening the soul; and the other, tending to self-culture, but leading to no single practical advantage? Shall we believe that the God and Father of all has made the many to labour by blind rules for the good of the few, without the possibility of spiritual elevation; and the few to learn nothing that shall promote the happiness of the whole, living on the labours of others, selfishly building themselves up in intellectual superiority? Is it not rather to be believed, that He has made each of these ends to harmonize with the other, so that all intellectual culture shall issue in knowledge which shall confer benefits on the whole; and all knowledge properly acquired, shall in an equal degree tend to intellectual development?

These expectations seem to me to be reasonable. If so, we might surely anticipate that all knowledge acquired according to the established laws of mind, would be productive of self-culture. Nay, we might suppose that that which God had made most necessary to our existence, would be, in the highest degree, self-disciplinary. Thus every one, whatever his position, may well be supposed to possess the means of developing his own powers, and arriving at the standing of an intellectual man. There is nothing in the nature of any occupation that renders such an expectation extravagant. The uncles of Hugh Miller were highly cultivated men, reading the best books, concerning one of whom he remarks, "there are professors of natural history who know less of living nature than was known by uncle Sandy;" and yet one of them was a harness-maker, and the other a stone-mason; each labouring industriously at his calling, for daily bread, for six days in the week.

But if we take no account of the acquisition of knowledge and confine ourselves simply to intellectual culture, I apprehend that we shall arrive at substantially the same result. Suppose that our sole object is to develop the powers of the human mind. We must then first ask what are these powers. It will be sufficient for our present purpose to consider the following, as they are allowed to be the most important: Perception, by which we arrive at a knowledge of the phenomena of the world without us; Consciousness, by which we become aware of the changes in the world within us; Abstraction and Generalization, by which our knowledge of individuals becomes the knowledge of classes; Reasoning, by which we use the known to discover the unknown; Imagination, by which we construct pictures in poetry and ideals in philosophy; and Memory, by which all these various forms of past knowledge are recalled and made available for the present.

Now, if such be the powers conferred on us by our Creator, it must, I think, be admitted that each of them is designed for a particular purpose, and that a human mind would be fatally deficient were any one of them wanting. In our cultivation of mind, then, we must have respect not to one or two of them, but to all; since that is the most perfect mind in which all of them are the most fully developed.

If, then, we desire to improve the intellect of man by study, it is obvious that that study will be the best adapted to our purpose which cultivates not one, but all, of these faculties, and cultivates them all most thoroughly. We cultivate our powers of every kind by exercise, and that study will most effectually aid us in the work of self-development, which requires the original exercise of the greatest number of them.

Supposing this to be admitted, which I think will not be denied, the question will arise what studies are best adapted to our purpose. This is a question which cannot be settled by authority. We are just as capable of deciding it as the men who have gone before us. They were once, like ourselves, men of the present, and their wisdom has not certainly received any addition from the slumber of centuries. They may have been able to judge correctly for the time that then *was*, but could they revisit us now, they might certainly be no better able than ourselves to judge correctly for the time that *now is*. If any of us should be heard of 200 years hence, it would surely be strange folly for the men of A.D. 2054 to receive our sayings as oracles concerning the conditions of society which will be then existing. God gives to every age the means for perceiving its own wants and discovering the best manner of supplying them; and it is, therefore, certainly best that every age should decide such questions for itself. We cannot, certainly, decide them by authority.

There are two methods by which we can determine the truth in this matter. First, we may examine any particular study and observe the faculties of mind which it does and which it does not call into action. Every reasonable man, at all acquainted with the nature of his own mind, will be able to do this. Take, for instance, the studies which are pursued for the sake merely of discipline. Do they call into exercise one or many of our faculties? Suppose they cultivate the reasoning power, and the power of poetic combination; do they do anything else? If not, what have we by which to improve the powers of observation, of consciousness, of generalization, and combination, these most important and most valuable of our faculties? If, then, their range be so limited, it may be deserving of inquiry whether some studies which can improve a larger number of our faculties might not sometimes take their places; and yet more, whether they should occupy so large a portion of the time devoted to education.

But we may examine the subject by another test. We may ask what are the results actually produced by devotion to those studies which are allowed to be merely disciplinary. We teach the mathematics to cultivate the reasoning power, and the languages to improve the imagination and the taste. We then may very properly inquire, are mathematicians better reasoners than other men, in matters not mathematical? As a student advances in the mathematics, do we find his powers of ratiocination, in anything but the relations of quantity, to be visibly improved? Are philologists or classical students more likely to become poets, or artists, than other men; or, does their style by this mode of discipline approach more nearly to the classical models of their own, or of any other language?

It is by such considerations as these that this question is to be answered. We have long since abjured all belief in magical influences. If we cannot discover any law of nature by which a cause produces its effect, and are unable to perceive that the effect is produced, we begin to doubt whether any causation exists in the matter.

If there be any truth in the foregoing remarks, they would seem to lead us to the following conclusions :—

First, that every branch of study should be so taught as to accomplish both the results of which we have been speaking; that is, that it should not only increase our knowledge, but also confer valuable discipline; and that it should not only confer valuable discipline, but also increase our knowledge; and that, if it does not accomplish both of these results, there is either some defect in our mode of teaching, or the study is imperfectly adapted to the purposes of education.

Secondly, that there seems no good reason for claiming pre-eminence for one study over another, at least in the manner to which we have been accustomed. The studies merely disciplinary have valuable practical uses. To many pursuits they are important, and to some indispensable. Let them, then, take their proper place in any system of good learning, and claim nothing more than to be judged of by their results. Let them not be the unmeaning shibboleth of a caste; but, standing on the same level with all other intellectual pursuits, be valued exactly in proportion to their ability to increase the power and range and skill of the human mind, and to furnish it with that knowledge which shall most signally promote the well-being and happiness of humanity.

And, thirdly, it would seem that our whole system of instruction requires an honest, thorough, and candid revision. It has been for centuries the child of authority and precedent. If those before us made it what it is, by applying to it the resources of earnest and fearless thought, I can see no reason why we, by pursuing the same course, might not improve it. God intended us for progress, and we counteract his design when we deify antiquity, and bow down and worship an opinion, not because it is either wise or true, but merely because it is ancient.

ON THOROUGHNESS OF INTELLECTUAL ATTAINMENT.

(*Extract from a Lecture delivered at University College, London by* PROFESSOR A. DE MORGAN.)

THERE are two ways in which education is to be considered: that is to say, with reference to its effect upon the character and disposition of the individual, and also with reference to the degree of power and energy which is communicated to the mind. Now, firstly, with respect to character as formed by education, it is hardly necessary to say that knowledge, to be useful in its effect upon habits, must be both liberal and accurate—must deal in reasoning and inference, and in sound reasoning and correct inference. So much is admitted by all; but I desire to be understood as going further. In looking over the various branches of human inquiry, I do not find that what is learned in a second period is merely a certain portion added to that which was acquired in the first. If I were to teach geometry for two months, I conceive that the geometry of the second month would not merely double the amount which the student gained in the first, but would be, as it were, a new study, showing other features and giving additional powers, with the advantage of its being evident that the second step is the development and consequence of the first. Suppose that, instead of employing the second month in geometry, I had turned the attention of the student to algebra, would he have been a gainer by the change? I answer confidently in the negative.

To carry this further, let us take the whole career of the learner, and apply the same argument. There is in every branch of knowledge a beginning, a middle, and an end: a beginning, in which the student is striving with new and difficult principles, and in which he is relying in a great measure on the authority of his instructor; a middle, in which he has gained some confidence in his own knowledge, and some power of applying his first principles. He is now in a state of danger, so far as the estimate which he is likely to form of himself is concerned. He has as yet no reason to suppose that his career can be checked—nothing to humble the high notion which he will entertain of himself, his teachers, and his subject. Let him only proceed, and he will come to what I have called the end of the subject, and will begin to see that there is, if not a boundary, yet the commencement of a region which has not been tracked and surveyed, and in which not all the skill which he has acquired in voyaging by the chart will save him from losing his way. It is at this period of his career that he will begin to form a true opinion of his own mind, which, I fully believe, is not done by many persons, simply because they have never been allowed to pursue any branch of inquiry to the extent which is necessary to show them where their power ends.

For this reason I think that, whatever else may be done, some one subject, at least, should be well and thoroughly investigated, for the sake of giving the proper tone to the mind upon the use, province, and extent of knowledge in general. I might insist upon other points connected with the disposition which a want of depth upon all subjects is likely to produce; but if what I have said be founded in reason, it is amply sufficient to justify my recommendation that, for character's sake, there should be in every liberal education at least one subject thoroughly studied. What the subject should be is *comparatively* of minor importance, and might, perhaps, be left in some degree to the student himself.

Neither is it necessary, as to the point just considered, that every study which is undertaken should be pursued to the same depth. Convince the mind by one example, and the similarity which exists between all branches of knowledge will teach the same truth for all. I now proceed with the consideration of the subject, in connexion with the power which is derived from deep study, and which is not to be obtained without.

The powers which we expect to give by liberal education, or at least a very considerable portion of the whole, may be comprised under two heads, which I will take separately.

Firstly, it is one of the most important points of education that the subject of it should be made a *good learner*. What is it that can be done before the age of twenty-one, either at school or college? Is the education then finished? Is the pupil to pursue no branch of study further? Nay, does not a professional career open upon him immediately? He is thrown upon the world to learn, with the resources of his education to rely on, and little other help; for it is well known that, throughout our different plans of professional education, there is found but a small amount of teaching, with free permission for the aspirant to teach himself. Now, in this new career there is no stopping half way, in accordance with a previous system of education, in which many subjects were only half taught. The lawyer or physician must be a finished lawyer or physician, able to investigate his subjects at the boundaries of knowledge, and to carry his previous studies successfully up to that point. So soon as either has arrived at the height where his education left him, as to the species of mental effort requisite to carry on his subject, from that moment his future professional study becomes, in point of fact, an awkward substitute for the education which his former teachers professed to supply. He must apply himself with pain to an isolated subject, under great difficulties and with small helps, to gain that power which might so much more easily have been gained when the mind was more supple, and formation of habits more easy. Seeing, then, that the future business of life will require a knowledge of the way to go *through* with a branch of inquiry, I submit that such a process should form, in one instance at least, the exercise of preceding years. The steady habit of reading, which extends over a long period; the practice of retaining difficulties in mind to be considered and reconsidered, to be taken up at the leisure moment, and laid down as deferred but not abandoned; the method of laying aside that which presents an obstacle insuperable for the time, but always bearing the point in mind in subsequent study, waiting to catch the moment at which more extensive reading will furnish the clue required;—all these most essential requisites for successful prosecution of professional studies are not to be learnt by anything but practice; nor can they be practised upon the first half, so to speak, of a branch of knowledge. To make a subject teach the mind how to inquire, it must be carried beyond the point at which the necessity for inquiry commences. I might, were it necessary, insist upon the success which so frequently in after life attends those who have exerted their juvenile powers in the thorough mastery of some main branch of knowledge, so far as their years rendered it practicable. But this would lead me too far, and I shall, therefore, proceed to the second quality of mind in question.

Among the educated classes we find those who can readily combine the ideas which they possess, and can turn their previous acquirements to the original consideration of such questions as arise; and we also find those who are slow at such exercise, or almost altogether incapable of it. In the latter class we often meet with persons who receive what is submitted to them with sufficient readiness of perception, and decide upon it with judgment, but, nevertheless, seem incapable of making one step in advance, or, as we should say in conversation, "out of their own heads." That the faculty of thinking easily, and originating thought, should be carefully cultivated, needs not to be maintained; and it cannot be effectively done without a considerable degree of attention paid to the method of thinking which is chosen. Would you train a youth to discriminate nicely by aid of the study of etymology and verbal criticism, and by habituating him to recognise the very nice, but very true, distinctions which that study points out? Then he must leave his accidence far behind, and become well practised in the routine of language: the beginner is not made ready to approach his ultimate object in a twelvemonth. Is it desired to sharpen his power of suggesting methods of deduction by means of mathematical studies? He must go through the elements, during which he will find neither the materials for his original investigations, nor power to pursue them. He must first patiently collect knowledge, and the power of application will come by very slow degrees, and will not be in that state of activity which will answer the purpose, until something more than mere elements is effectively learnt. Considerations of the same character apply to every department of knowledge: there is a lower stage in which the pupil can do little more than collect; there is a higher state of knowledge in which he can begin effectively to apply thought to his collected stores, and thus make them help him to useful habits of mind. If it be desired to train the power of investigation, and to enable the student to do something for himself, it must be by following up one subject at least, to the extent just described.

I might, further, instance the tendency to create power of perseverance which must exist in sustained and digested study, and the habit of steady application thereby fostered. But upon these points there will be no dispute. I will only observe, that accuracy is seldom the fruit of an attention much divided in early years. Generally speaking, correctness in any branch of knowledge is a result only of much study. However simple the subject may be, however absurd the only possible mistake may be, I believe it may be taken as an axiom that the beginner is always inaccurate, and remains subject to this defect until he has acquired something more than elements. It has always appeared to me that the value of accuracy does not begin to be soon felt, and that it is only when the student has something of considerable extent to look back upon, that he begins to understand how much depends upon correctness. The same may be said as to lucid arrangement, of which it is clear that the learner will never see the value, until he has a considerable quantity of matter on which to employ himself.

On such grounds as these I form my opinion that the ancient universities, in laying down, as it were, few and distinct objects of study, did not pursue a course for which they deserve to be the objects of censure. Opinions may differ as to the subjects chosen: some may conceive that the fundamental studies should be literary, others scientific; some may think the details of the system of education faulty in a high, others in a low, degree. With these and similar questions I have here nothing to do, but only with the principle of not turning the attention of the student to a wide variety of subjects. If the universities have erred in not encouraging a minor degree of attention to subjects not yet comprehended in their course—and I am far from saying that they have not erred—still I think that their error has been venial compared with that committed by the advocates of too extensive an education. Now, I would charge no one with being the favourer of either the existing extreme, or that which has been proposed; perhaps the ultras of either side are few in number. But having given some reasons why the existing system in its worst form secures several great points, and provides for several important wants, I turn to an equal excess on the other side, and I ask what is the counterbalancing advantage? When the student has occupied his time in learning a moderate portion of many different things, what has he acquired—extensive knowledge, or useful habits? Even if he can be said to have varied learning, it will not long be true of him, for nothing flies so quickly as half-digested knowledge; and when this is gone, there remains but a slender portion of useful power. A small quantity of learning quickly evaporates from a mind which never held any learning except in small quantities; and the intellectual philosopher can perhaps explain the following phenomenon,—that men who have given deep attention to one or more liberal studies, can learn to the end of their lives, and are able to retain and apply very small quantities of other kinds of knowledge; while those who have never learnt much of any one thing, seldom acquire new knowledge after they attain to years of maturity, and frequently lose the greater part of that which they once possessed.

ON THE EDUCATIONAL USES OF MUSEUMS

(*Extract from a Lecture by* EDWARD FORBES, F.R.S.)

MUSEUMS, of themselves alone, are powerless to educate. But they can instruct the educated, and excite a desire for knowledge in the ignorant. The labourer who spends his holiday in a walk through the British Museum, cannot fail to come away with a strong and reverential sense of the extent of knowledge possessed by his fellow-men. It is not the objects themselves that he sees there and wonders at, that make this impression, so much as the order and evident science which he cannot but recognise in the manner in which they are grouped and arranged. He learns that there is a meaning and value in every object however insignificant, and that there is a way of looking at things common and rare distinct from the regarding of them as useless, useful, or curious,—the three terms of classification in favour with the ignorant. He goes home and thinks over it; and when a holiday in summer or a Sunday's afternoon in spring tempts him, with his wife and little ones, to walk into the fields, he finds that he has acquired a new interest in the stones, in the flowers, in the creatures of all kinds that throng around him. He can look at them with an inquiring pleasure, and talk of them to his children with a tale about things like them that he had seen ranged in order in the Museum. He has gained a new sense,—a thirst for natural knowledge, one promising to quench the thirst for beer and vicious excitement that tortured him of old. If his intellectual capacity be limited and ordinary, he will become a better citizen and happier man; if in his brain there be dormant power, it may waken up to make him a Watt, a Stephenson, or a Miller.

It is not the ignorant only who may benefit in the way just indicated. The so-called educated are as likely to gain by a visit to a Museum, where their least cultivated faculties, those of observation, may be healthily stimulated and brought into action. The great defect of our systems of education is the neglect of the *educating* of the observing powers,—a very distinct matter, be it noted, from scientific or industrial *instruction*. It is necessary to say this, since the confounding of the two is evident in many of the documents that have been published of late on these very important subjects. Many persons seem to fancy that the elements that should constitute a sound and manly education are antagonistic, – that the cultivation of taste through purely literary studies and of reasoning through logic and mathematics, one or both, is opposed to the training in the equally important matter of observation through those sciences that are descriptive and experimental. Surely this is an error; partizanship of the one or other method or rather department of mental training, to the exclusion of the rest, is a narrow-minded and cramping view, from whatsoever point it be taken. Equal development and strengthening of all are required for the constitution of the complete mind, and it is full time that we should begin to do now what we ought to have done long ago. Through the teaching of some of the sections of natural history and chemistry,—the former for observation of forms, the latter of phenomena,—I cannot but think the end in view might be gained, even keeping out of sight altogether, if the teacher holds it best to do so, what are called practical applications. For this branch of education Museums are the best text-books; but, in order that they should be effectively studied, they require to be explained by competent teachers. Herein at present lies the main difficulty concerning the introduction of the science of observation into courses of ordinary education. A grade of teachers who should be able and willing to carry science into schools for youth has hardly yet appeared. Hitherto there have been few opportunities for their normal instruction.

ON THE CLAIMS OF SCIENCE IN EDUCATION.

(*Extract from an Address delivered at Birmingham by his Royal Highness* PRINCE ALBERT.)

NO human pursuits make any material progress until science is brought to bear upon them. We have seen, accordingly, many of them slumber for centuries upon centuries; but, from the moment that science has touched them with her magic wand, they have sprung forward, and taken strides which amaze and almost awe the beholder. Look at the transformation which has gone around us since the laws of gravitation, electricity, magnetism, and the expansive power of heat have become known to us. It has altered our whole state of existence—one might say, the whole face of the globe. We owe this to science, and to science alone; and she has other treasures in store for us, if we will but call her to our assistance.

It is sometimes objected by the ignorant, that science is uncertain and changeable, and they point with a malicious kind of pleasure to the many exploded theories which have been superseded by others, as a proof that the present knowledge may be also unsound, and, after all, not worth having. But they are not aware that, while they think to cast blame upon science, they bestow, in fact, the highest praise upon her. For that is precisely the difference between science and prejudice; that the latter keeps stubbornly to its position, whether disproved or not, whilst the former is an unarrestable movement towards the fountain of truth, caring little for cherished authorities or sentiments, but continually progressing, feeling no false shame at her shortcomings, but, on the contrary, the highest pleasure, when freed from an error, at having advanced another step towards the attainment of Divine truth—a pleasure not even intelligible to the pride of ignorance.

We not unfrequently hear, also, science and practice, scientific knowledge and common sense, contrasted as antagonistic. A strange error! for science is eminently practical, and must be so, as she sees and knows what she is doing, whilst mere common practice is condemned to work in the dark, applying natural ingenuity to unknown powers to obtain a known result.

Far be it from me to undervalue the creative power of genius, or to treat shrewd common sense as worthless without knowledge. But nobody will tell me that the same genius would not take an incomparably higher flight if supplied with all the means which knowledge can impart; or that common sense does not become, in fact, only truly powerful when in possession of the materials upon which judgment is to be exercised.

The study of the laws by which the Almighty governs the Universe is therefore our bounden duty. Of these laws, our great academies and seats of education have, rather arbitrarily, selected only two spheres or groups (as I may call them), as essential parts of our national education: the laws which regulate quantities and proportions, which form the subject of mathematics; and the laws regulating the expression of our thoughts, through the medium of language, that is to say, grammar, which finds its purest expression in the classical languages. These laws are most important branches of knowledge, their study trains and elevates the mind, but they are not the only ones; there are others which we cannot disregard, which we cannot do without.

There are, for instance, the laws governing the human mind and its relation to the Divine Spirit (the subject of logic and metaphysics); there are those which govern our bodily nature, and its connexions with the soul (the subject of physiology and psychology); those which govern human society, and the relations between man and man (the subjects of politics, jurisprudence, and political economy); and many others.

ON THE CULTURE OF THE SENSES.

(*Extract from an Address on Integral Education by* DR. THOMAS HILL, *President of Harvard University, Mass.*)

BEGINNING, then, with this body, in which it has pleased our Creator to give us our earthly dwelling, it evidently needs a careful training to develop its full capacities and powers. The senses are capable of education, even smell, taste, and touch, much more hearing and sight. Our ordinary modes of education do not do justice to these powers; but, on the contrary, ordinary schooling, by confining children to books, and withdrawing their attention from visible objects, rather tends to render the senses less useful in conveying impressions to the mind.

It is frequently thought that cultivation renders the sense itself more acute. Thus the blind are popularly supposed to have a more delicate touch, and a sharper sense of hearing, than those who see. But in a long course of experiments, which I once had the opportunity of making, upon a friend blind from birth, I found that neither his touch nor his hearing was so acute as mine; I could hear faint sounds which he could not hear, and he never heard those which I could not; I could feel roughnesses on a smooth surface so slight that he could not detect them. Yet he could read fluently the raised printing for the blind, by passing his fingers over it, while I could not, in that way, decipher one word. He could, from the echo of his footsteps, detect the position of the smallest sapling planted by the roadside, while I could not, with my eyes shut, tell from such echoes, the position of the largest tree. His hearing and touch were educated,—his judgment was practised, and he decided instantly upon the meaning of sounds which I doubtless heard, but could not interpret.

Now this case of the blind is quoted merely to show the possibility of educating the senses, not to show the kind or degree of education for those who have sight. But that some systematic training of the eye and the ear is desirable, as well as possible, is evident from many considerations. If we wish a child to enjoy life, we must not allow it to go through the world with these great avenues for all joyous influences to enter, closed. There is a little dialogue in Mrs. Barbauld's "Evenings at Home," called "Eyes and no Eyes," which ought to be made familiar, not only to every child, but more especially to every teacher of children. Two boys take a walk. One sees nothing, and returns complaining of the dulness and tediousness of the way. The other, taking precisely the same road, brings home a variety of strange and beautiful plants, sees curious birds, observes their odd ways, converses with workmen about different branches of human industry, and returns full of joyous enthusiasm. The tale illustrates the daily experience of life. One man finds it all a dull, weary round of toil and sorrow, sees nothing and hears nothing that can cheer and enliven him; another, having precisely the same fortunes, will see in each day's experience, lessons of wisdom and pictures of beauty, and will find, in all sounds, music to lift his heart into hymns of thanksgiving.

As a source of happiness, therefore, I would have a child cultivate quickness and truthfulness of observation, to see everything, and to see accurately,—to hear everything, and to hear exactly. But this habit of accurate observation is not only a source of happiness, it is a means of usefulness. The errors in the world come less from illogical reasoning than from inaccurate observation and careless hearing. A clear and intelligent witness, who can state precisely what he saw, and who saw everything that there was to see, who can repeat exactly what he heard, and who heard everything that was said, is rarer than a sound lawyer or judge. Most men see as much with their preoccupied imagination as with their eyes, and do not know how to separate their own fancies, or their erroneous interpretation of a fact, from the observed fact itself. Physicians can rarely obtain from the patient a statement of his symptoms, unmingled with theories as to their cause; lawyers cannot get a statement of what a man did, uncoloured by the imputation of motives for his action; scientific men are well aware that popular testimony to any minute phenomenon is wholly untrustworthy. In short, we should benefit science, art, jurisprudence, therapeutics, literature, and the whole intellectual and moral state of the community, if we could raise up a generation of men who would make it a matter of conscience to use their five senses with fidelity, and give report of their testimony with accuracy.

I would not here fail to call your attention to the fact that, in the education of the senses, it is not simply power that is increased. It is indeed doubtful, as I have already said, whether actual power of sense can be materially increased; that is, whether the eye, the ear, and the fingers can be rendered more sensitive to impressions from the external world. The need is of skill rather than of power; of skill which arises from habit, and consists in part of habit; which, being the result or remembrance of previous efforts, is precisely analogous to knowledge.

When a philosopher asserts that there is more happiness in the pursuit of truth than in the possession of it, he either implies that there is truth to be pursued and to be obtained, and that its possession is a good in itself, or else he asserts a most pernicious falsehood. The pursuit of truth has been likened to the chase, in which the value to the participant consists not in the paltry fox which is made the sufferer, and which could have been easily slain as it was unkennelled, but the exhilaration of the ride in the fresh morning air, and in the emulation between the horses and the hounds. Thus also in the ingenious disputations and paradoxical arguments of the metaphysicians, by which they used to endeavour to prove that there is no motion, or that there is no rest, that a hare cannot overtake a tortoise, or in the more serious debates concerning psychological and theological disputes, it is not the truth which is of importance, but the invigoration of a man's powers of argument. But of what value is fox-hunting to a man who makes no use of his health and strength gained on the saddle,—and what estimate should we make of the man's own character, if he felt no enjoyment in anything else than the chase? Neither would there be the least value in increased power of argument, if there is no truth to be defended; nor should we have any more respect for the man whose sole delight is in argumentation, than we have for a man who only lives for fox-hunting.

If education is to develop the mental powers, then those powers must have a legitimate field of exercise. There must be truth that is worth knowing, and work that is worth doing, and that work cannot be done unless the student gain knowledge to guide his power. The acquisition of power without knowledge is not therefore desirable.

No man can be induced to study and to exercise his intellectual powers in a healthy and vigorous way, unless he devoutly believes that objective truth is attainable by man. A story is told of a benevolent Quaker who hired a man asking for work to move a pile of stones, which he did not care to have moved, and on the man asking for more work, the Friend hired him to move the stones back to their original position, which the poor fellow gladly did, and received his wages thankfully. Now it is evident, that, if this story be true, the man out of employment was not of Yankee birth, else he never would have been willing to move the stones back again. No true American, with the spirit of manhood in him, could be hired to do work that is absolutely useless when finished. A young man, whose intellectual powers are worth cultivating, cannot be willing to cultivate them by pursuing phantoms,—he may be willing to pursue trifles at times for relaxation, for this is evidently a part of the Divine plan of life, that we should have our recreations as well as our tasks,—but he cannot make it his business, for seven years or more, to study what he does not believe to be absolutely true, and worth learning. Nor can he so insult the majesty of Truth as to doubt that there is a scheme of truth laid before us by our beneficent Father for our study, and for the reward of our labour, which is attainable by man, and towards a knowledge of which it is the duty of every man to struggle with lifelong zeal.

But I have recently, on several occasions, expressed myself so fully on this scheme of Truth which has been laid before us, that I am inclined to pass it by with only one additional remark, and that is, that it is, to my mind, probable that intellectual power is not capable of so much increase by culture as is usually supposed ; but, as we erroneously think the blind man's acuteness of hearing has been increased, simply because his skill in interpreting the meaning of sounds has been improved by practice, so we attribute to an increase of intellectual power, in the educated man, the results which arise chiefly, if not altogether, from the increased skill with which he uses his powers. Practically the increased skill is equivalent to strength, even in physical exertions, according to the Scripture, "If the iron be blunt, and he do not whet the edge, then must he put to more strength : but wisdom is profitable to direct." But no amount of skill acquired by training can compensate, in full, for any great deficiency of original power. We must beware also of comparing the development of intellectual power by study to the development of muscular power by exercise. The blacksmith's arm and the student's brain are made of different materials, and the law of muscular growth cannot be extended to the nervous system without a breach of continuity that vitiates all inference and comparison. Both doubtless gain skill from habit, and this likeness may come from the fact that the arm is stimulated by nerves, and the nerves are one with the brain,—it may be only the nervous system which is capable of acquiring habits. But the part of the arm that grows by exercise is the muscle, and there is no muscle in the brain. The stories which phrenologists give us of the growth of particular organs by exercise are to be received and sifted with extreme caution.

I make these remarks because I fear, that, in asserting, as I do, that education increases our intellectual *power*, I may be misunderstood to say that it increases our intellectual *powers*. I doubt whether any training can materially augment the actual strength of a man's imagination or reason, or any other mental faculty ; but I do not doubt in the least, on the contrary I earnestly maintain, that education may give a man such skill in the use of his faculties, that, for all practical purposes, they shall be tenfold their original value.

CLASSICAL AND MODERN CULTURE.

(*By* PROF. GOLDWIN SMITH. *From the "Lectures on History."*)

THE nobility and gentry, as a class, seem to have been certainly more highly educated, in the period of the late Tudors and the earlier Stuarts, than in any other period of our history. Then education was classical, but classical learning was then, not a gymnastic exercise of the mind in philology, but a deep draught from what was the great and almost the only spring of philosophy, science, history, and poetry, at that time. It is not to philological exercises that our earliest Latin grammar exhorts the student ; nor is it a mere sharpening of the faculties that it promises as his reward. It calls to the study of the language, wherein is contained a great treasure of wisdom and knowledge, and the student's labour done, wisdom and knowledge were to be his meed. It was to open that treasure, not for the sake of philological niceties or beauties, not to shine as the inventor of a canon, or the emendator of a corrupt passage, that the early scholars undertook the ardent, life-long, and truly romantic toils, which their massy volumes bespeak to our days,—our days, which are not degenerate from theirs in labour, but in which the most ardent intellectual labour is directed to a new prize. Besides, Latin was still the language of literary, ecclesiastic, diplomatic, legal, academic Europe ; familiarity with it was the first and most indispensable accomplishment, not only of the gentlemen, but of the high-born ladies of the time. We must take all this into account when we set the claims of classical against those of modern culture, and balance the relative amount of motive power we have to rely on for securing industry in either case. In choosing the subjects of a boy's studies, you may use your own discretion ; in choosing the subjects of a man's studies, if you desire any worthy and fruitful effort, you must choose such as the world values, and such as may receive the allegiance of a manly mind. It has been said that six months of the language of Schiller and Goethe will now open to the student more high enjoyment than six years' study of the languages of Greece and Rome. It is certain, that six months' study of French will now open to the student more of Europe, than six years' study of that which was once the European tongue. There are changes in the circumstances and conditions of education, which cannot be left out of sight, in dealing with the generality of minds. Great discoveries have been made by accident; but it is an accidental discovery, and must be rated as such, if the studies, which were first pursued as the sole key to wisdom and knowledge, now that they have ceased not only to be the sole, but the best key to wisdom and knowledge, are still the best instruments of education.

HINTS ON EARLY PHYSIOLOGICAL STUDY.

(*By* PROFESSOR H. W. ACLAND, *of Oxford.*)

GENERAL physiological questions will, in a few years, become so universally understood, that much ordinary literature will be unintelligible to those wholly unacquainted with them. Advanced physiological problems are already discussed in reviews, in this and other countries. Sanitary inquiries, of all kinds, now come within the range of town-councils and officials in every class of society. The standard of medical knowledge, and medical practice, will be raised in proportion to the diffusion of physiological knowledge among the general public. I look, therefore, to the increase of a general knowledge of physiology and hygiene as one of the greatest benefits, which will conduce, through science, to the temporal interests of mankind. Every form of quackery and imposture in medicine will, in this way, and in this way only, be discouraged. It is in great part on this ground—on the ground of the future benefit of the people, through dissemination of true perceptions of the *groundwork* of practical medicine—that I have laboured, for many years to promote physiological knowledge in this University, among students of whatever rank and destined for whatever occupation. . . .

Probably no kind of literary composition will tend more to precision of thought and statement, than the early habit of describing correctly natural objects. Without precision of ideas, and accuracy of expression, true physiological science does not exist, and can neither be taught nor learnt. That this *is* so will appear more and more as time goes on—the ideas and the language of my own hitherto most loosely worded art will become every year more definite and significant. Its dogmas are becoming either precise or worthless.

Dr. Acland makes the following suggestions to teachers, as to the mode of teaching physiology :—

I. For the sake of precision in a subject which contains necessarily many doubtful points, introduce, where you can, precise definitions and numerical calculations, weights, dimensions, micrographic and others.

II. For the study of external characters, encourage the collection of Fauna and Flora of the neighbourhood, including, in the case of all the boys, microscopic species. For the study of organs and functions, show dissections where you can. A rabbit, a rat, a sparrow, pig, perch, snail, bee, a few infusoria will enable you, at any time of the year, to show some of the most important types of structure in the animal kingdom.

III. Encourage the boys to put up microscopic objects. The minute manipulations will give neatness and precise habits. Little apparatus is required, and no "mess" need be made.

THE STUDY OF CLASSICAL LANGUAGES.

(*From the "Essay on the Athenian Orators,"* *by* LORD MACAULAY.)

MODERN writers have been prevented by many causes from supplying the deficiencies of their classical predecessors. At the time of the revival of literature no man could, without great and painful labour, acquire an accurate and elegant knowledge of the ancient languages; and unfortunately those grammatical and philological studies, without which it were impossible to understand the great works of Athenian and Roman genius, *have a tendency to contract the views and deaden the sensibility* of those who follow them with extreme assiduity. A powerful mind which has been long employed in such studies may be compared to the gigantic spirit in the Arabian tale, who was persuaded to contract himself to small dimensions in order to enter within the enchanted vessel, and when his prison had been closed upon him fancied himself unable to escape from the narrow boundaries to the measure of which he had reduced his stature. When the *means* have long been the objects of application, they are naturally substituted for the *end.* It was said by Eugene of Savoy, that the greatest generals have commonly been those who have been at once raised to command, and introduced to the great operations of war without being employed in the petty calculations and manœuvres which employ the time of an inferior officer. In literature the principle is equally sound. The great tactics of criticism will, in general, be best understood by those who have not had much practice in drilling syllables and particles. I remember to have observed among the French authors a ludicrous instance of this. A scholar, doubtless of great learning, recommends the study of some long Latin treatise, of which I now forget the name, on the religion, manners, government, and language of the early Greeks. "For there," says he, "you will learn everything of importance that is contained in the Iliad and Odyssey, without the trouble of reading two such tedious books." Alas! it had not occurred to the poor gentleman, that all the knowledge to which he attached so much value *was useful only as it illustrated the great poems which he despised, and would be as worthless for any other purpose as the mythology of Caffraria, or the vocabulary of Otaheite.*

EXTRACTS FROM THE EVIDENCE GIVEN BEFORE THE ENGLISH PUBLIC SCHOOLS' COMMISSION.

Evidence of Professor William B. Carpenter.

Q. I believe, Dr. Carpenter, you are Registrar of the London University?—*A.* I am. *Q.* How long have you been Registrar? —*A.* Six years. *Q.* I believe you are likewise a member of the Council of the Royal Society?—*A.* Yes. *Q.* Have you been able to form any opinion as to the use of the physical sciences, as a training of the mind, as compared with pure mathematics?—*A.* I think that their function is quite different. I think that each is a supplement to the other. I should be very sorry to see either left out. It appears to me, that the use of the physical sciences is to train a class of mental faculties, which are ignored, so to speak, by a purely classical or a purely mathematical training, or by both combined. The observation of external phenomena, and the exercise of the reasoning faculties upon such phenomena, are matters altogether left out of the ordinary public-school education. I am speaking of schools in which classics and mathematics are the sole means of mental discipline. Mathematical training is limited to one very special kind of mental action.

Q. In the schools?—*A.* I mean that mathematical training exercises the mind most strenuously in a very narrow groove, so to speak. It starts with axioms which have nothing to do with external phenomena, but which the mind finds in itself; and the whole science of mathematics may be evolved out of the original axioms which the mind finds in itself. I do not go into the question, whether they are intuitive, or whether they are generalizations of phenomena, found at a very early age; in either case, the mind finds it in itself. Now, it is the essence of scientific training, that the mind finds the objects of its study in the external world. As Bacon says, *Homo minister et interpres naturæ;* so it appears to me, that a training which leaves out of view the relation of man to external nature is a very defective one, and that the faculties which bring his intelligence into relation with the phenomena of the external world are subjects for education and discipline equally important with the faculties by which he exercises his reason purely upon abstractions.

Q. Then you consider that the mind, if it only had the training that could be given by close study of classics and of pure mathematics, has not had so great an advantage in training, as if the study of physical science had been added?—*A.* I am quite of that opinion; and I may add, that, having given considerable attention to the reputed phenomena of mesmerism, electro-biology, spiritualism, &c., I have had occasion to observe, that the *want of scientific habits of mind* is the source of a vast amount of prevalent misconception as to what constitutes adequate proof of the marvels reported by witnesses, neither untruthful nor unintelligent as to ordinary matters. I could name striking instances of such misconception in men of high literary cultivation, or high mathematical attainments; whilst I have met with no one, who had undergone the discipline of an adequate course of scientific study, who has not at once recognised the fallacies in such testimony when they have been pointed out to him.

Q. I observe, Dr. Carpenter, that your matriculation examinations do not take place till the applicant is past sixteen?—*A.* Yes. *Q.* Being of that age, you see great benefit in making natural philosophy and chemistry part of that examination, in addition to a certain examination in classics; and you consider that not merely as fitting a boy for success in the active business of life, but also as a means of training the mind, and that much benefit results from such combination. I should like to ask you, whether you consider that similar recommendations exist to the introduction of physical sciences at an early age? You applied your observations to your own candidates for matriculation?—*A.* I think that there is great advantage in commencing very early. I have commenced with my own children at a very early period in training their observing faculties, simply to recognise and to understand, and to describe correctly what they see,—showing them simple experiments, and desiring them to write down an account of them; and, from my own experience, I should say, that a boy of ten years old is quite capable of understanding a very large proportion of what is here set down under the head of natural philosophy.

Q. Is there not a danger of disturbing the power of sustained attention, if too many subjects of instruction are brought before boys at an early age?—*A.* I think that very much depends on the manner in which it is done. A good teacher need never forfeit the training of sustained attention by directing the attention to the facts of nature, because the attention is as healthfully exercised in what is going on before the child, as it is in the study of a book.

Q. Were you at a public school yourself?—*A.* I was not.

Q. You were at a large classical school, were you not?—*A.* I was brought up in a private school. *Q.* A large school?—*A.* About twenty was the average number.

Q. Should you, from your experience as a boy, confirm the opinion you have now expressed?—*A*. In the school in which I was brought up, all these subjects were taught systematically; and I certainly believe, that there was no deficiency there of power of attention, and that the training which was given in classics and mathematics—which was a very substantial one—was not at all impaired by the attention to these other subjects.

Q. At what age did attention to these subjects commence at your school?—*A*. I should think that about twelve years might be taken as the average. *Q*. Have you any practical acquaintance with the system of our public schools?—*A*. Not practically: I know the system generally. *Q*. You know the amount of time, perhaps, given to particular subjects, speaking generally?—*A*. Yes.

Q. Have you formed any opinion as to whether it would be desirable to diminish the proportion of time given, say to classics or mathematics, for the purpose of introducing physical science?—*A*. I have formed an opinion, that at the earlier age, say from ten to twelve or thirteen, the amount of study given to classics may be advantageously diminished. I have been led to conclude, from considerable opportunities of observation, that those who have commenced classics later than usual, and have been of average intelligence, have, by the age of sixteen, acquired as good a classical knowledge as those who have begun earlier,—whose minds have been fixed upon classical study for two or three years longer. I may state, that that is quite the opinion of many gentlemen of very large experience in education; and, I believe, I may quote Professor Pillans, of Edinburgh, as entertaining it. Dr. Hodgson, who had for a long time a large public school in the neighbourhood of Manchester, wrote a pamphlet some years ago in defence of that opinion. . . . I could quote several instances of young men who have shown very remarkable proficiency in classical study at the age of sixteen and seventeen, who began very late—at thirteen and fourteen.

Q. I understand you to attach very high importance to the philosophical study of language?—*A*. Yes. *Q*. And to its being commenced early?—Yes. *Q*. I believe you are author of works called "The Principles of Physiology, General and Comparative," "The Microscope and its Revelations," and of "An Introduction to the Study of Foraminifera"?—*A*. Yes.

Q. Do you consider that your taste for those studies was awakened at school?—*A*. My taste for physical and chemical science was certainly awakened at school. The training that I had in my school-course, and the advantages which I had of attending lectures at the Philosophical Institution at Bristol, at the time that I was going through that course, certainly tended to develop my taste for science generally. At that time, I knew next to nothing of natural history; and I suppose it was the circumstance of my having entered the medical profession, and being led to seek for scientific culture in the subjects on which medicine is founded, that caused me to direct my attention to natural history and physiology—physiology as based on natural history, in fact.

Q. You were likewise instructed in mathematics at school?—*A.* Yes. *Q.* Had you any occasion to observe at school that there was one class of minds which had a great aptitude for mathematics, another for the physical sciences, and another for the classics; so that there were three different types of mental intelligence?—*A.* Yes.

Q. Do you not consider, that it is an injury to a boy who may have a turn for the sciences of observation, or for other natural sciences, that he has no instruction in them whatever up to the time he is eighteen—up to the time of his going to the University?—*A.* I feel that very strongly. I am quite satisfied that there is such a class of minds. I see it in the candidates for our degrees in sciences. Though the degrees have only been instituted two or three years, yet I am quite certain, from what I have seen of those who have become candidates for them, that there is a very decided aptitude for physical sciences; and that those generally are persons who have a distaste for classics. I may say, with regard to myself, that I never had any taste for classics. I went through a very long course of classical training; and I feel very strongly indeed the value of the discipline which it gave me: but I never, as a boy, had any taste for classics (though now I can come back and read a classical author with pleasure), because I was weary of the drudgery of the ordinary routine of instruction (to which I had been subjected from an unusually early age), whilst at sixteen my mind was not sufficiently advanced in that direction to appreciate the higher beauties of a classical author. For instance, I could then read the "Prometheus;" but I did not understand its argument.

Q. It would be an injury to the mental capital of a nation, so to say, to give no instruction to boys in the physical sciences up to eighteen?—*A.* I should certainly consider that it leaves that branch of the mental faculties, which every individual has in a certain degree, uncultivated, and would leave without cultivation those powers which certain individuals have in a very remarkable degree.

Q. Is it not the case, that there are some boys at school who have only a slight aptitude for classical studies, who have an aptitude for the sciences of observation and the experimental sciences?—*A.* I am quite certain of that. I have five sons; and, in their education, I endeavour to train what I perceive to be the special aptitude of each. Thus, my eldest son has shown a decided aptitude for the physical and chemical sciences: he has taken his Bachelor of Arts degree in the University, and has now taken that of Bachelor of Science. He took the Bachelor of Arts degree, because, at that time, there was no degree in science; he went through the classical training required for it, but his whole bent is for the exact sciences. On the other hand, my second son has as strong a turn for literary culture as my eldest son has for scientific, and I have encouraged that just as I would the scientific culture—

taking care, however, in each case, that the other subjects were not neglected.

Q. I think you mentioned that you considered that the study of physical science at an early age was conducive to the cultivation of the intellectual faculties as well as of the senses?—*A.* I think so, decidedly, if it is rightly taught. I think very much depends upon the teacher.

Q. Do you think that the mind, ordinarily speaking, is as apt for the exercise of its faculties upon the subjects of natural science as upon grammar and mathematical subjects at the early period of life?—*A.* I should say, more so; that it is more easy to fix a child's attention upon something which it sees than upon an abstraction.

Q. Do you think that in that point of view, in fact, it is so far a subject better calculated to call out a healthy action of the reasoning powers than the more abstract subjects of grammar and mathematics?—*A.* I think it is at the early period. I think that a lad of from ten to twelve years of age is better fitted to be led to observe and reason upon what he observes in objective phenomena than he is to reason upon abstractions. I think that, from say twelve years of age, the powers may be healthfully exercised upon abstractions; but, as far as I can judge, a child in learning a language learns by rote purely, or almost purely, up to say twelve years of age; but after that he begins, if he is well taught, to understand the *rationale* (so to speak) of the rules; but it is a mere matter of memory with him up to that time.

Q. In fact, you doubt whether, in the cultivation of language the reasoning powers are much exercised at all at that time?—*A.* Yes.

Q. Have you been sufficiently in company with youths emerging from childhood to say whether there is, in your opinion, at all a natural curiosity which arises at that time for the observation and comprehension of the phenomena of nature?—*A.* I should say there is. I have seen a great deal of youths of different ages in the course of my life. I have been always interested in education, and have seen and known a great deal of what takes place in education among the humbler classes; and amongst them there is most decidedly a readiness of observation, and a readiness of power of apprehension and of reasoning upon phenomena of nature, which shows that that must be universal.

Q. Have you observed, that, besides that power, there is a curiosity with regard to the phenomena, and an interest in that sense with regard to the phenomena of the outward world?—*A.* I think there is, if it is not repressed. My opinion is, that the tendency of public-school education is to repress all that curiosity,—to withdraw the attention so completely from those subjects that it has no development.

Q. With regard to the study of language, I think you said, that you had had some opportunity of observing that youths who began later could make so much progress, owing to the different state of their faculties then, as that they could recover the amount that had been lost to the study of language by deferring it?—*A.* Yes: providing always that their mental habits have been properly trained; that the power of sustained attention, for instance, has been exercised in other ways. . . .

Q. With regard to their bearing on literary studies, do you think that the mixture of the physical sciences with the literary studies would be a mixture which would be conducive of benefit to both, or otherwise?—*A.* I think decidedly conducive of benefit, because I cannot think that any mental training can be really adequate which is one-sided; and, again, all experience shows that a change of study from one subject to another is advantageous in this way,—that it is a positive refreshment to the mind. I believe, that a lad who has been exercised a certain number of hours in the study of language, or in the study of mathematics, would enjoy going to the study of physical science. If it is properly handled, by a good teacher, he would enjoy that as much as he would enjoy going into some desultory course of reading for recreation.

Q. In fact, the exchange would produce very much less physical exhaustion than the continuance of the same study for the same number of hours?—*A.* Yes: I feel sure of that. I may mention, that there is at present going on a good deal of inquiry in regard to the number of hours which can be healthfully employed in study by the class of children who attend the National and British schools; and it is a subject in which I have taken a great deal of interest. I have happened to come in contact with a good many individuals who are working out experiments in different ways; and there is a very general conviction amongst the better and more intelligent class of masters in those schools, that four hours a day is as much as can be healthfully employed in purely intellectual acquirements by children of that class. Now, I believe that the allowance which is healthful for children of that class may be, perhaps, double for those of an educated class.

Q. At what age?—*A.* Say from eight to twelve; but the prevalence of this conviction shows, that the masters, practically, do not find that the children learn more who are at school for six or seven hours than those who are at school only from three and a half to four hours. *Q.* Do you think that you would find a different, that is, a larger measure of hours suitable to health, if there was this difference in studies at different times of the day?—*A.* Yes: I feel sure of it. *Q.* I suppose you say that as a physiologist? . . . *A.* Yes; I am speaking as a physiologist decidedly. I am quite satisfied of it as a fact in our mental constitution. . . .

Q. You said just now, that you thought there were instances of boys taking up the study of classics late, and, if they were properly trained in other ways, making up for the lost time by the superiority of their power of application and of learning. Do you think that that might be the case also in the study of physical science; that a boy taking to study physical science late might make up for lost time by beginning at an age at which his powers were more developed?—*A.* I have no doubt that he might make up for lost time: but I think that the natural period for commencing the study of physical science is at an earlier age, because I think any right system of education will take up the faculties in the order of their development; and it is quite certain, that the observing faculties are developed before the reasoning powers. An infant, during the first year of its life, is educating its observing faculties in a way we really scarcely give it credit for; and the training of the observing faculties, by attention to the phenomena of nature, both in physical and in natural science, seems to me to be the natural application of time at the age of say from eight to twelve.

Q. You supported your argument by the case of a boy who had studied French as an introduction to the study of Latin and Greek, and had not suffered in his classical studies by deferring them: would you not think, that a boy would suffer in the study of languages by wholly giving his early years to the study of physical science, and not taking up language at all till he got to the age, say of twelve?—*A.* Yes, I think he would. I think that neglecting the study of language altogether would be a very undesirable thing; but what I mean is this: I should prefer to see the faculties which are concerned in the cultivation of physical science trained at the earlier period, because I believe that is the natural period in which the observing faculties and the elementary reasoning processes may be best cultivated, and the period at which the mind is not prepared for the more advanced culture of language.

Q. But is it not the period at which it is also prepared for the commencement of the culture of language?—*A.* Certainly; but, then, I think all that the culture of language may give at that period may be given in a smaller number of hours than are usually devoted to it.

Q. A question was asked as to the possibility of a boy, well cultivated in classics, making up afterwards for deficiency in the natural sciences. Would there not be a distinction between the sciences of observation and the sciences of experiment? Is it likely that a grown-up person, or a boy beyond a certain age, would make up for the neglect of the faculty of observation?—*A.* I think not so well. If I am allowed to do so, I may mention my own experience in the matter. My greatest difficulty in the pursuit of systematic zoology and botany has arisen, I am quite satisfied, from the circumstance, that I was not early trained in those sciences. I can recognise a flower or an animal when I see them, and I can remember their names. I have no difficulty as to verbal memory; but I have a difficulty in connecting the two things, the flower or the animal and the name; and I believe, that, if I had had an early training in the habit of systematic nomenclature, I should not have experienced that difficulty in later life.

Q. Is it not, to a certain extent, the case with regard to the faculty of observation, as with regard to aptness for rapid calculation in arithmetic, that the habit should be acquired early?—*A.* Yes: I am very strongly of that opinion; and I know that it is very easily acquired under proper training. The late Professor Henslow studied the method of teaching natural science, I believe, as carefully as any one; and he was wonderfully successful in training that order of faculties.

Q. Is it the result of your experience, that, by the exclusion of the physical sciences and of the methods of investigation employed in their study, the mind does not receive as good a training as it might do?—*A.* I have been acquainted with several gentlemen who have passed with distinction through a course of public school and University training, and who have confessed to me with regret their inaptitude to understand any scientific subject whatever,—their want, not only of the knowledge, but of the mental aptitude.

Q. That is to say, that you consider that the physical sciences and methods of investigation call forth different faculties of the mind from those which are developed by the studies of mathematics and classics?—*A.* Yes: I think so very decidedly.

Q. And that, therefore, by neglecting the physical sciences, those faculties lie dormant if they existed?—*A.* Yes.

EVIDENCE OF SIR CHARLES LYELL.

Q. As we know your attention has long been turned to this subject, I would beg to ask you, as the result of your observation and experience, what you consider to be the position of physical science and natural history in this country, as far as regards our educational system?—*A.* I think it is hardly too strong a term to say, that they have been ignored. There has been a move of late in the Universities to restore them somewhat to that place which they formerly held, when the sciences were much less advanced, but when, in proportion to what was then known, they held a very fair position; and within the last two hundred years I consider them to have been deprived of the proper position which they once held. The public schools being modelled in a great measure on the system of the Universities, they have, in like manner, entirely neglected them, even in those schools where they are educated sometimes up to the age of seventeen or eighteen. I think, therefore, that in that period of the progress of the nation, when these branches have been acquiring more and more importance, both theoretically and practically, that has been precisely the time when they have been more and more excluded from the teaching of the higher classes of this country.

Q. To what would you attribute the neglect of these studies that has been shown at the schools in particular?—*A.* I think that the schools being preparatory, in a great measure, to the Universities, they frame their system in regard to those subjects which are to obtain the chief rewards, prizes, and honours at the University. Although a large proportion of the boys at our larger schools do not go to the University (I do not know what proportion, but I know that it is very large), nevertheless, the system is planned as if they were all going there; and whatever be the plan adopted at the Universities, and, particularly, whatever may be the matriculation, the entrance examination to the University, that will in no small degree govern what is taught in public schools, if any branch of knowledge is entirely omitted.

Q. You consider, then, that as there is no demand for physical sciences and natural history at the Universities, there is no attempt to supply them at the schools?—*A.* Exactly: that is a great reason. However, it must not be forgotten, that those schoolmasters are brought up in the Universities without a knowledge of the sciences and natural history; and, having no such knowledge, it is very natural that a great number of them should entertain some prejudice, or think very slightingly of them.

Q. You would consider, then, that although the great majority of boys educated at our public schools do not go to the Universities, yet the requirements of those who do go to the Universities do, in fact, regulate the system of the school?—*A.* Quite so.

Q. Therefore, you would say, that the majority do not have the education that would be best for them; and, in fact, are sacrificed to the minority who are proceeding to the University?—*A.* Yes....

Q. At our public schools, it is generally considered that the study of the classics is the best possible training for the mind; but would you consider that the mind does not get the best possible training, if the study of the physical sciences is omitted? and would you consider that the study of physical science calls into operation and develops faculties of the mind that are not called into activity by classics or mathematics?—*A.* Yes: I do most decidedly. I think the reasoning powers and the judgment are more cultivated by these subjects than by the exclusive study of the classics.

Q. Of classics and mathematics?—*A.* Yes.

Q. Pure mathematics?—*A.* Yes. I think mathematics applied often does that which pure mathematics will not do....

Q. It is sometimes said, with great force, that the faculties of observation ripen, so to say, at an earlier period than the reasoning powers?—*A.* Yes.

Q. Do you think that that would or would not point to the conclusion, that such sciences as botany and chemistry, perhaps, and so on, should be communicated at an earlier period?—*A.* Yes. I have no children of my own, but I have nephews in whom I take much interest; and I certainly have observed that the powers of observation, and the interest of observing with accuracy, are very early developed,—indeed, at nine or ten; and they learn a vast deal of other things in consequence, if they be taught any of these branches.... *Q.* You would prefer their beginning at an early period?—*A.* Yes, indeed I should.... *Q.* Do you think that purely literary pursuits, and the literature of the country generally, would receive benefit by a degree of scientific education and instruction being given in the public schools and the Universities in conjunction with a literary education?—*A*. Indeed, I think it would. I think the literature would gain. I think the literary writings of a man like Hallam, for instance, who had taught himself science and natural history, are of a higher stamp than they would have been if he had not had that knowledge. . . .

Q. In your geological investigations in Germany, have you become acquainted with many literary men there?—*A*. Yes.

Q. Among the class of literary men, is there greater or less knowledge of the physical sciences than in England?—*A*. There is decidedly more general knowledge, even where there is no special knowledge. They understand a great deal more what we are about than the literary men and classical scholars of this country do. . . .

Q. With regard to the clergy, have you seen anything of the clergy in Germany? Would you say that they were better acquainted with such subjects?—*A*. Yes, indeed, I think they are. I think there is a great advantage in that respect in Germany. In fact, it was an observation of Baron Von Buch, when he came over here, "In regard to Church matters, or the connexion of science and religion, you are as much behind us in freedom, as you are ahead of us in your political institutions;" and I attribute that, in some measure, to there being a better general notion of science among the clergy. . . .

Q. Have you any means of knowing whether, in the middle classes, there is a greater knowledge on these subjects at present than in the upper classes?—*A*. It is a very remarkable fact, that, if a scientific book is published, it depends more for its sale on the middle classes of the manufacturing districts than on the rich country gentlemen and clergy of the agricultural parts of the country; and therefore, if there is distress, like the present in Lancashire, the publisher would say, "Do not bring out your book now."

Q. In a political point of view, is not that not only an unhealthy, but a dangerous state of things, in some repects, that the material world should be very much better known by the middle classes of society than by the upper classes?—*A*. Certainly; and I think it is particularly so in reference to the teaching in this country by the clergy; and a vast proportion of the University men are going into the Church. . . .

Q. But if the upper classes, in acquiring a greater amount of this knowledge of the physical world, were to lose any of their literary and intellectual superiority, might they not thereby endanger their pre-eminence as much in the one way as they would gain in the other?—*A*. In answer to that question, I think I could say, from my own experience, that, in consequence of narrowing the number of subjects taught, a large portion of those who have not a particular aptitude for literary pursuits, but who would have shown a strong taste for the sciences, are forced into one line; and, after they leave their College, they neglect branches they have been taught, and so cultivate neither the one nor the other. I have known men, quite late in life, who have forgotten all the Latin and Greek which they spent their early years in acquiring, hit upon geology or some other branch, and all at once their energies have been awakened, and you have been astonished to see how they came out. They would have taken that line long before, and done good work in it, had they been taught the elements of it at school.

Q. So that there was a mental waste in their youth?—*A.* Quite so.

EVIDENCE OF DR. M. FARADAY.

Q. Will you have the goodness to give us your opinion, as the result of your observation and experience, upon the state of knowledge of the physical sciences and natural history in this country, with reference to our educational system?—*A.* I can give you my impression, as far as that is permissible, independent of any comparison between that part of knowledge and other branches. I am not an educated man, according to the usual phraseology, and therefore can make no comparison between languages and natural knowledge, except as regards the utility of language in conveying thoughts; but that the natural knowledge which has been given to the world in such abundance during the last fifty years should remain, I may say, untouched, and that no sufficient attempt should be made to convey it to the young mind, growing up and obtaining its first views of these things, is to me a matter so strange that I find it difficult to understand it. Though I think I see the opposition breaking away, it is yet a very hard one to overcome. That it ought to be overcome, I have not the least doubt in the world. . . .

Q. You probably are aware that what our great schools profess and aim at most, is to give a good training to the mind; and it is there considered, perhaps, as you were saying just now, from habit and from prestige, that that is effectually done by the study of the classics and of pure mathematics, and that in that way they furnish the best training of the mind that can be given. Now, I would ask you, whether you think, supposing the training of the mind is the object in the public schools, that that system of training the mind is complete which excludes physical science? whether the study of physical science would call into activity faculties of the mind that are not so developed by studies confined to classics and mathematics?—*A.* The phrase, "training of the mind," has to me a very indefinite meaning. I would like a profound scholar to indicate to me what he means by "training of the mind;" in a literary sense, including mathematics. What is their effect on the mind? What is the kind of result that is called the "training of the mind"? Or what does the mind learn by that training? It learns things, I have no doubt. By the very act of study, it learns to be attentive, to be persevering, to be logical, according to the word "logic." But does it learn that training of the mind which enables a man to give a reason, in natural things, for an effect which happens from certain causes; or why, in any emergency or event, he does, or should do, this, that, or the other? It does not suggest the least thing in these matters. It is the highly educated man that we find coming to us, again and again, and asking the most simple questions in chemistry and mechanics; and when we speak of such things as the conservation of force, the permanency of matter, and the unchangeability of the laws of nature, they are far from comprehending them, though they have relation to us in every action of our lives. Many of these instructed persons are as far from having the power of judging of these things as if their minds had never been trained.

Q. You would not consider that the minds of such men as you allude to, who have been highly trained, and who have great literary proficiency, are in a state readily to receive such information as they are deficient in?—*A.* I find them greatly deficient; not in their own studies, or in their applications of them, but when taken out of that into natural sciences. Ask what is the reason of this or that,—they have a difficulty in giving the reason. If they are called upon to judge in a case of natural science, they find it difficult to give a judgment; they have not studied it.

Q. You do not find any particular aptitude in those minds for grasping a new subject?—*A.* I do not. Take those minds, and apply them to the special subjects which they have never touched upon or known of, and they have to go to the beginning, just as the juvenile does. They are no more ready. The young mind, as I find it, formed by habits, forced this way and that way, is very observant, and asks most acute questions. I do not find that mind, generally speaking, backward in understanding the statement I make to him in simple language; and if I tell him this or that,—if I tell him that the atmosphere is compounded of oxygen, nitrogen, and so on, and then shape it into a question,—he can generally answer me. I must confess to you, that I find the grown-up minds coming back to me with the same questions over and over again. They ask, What is water composed of? though I have told the same persons, a dozen years in succession, that it is composed of oxygen and hydrogen. Their minds are not prepared to receive or to embody these notions; and that is where you want education,—to teach them the A B C of these things.

Q. You think that exclusive attention to one set of studies during early life rather precludes the ready adoption of these ideas?—*A.* Yes. It does not blunt the mind—I do not think it does—but it so far gives the growing mind a certain habit, a certain desire and willingness to accept general ideas of a literary kind, and to say all the rest is nonsense, and belongs to the artisan, that it is not prepared to accept, and does not accept, the other and greater knowledge.

Q. So that the mind runs in a particular groove, from which it does not extract itself easily?—*A.* Yes: by that degree of habit, the mind, I do think, is really injured for the reception of other knowledge. . . . *Q.* Supposing the one main object of education to be to train the mind to ascertain the sequence of a particular conclusion from certain premises; to detect a fallacy; to correct undue generalization; or generally to prevent the growth of mistakes in reasoning,—should you consider physical science is as valuable for that object as classical instruction is?—*A.* I do not see clearly how classical studies do educate the mind for that kind of judgment; but, as regards the exercise of the judgment on the laws of matter, it is to me the most fertile source of the exercise of that judgment, and the true logic of facts, which I can conceive of, and which enables the man, when he has the facts in his hand, to apply them in every form and shape. . . . I think I see a most lamentable deficiency, even in the highly educated men, of that kind of logic. . . . I hope I shall offend nobody if I try to illustrate my feeling in that respect. Up to this very day, there come to me persons of good education, men and women, quite fit for all that you expect from education: they come to me, and they talk to me about things that belong to natural science; about mesmerism, table-turning, flying through the air; about the laws of gravity: they come to me to ask me questions; and they insist against me, who think I know a little of these laws, that I am wrong and they are right, in a manner which shows how little the ordinary course of education has taught such minds. Let them study natural things, and they will get a very different idea from that which they have obtained from that education. It happens up to this day. I do not wonder at those who have not been educated at all; but such as I refer to, say to me, "I have felt it, and done it, and seen it; and, though I have not flown through the air, I believe it." Persons who have been fully educated, according to the present system, come with the same propositions as the untaught and stronger ones, because they have a stronger conviction that they are right. They are ignorant of their ignorance at the end of all that education. It happens even with men who are excellent mathematicians. They and you will say, "But you are most likely wrong, and they right." It may be so; at all events, the education we speak of in natural things, will be something in addition to that which they gain by their study of the classics. Until they know what are the laws of nature, and until they are taught by education to see what are the natural facts, they cannot clear their minds of these, as I say, most absurd inconsistencies; and I say again, as I said once before, that the system of education that could leave the mental condition of the public body in the state in which this subject has found it, must have been greatly deficient in some very important principle.

Q. When you say that you have not been able to understand in what way classical instruction trains the mind, you are aware that many, perhaps most, of the defenders of classical education defend it on the ground, not that it teaches certain things, nor that the classics, as classics, have any peculiar value; but that, through the classics, both the laws of language and the structure of language are studied; and that it is the study of the laws of language which is held best to develop and strengthen the mental faculties?—*A*. That is narrowing the question this way, that, in place of saying you are taking the classics, you take the laws of language; and no doubt they give that education, as far as I can see. I am reasoning in the dark, because I have not had the opportunity, and have not the right, to speak of these things. I confess all that; but although it be a very important thing to know language perfectly, and to know its laws, or to carry it out, as the most profound scholar would do, by tracing all languages to an original one, or what not,—Max Müller or anybody else,—that is not all knowledge. I am not attacking the classics at all. I am only putting in a plea for that other knowledge which belongs to our absolute nature, and, in fact, which language only helps to describe.

Q. What is held, I believe, by the defenders of classical literature is, that the study of language strengthens the general powers of the mind in its application to any other subjects whatever which may come before it, and that in that way the mind is best strengthened as an instrument for acquiring any other kind of knowledge whatever?—*A*. I see the value of those studies which do lead to such a result; but I think that, at present, society at large is almost ignorant of the like and greater value of the kind of studies which I recommend. . . . I say, that these physical sciences, in my opinion, ought to be brought forward also; and I say it the more boldly, because the learned men who have been so educated in languages do *not* show any aptness to judge of physical science. In matters of natural knowledge, and all the uses and applications derived from it, I should turn to a man, untaught in other respects, who I knew was acquainted with these subjects, rather than to a classical scholar, as expecting to find within his range that mode of mind, or that management of the mind, which would enable him to speak with understanding. Any word that I have said that has led you to think that I am opposed to classics, I must withdraw. I have no such feeling.

EVIDENCE OF PROFESSOR RICHARD OWEN.

Q. The result of your observation, coming in communication, as you must have done, with various classes,—the wealthy, the middle, and the poor,—I suppose is, that there exists a complete deficiency in knowledge of physical science and natural history?—*A*. The absence of a knowledge of the main end, methods, and application of natural history, has appeared to me to be greater in the higher and more refined classes of the community, than in the middle, or, perhaps, even, as regards details or species, than in the lower classes. If I were to select a particular group, it would be the governing and legislative class; which, from the opportunities I have had of hearing remarks in conversation or debate, appears to be least aware of the extent of the many departments of natural-history science, of the import of its generalizations, and especially of its use in disciplining the mind, irrespective of its immediate object of making known the different kinds of animals, plants, or minerals.

Q. I suppose, when you attribute this state of ignorance to the higher classes, you allude to the absence of instruction, both at the public schools and the Universities, at which these classes, in particular, are educated?—*A.* More especially at the public schools. . . .

Q. I suppose you would consider that is not the best training which omits the physical sciences?—*A.* Not the completest. Grammar and classics, arithmetic and geometry, may be the most important disciplinary studies. We know the faculties of the mind they are chiefly calculated to educe; but they fail in bringing out those which natural-history science more especially tends to improve. I allude now to the faculty of accurate observation, of the classification of facts, of the co-ordination of classes or groups; the management of topics, for example, in their various orders of importance in the mind, giving to a writer or public speaker improved powers of classifying all kinds of subjects. Natural history is essentially a classifying science. Order and method are the faculties which the elements and principles of the science are best adapted to improve and educe. . . . In every community of two hundred or more youths, there must be some few, the constitution of whose minds is specially adapted to the study of natural history, to the work of observation and classification, who consequently are impelled by innate aptitude to that kind of study, but who are not at present afforded the slightest opportunity of working their minds in that way; so that it may happen that the faculty or gift for natural history, if it be not actually destroyed by exclusive exercise in uncongenial studies, is never educed. What is the result? In all our great natural-history movements, we have looked in vain, since the death of Sir Joseph Banks, for any man having a sufficient standing in the country to fraternize with us, to understand us, to help us in debate or council, in questions most vital to the interests of natural history. It has often occurred to me to ask how such should be the case; and my answer has been, that, in the education of noblemen and gentlemen, the great landed proprietors of England, of those destined to take part in the legislation and government of the country, there has been a complete absence of a systematic imparting of the elements of natural history; no demonstrations of the nature and properties of plants and animals; no indication of the aims and importance of natural history; no training of the faculties, for which it affords the healthiest exercise: consequently they have not been educed. I cannot doubt that this must have been the effect of the present restricted system. There must have been by nature many Sir Joseph Banks's since he died: but they have been born, have grown up, and passed away without working out their destined purpose; their peculiar talent has never been educed; their attention has never been turned to those studies: but they have been wholly devoted to classics. It must be remembered, that minds of this class are usually very averse to classical studies, and mere exercises of memory and composition: they never take to them; they get through them as well or as ill as they can, doing little or nothing to the purpose; and they fail to achieve that for which they are naturally fitted, from the want of having their special faculties educed. I consider it a loss to the nation, that, in our great educational establishments for youth, there should be no arrangements for giving them the chance of knowing something of the laws of the living world, and how they are to be studied. . . .

Q. Do you think there would be much difficulty in getting teachers, say for the seven or eight principal schools of the country, to undertake that work?—*A.* I am afraid at the present time that there would be, arising from the general defects of our teaching arrangements, especially the want of systematic teaching of the elements of natural history in schools. We are all of us, as it were, naturalists by accident. It is the perception of that difficulty which has led me, on every occasion when I have been called upon to give evidence on the subject, to urge the giving of elementary instruction in natural history as one of the duties that should be attached to the keeper of each secondary or subordinate department in great national museums of natural history. . . .

Q. You say that many of those sciences are in a progressive state?—*A.* Every science we are acquainted with is one of progress.

Q. But the principles of some of the sciences are determined; such as those of mathematics, for instance?—*A.* The fundamental principles of classification in natural history are as certain.

Q. Take this case: fifty years ago, supposing zoology to have been taught in schools, would not the Linnæan system have been adopted?—*A.* You might teach the main part of that system, in reference to botany, as a disciplinary science at the present day.

Q. I was thinking of the study of zoology?—*A.* In zoology, although of course there has been a great increase in the knowledge of the structure of animals since the time of Linnæus, still the principles laid down in Linnæus's immortal work, "Philosophia Botanica," are really those that cannot be deviated from, whether the elements of zoology or botany be imparted.

Q. You do not think there is any objection to the educational use of the physical sciences in consequence of the fluctuating or speculative character of those sciences?—*A.* I deny the "fluctuating character:" it is not applicable to natural history. The zoological system of Ray is the basis of the system of Linnæus. It forms an essential part of the Linnæan system. There is neither fluctuation nor speculation. The principles of natural history are already as settled and fixed as can be needed for its use as a disciplinary science. Modification of details would never affect its value in relation to elementary teaching.

Q. The zoological classifications of the ancients were somewhat puerile, were they not, even the classification of Aristotle?—*A.* No: it is surprising how much of Aristotle's system is really retained; how much is founded on truth, and is the basis of the modern classification.

Q. Plato was the first writer on classification, I think: Aristotle is very severe on him, if I remember rightly?—*A.* I am not sure. But the improvement that Cuvier made on the zoological system of Linnæus was mainly a revival of the Aristotelian principles, because Cuvier was the first modern systematist who had anything like the same amount of knowledge of the structure of animals which that wonderful man, Aristotle, possessed.

Q. I suppose that, if we were to wait in order to teach the subject until we entirely escaped the possibility of there being some change in the form and substance of the truths taught, we should have to wait for ever, in all sciences: should we not?—*A.* We should certainly have to wait for the termination of our existence as a species.

Q. Not with respect to arithmetic, for instance?—*A.* In Transactions of Societies and Academies of the Natural Sciences, we see annual progress and discoveries in mathematics; the sciences, in regard to the works of nature or of the Author of nature, are more incomplete; and the more we know of them, the more we get impressed with the small amount of knowledge we possess. But that amount, compared with ignorance, is so great, and the principles that we are enabled to educe from the little that we do know are so sure, that, taking them at the present very imperfect standard, whether in respect to zoology, or botany, or geology, they are as good for the purposes of elementary instruction and discipline as they will perhaps be ten thousand years hence.

Q. There is another point upon which I should like to have your opinion, which is a practical matter entirely, with reference to natural history and philosophy. Has it occurred to you to observe, whether persons in the upper classes of society, and other members of society, are well or ill acquainted with the physiological laws of the human structure?—*A.* No: it is a knowledge very rarely possessed, as far as my experience goes, very rarely indeed; and I believe that it is chiefly upon that general ignorance that the success of spurious systems of medicine have their dependence. It is upon the general ignorance of the population that the empiric bases his pretensions, and has an influence for a certain time, till one subsides, and is succeeded by another. . . . In reference to the conclusion to which I have come in regard to the importance of natural history as an element of school instruction, and the time to be given to it in beginning the experiment, I would ask leave to read a passage from the address of a gentleman who fills a very eminent position,—that of Local Director of the Geological Survey of

Ireland, and Lecturer on Geology to the Museum of Irish Industry, Mr. J. B. Jukes; who, in opening the business of the Geological Section of the British Association, over which he presided at Cambridge, made these remarks: "The natural sciences are now considered as worthy of study by those who have a taste for them, both in themselves and as a means of mental training and discipline. In my time, however, no other branches of learning were recognised than classics and mathematics; and I have, with some shame, to confess, that I displayed but a truant disposition with respect to them, and too often hurried from the tutor's lecture-room to the river or field to enable me to add much to the scanty store of knowledge I had brought up with me. Had it not been then for the teaching of Professor Sedgwick in geology, my time would have been altogether wasted." So that it was just the accident, so to speak, of one short course on a branch of natural history, grafted through an old bequest upon the main studies of his University, that led Professor Jukes to his appreciation of the method of study and value of the science which owes so much to his labours. I could also, with your permission, adduce a higher authority on the main point, and that is Baron Cuvier's; who, in the preface to the first edition of his elementary book on Natural History, expresses himself as follows: "The habit, necessarily acquired in the study of natural history, of mentally classifying a great number of ideas, is one of the advantages of this science which is seldom spoken of, and which, when it shall have been generally introduced into the system of common education, will perhaps become the principal one: it exercises the student in that part of logic which is termed 'method,' as the study of geometry does in that which is called 'syllogism;' because natural history is the science which requires the most precise methods, as geometry is that which demands the most rigorous reasoning. Now, this art of method, when once well acquired, may be applied with infinite advantage to studies the most foreign to natural history. Every discussion which supposes a classification of facts, every research which requires a distribution of matters, is performed after the same manner; and he who has cultivated this science merely for amusement, is surprised at the facilities it affords for disentangling all kinds of affairs. It is not less useful in solitude; sufficiently extensive to satisfy the most powerful mind; sufficiently various and interesting to calm the most agitated soul: it consoles the unhappy, and tends to allay enmity and hatred. Once elevated to the contemplation of the harmony of nature, irresistibly regulated by Providence, how weak and trivial appear those causes which it has been pleased to leave dependent upon the will of man! How astonishing to behold so many fine minds consuming themselves, so uselessly for their own happiness and that of others, in the pursuit of vain combinations, the very traces of which a few years suffice to obliterate! I avow it proudly, these ideas have always been present. my mind, the companions of my labours; and if I have endeavoured, by every means in my power, to advance this peaceful study, it is because, in my opinion, it is more capable than any other of supplying that want of occupation which has so largely contributed to the troubles of our age."

EVIDENCE OF DR. JOSEPH HOOKER.

Q. I believe you are a Fellow of the Royal Society, Assistant-Director of the Botanical Gardens at Kew, and the author of "Travels in the Himalaya"?—*A.* Yes.

Q. From your experience, and the means of observation you have had, have you formed any opinion as to the state of knowledge in natural and physical science, with respect to the education of the upper and middle classes, as it exists at present?—*A.* At Kew, we are thrown into contact with persons belonging to the middle and upper classes in very large numbers; and I think the regret that they know nothing of botany is quite apparent in all their communications with us. Hardly a day passes but what we receive communications from some part of the world in which such regret is expressed.

Q. What is the nature of the communications into which you are brought with these classes at Kew?—*A.* Most prominently now with regard to vegetable fibres. Sometimes two or three letters a day come to us requiring information with regard to well-known fibres, which the slightest habit of observation, or the slightest knowledge, would assure the persons who send them that they cannot, in any way, be used for cotton.

Q. Then these have been comparatively recent communications?—*A.* No: they have gone on for the last twenty years of my father's experience, and the last ten years of my own; not so much formerly with regard to cotton fibre for the use of yarns as for making paper, and for many other purposes to which cotton is applied.

Q. In fact, you say, that the upper and middle classes in this country are in the habit of constantly consulting either your father or yourself at Kew?—*A.* Yes, both officially and unofficially. *Q.* And both the subjects upon which they wish to have knowledge, and their mode of inquiry, lead you to think that they are in a state of great ignorance?—*A.* Yes. *Q.* That that study in particular has been greatly neglected by those classes?—*A.* Very greatly. *Q.* And they have generally expressed their regret that it has been so neglected?—*A.* Universally, I may say. *Q.* You have probably considered that the neglect of this important study is a matter of national regret?—*A.* I have always thought so.

Q. Have you ever turned your attention at all to the possibility of teaching botany to boys in classes at school?—*A.* I have thought that it might be done very easily; that this deficiency might be easily remedied. *Q.* What are your ideas on the subject?—*A.* My own ideas are chiefly drawn from the experience of my father-in-law, the late Professor Henslow, Professor of Botany at Cambridge. He introduced botany into one of the lowest possible class of schools,—that of village labourers' children in a remote part of Suffolk.

Q. Perhaps you will have the goodness to tell us the system he pursued?—*A.* It was an entirely voluntary system. He offered to enrol the school children in a class to be taught botany once a week. The number of children in the class was limited, I think, to forty-two. As his parish contained only 1,000 inhabitants, there never were, I suppose, the full forty-two children in the class; their ages varied from about eight years old to about fourteen or fifteen. The class mostly consisted of girls. . . . He required, that, before they were enrolled in the class, they should be able to spell a few elementary botanical terms, including some of the most difficult to spell, and those that were the most essential to begin with. Those who brought proof that they could do this were put into the third class; then they were taught once a week, by himself generally, for an hour or an hour and a half, sometimes for two hours (for they were exceedingly fond of it).

Q. Did he use to take them out in the country, or was it simply lessons in the school?—*A.* He left them to collect for themselves; but he visited his parish daily, when the children used to come up to him, and bring the plants they had collected; so that the lessons went on all the week round. There was only one day in the week on which definite instruction was given to the class; but on Sunday afternoon he used to allow the senior class, and those who got marks at the examinations, to attend at his house. . . .

Q. Did he find any difficulty in teaching this subject in class?—*A.* None whatever; less than he would have had in dealing with almost any other subject.

Q. Do you know in what way he taught it? did he illustrate it?—*A.* Invariably: he made it practical. He made it an objective study. The children were taught to know the plants, and to pull them to pieces; to give their proper names to the parts; to indicate the relations of the parts to one another; and to find out the relation of one plant to another by the knowledge thus obtained.

Q. They were children, you say, generally from eight to twelve?—*A.* Yes, and up to fourteen. *Q.* And they learnt it readily?—*A.* Readily and voluntarily, entirely. *Q.* And were interested in it?—*A.* Extremely interested in it. They were exceedingly fond of it.

Q. Do you happen to know whether Professor Henslow thought that the study of botany developed the faculties of the mind,—that it taught these children to think? and do you know whether he perceived any improvement in their mental faculties from that?—*A.* Yes: he used to think it was the most important agent that could be employed for cultivating their faculties of observation, and for strengthening their reasoning powers.

Q. He really thought that he had arrived at a practical result?—*A.* Undoubtedly; and so did every one who visited the school or the parish. *Q.* They were children of quite the lower class?—*A.* The labouring agricultural class. *Q.* And in other branches receiving the most elementary instruction?—*A.* Yes.

Q. And Professor Henslow thought that their minds were more developed; that they were become more reasoning beings, from having this study superadded to the others?—*A.* Most decidedly. It was also the opinion of some of the inspectors of schools, who came to visit him, that such children were in general more intelligent than those of other parishes; and they attribute the difference to their observant and reasoning faculties being thus developed. . . .

Q. So that the intellectual success of this objective study was beyond question?—*A.* Beyond question. . . . In conducting the examinations of medical men for the army, which I have now conducted for several years, and those for the East-India Company's service, which I have conducted for, I think, seven years, the questions which I am in the habit of putting, and which are *not* answered by the majority of the candidates, are what would have been answered by the children in Professor Henslow's village school. I believe the chief reason to be, that these students' observing faculties, as children, had never been trained,—such faculties having lain dormant with those who naturally possessed them in a high degree; and having never been developed, by training, in those who possessed them in a low degree. In most medical schools, the whole sum and substance of botanical science is crammed into a few weeks of lectures, and the men leave the class without having acquired an accurate knowledge of the merest elements of the science. . . .

Q. At the High School in Glasgow, did you observe among the boys a difference of aptitude for the three branches of languages, mathematics, and the sciences of observation?—*A.* Very great.

Q. A boy who distinguishes himself in classics might have an inaptitude for mathematics and natural science, and *vice versâ*?—*A.* Yes. One of my own classmates was a dull boy in the High School, where mathematics were not then taught, except in the senior class, which I did not attend. He was the best mathematician of his year at the University afterwards.

Q. Do you not think that it is very undesirable that a boy at school, having faculties of a particular kind, should have them wholly neglected? Take the example of a boy who has really an aptitude for the natural sciences; do you not think it a very hard case that his faculties should be wholly neglected?—*A.* I think it is very hard. Nothing is more destructive to his whole education.

Q. Supposing that a boy happened not to have a turn for languages, his place in school would be very low down. Would it not have an injurious moral effect habitually for him to be regarded as stupid, because he had no talent for languages?—*A.* Yes.

Q. It would have a tendency to impair his self-respect?—*A.* Yes.

Q. The same boy, if he had an opportunity of cultivating his faculties in the natural sciences, and using his abilities there, would be likely to become a much more useful member of society?—*A.* Yes, much more....

Q. The majority of the young men who are intended for the medical profession, and who come from the various public schools of the country, scarcely ever bring with them any physical science, do they?—*A.* None whatever, or very rarely.

Q. As far as your observation goes, that is generally neglected in your profession?—*A.* Yes; and it is a want more felt by medical men than by any others. The amount of botany and chemistry required by the medical man might be as easily obtained at school as during the time he is undergoing his medical curriculum.

Q. I suppose you have found a sentiment of regret prevailing amongst them at the manner in which those valuable years of their lives had been employed?—*A.* Very generally.

Q. And they would have liked to have spent them differently?—*A.* Yes, to a great extent. I never knew them regret their classics and mathematics; quite the contrary: but they do regret very much that their faculties were not early trained to habits of observation. When they go round the hospitals, they have felt that they have not been taught to observe, and to reason upon what they observe, as they might have been.

Q. Do you think there is a general feeling amongst those men, that the study of physical science might have been added to the classics, without impairing that knowledge which they would be glad to have acquired?—*A.* That was the universal feeling.

THE END.

ESSAYS:

MORAL, POLITICAL, AND ESTHETIC.

In one Volume. Large 12mo. 386 pages.

CONTENTS:

I. The Philosophy of Style.
II. Over-Legislation.
III. Morals of Trade.
IV. Personal Beauty.
V. Representative Government.
VI. Prison-Ethics.
VII. Railway Morals and Railway Policy.
VIII. Gracefulness.
IX. State Tamperings with Money and Banks.
X. Reform; the Dangers and the Safeguards.

"These Essays form a new, and if we are not mistaken, a most popular installment of the intellectual benefactions of that earnest writer and profound philosopher, Herbert Spencer. There is a remarkable union of the speculative and practical in these papers. They are the fruit of studies alike economical and psychological; they touch the problems of the passing hour, and they grasp truths of universal application; they will be found as instructive to the general reader as interesting to political and social students."—*Boston Transcript.*

"These Essays exhibit on almost every page the powers of an independent humanitarian thinker. Mr. Spencer's ethics are rigid, his political views liberalistic, and his aim is the production of the highest earthly good."—*Methodist Quarterly Review.*

"It abounds in the results of the sharp observation, the wide reach of knowledge, and the capacity to write clearly, forcibly, and pointedly, for which this writer is preeminent. The subjects are all such as concern us most intimately, and they are treated with admirable tact and knowledge. The first essay on the Philosophy of Style is worth the cost of the volume; it would be a deed of charity to print it by itself, and send it to the editor of every newspaper in the land."—*New Englander.*

"Spencer is continually gaining ground with Americans; he makes a book for our more serious moods. His remarks upon legislation, upon the nature of political institutions and of their fundamental principles; his elucidation of those foundation truths which control the policy of government, are of peculiar value to the American student."—*Boston Post.*

"This volume will receive the applause of every serious reader for the profound earnestness and thoroughness with which its views are elaborated, the infinite scientific knowledge brought to bear on every question, and the acute and subtle thinking displayed in every chapter."—*N. W. Christian Advocate.*

"A more instructive, suggestive, and stimulating volume has not reached us in a long time."—*Providence Journal.*

A NEW SYSTEM OF PHILOSOPHY.

PRINCIPLES OF BIOLOGY.

This work is now in course of publication in quarterly numbers (from 80 to 100 pages each), by subscription, at $2 per annum. It is to form two volumes, of which the first is nearly completed, four numbers having been issued. While it comprises a statement of those general principles and laws of life to which science has attained, it is stamped with a marked originality, both in the views propounded and in the method of treating the subject. It will be a standard and invaluable work. Some idea of the discussion may be formed by glancing over a few of the first chapter headings.

PART FIRST.—DATA OF BIOLOGY.

I. Organic Matter; II. The actions of Forces on Organic Matter; III The Reactions of Organic Matter on Forces; IV. Proximate Definition of Life; V. The Correspondence between Life and its Circumstances; VI. The Degree of Life Varies with the Degree of Correspondence; VII Scope of Biology.

PART SECOND.—INDUCTIONS OF BIOLOGY.

I. Growth; II. Development; III. Function; IV. Waste and Repair; V. Adaptation; VI. Individuality; VII. Genesis; VIII. Heredity; IX. Variation; X. Genesis, Heredity, and Variation; XI. Classification; XII. Distribution.

Mr. Spencer is equally remarkable for his search after first principles; for his acute attempts to decompose mental phenomena into their primary elements; and for his broad generalizations of mental activity, mind in connection with instinct, and all the analogies presented by *life* in its universal aspects.—*Medico-Chirurgical Review.*

ESSAYS:

MORAL POLITICAL, AND ESTHETIC.

In one Volume. Large 12mo.

CONTENTS:

I. The Philosophy of Style.
II. Over-Legislation.
III. Morals of Trade.
IV. Personal Beauty.
V. Representative Government.
VI. Prison-Ethics.
VII. Railway Morals and Railway Policy.
VIII. Gracefulness.
IX. State Tamperings with Money and Banks.
X. Reform; the Dangers and the Safeguards.

ALSO,

SOCIAL STATICS;

OR,

THE CONDITIONS ESSENTIAL TO HUMAN HAPPINESS SPECIFIED, AND THE FIRST OF THEM DEVELOPED.

In one Volume. Large 12mo.

All these works are rich in materials for forming intelligent opinions, even where we are unable to agree with those put forth by the author. Much may be learned from them in departments in which our common Educational system is very deficient. The active citizen may derive from them accurate systematized information concerning his highest duties to society, and the principles on which they are based. He may gain clearer notions of the value and bearing of evidence, and be better able to distinguish between facts and inferences. He may find common things suggestive of wiser thought —nay, we will venture to say of truer emotion—than before. By giving us fuller realizations of liberty and justice his writings will tend to increase our self-reliance in the great emergency of civilization to which we have been summoned.—*Atlantic Monthly*

THE CORRELATION AND CONSERVATION

OF

FORCES.

A SERIES OF EXPOSITIONS BY GROVE, MAYER, HELMHOLTZ, FARADAY, LIEBIG, AND CARPENTER.

WITH

AN INTRODUCTION.

BY E. L. YOUMANS.

The work embraces:

I.—THE CORRELATION OF PHYSICAL FORCES. By W. R. Grove. (The complete work.)

II.—CELESTIAL DYNAMICS. By Dr. J. R. Mayer.

III.—THE INTERACTION OF FORCES. By Prof. Helmholtz.

IV.—THE CONNECTION AND EQUIVALENCE OF FORCES. By Prof. Liebig.

V.—ON THE CONSERVATION OF FORCE. By Dr. Faraday.

VI.—ON THE CORRELATION OF PHYSICAL AND VITAL FORCES. By Dr. Carpenter.

The Philosophy of Herbert Spencer.

FIRST PRINCIPLES;

IN TWO PARTS:

I. THE UNKNOWABLE. II. LAWS OF THE KNOWABLE.

In one Volume. 518 pages.

"Mr. Spencer has earned an eminent and commanding position as a metaphysician, and his ability, earnestness, and profundity, are in none of his former volumes so conspicuous as in this. There is not a crude thought, a flippant fling, or an irreverent insinuation in this book, notwithstanding that it has something of the character of a daring and determined raid upon the old philosophies."—*Chicago Journal.*

"This volume, treating of First Principles, like all Mr. Spencer's writings that have fallen under our observation, is distinguished for clearness, earnestness, candor, and that originality and fearlessness which ever mark the true philosophical spirit. His treatment of theological opinions is reverent and respectful, and his suggestions and arguments are such as to deserve, as they will compel, the earnest attention of all thoughtful students of first truths. Agreeing with Hamilton and Mansel in the general, on the unknowableness of the unconditioned, he nevertheless holds that their being is in a form asserted by consciousness."—*Christian Advocate.*

"The literary world has seen but few such authors as Herbert Spencer. There have been metaphysical writers in the same exalted sphere who before him have attempted to reduce the laws of nature to a rational system. But in the highest realm of philosophical investigation he stands head and shoulders above his predecessors; not perhaps purely by force of superior intellect, but partly owing to the greater aid which the light of modern science has afforded him in the prosecution of his difficult task."—*Boston Bulletin.*

"Mr. Spencer is achieving an enviable distinction by his contributions to the country's literature; his system of philosophy is destined to become a work of no small renown. Its appearance at this time is an evidence that our people are not *all* absorbed in war and its tragic events."—*Ohio State Journal.*

"Mr. Spencer's works will undoubtedly receive in this country the attention they merit. There is a broad liberality of tone throughout which will recommend them to thinking, inquiring Americans. Whether, as is asserted, he has established a new system of philosophy, and if so, whether that system is better than all other systems, is yet to be decided; but that his bold and vigorous thought will add something valuable and permanent to human knowledge is undeniable."—*Utica Herald.*

"Herbert Spencer is the foremost among living thinkers. If less erudite than Hamilton, he is quite as original, and is more comprehensive and catholic than Mansel."—*Universalist.*

A NEW SYSTEM OF PHILOSOPHY.

FIRST PRINCIPLES.

1 Vol. Large 12mo. 515 Pages. Price $2 50.

CONTENTS:

PART FIRST.—*The Unknowable.*

Chapter I. Religion and Science; II. Ultimate Religious Ideas; III. Ultimate Scientific Ideas; IV. The Relativity of all Knowledge; V. The Reconciliation.

PART SECOND.—*Laws of the Knowable.*

I. Laws in General; II. The Law of Evolution; III. The same continued; IV. The Causes of Evolution; V. Space, Time, Matter, Motion, and Force; VI. The Indestructibility of Matter; VII. The Continuity of Motion; VIII. The Persistence of Force; IX. The Correlation and Equivalence of Forces; X. The Direction of Motion; XI. The Rhythm of Motion; XII. The Conditions Essential to Evolution; XIII. The Instability of the Homogeneous; XIV. The Multiplication of Effects; XV. Differentiation and Integration; XVI. Equilibration; XVII. Summary and Conclusion.

In the first part of this work Mr. Spencer defines the province, limits, and relations of religion and science, and determines the legitimate scope of philosophy.

In part second he unfolds those fundamental principles which have been arrived at within the sphere of the knowable; which are true of all orders of phenomena, and thus constitute the foundation of all philosophy. The law of Evolution, Mr. Spencer maintains to be universal, and he has here worked it out as the basis of his system.

These First Principles are the foundation of a system of Philosophy bolder, more elaborate, and comprehensive perhaps, than any other which has been hitherto designed in England.—*British Quarterly Review.*

A work lofty in aim and remarkable in execution.—*Cornhill Magazine.*

In the works of Herbert Spencer we have the rudiments of a positive Theology, and an immense step toward the perfection of the science of Psychology.—*Christian Examiner.*

If we mistake not, in spite of the very negative character of his own results, he has foreshadowed some strong arguments for the doctrine of a positive Christian Theology.—*New Englander.*

As far as the frontiers of knowledge, where the intellect may go, there is no living man whose guidance may more safely be trusted.—*Atlantic Monthly.*